ON THE WAY TO NINEVEH

Studies in Honor of George M. Landes

ASOR Books Volume 4

Victor Matthews, editor

ON THE WAY TO NINEVEH

STUDIES IN HONOR OF GEORGE M. LANDES

edited by

Stephen L. Cook and S. C. Winter

Scholars Press • Atlanta, Georgia

ON THE WAY TO NINEVEH
Studies in Honor of George M. Landes

ASOR expresses appreciation to the University Seminars at
Columbia University for assistance in the preparation of the manuscript
for publication. Material published in this work was presented to the
University Seminar on the Hebrew Bible.

Library of Congress Cataloging-in-Publication Data

On the way to Nineveh : studies in honor of George M. Landes /
   edited by Stephen L. Cook and S.C. Winter.
      p.   cm. — (ASOR books : v. 4)
   ISBN 0-7885-0585-8 (pbk. : alk. paper)
   1. Bible. O.T.—Criticism, interpretation, etc. 2. Bible. O.T.
Jonah—Criticism, Interpretation, etc. I. Landes, George M.
II. Cook, Stephen L., 1962–   . III. Winter, S. C. (Sara C.)
IV. Series.
BS1171.2.044   1999
221.6—dc21   99–43279
                                    CIP

Printed in the United States of America
on acid-free paper. ∞

For Our Parents

דּוֹר לְדוֹר יְשַׁבַּח מַעֲשֶׂיךָ וּגְבוּרֹתֶיךָ יַגִּידוּ:

Let one generation to another praise your works,
and your mighty acts they shall make known.

—Psalm 145:4

George M. Landes

Contents

PREFACE

This Festschrift is presented with respect and affection to George M. Landes. May it convey to both him and to his wife Carol the esteem and the affection we all feel for them.

The editors wish to thank all of the contributors for their thoughtful participation in the project. Yochanan Muffs of the Jewish Theological Seminary of America deserves special thanks for ensuring that we embarked on this project. We are also especially grateful to and wish to recognize our panel of consultants: Richard W. Corney, David Marcus, and Robert R. Wilson, who gave so generously of their time. They provided helpful advice, including suggesting the title for this volume, and critical acumen at all stages of the project. Credit also goes to Herbert B. Huffmon and Edward F. Campbell, Jr. for their editorial advice. We thank Carol Landes for her steady encouragement and for providing the portrait of George for this volume.

Aaron W. Warner and the University Seminars at Columbia University provided the financial underpinning for the publication of this project through a grant from the Leonard Hastings Schoff Publication Fund. We gratefully acknowledge this support. Additional financial support for the volume came from Union Theological Seminary in the City of New York, and we extend our thanks to Holland L. Hendrix.

We were privileged to have had the support from the start of this project of the American Schools of Oriental Research. Warm thanks go to R. Thomas Schaub, former chair of ASOR's Committee on Publications, Victor H. Matthews, ASOR Books Series Editor, and Billie Jean Collins, ASOR Director of Publications.

Many people have provided encouragement and assistance over the several years that we were working towards the publication of this volume. Our colleagues at Virginia Theological Seminary, the Jewish Theological Seminary, and Lang College have provided us supportive environments in which we are able to be productive. Christopher Cunningham, Head of Information Technology at Virginia Theologi-

x   *ON THE WAY TO NINEVEH*

cal Seminary, contributed valuable technical assistance, as did his aides, especially James Beck.

Stephen would like to express his indebtedness to his wife, Catherine, for her praiseworthy forbearance. He thanks her with all his heart. Sara would like to thank Robert P. Boyer for his encouragement and support and Larry Kravitz for his good advice. She also thanks Catherine E. Cook for her gracious hospitality.

This volume is dedicated to Sara's parents, Gibson and Blair Winter, and to Stephen's and Catherine's parents, Dr. and Mrs. William and Dorothy Cook, and Dr. and Mrs. Arthur and Marilyn Jacobs.

George M. Landes:
An Appreciation

ROBERT R. WILSON

The impetus for this celebratory volume arose in the Columbia University Seminar for the Study of the Hebrew Bible, of which George Landes was a founding member. To honor his faithful service to the Seminar over the years and to wish him well on the occasion of his retirement from Union Theological Seminary, where he had taught for his entire career, the editors invited colleagues and former students to contribute essays that would reflect something of the range of George's interests. That range turned out to be very wide indeed. Many of the younger members of the Seminar first knew George not in person but through the publication of his helpful word-frequency list, which over the years has helped to teach generations of students the vocabulary of Biblical Hebrew. Only later did we learn that he was also a master of other Northwest Semitic languages and had written what was at the time of its creation the definitive work on Ammonite. But his heart always seemed to lie with Hebrew, and those fortunate enough to have studied with him at Union know that throughout his career he remained a systematic and dedicated teacher of the intensive elementary Hebrew course. Over the years he was always seeking to improve the standard techniques for presenting the language, and he carefully tracked student performance in order to see which approaches worked and which did not. Characteristically, toward the end of his teaching career he passed on what he had learned to a new generation of teachers to be sure that his legacy of solid language training would be safe for generations to come.

Less well-known to members of the Seminar were George's archaeological interests. He has been a long-time member of the American Schools of Oriental Research, and over the years he has participated in their excavations and contributed to their publications. As he has done

1

in so many other contexts, he also cheerfully served the Schools in a number of administrative capacities, calmly riding out the storms that have washed over the archaeological guild over the years.

However, Seminar members knew George best through the scholarly papers that he shared from time to time. Usually they reflected his most recent work on the Book of Jonah, in which he has had a life-long interest. As is characteristic of all of his work, his presentations were always thorough, well-researched, and creative, reflecting fully his literary and theological interests. Unlike some senior scholars, his criticisms of his colleagues' work were never dismissive or vindictive but always fair and helpful, an attitude that I am sure he always exhibited in the classroom. In the lively discussion sessions that always followed his papers, he was never defensive but always willing to consider objections and to entertain modifications to his theses. In short, for his younger colleagues in particular he was a model of what a professional, engaged scholar should be. With happy memories of their past associations with him, and with eager anticipation of continued conversations in the future, his colleagues and former students take great pleasure in presenting him with this volume in his honor.

A Personal Reminiscence of a Path Trod Together

EDWARD F. CAMPBELL, JR.

In the years 1953 through 1956, George Landes and I found ourselves traveling parallel but not yet engaged paths. He had graduated from McCormick Theological Seminary in 1952, a year before I enrolled. Both of us had fallen under the spell of G. Ernest Wright and Frank Moore Cross, Jr., who, along with Ovid Sellers, made up the Old Testament field there. McCormick, committed to educating students for ministry in an inner-city setting, also sought to pursue the disciplines that characterize a graduate school of theology. It encouraged some of its students to go on to Ph.D. studies as a ministry for the church.

So it was that George and I became part of a stream of students Wright and Cross pushed to follow up on our seminary careers with the trek to The Johns Hopkins University to study with the legendary William Foxwell Albright. George was vanguard for a burst of McCormick people, followed soon by Orval Wintermute. George and Carol and the Wintermutes, along with Lawrence Sinclair, Nancy Renn Lapp, and Robert Boling and their spouses, were there to greet my wife Phyllis and me. In those days a number of courses were what Albright, with a twinkle in his eye, called "auto-didactic"—teach it to yourself—but we also worked with Samuel Rosenblatt on Arabic, Sam Iwry on Dead Sea Scrolls and the world of Hebrew Bible in general, Tom Lambdin on just about anything having to do with Semitic languages, Gus van Beek on archaeology, and (in George's case) Frank Blake on historical Hebrew grammar. It seemed that the whole world of Near Eastern historical scholarship passed through Baltimore and gave us seminars.

Albright, appropriately absent-minded, had a great ally in George, who kept two sheets of paper in the drawer of the seminar-room table close to where Albright sat; one said "history" and one said "archaeology," and George would produce one or the other on the appropriate day (especially if Albright's content was clearly out of sync) to remind the "Old Man" in which class it was that he was now lecturing.

Most important, we taught one another. It was essential that we do that. An hour in a classroom with any of those teachers required a week to absorb, so we went to our elder student colleagues and got help. That's how I first became a friend of George Landes—who was around for my first months of immersion at Hopkins. George and Carol then set out for Union, while the rest of us finished up during the final years of Albright's presence in Baltimore.

They were halcyon days, and we thought we could learn everything having to do with the ancient Near East! There weren't many who had the breadth to tell us what a foolish notion that was, although Albright himself was observing that the study of the atom and the study of the ancient Near East were the two fastest-moving fields in the contemporary world.

"Everything" included archaeology. George and Carol were not able to go with the rest of us to the 1957 campaign at Tell-Balâtah/Shechem, but by 1962 they did join the staff, working in the registry. Few of that staff will ever forget Carol singing the role of Miss Katherine Kanyon to Carl Graesser's Hartley Evers Wrong in the opera that decorated the season-ending party that summer, a composition of our friend Delbert Hillers. If memory serves, George was part of the Wall that separated Primus and Thistlebe, two "wogs" on the dig staff in the opera. After this high point of their archaeological careers, the Landeses stayed on in Jerusalem during his first Union sabbatical as "Shechem fellow," organizing the pottery finds and drawing pottery plates.

In 1967–1968 George was again in Jerusalem, and again served the expedition by using some of his sabbatical time to expand the regional survey around the Shechem vale. During that year he conducted a project of his own near Jericho, because events had precluded his working out of Jerusalem on his special interest in the Ammonites (in Jordan). He published his project in an ASOR Annual, in which he also edited Boling's report on a facet of the Shechem dig.

One venue of our by-now mutual paths was Biblical Colloquium, a group of roughly fifteen formed by Ernest Wright of mostly Albright students who met each Thanksgiving weekend to "read at" one another— papers of three hours' duration that no presenter ever got through because of all the discusion and head-butting that began after the first sentence was read. By the time turmoil gripped the academic world in the late 1960s, George and I shared with about half of the members of Colloquium that we were becoming veterans in the chaos called theological education while trying to keep abreast of the dimensions of philology, archaeology, and historical reconstruction that were all burgeoning in scope and rendering the enterprise next to impossible to manage! We shared a passion for exegetical inquiry and a generalist's vision, and sought to find methodological pathways to do all that. We've tried to keep going through post-modern and post-processual, and post-most-everything-else movements ever since. George focussed on Jonah a lot, as I did on Ruth—both books we frequently read with our introductory exegesis classes at Union and McCormick. We saw each other from time to time, but I think we simply took comfort in knowing that each was at work on what needed doing, and trusted we were doing it as best we could and on similar wave-lengths.

Prescott Williams and the late Robert Boling are two more friends who worked this way; since I have shared my collegiality with George in conversations with each of them, they participate in this tribute. One result of this style we sought to practice was a relatively limited list of major publications. Greater satisfaction came from the discoveries made when groups of students sit down and try to make not only philological but rhetorical, aesthetic and theological sense of an ancient text from a very different society that is expected to have pertinence to our own times.

George Landes throughout his career has been one of those admirable people who does his work well and thoroughly, keeps his commitments strongly, and does not seem to care who gets the accolades. When one serves as secretary of the Board of Trustees of the American Schools of Oriental Research for twenty-two years and the minutes are always correct and have just the right amount of detail, people take it for granted. When an ASOR Annual gets edited properly, it is nice to have the citation as editor, but the editor goes relatively unheralded. When one contributes but does not try to be the one to occupy the limelight, it is barely noticed. Without this, though, a field does not move and students do not get moved. Most of George Landes's "publications" are his students; I'm honored to have been one of the first to learn from him at Hopkins in formal graduate education and honored now to join in felicitating him. And I am equally delighted to commend Carol's and George's having the good judgment to find one another. What a fine team they have been—and as my own contribution to this volume may suggest, such teams are a blessing beyond words to express.

Thank you, Steve and Sara, for putting this tribute volume together. George and Carol deserve the best we can give them.

1 Introduction: Contemporary Methods and the Place of Philology and Archaeology in Biblical Studies Today

STEPHEN L. COOK and S. C. WINTER

Contributors responded with enthusiasm and appreciation to our plans for this volume to honor our friend and colleague, George M. Landes. Our planning commenced with George's retirement in 1995 from Union Theological Seminary in the City of New York, after thirty-nine years of service to the field of biblical studies. In response to our request for an article in honor of George, contributors told us how much they thought George deserved this honor and how pleased they would be to participate in a publication project dedicated to him. Their correspondence and articles speak of George's qualities as a scholar, as a teacher, and as a person.

Contributors have reminded us of the exhaustive diligence of George's scholarship. Baruch Levine, in his essay, rightly refers to George as the "persistent scholar." George is not one to leave any stone unturned. He takes the time to gather all of the evidence pertaining to his topics and shows in all of his research the kind of patience required to compile the word frequency and cognate lists for his *A Student's Vocabulary of Biblical Hebrew.*

Contributors also have frequently noted George's warm collegiality. We all understand what James Sanders means when he writes that it was his years with George on the Union faculty "that taught me what real collegiality is about." At an educational institution where many faculty chose to work most of the time in their home offices, George

7

was consistently "in." He could almost always be found working in his office atop Union's Brown Tower, his door open, sometimes just a crack, but most often fully open, inviting the passer-by to drop in for a collegial chat.

George is known to all of us as a model teacher, committed to pedagogical excellence. Those of us who have studied with him, co-taught with him, or been tutors in his intensive Hebrew course know first hand his love of teaching every aspect of Hebrew language from Comparative Semitics to "Hebrew for Homiletics." He strived to solve pedagogical problems, including how best to structure class time in an intensive language course, and how best to evaluate the progress of students and communicate that evaluation to them. George devised a means for diagnosing in advance each student's own strengths and weaknesses for learning languages to help them over the difficult points in introductory Hebrew. A career-long commitment to preparing seminarians for ministry meant that he frequently made Christian theological and homiletical use of the Bible. In his "Hebrew for Homiletics" class, he even taught students how knowing the original language of the weekly lectionary texts enhanced their appropriation of them for preaching. Edward F. Campbell expresses well George's commitment to teaching when he writes, "Most of George Landes's 'publications' are his students."

It is a measure of the high esteem in which George is held by his colleagues that the contributions to this volume are in a sense very personal. That is, contributors have written on topics chosen with a personal connection with George in mind. Five of the papers in this volume are on Jonah, George's longtime love for which is well-known. Indeed, many who have studied or worked with George have accumulated private collections of whale miniatures and knickknacks in celebration of an enjoyment of Jonah. Roger Boraas publishes here some results from the Drew-McCormick expeditions at Shechem, in which George participated in the 1962 and 1968 seasons. Edward Campbell writes that his essay on Ruth stems from an approach to a career in biblical studies that in many ways parallels George's own vocational journey. And knowing George's conviction that archaeology and exegesis are mutually illuminating, several writers untangle exegetical problems through examining ancient Near Eastern artifacts, iconography, and texts. Some of the articles in this volume grew out of papers given at the Columbia University Seminar on the Study of the Hebrew Bible, of which George is a longtime member and former chair. In other instances, conversations with George—during graduate studies, seminar discussions, or collegial interactions—influenced how contributors chose and developed their topics.

The theme of this volume grows out of George's career-long commitment to the study and teaching of language and biblical archaeology. Contributors were asked to comment on the role of philology and archaeology in their approaches, when appropriate, or to reflect upon how their work has moved in reliance on these methods.

George Landes was a student of W. F. Albright, the "dean" of twentieth-century American biblical studies from the 1920s through the 1950s and 1960s. Albright developed and defined biblical scholarship in America in specifically philological, archaeological, and historical terms. George imparted to his own students the strengths of the Albright School. But between the time George finished his graduate studies and today, the "normative" approach developed by Albright has been replaced by a plurality of methods, a range of new social questions that are being posed both to the text and its context, and a new self-consciousness regarding method. George's career has spanned these decades of major shifts in biblical studies. Recently also the legacy of Albright has been under new scrutiny. In fact, a special session evaluating Albright formed part of the Annual Meeting of the American Schools of Oriental Research (ASOR) in 1991, Albright's birth-centennial.

In George Landes's own work one sees both his training in philology and archaeology and ways in which he built on his training. At the beginning of his career, George's explorations into the history of the biblical world took a largely archaeological tack. Later, when it became clear that Union Seminary was not able financially to support a field-archaeology program, George concentrated his scholarship on biblical exegesis and also contributed his philological expertise to the field in his capacity as a translator of the New Revised Standard Version (NRSV). Although not engaged directly in field archaeology, George remained immersed in Near Eastern studies through his longtime position as Secretary for ASOR and through his active membership in the Biblical Colloquium, a group carrying forward the general "conversation" initiated by Albright and his students. But, as was inevitable given his institutional position, George's own teaching and writing also moved in conversation with changes in society and the guild in the post-Albright era. Social and theological changes and challenges within the American scene had a particularly powerful impact at Union Seminary over the course of George's career.

The contributions to this volume cover a wide variety of topics but all illustrate the interplay between the Albrightian heritage and new methods. Some authors reflect explicitly on that interplay, but others illustrate it indirectly through particular, concrete studies, including many exegetical studies. The selection of essays is arranged in overlapping groups, primarily according to the methods of interpretation employed by the authors and secondarily according to the issues and concerns that they raise. The contributions illustrate quite fully, even in this small sample, how scholarship rooted in the American archaeological approach has flourished, how it has diversified by building on and extending philological and archaeological methods, and how it has refined itself through self-consciousness of method. These essays also demonstrate how various critical methodologies may or may not work together effectively, an issue in light of the current seemingly endless burgeoning of new approaches. Several of these essays, looking at the Bible through a lens of new social questions, bring new facets of the text to light. Others raise hermeneutical questions about the nature of the biblical text and its interaction with its readers.

The first three articles, by Roger S. Boraas, Richard W. Corney, and David Marcus, make use of archaeology and philology to yield new insights into the biblical text and its context. These three articles demonstrate that archaeology and the comparative study of ancient Near Eastern texts remain essential to biblical studies.

Roger Boraas offers an initial publication of a locus of pottery from the Shechem excavation. As Edward Campbell's felicitation of George reminds us, many of the participants in the Shechem excavations under the leadership of G. E. Wright, including both Campbell and Landes, understood their engagement in field archaeology as an intrinsic facet of their biblical scholarship.

The articles by Corney and Marcus apply the fruits of archaeological discovery to exegesis. Corney clarifies Psalm 23 through study of ancient Near Eastern motifs and symbols, arguing for a coherent reading of the two sections of the psalm that has otherwise eluded interpreters.

Marcus' contribution also relies on ancient Near Eastern and philological study. He argues for a new interpretation of the "three days' walk" of Jonah 3:3 based on examination of this verse's language and of comparable diction in texts from the ancient world.

The three essays show that archaeological work, especially discoveries of ancient texts and images, continues to be a necessary element in exegesis. Recourse to archaeological finds and comparative ancient Near Eastern texts, with their attestations to Semitic diction, symbols, and constructs, is still an aid in biblical interpretation. Corney's article, for example, illustrates how such study can uncover coherence in a seemingly disjointed text.

The next three contributions, those of Edward F. Campbell, Jr., Ee Kon Kim, and Thomas B. Dozeman, take an Albrightian approach to the biblical text as a starting point for branching out methodologically. These contributions also show a common interest in form-critical questions.

Edward Campbell's essay relies on the American, archaeological approach in its study of the language and social customs of the biblical narrative. But Campbell explains how he has modified and changed some of his exegetical conclusions about Ruth over time, in conversation with other scholars and with currents in the field. Campbell's methodology has been particularly influenced by conversation with feminist interpretations of Ruth throughout his career. In this connection Campbell pays attention to the role of women in the generation of folk traditions. Further, he discusses the thesis that in the folk-story of Ruth the type of moral decision making that is highlighted indicates that this book is a product of women's culture.

Ee Kon Kim's article, like Campbell's, has solid roots in philological and related methods. His intensive study of the shift of mood in lament psalms relies on philological study, as his contribution to this volume illustrates. His essay closely examines terminology in the lament psalms as one of three key indicators for establishing the provenance of the major influence in these psalms' formation. But to an even greater extent, Kim's work exemplifies form-critical methodologies. At least through the 1960s and early 1970s, the German form-critical approach constituted the major alternative in twentieth-century biblical scholarship to the American approach, and Kim's article illustrates these two methodological approaches working compatibly together. At those points where its differing understandings of the nature of biblical texts come to the fore, however, the German stance has also represented more a challenge than a companion to the American brand of biblical research. Thomas Dozeman's contribution to this volume goes further towards illustrating the aspect of challenge to the American approach inherent in form criticism.

Dozeman traces a history of tradition in the development of the Song of the Sea in Exod 15:1–18. The Albright School had held that this text was composed in early Israel in roughly the form of its current coherence; and the Albright School saw its significance to derive from its original, early meaning. Dozeman, in contrast, takes a tradition-history approach that attempts to elucidate biblical texts in terms of their ongoing life and growth within Israelite history. This represents a distinct move beyond viewing biblical texts as artifacts from single historical strata.

Dozeman critiques one of the major results of the Albright School—the early dating of the salvation-history outline presented by Exodus 15's Song of the Sea. His conclusion, which would make salvation history a late, Deuteronomistic reinterpretation of Israel's archaic hymnody, resonates with a wider movement within the field. This movement, which tends to take the Bible's surface presentation as a late, secondary development, stands in sharp contrast to the Albright School and its successors.

The next two essays are by Robert R. Wilson and Naomi Steinberg. Wilson and Steinberg have both made use of a sociological approach to move beyond strictly philological and historical work. Their articles in this volume differ, however, in their stances toward earlier methodology. Steinberg's stance presupposes a disjuncture between a sociological approach and two main Albrightian types of interests, the interest in the historical dimension of the Bible and the interest in its modern religious significance. Steinberg brackets the question of what actual events lie behind the story of Jephthah's vow and the question of the insight of the story into "eternal reality," focussing instead on the meaning of human sacrifice within Israelite social structure and religious culture. She draws on contemporary anthropological theories of sacrificial ritual to argue for a connection between human sacrifice in Israel and Israelite understandings of kinship relations.

Wilson by contrast presupposes little disjuncture between Albrightian interests and a sociological approach. He argues for a historicizing focus within the book of Jeremiah that can be seen to function both theologically and sociologically. Historical narratives in Jeremiah serve sometimes to illustrate and vindicate theological points made in earlier Jeremianic oracles. At other times, the historical narratives serve the definite sociological function of establishing group identity within the exile. This identity must often have turned on the careful records kept by the Jeremianic narratives about the sides taken by the exiles' various ancestors in the fateful social conflicts preceding Jerusalem's fall.

Though Wilson's sociological approach is apparent in his essay, the focus of his contribution to this volume lies elsewhere—in the substantial support he unearths in Jeremiah for the Albrightian connection between exegesis and history. According to Wilson, a methodological conviction central to George Landes' work has been that biblical exegesis and the study of Israel's history should be held together. Wilson finds in Jeremiah support for that tenet in that Jeremiah, at least, will just not allow for the various programs, many of recent years, that compartmentalize these two areas of investigation. In Jeremiah, Wilson sees biblical literature specifically historicized. Such historicizing within a text, whether for sociological or theological reasons, or both, means that interpretation of the text must retain history and literature together as "dialog partners."

The next two articles, by Edward L. Greenstein and Herbert B. Huffmon, take a literary approach to the text. Each analyzes a specific rhetorical device in detail, and each attempts to ascertain the significance of the device in its larger biblical context. The two contributors differ, however, in the extent to which they depart from the modernist concern with texts' diachronic dimensions.

Greenstein begins his article, on wordplay in Exodus 18, with reflections on method that situate his approach. Whereas Exodus 18, he points out, has evoked mostly diachronic discussion, his approach is oriented towards Exodus 18's present form. Moreover, he notes examples in his article that illustrate inevitable tensions between a diachronic approach and his own synchronic analysis. Greenstein's concern with the hermeneutical interaction of texts and readers further differentiates his methodology. In contrast to the essays in this volume that employ text-centered, canonical approaches, Greenstein's method stresses the interpretive efforts of readers in making sense of texts.

Huffmon examines a specific literary topos in Jer 31:35–37, and like Greenstein, he explores its function within its biblical context as a whole.

Huffmon's approach, however, is much more Albrightian in that his argument deals at length with text criticism and with the comparison of Near Eastern parallels. Tellingly, he is interested in diachronic problems, including the question of the authenticity of his passage to the prophet Jeremiah and the question of its chronological relationship with other biblical literature, such as Second Isaiah.

The next three papers are by Phyllis Trible, Baruch A. Levine, and Johanna W. H. van Wijk-Bos. They each illustrate the impact of cultural and political contexts and interests on the interpretation of biblical texts. All three papers discuss the book of Jonah, and all three show how a located stance shapes the lens through which the interpreter views the text.

With "ecological soundings" of the book of Jonah, Trible examines the book in light of a set of questions that have emerged only in the past three decades. Contexts of interpretation constantly raise new questions of texts, motivating examinations of the text in a new light. In her examination of Jonah from an ecological perspective, Trible's "soundings" explore new horizons of the text. This type of expository voice, advocating concern for nature, may become more prominent as our ecological crisis intensifies.

The essays by Levine and van Wijk-Bos put in sharp relief the importance of positionality in interpretation. Levine, situating his reading in conversation with Jewish interpretation, explores how the theme of repentance in Jonah resonates with passages in Genesis, Exodus, and the prophets. Van Wijk-Bos situates her exploration of the theme of the Ninevites' repentance and of Jonah's response within the history of Christian lines of interpretation, with attention to Jonah's impact on Christian views of Judaism. Although Levine and van Wijk-Bos both take the theme of repentance as central to the book of Jonah, by examining this theme within two distinct religious traditions they produce treatments of Jonah with divergent foci.

The next two contributions are by S. C. Winter and Gerald T. Sheppard. Winter and Sheppard discuss two different periods of premodern biblical interpretation, late antiquity and the seventeenth-century Age of Discovery, respectively. This interest in the history of interpretation represents another side of the contemporary awareness of the situatedness of all exegesis. Scholars today, rather than valuing earlier interpretation only in terms of how closely it came to adumbrating historical-critical methods, want to understand methods of exegesis from earlier periods on their own terms and with regard for their own integrity. This endeavor, in turn, contributes to greater awareness of our own, present-day methodological assumptions and focal issues in interpretation.

In some ways, of all the contributions to the present volume, the articles by Winter and Sheppard are most suggestive of how biblical study has moved in relation to the methods and presuppositions of the Albright School. As Sheppard writes, we stand today in "a period of disequilibrium between epochs of confidence." This characterization of our present situation is true in several respects, one of which being that as a guild we no longer have the self-confidence of the Albright era. Such a reduction in confidence can have its advantages, one of which being that we may judge less harshly and attempt to appreciate more the efforts of earlier epochs of biblical interpretation.

Winter writes about a commentary on Jonah attributed to the Christian school of exegesis at Antioch. She explores what light the commentary sheds on how Antiochene method was shaped by its context. Moreover, she analyzes how the method of the Antiochene school was informed by traditions borrowed from Jewish interpretation and some principles taken from Hellenistic moral philosophy.

Sheppard's contribution not only appreciates premodern interpretation on its own terms but also finds two of its concepts helpful for a late-modern approach to the biblical texts: the notion of biblical writers as "inditers" and the idea of texts as territorial "places." The concept of "inditers" of texts is helpful for moving beyond the modern period's historicist model for understanding authorship. The concept helps us replace our modern preoccupation with the historical intentionalities and conditionalities behind texts with a recognition that prevailing canonical forces (i.e., forces shaping biblical literature as Scripture) strongly influenced the work of the biblical writers. The concept of texts as "territories" is helpful for moving beyond the modern period's overly simple notions of secular objectivity in interpreting the historical sense of texts. A putatively objective, external vantage from which one is able to historicize a text is not necessarily a preferable perspective for appreciating a text's literal meaning. A text's authentic plain sense may relate much more to what premoderns considered as its territorial "circumstances," that is, its "historical" sense as defined by its inner-biblical context. The premoderns often correctly intuited that it is the biblical "circumstances" of texts, illuminable through cross-referencing within Scripture, that govern the provenance of language within biblical passages and thus their plain, biblical sense.

The final two essays in the volume, by Stephen L. Cook and James A. Sanders, take a canonical approach to biblical study, just as Sheppard's essay does. A characterization first made by W. C. Smith clarifies well the distinctiveness of canonical approaches. On the one hand, the American archaeological approach reads the biblical texts "prebiblically," as sources for reconstructing the ancient history and religion behind the texts. On the other hand, recent literary approaches understand the texts "postbiblically," in their interactions with readers—dynamics that may be non-religious. But in contrast to both of these stances, canonical approaches attempt to understand the texts "biblically," as the Scriptures of Judaism and Christianity. That is, canonical approaches attempt to understand the texts in terms of their interaction with faith communities, how they form and nourish the experience and theology of Synagogue and Church.

Contrary to a common view, canonical approaches go beyond a mere focus on the biblical materials in their present literary (synchronic) forms. Canonical approaches focus on the effectual or generative propensities of biblical materials, their time-tested capacities for the creation of religious communities around them and for impacting and forming the continuing life and experience of those communities. That is, canonical methods view biblical texts as active forces in the creation of the religious experience of communities. This is in contrast to methods that focus either on readers' contemporary interactions with biblical texts or on the religion and history that stands behind biblical texts.

Cook and Sanders make use of canonical approaches to consider two very different problems. Cook explores the prehistory of a sample biblical tradition from a canonical perspective, in order to probe the nature of the prevailing impact on tradents and redactors of canonical traditions, which impact caused them to be forwarded into the future (i.e., preserved and archived) as scriptural texts. Taking up the same text in Exodus 18 that Greenstein's essay in this volume treats, Cook examines the impact and the challenge that the Mosaic-judges tradition presented in the various historical circumstances and settings of its history of transmission. That this exercise proves both possible and constructive suggests that historical (diachronic) methods and canonical methods of studying traditions may be fruitfully paired in critical scholarship. Some canonical contexts cannot be described in mere synchronic, literary terms but extend through time. To borrow a phrase from James Sanders' essay, some traditions early on earned a "tenure track" position towards a canonical status as Scripture.

Sanders' article steps back to take a macro-view of the final forms of the Jewish and the several Christian canons. His contribution is a study of intertextuality, in the sense of the interrelation of biblical texts, and a study of the structures of canons as they have been fixed by canonical closure. Sanders analyses the individual theological statements made by the canons presented, arguing that the variant order of biblical books in these canons conveys a radical difference in their messages.

Readers may come to this volume for several reasons. Some will be drawn by an interest in Jonah. Others will be interested in the volume's theme of how contemporary methodology relates to earlier approaches, such as the approach of the Albright School of the preceding epoch. Readers will differ immensely in terms of which contemporary approaches to and stances toward the biblical text they will find congenial. There will be even more disagreement about which approaches in biblical scholarship represent the inevitable wave of the future. Nevertheless, it is hoped that all readers will appreciate this volume for the diversity of contemporary methods that it maps and for the tribute to George Landes that it attempts to render.

2   Shechem Pottery— Locus 14.132

ROGER S. BORAAS

In grateful recognition of the contributions of Prof. George Landes as a staff member of the Drew-McCormick Joint Expedition to Tell Balâṭah, Jordan (biblical Shechem), and of Mrs. Landes in ceramic conservation for the expedition, I offer the following as a modest additional step in publishing the pottery of the site. I also wish to express gratitude for the long association with Prof. Landes at the Columbia Seminar on the Study of the Hebrew Bible.

Publication of the ceramic corpus of the transitional period from Late Bronze to Iron Age I at this site has been minimal to date (Boraas 1986).[1] This article will supplement the previously published material, adding a horizon of ceramics from a single locus dated to the period on stratigraphic grounds.

The basis of selection of the locus in this instance rests on the following descriptive details currently available. Field VII was an extensive zone of excavation on the center of the main mound, and was opened and expanded by the Drew-McCormick team to carry on from the previously reached levels of occupation left by earlier excavators. Analysis of the stratigraphy reported by Edward F. Campbell, Jr. in private correspondence dated 19 September 1996 indicated that the relevant transitional materials occurred in Strata XIA (uppermost) and XIB (lower and above Stratum XII, Late Bronze material). They correspond to Layers mentioned in preliminary reports as Layers 3 and 4. A list of "confident Stratum XI pottery" includes the comment, "In the north of [B.64, Field VII] Area 5 this system is lumped as [Locus] 14.132: see #39 on BB [S]ection [drawing]" (Campbell 1996b: 1–3). The reference to the layer identification as #39 applies only to the Section Drawing BB from Field VII for excavation work in 1964.

Verbal description of the context is provided by Prof. Campbell in the draft text of a book in preparation at this point. I cite below the relevant portion, realizing the tentative nature of the comments. Layer numbers are those used in the Section BB drawing to identify the Loci.

> Section BB provides the best evidence for relating the banded accumulation to the structures to the south. The banded layers are 14.132 (layer 39) covering Stratum XII Wall 14.146 and beginning from Stratum XII Floor 14.144 (layer 44). As noted earlier, the segment of flagstones [Locus] 14.141A is a feature of one of the intermediate bands. Topping 14.132 was Stratum XIA Floor 14.124 (layer 34) at elevation [above sea level] sloping from 15.04 to 14.59. On 14.124 just to the south of the balk, and interrupting it at places suggesting that the last of the bands may have been laid just after the destruction, is the 14.139 destruction debris. The logical, but not stratigraphically firm, conclusion is that the accumulation of banded layering is coterminous with all the Stratum XI developments in the south, with the possible exception of the uppermost band (fig. 1; Campbell 1996a: 91).

The arrangement of the ceramics portrayed below follows the general typology for the period tentatively established by this writer in the prior published and some unpublished material (Boraas 1986: 251–55; Boraas 1965[2]). The figures are arranged to show minor variations of the major Types, and the text following each figure provides the details concerning the sherds portrayed. Color determinations were used employing the standards in Munsell Soil Color Charts (Munsell 1973). Drawings reflect the corpus of 1:1 drawings I prepared since the excavation season, 1964.[3] Sherd numbers within each figure for each item are strictly for correlation with the details which follow, and have no reference to either Field Report identifications or other numerical indications.

For general perspective, I note that the total registered and unregistered sherd drawings for the Locus 14.132 from B 64, Field VII, Area 5, runs to 251 from 25 baskets in sequence as registered. Of these, 130 drawings have been omitted from this study for various reasons (no sure stance possible, no radius measurable, unregistered material, balk scraping material, chipped profile). All materials presented are from

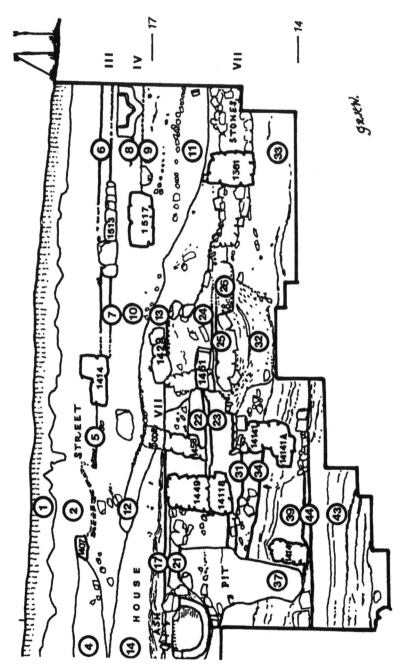

Fig. 1. B 64, Field VII, Area 5, Section BB.

B 64, Field VII, Area 5, Locus 14.132. Clearly here I have selected representative items, many of which occur in multiple attestation within the Locus. I believe the representation is an accurate reflection of the materials recovered from the Locus. Comparative data is lacking except as the correlation with the 1986 published corpus may obtain. The presentation of this data is viewed as one additional step toward establishing the horizon for the period. Comparative data from other Fields, Areas and Loci, or from other published sites, is yet to be noted. I can only underscore the modesty of this step, but it is considered worthwhile en route to final publication of the materials.

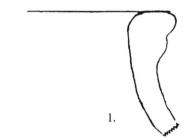

1.

Item	Type	Sherd No.	Radius (m)	Munsell Color Code
1.	I A	22,331	.07	5YR 7/3

Fig. 2. Store Jar Rim

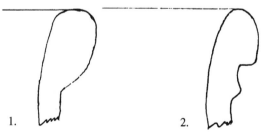

1.   2.

Item	Type	Basket	Sherd No.	Radius (m)	Munsell Color Code
1.	I B	165	22,432	.10	Ware 10YR 5/1 Slip 7.5YR 7/2
2.	I B	163	22,3[3]1	.10	5YR 7/4

Fig. 3. Store Jar Rim

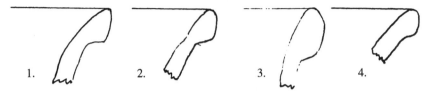

Item	Type	Basket	Sherd No.	Radius (m)	Munsell Color Code
1.	II A	156	22,282	.06	10YR 7/3
2.	II A	285	26,175	.045	10YR 5/2
3.	II A	164	22,350	.06	7.5YR 5/0
4.	II A	285	26,177	.06	5YR 7/3

Fig. 4. Jar/Jug/Pitcher Rim. Thirteen samples.

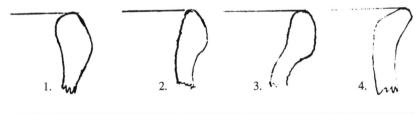

Item	Type	Basket	Sherd No.	Radius (m)	Munsell Color Code
1.	II E	161	22,321	.04	7.5YR 6/4
2.	II F	198	22,891*	.05	10YR 7/2
3.	II F	170	22,493	.05	10YR 7/1
4.	II F	188	22,835*	.07	10YR 5/1

Fig. 5. Jar/Jug/Pitcher Rim.

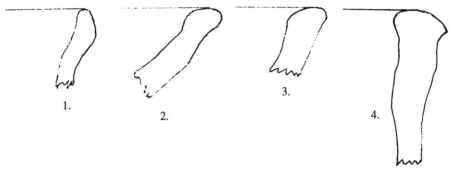

Item	Type	Basket	Sherd No.	Radius (m)	Munsell Color Code
1.	III B	193	22,862*	.12	2.5Y 7/2
2.	III B	169	22,473	.15	10YR 2/1
3.	III B	168	22,461	.13	10YR 5/1
4.	III B	156	22,281	.14	10YR 6/4

Fig. 6. Bowls—Heavy. Eight samples.

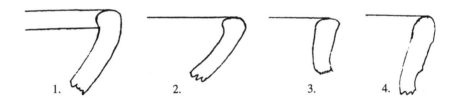

Item	Type	Basket	Sherd No.	Radius (m)	Munsell Color Code
1.	III A	159	22,301	.11	10YR 7/1
2.	III A	161	22,319	.10	7.5YR 7/4
3.	III D	162	22,330	.12	10YR 6/1
4.	III D	163	22,3[2]9	.13	10YR 7/3

Fig. 7. Bowls—Heavy, Wide and Deep.

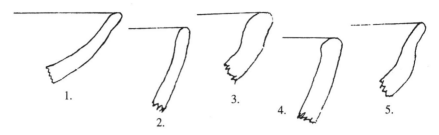

Item	Type	Basket	Sherd No.	Radius (m)	Munsell Color Code
1.	III C	162	22,327	.09	2.5Y 7/0
2.	III C	183	22,826*	.13	5YR 7/2
3.	III C	170	22,495	.09	7.5YR 7/3
4.	III C	189	22,843*	.09	10YR 7/2
5.	III C	189	22,848*	.07	10YR 7/3

Fig. 8. Bowls—Small and Medium, Rims. Twenty-eight samples.

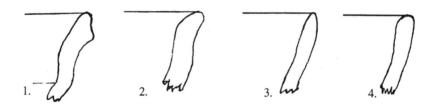

Item	Type	Basket	Sherd No.	Radius (m)	Munsell Color Code
1.	III K	159	22,309	.035	10YR 6/2
2.	III K	196	22,881*	.04	7.5YR 8/2
3.	III K	271	26,095	04	2.5YR 6/4
4.	III K	284	26,172	.04	2.5YR 6/4

Fig. 9. Bowls—Cup Rims.

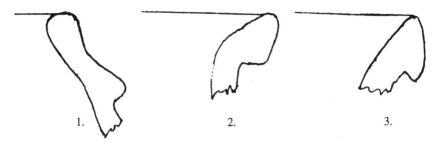

Item	Type	Basket	Sherd No.	Radius (m)	Munsell Color Code
1.	IV A	171	22,502	.10	10R 5/4
2.	IV B	283	26,167	.11	5YR 6/3
3.	IV B	193	22,859*	.13	5YR 5/2

Fig. 10. Cookpot Rims.

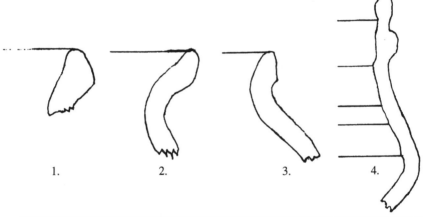

Item	Type	Basket	Sherd No.	Radius (m)	Munsell Color Code
1.	IV D	166	22,440	.14	7.5YR 4/0
2.	IV D	170	22,501	.09	10YR 7/2
3.	IV D	156	22,280	.08	7.5YR 6/4
4.	IV D	170	22,498–99	.15	7.5YR 6/3

Fig. 11. Cookpot Rims. Nineteen Samples.

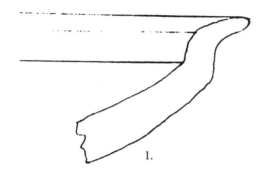

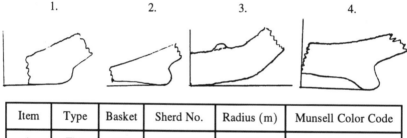

1.

Item	Type	Basket	Sherd No.	Radius (m)	Munsell Color Code
1.	Lamp	170	22,494	.08	10YR 5/1

Fig. 12. Lamp Rim.

1.   2.   3.   4.

Item	Type	Basket	Sherd No.	Radius (m)	Munsell Color Code
1.	Flat	159	22,313	.03	10YR 7/3
2.	Disc	159	22,314	.035	7.5YR 7/4
3.	Round	164	22,355	NA	10YR 8/3
4.	Ring	183	22,825*	.035	5YR 3/1

Fig. 13. Bases: Flat-15; Disc-6; Round-2; Ring-9 Samples.

CONCLUSIONS

Three significant observations can be made from this data. First, every sample shown has counterparts that have appeared in at least one and in some cases two other Fields on the site. They probably, then, comprise a set of forms in use throughout the site in this period.

Second, it would seem warranted from that fact to assert that these forms represent common ceramic products in use in the period. This second observation is evident especially in particular bulk quantities found in the Cookpot, Small and Medium Bowls, Heavy Bowls, and Jug/Jar/Pitcher forms. (Note sample counts in figs. 4, 6, 8, and 11.)

Third, it would seem warranted from that fact that the dominant artifact recoveries thus indicated comprised a domestic economy sample, as over against industrial materials. This conclusion remains tentative pending completion of the comparative studies on the thirty remaining unpublished sherds from this locus. If they indicate particular industrial forms, this conclusion will need to be revised. Preliminary visual assessments indicate that they fall within the horizon of domestic forms in use in the period.

NOTES

1. This is the only primary data from the site for the period on published record to date.
2. Chapter IV of the treatment presented the relevant Iron IA materials from the site available through the 1962 season.
3. The assistance of Cynthia Walton and William Walton in the preparation of some of these drawings is hereby gratefully acknowledged.

REFERENCES

Boraas, R. S.
   1965   Judges IX and Tell Balatah. Unpublished Ph.D. Dissertation, Drew University.
   1986   Iron IA Ceramics at Tell Balatah: A Preliminary Examination. Pp. 249–63 in *The Archaeology of Jordan and Other Studies*, eds. L. T. Geraty and L. G. Herr. Berrien Springs, MI: Andrews University.
Campbell, E. F.
   1996a   *Shechem III: Site Stratigraphy and Architecture.* Unpublished draft manuscript.
   1996b   Letter of Sept 19, 1996 to Roger Boraas.
Munsell
   1973   *Munsell Soil Color Charts.* Baltimore MD: Munsell Products, Macbeth Color & Photometry Division of Kollmoregen Corporation.

3 "Rod and Staff" (Psalm 23:4): A Double Image?

RICHARD W. CORNEY

"It seemed to us," said William Allen Knight, speaking on behalf of his family to their Syrian guest about Psalm 23, "to lose the sweet simple melody ... when it changes to a scene of banquet hospitality" (Knight 1904: n.p.). What bothered the Rev. Dr. Knight and his family around the turn of the century has continued to bother a number of commentators on this psalm. Such commentators think Psalm 23 is much too brief to sustain the two[1] or even three[2] images that other scholars have discerned in it. To such commentators "any division of such a short psalm is out of the question" (Lundbom 1971: 11 n. 7; similarly Asensio 1959: 244 n. 7).

Some have sought the unity of Psalm 23 in the same manner as Dr. Knight's Syrian guest, who explained the entire psalm to the Knight family in terms of a shepherd tending a flock. On such a reading, for example, the preparation of a table over against the psalmist's adversaries (v. 5) becomes the preparation of the sheepfold for the bedding down of the flock at night (e.g., Sauer 1971: 489–90). But such explanations for the imagery in vv. 5–6 seem more than a little forced even to some who themselves believe that the image of sheep-herding governs the entire psalm. These commentators prefer to eliminate the table by emendation of the text, thereby transforming the table into a weapon the shepherd prepares in order to ward off predators (Power 1928: 439; his emendation has been accepted by Morgenstern 1946: 15 and Koehler 1956: 232).[3] But total lack of textual support for such an emendation has led to its general rejection (e.g., Vogt 1953: 197; Kraus 1978: 335).[4]

The difficulty of interpreting vv. 5–6 in terms of shepherd and sheep has led others to search for a topos beneath the surface imagery of Psalm 23 in which the diverse images of shepherd and host are united.

Some have found this unifying topos in the biblical accounts of and allusions to the nexus of events from the Exodus to Conquest. Tournay writes, "la typologie de l'Exode ... enveloppe l'ensemble du Ps XXIII (berger, eaux, chemin, ténèbre, table)" (Tournay 1956: 511). Freedman, noting that the presentation of the Exodus-Conquest nexus found in Psalm 78 employs both shepherd and host imagery, suggests that Psalm 23 utilizes such imagery both to personalize and to universalize Israel's experience of those events (Freedman 1980: 276). Freedman's argument has been further developed by Barré and Kselman, who find in v. 6a a reference to the new covenant (Barré and Kselman 1983: 98). But even if such scholars are correct in their identification of the psalm's underlying topos (Pardee has pointed out that "it requires a multileveled application, *by allusion only*" [Pardee 1990: 276–77]), it still does not alter the fact that two or three different images are present on the surface of the text. As Milne, who herself hears echoes of the Exodus in Psalm 23, admits, the assertion that the overall motif of the psalm is the Exodus in no way denies the images of shepherd and host in the poem (Milne 1974/75: 245).

A third route followed by those disturbed by the diversity present in Psalm 23 is to find its unity in the poet's personal experience. These commentators treat at least part of the psalm as non-metaphorical, usually by explaining vv. 5–6 as a description of an actual event occurring in the cult. Thus Mittmann writes that these verses "ungeachtet der metaphorischen Diktion eine Realität beschreibt" (Mittmann 1980: 2); for him the described reality is the meal accompanying a thanksgiving sacrifice. Earlier Vogt had suggested that v. 5 was "a short description of a real meal in which the psalmist had participated" in the Temple (Vogt 1953: 201).[5] In this approach vv. 1–4 are read as a metaphorical description of the actual cultic situation set forth in the psalm's concluding verses (similarly Stamm 1966: 127; Oost 1986: 98). M. E. Smith takes this experiential approach a step further. For him Psalm 23 is a pilgrimage psalm; vv. 1–4 reflect the psalmists's journey to Jerusalem, while vv. 5–6 describe what happened after he got there. Smith reads the psalm as a merging of the psalmist's external and internal experience; pasture, waters, valley, table, and Temple are all to be understood as phenomena experienced personally by the pilgrim poet (Smith 1988: 63–64). There are, however, certain difficulties with reading v. 5 as a reference to a sacrificial meal. Spieckermann has pointed out that in Ps 23:5, in contrast to the description of sacrifice and sacrificial meal in Leviticus 7, everything is done by Yahweh alone; the psalmist is a completely passive recipient of Yahweh's largesse (Spieckermann 1989: 271 n. 28). Nor does the view that v. 5 describes a cultic sacrifice provide an adequate explanation for the fact that the table is prepared in the presence of the psalmist's adversaries (Sylva 1990: 112–13).

Another who finds the unity of Psalm 23 in a cultic context is Merrill. He locates the psalm in the coronation ritual and understands its speaker to be the king. On Merrill's reading, the psalm, in which he sees a reflection of the Jerusalem royal ideology, relates to a procession that circumambulated the capital city. Behind the shepherd and possibly the guide imagery of vv. 1–4 lies material associated with the monarchy. For example, the "tracks" (*ma ʿgĕlê*, v. 3) on which Yahweh leads the psalmist echo the transportation of the ark to Jerusalem on a cart (*ʿăgālâ*, 2 Sam 6:3), and the "waters of a resting place" (v. 2) become those of "the resting place, the temple of Jerusalem" (Merrill 1965: 358). But as with the Exodus-Conquest topos, so too Merrill's approach to the material in vv. 1–4 relies on allusion, and these allusions seem quite remote.

The same criticism applies to Lundbom's presentation of Psalm 23 as a recounting of "David's passage out of Jerusalem into the wilderness, and back to Jerusalem once again" (2 Sam 15–19) "written from the perspective of the crisis being over, but David has not yet come to Jerusalem" (Lundbom 1986: 14–15). Since Lundbom is "uncertain" about Davidic authorship of the psalm (Lundbom 1986: 12), it is not clear whether he thinks we should understand the psalm as David's personal account of his own experience, as was the case with Smith's pilgrim, or believes that we should treat the events described in 2 Sam 15–19 as the same sort of topos that others have found in the events of the Exodus-Conquest. In either case Lundbom's argument depends on the reader's awareness of allusions to the events of Absalom's revolt, and once again these allusions appear remote. For example, "I shall not lack" (v. 1b) refers to the provisions brought to David by Ziba (2 Sam 16:2), the "still waters" which restore the psalmist's vitality (vv. 2b–3a) reflect the revival of David and his companions when they reach the Jordan (2 Sam 16:5–13), and the prepared table signifies the provisions brought to David at Mahanaim (2 Sam 17:27–29) (Lundbom 1986: 13).[6]

Neither single metaphor nor underlying topos nor the psalmist's own experience seems to provide an adequate basis for discerning unity in Psalm 23. Does this mean that there is no metaphorical consistency in the poem and that all attempts to discern such unity are the result of modern prejudices (so Eaton 1965: 172)? Or is there a common ground on which the different metaphors of shepherd and host can come together? Such a common ground exists, I believe, in the two-fold character of the term "shepherd" in v. 1b and in the same double signification of the words "your mace and your staff" in v. 4b; vv. 2–4a can be read as a metaphorical exposition of one aspect of the double image, vv. 5–6 as a metaphorical exposition the other.[7]

That "shepherd" in the biblical world can both designate one who is a herder of sheep and goats (e.g., Gen 4:2) and signify one who is a ruler (e.g., Isa 44:28)[8] has long been recognized. This two-fold character of the term is reflected, for example, in the different translations given by St. Jerome for Psalm 23:1b. In *Psalterium iuxta Hebraeos* he renders the verse as *Dominus pascit me* ("the Lord pastures me") while in the Vulgate he translates it as *Dominus regit me* ("the Lord rules me") (see Asensio 1959: 237 n. 2).

When we come to the mace (*šēbeṭ*) and staff (*miš'enet*), however, commentators for the most part have treated these instruments as having only a single signification.[9] Usually they are read in terms of the preceding pictures of shepherd and sheep (e.g., Stamm 1966: 121; Auffret 1985: 60); Spieckermann, for example, maintains that mace and staff concretize the shepherd motif (1989: 270–71). To demonstrate that both mace and staff are carried by shepherds, commentators have looked to descriptions of life in Holy Land around the turn of the century (Power 1928: 435–36)[10]; descriptions of shepherds in other cultures have also been cited.[11] Evidence for the use of these two implements by shepherds in the ancient Near East is slight. However, Keel has called attention to a cylinder seal from third millennium Uruk on which is portrayed a shepherd leading a flock, with a staff over one shoulder and a club in the other hand (Keel 1978: 229–30).[12] A similar staff carried in a similar manner can be seen in a photograph taken by Dalman in the plain of Jezreel in 1900 C.E., and a similar club appears in the hand of a shepherd in other photographs of Dalman (Dalman 1939: figs. 30, 34). The fact that early in this century shepherds in the Holy Land were using instruments identical with those of shepherds in

third millennium Uruk justifies in this instance the reading back of
early twentieth century descriptions of pastoral practice into the days
of the psalmist.[13]

In addition to their use by shepherds, mace and staff were carried by
monarchs. In fact, evidence for their employment as royal regalia in
antiquity is much more plentiful than the evidence for their pastoral
use. Of the many portrayals of ancient Near Eastern monarchs with
scepter and/or staff, two may be cited. From Egypt there is the statue
of Tut-ankh-Amon standing with a golden mace in his right hand and a
golden staff of the *mekes* type in his left (Pritchard 1954: fig. 414),[14]
and from Assyria there is the stele discovered in 1951 at Nimrud
(Kalḫu), on which Ashurnaṣirpal II is portrayed with a mace in his
right hand and a staff in his left (Wiseman 1952: pls. II, III, VII). The
association of these shepherds' implements with royalty is also attested
in written documents. Thus we read in the Old Babylonian version of
the Legend of Etana that before kingship was established on earth "scepter (*ḫaṭṭu*), crown, headcloth and staff (*šibirru*) lay before Anu in
heaven" (tablet 1/A, 10–11; Kinnier-Wilson 1985: 30), while in the
Neo-Babylonian period Nabonidus prays that he may possess "scepter
(*ḫaṭṭu*) and just staff (*šibirru kînum*) for ever" (Langdon 1912: 226;
iii, 20).[15] Similarly in Gen 49:10 mace (*šēbeṭ*) and staff (*mĕḥōqēq*)
appear together as insignia of a ruler. To be sure, the staff in Gen
49:10 is designated by a term different from the one used in Ps 23:4;
however, in Egypt ceremonial staffs of different sorts, designated by
different names, were used as symbols of authority (Hayes 1990:
284–86), and the same may have been true in ancient Israel.

There are indications in the language and structure of Psalm 23 that
v. 4b, with its image of mace and staff, is not, as many commentators
maintain (e.g., Oesterley 1955: 184; Kraus 1978: 339; Spieckermann
1989: 265), simply the conclusion of the first part of the psalm, but
rather that it stands between the first and the second parts as an independent bicolon. If we treat v. 1b and v. 4b as independent bicola, each
would be followed by eight lines of exposition, though in vv. 2–4a this
would break down as tricolon (vv. 2–3a), bicolon (v. 3b) and tricolon
(v. 4a), while in vv. 5–6 there are four bicola (vv. 5a, 5b, 6a, 6b).[16]
Moreover Steingrímmson has pointed out that v. 4a, the final tricolon
of the first exposition, is one of only two verses in Psalm 23 where a
sentence is introduced by a conjunction; the other occurrence is in v.

6b, where the conjunction introduces the final verse of the psalm. He argues that in a psalm that is largely asyndetic this use of conjunctions indicates that vv. 4a and 6b are linked texts (Steingrímmson 1991: 485). I would suggest that what links them is their function as the concluding lines of their respective expositions, with v. 4a ending the exposition of v. 1b and v. 6b closing that of v. 4b.[17]

There are marked similarities between the independent bicola v. 1b and 4b. The first colon of each consists entirely of two substantives, differing, to be sure, in syntax (in v. 1b the substantives constitute a nominal sentence; in v. 4b they function as a *casus pendens*), but conveying essentially the same information, namely that YHWH is shepherd/king. V.1b does this directly through its use of the term *rō'eh*; v. 4b conveys the information by its depiction of implements which both shepherd and king employ. Likewise in each of these independent bicola, the second colon is a verbal sentence in which the impact on the psalmist of the information given in the preceding colon is set forth. These similarities in form and content suggest a similarity in function. That function, I believe, is to present in each instance the double image that will be exposited in the following lines.

Psalm 23 opens, then, with the statement that YHWH is sheep herder/ monarch (v. 1b). Vv. 2–4a expound and expand on this statement in sheep herder terms. YHWH is the shepherd, the psalmist a sheep.[18] In this section, as Pardee has pointed out, the verbs with the first common singular suffix are verbs closely linked to the tending of animals, while "pastures," "paths," and "valleys" are geographical terms for places where flocks are led (Pardee 1990: 247–49, 273).[19]

When the reader reaches v. 4b with its mace and its staff, the reader would first understand these implements in the light of the sheep herding exposition that precedes them. The connection of *"your* mace and *your* staff" with what has gone before is strengthened by a shift encountered in the last line of the preceding exposition. Until this point references to YHWH have been in the third person; in v. 4a YHWH is referred to in the second person ("for *you* are with me"). But, as Pardee notes, when the reader reaches the verb *nhm*, a verb not applicable to sheep, the image shifts (Pardee 1990: 272, 275)—mace and staff are transformed, by backreading, into royal regalia, and the double image of v. 1b is thereby reconstituted. "Your mace and your staff" now function as a metonym for YHWH, both sheepherder and monarch.

In vv. 5–6 the psalmist, having reconstituted the double image, proceeds to expound its royal aspect, using language appropriate for humans, not animals (Pardee 1990: 276). YHWH is the monarch, the psalmist an important retainer of the monarch, one of those who like Mephibosheth (2 Sam 9:7, 10, 11, 13; 19:29) or the sons of Barzillai (1 Kgs 2:7) are invited to eat at the king's table,[20] while those who have been the psalmist's adversaries are treated like the seventy kings who scavenged under the table of Adonizedek (Judg 1:7), or like those uninvited guests who arrived at a banquet given by El for the other gods and whom he beat "with a mace under the table" (RS 24.258:8).[21] The psalm concludes with the psalmist's/retainer's conviction that, like Mephibosheth who ate at the king's table "continually," he or she will dwell[22] forever in the palace of King YHWH.[23] Psalm 23, then, is a unified work, and what unites its two sections is the two-fold nature of the opening image of shepherd/king and the reiteration of that image in the shepherd/royal implements of mace and staff.

NOTES

1. Usually shepherd (vv. 1–4) and host (vv. 5–6) (e.g., Baethgen 1892: 67; Oesterley 1955:183; Kraus 1978: 337–40; Steingrímmson 1991); a division between the Elysian Fields (vv. 2–3) and life on earth (vv. 4–5) has been suggested by Dahood (1966: 145–6).

2. Shepherd (vv. 1–3a), guide (vv. 3b–4), and host (vv. 5–6) (Briggs 1906: 207; similarly Loretz 1993: 115). Some who find shepherd imagery throughout vv. 1–4 nevertheless subdivide that image into shepherd as nourisher and shepherd as guide (e.g., Weiser 1962: 228–29; Sauer 1971: 489; Auffret 1985: 58) or into the happy state of being herded by YHWH and the dangers of that state (Pardee 1990: 274).

3. Power suggested that the final *nun* of *šulḥān* is a dittography of the first letter of the following *neged*. The restored consonantal text is then read as *šelaḥ* "throwing spear" (Power 1928: 439).

4. While interpreting the entire twenty-third Psalm in terms of a shepherd metaphor has not received wide scholarly support, it is common in the popular press (e.g., Keller [1970: 99–100], who understands the "table" of v. 5 as a reference to the "tableland," the high range where the sheep are herded in the summer months).

5. Some who find in v. 5a a reference to a cultic meal also treat the description in a quasi metaphorical manner (e.g., Weiser 1962: 230).

6. Tournay also finds "Davidic echoes" in the psalm, but considers them to be supplemental to the underlying Exodus imagery (Tournay 1956).

7. Van Uchelen (1989) also sees this psalm in terms of what he calls *modus ponens* followed by *modus exponens*; for him the first *modus ponens* is "YHWH is my shepherd" (v. 1b); the second is "you are with me" (v. 4a).

8. Mittmann points out that "shepherd" was not a royal title in Israel, but that it functions as a metonym for "ruler," especially the king (Mittmann 1980: 20 n. 55).

9. Pardee is an exception. He notes that v. 4b contains two terms that from the preceding image, should be expected to denote the shepherd's staff, but the first of which, especially, is susceptible of being interpreted as the judge's rod or the king's scepter (Pardee 1990: 275). Where what is presented here differs from Pardee is in its isolation of v. 4b, which for Pardee is the middle colon of a tricolon beginning with *kî ʾattâ ʿimmādî* (v. 4a), and in its understanding of v. 4b as a resumption of v. 1b.

10. Power correctly notes, against an earlier view that understood *šēbeṭ* and *mišʿenet* as parallel terms signifying the same instrument (e.g., Baethgen 1892: 439), that the following *hēmâ* shows that we have here two different implements, not the same implement under two different names (Power 1928: 439).

11. Thus Keller writes, "Some of my most vivid boyhood recollections are those of watching the African herdsmen shepherding their flock with only a long slender stick and a rough *knob-kerrie* in their hand" (Keller 1970: 86).

12. The seal is VA 7334. A clear photograph of an impression of this seal may be found in Moortgat (1940: pl. 1,4).

13. Merrill, who argues that *only* royal regalia are signified by mace and staff in Psalm 23, maintains correctly that *mišʿenet* is never associated with shepherds in the Hebrew Bible, but that it is associated with nobles (Num 21:18; Merrill 1965: 358–59). However, the *mišʿenet* also designates a simple walking stick, with no noble associations (Exod 21:19), and as such would be a suitable implement for a shepherd. For the use of *šēbeṭ* with the flock, see Lev 27:32.

14. For a discussion of the different types of staff used in Egypt, see Hayes (1990, I: 284–85).

15. *CAD* VI, 155 lists only figurative usages of *ḫaṭṭu* as a shepherd's implement. But the existence of a plant called *ḫaṭṭu reʾi* would seem to indicate that it was carried by sheep herders as well as monarchs. For *šiburri* as a shepherd's implement note the line *ri-e-u ina ši-bir-ri-šu li-duk-ši* ("a shepherd with his staff slew her") (Haupt 1881: 120.16).

16. There is little agreement about the strophic structure and meter of Psalm 23. Among those who treat v. 1b as a 2+2 bicolon are: Morgenstern (1946: 22), Stamm (1966: 120), and Foley (1978: 365–66); those who treat v.

4b as a 2+2 bicolon include Rinaldi (1961: 81) and Loretz (1993: 105).

17. Van Uchelen also sees v. 4b as the beginning of the final section of Psalm 23, but he treats the entire section as *modus exponens* (see above, n. 7; van Uchelen 1989: 159). Other evidence in the text for the treatment of vv. 1b–4a as a unit has been noted. There is, for example, a chiastic relationship between v. 1b and 4a (Foley 1978: 373; Mittmann 1980: 11; Steingrímmson 1991: 486). Auffret's understanding of the structure of vv. 1–4, apart from his treatment of v. 4b as the closing line of the first section, is likewise similar to the one suggested here (Auffret 1985).

18. It is often said that Ps 23:1 is the only place in the Hebrew Bible where YHWH is portrayed as the shepherd of an individual. This has then been used as a basis for arguing that the "I" of this psalm is the king, who as the embodiment of his people "reconciles the prominence of the I with the … fact that conception of God as shepherd should refer, as elsewhere, to the rule and care of a collective …" (Eaton 1965: 175; see also Stenger 1987: 446). But Steingrímmson has pointed out that in Gen 48:15 the relation of God, "the one shepherding," is to Jacob as an individual (1991: 490). Of course, both individual sheep and the individual royal retainer (see below) are themselves part of a larger collective (Baethgen 1892: 68).

19. This is not to deny that the words of this psalm operate on other levels as well; it is only to claim that on the level of the metaphor governing this section of the psalm the language is appropriate for the herding of sheep. On other levels of interpretation the words may bear other significations as well. Thus the "right paths" (v. 3) on which the shepherd leads the sheep can at the same time be "paths of righteousness" (see Asensio 1959: 241; Eaton 1965: 172–73; Spieckermann 1989: 268; contra Lundbom 1986: 13). Nor does it deny that this language may also carry an echo of other traditions, such as some of those discerned by advocates of the Exodus-Conquest topos.

20. Honored retainer seems to me to fit the tone of the metaphor here better than vassal king, as suggested by Barré and Kselman 1983:105–106 (similarly Pardee 1990: 270; Loretz 1993: 115).

21. *wlmn.ḥtm.tḥt.tlḥn* (Virolleaud 1968: 545). The understanding of the verb as "beat" is that of Gaster (1969: 417), who cites this text in connection with Judg 1:7. For the translation of *ḥtm* as "with a mace," see Gray (1955: 56). A frequently cited parallel to this verse of the psalm, first pointed out in Gunkel 1926: 100, is EA 100:33–35 (Pharaoh "gives to his servants while our enemies look on").

22. Of the various suggestions for the commonly accepted alteration of MT "I shall return" into "I shall dwell," namely understanding MT *wĕšabtî* as a contraction or by-form from *yšb* (Dahood 1966: 148) or emending MT

either to *wĕyāšabtî* (see Jerome, Syriac, Targum; so, e.g., Power 1928: 442; Kraus 1978: 335) or *wĕšibtî*, I prefer the last. Tournay suggests MT arose from "une relecture davidique," which understood the verse to refer to David's temporary absence from Jerusalem during Absalom's revolt (Tournay 1956: 506, 509; see also Lundbom 1986: 14).

23. I would side with those who hold that the metaphorical language continues to the end of the psalm (e.g., Herkenne 1936: 112) and against those who find in v. 6 direct theological speech (e.g., Spieckermann 1989: 273).

REFERENCES

Asensio, F.
    1959   Entrecruce de Simbolos y Realidades in Salmo 23. *Biblica* 40: 237–47.
Auffret, P.
    1985   Essai sur la structure littéraire du Psaume 23. *Estudios Biblicos* 43: 57–88.
Baethgen, F.
    1892   Die Psalmen. Handkommentar zum Alten Testament, II/2. Göttingen: Vandenhoeck & Ruprecht.
Barré, M. L., and Kselman, J. S.
    1983   New Exodus, Covenant, and Restoration in Psalm 23. Pp. 97–127 in *The Word of the Lord Shall Go Forth. Essays in Honor of David Noel Freedman in Celebration of His Sixtieth Birthday*, eds. C. L. Myers and M. O'Connor. Winona Lake, IN: Eisenbrauns.
Briggs, C. A. and E. G.
    1906   *A Critical and Exegetical Commentary on the Book of Psalms, I*. The International Critical Commentary. New York: Scribner's.
CAD
    1956–   *The Assyrian Dictionary of the Oriental Institute of the University of Chicago*. Chicago: The Oriental Institute.
Dahood, M.
    1966   *Psalms I. 1–50*. Anchor Bible 16. Garden City: Doubleday.
Dalman, G.
    1939   *Arbeit und Sitte in Palästina, VI*. Gütersloh: Bertelsmann.
Eaton, J.
    1965   Problems of Translation in Psalm 23:3–4. *Bible Translation* 16: 171–76.
Foley, C. M.
    1978   Pursuit of the Inscrutable: A Literary Analysis of Psalm 23. Pp. 363–83 in *Ascribe to the Lord. Biblical and Other Essays in*

Memory of Peter C. Craigie, eds. L. Eslinger and G. Taylor. Journal for the Study of the Old Testament-Supplement Series 17. Sheffield: JSOT.

Freedman, D. N.
1980   The Twenty-Third Psalm. Pp. 275–302 in *Pottery, Prophecy and Poetry. Studies in Early Hebrew Poetry*. Winona Lake, IN: Eisenbrauns.

Gaster, T. H.
1969   *Myth, Legend and Custom in the Old Testament*. New York: Harper and Row.

Gray, J.
1955   *The Krt Text in the Literature of Ras Shamra: A Social Myth of Ancient Canaan*. Documenta et Monumenta Orientis Antiqui 5. Leiden: Brill.

Gunkel, H.
1926   *Die Psalmen*. Göttingen: Vandenhoeck & Ruprecht.

Haupt, P.
1881   *Akkadische und sumerische Keilschrifttexte nach den Originalen im britischen Museum copirt* 4. Assyriologische Bibliothek, I. Leipzig: Hinrichs.

Hayes, W. C.
1990   *The Scepter of Egypt. A Background for the Study of the Egyptian Antiquities in the Metropolitan Museum of Art*. Revised edition. New York: Metropolitan Museum of Art.

Herkenne, H.
1936   *Das Buch der Psalmen*. Die Heilige Schrift des Alten Testaments. Bonn: Peter Hanstein.

Keel, O.
1978   *The Symbolism of the Biblical World: Ancient Near Eastern Iconography and the Book of Psalms*. New York: Seabury.

Keller, P.
1970   *A Shepherd Looks at Psalm 23*. New York: Harper Collins.

Kinnier-Wilson, J. V.
1985   *The Legend of Etana. A New Edition*. Warminster: Aris & Phillips.

Knight, W. A.
1904   *The Song of Our Syrian Guest*. Boston: Pilgrim.

Koehler, L. von
1956   Psalm 23. *Zeitschrift für die alttestamentliche Wissenschaft* 68: 227–34.

Kraus, H. J.
1978   *Psalmen*. Biblische Kommentar, Altes Testament, XV/1. Neukirchen-Vluyn: Neukirchener.

Langdon, S.
1912   *Die neubabylonischen Königsinschriften.* Vorderasiatische
        Bibliothek 4. Leipzig: Hinrichs.
Loretz, O.
1993   Marzihu im ugaritischen und biblischen Ahnenkult. Zu Ps 23;
        133; Am 6, 1–7 und Jer 16, 5. 8. Pp. 93–144 in *Mesopotamica,
        Ugaritica, Biblica: Festschrift für Kurt Bergerhof zur Vollendung
        seines 70. Lebensjahre am 7 Mai 1992,* eds. M. Dietrich and O.
        Loretz. Alter Orient und Altes Testament 232. Neukirchen-
        Vluyn: Neukirchener.
Lundbom, J. R.
1986   Psalm 23: A Song of Praise. *Interpretation* 40: 5–16.
Merrill, A. J.
1965   Psalm XXIII and the Jerusalem Tradition. *Vetus Testamentum*
        15: 354–60.
Milne, P.
1974/75 Psalm 23: Echoes of the Exodus. *Studies in Religion / Sciences
        Religieuse* 4: 237–47.
Mittmann, S.
1980   Aufbau und Einheit des Danklieds Psalm 23. *Zeitschrift für
        Theologie und Kirche* 77: 1–23.
Moortgat, A.
1940   *Vorderasiatische Rollsiegel: Ein Beitrag zur Geschichte der
        Steinschneidekunst.* Berlin: Mohr.
Morgenstern, J.
1946   Psalm 23. *Journal of Biblical Literature* 65: 13–24.
Oesterley, W. O. E.
1955   *The Psalms.* London: SPCK
Oost, R.
1986   De Structur van Psalm 23. *Amsterdamse Cahiers voor Exegese
        en Bijbelse Theologie* 7: 96–100.
Pardee, D.
1990   Structure and Meaning in Hebrew Poetry: The Example of Psalm
        23. Pp. 239–80 in *Sopher Mahir: Northwest Semitic Studies
        Presented to Stanislav Segert.* Winona Lake, IN: Eisenbrauns.
Power, E.
1928   The Shepherd's Two Rods in Modern Palestine and in Some
        Passages of the Old Testament. *Biblica* 9: 434–42.
Pritchard, J. B.
1954   *The Ancient Near East in Pictures Relating to the Old Testa-
        ment.* Princeton: Princeton University.

Rinaldi, G.
1961   Il Salmo 23 (Volg 22) (Dominus regit me). *Bibbia e Oriente* 3:
            81–85.
Sauer, A.
1971   Fact and Image in the Shepherd Psalm. *Currents in Theology
            and Mission* 42: 488–92.
Smith, M. E.
1988   Setting and Rhetoric in Psalm 23. *Journal for the Study of the
            Old Testament* 41: 61–66.
Spieckermann, H.
1989   *Heilsgegenwart: Eine Theologie der Psalmen*. Forschungen zur
            Religion und Literatur des Alten und Neuen Testaments 148.
            Göttingen: Vandenhoeck & Ruprecht.
Stamm, J. J.
1966   Erwägungen zu Psalm 23. Pp. 120–28 in *Freude am Evangelium.
            Alfred de Quervain zum 70 Geburtstag am 28 September 1966*,
            eds. J. J. Stamm and E. Wolff. Munich: Chr. Kaiser.
Steingrímmson, S. Ö.
1991   Der priestliche Anteil. Bedeutung und Aussageabsicht im Psalm
            23. Pp. 483–519 in *Text, Methode und Grammatik: Wolfgang
            Richter zum 65 Geburtstag*, ed. W. Gross. St. Ottilien: EOS.
Stenger, W.
1987   Strukturale "relecture' von Ps 23. Pp. 441–55 in *Freude an der
            Weisung des Herrn: Beiträge zum Theologie der Psalmen:
            Festgabe zum 70 Geburtstag von Heinrich Gross*, eds. E. Haag
            and L. Hossfeld. Stuttgart: Katholisches Bibelwerk.
Sylva, D. D.
1990   The Changing Images in Psalm 23, 5. 6. *Zeitschrift für die
            alttestamentliche Wissenschaft* 102: 111–16.
Tournay, R.
1956   En marge d'un traduction des Psaumes (suite) (1). *Revue
            Biblique* 63: 496–512.
van Uchelen, N. A.
1989   Psalm XXIII: Some Regulative Linguistic Evidence. Pp. 156–62
            in *New Avenues in the Study of the Old Testament: A Collection
            of Old Testament Essays Published on the Occasion of the Fifti-
            eth Anniversary of the Oudtestamentische Werkgezelschap and
            the Retirement of Prof. M. J. Miller*, ed. A. S. van der Woude.
            Oudtestamentische Studien 25. Leiden: Brill.
Virolleaud, C.
1968   Les nouveaux textes mythologiques et liturgiques de Ras Shamra
            (XXIVe campagne, 1961). *Ugaritica* V: 545–95.

Vogt, E.
  1953   The 'Place in Life' of Psalm 23. *Biblica* 34: 195–211.
Weiser, A.
  1962   *The Psalms: A Commentary.* Trans. H. Hartwell, from German.
             Old Testament Library. Philadelphia: Westminster.
Wiseman, D. J.
  1952   A New Stela of Assur-nasir-pal II. *Iraq* 14: 24–60.

4   Nineveh's "Three Days' Walk" (Jonah 3:3): Another Interpretation

DAVID MARCUS

The legendary sinful city of Nineveh is described in the Book of Jonah as being extraordinarily large. Four times the epithet עִיר גְּדוֹלָה "large city" is applied to it (1:2; 3:2; 3:3; 4:11), and on one of those occasions it is called עִיר גְּדוֹלָה לֵאלֹהִים (3:3). The addition of לֵאלֹהִים to the epithet magnifies the city even more. It is "an exceptionally large city," literally, "a great city to gods or to God." The force of לֵאלֹהִים is probably, as Winton Thomas (1953: 210–16) suggested, a form of the superlative "a divinely great city" as in our colloquial "godalmighty big city" (Day 1990: 34) or "a godawfully big city" (Vawter 1983: 105). In addition, as a sign of its enormity, it is said that Nineveh's population consisted of 120,000 people אֲשֶׁר לֹא־יָדַע בֵּין־יְמִינוֹ לִשְׂמֹאלוֹ "who do not know their right hand from their left" (4:11). The meaning of this phrase has been variously interpreted. Some believe it signifies "children," because little children don't know the difference between their right hand and their left hand (*Kimḥi* 1951; Bewer 1912: 64).[1] Others extend the analogy with children to include the entire population who lack knowledge or moral perception (Stuart 1987: 507; Alexander 1988: 130; and Freedman 1990: 31). Just as children do not know the difference between right and wrong and are thus not morally responsible, so too the Ninevites, like children, are morally obtuse. If the idiom refers to the Ninevites then the figure of 120,000 would refer to the total population of the city. But if the idiom refers only to the children then the 120,000 represents only a portion of the actual population, and some have speculated on numbers as high as 300,000 (see Sasson 1990: 311–12), or

42

even twice that amount as being the number of the total population (Bewer 1912: 64; Archer 1964: 299).

In his recent commentary Jack Sasson (1990: 315) has advanced a most original interpretation of the phrase. Nineveh was so large in size that the inhabitants literally did not know who was living on the right and left of them, that is, they did not know who their neighbors were. Support for Sasson's theory may be found in Akkadian, where the expression "to the right and the left" (*kīmma imitti u šumē ʾli*) is used for "neighbors to the right and left" (see *CAD*, I: 123). In any event, whatever the phrase means, the figure 120,000 seems to be another of the hyperbolic numerical expressions in the book indicating "a teeming population" (Allen 1976: 234).

It is commonly thought that another description of the enormity of the city is to be found in the phrase מַהֲלַךְ שְׁלֹשֶׁת יָמִים "a three days' walk," which occurs in chapter three, verse three. Nineveh was such a large city that it took a full three days in order to go from end to end or, according to some, to walk around its walls. It is with this common interpretation that this paper takes issue. It is my belief that the phrase מַהֲלַךְ שְׁלֹשֶׁת יָמִים, "a three days' walk," does not refer to the dimensions of Nineveh, but refers to the distance that Jonah has to travel in order to reach Nineveh. My arguments are threefold.

First of all, there are some problems with the standard interpretation that the phrase מַהֲלַךְ שְׁלֹשֶׁת יָמִים, "a three days' walk," refers to the dimensions of Nineveh. If one takes this as a description of the historical Nineveh, as many attempt to do, it does not fit. According to the latest surveys by Stronach and Lumsden (1992: 227), Nineveh, at its imperial height in the seventh century, measured 750 hectares or about 4 square miles.[2] Hence, at that time it would have been possible to walk around the city in a couple of hours or less, and one could certainly have gone from one end to another of imperial Nineveh in half an hour or so (Vawter 1983: 105; Day 1990: 34).

To counter this objection it has been proposed that we ought to think more of a greater Nineveh than simply the city itself. Nineveh's boundaries ought to be extended to include areas outside the city limits. Thus, on the analogy of "greater London," a term which includes the suburbs and denotes a much larger area than the actual city of London, André Parrot (1955: 85–86) suggested that greater Nineveh included every town from Khorsabad in the north to Nimrud in the south. This area, which he terms "the Assyrian triangle," covers a distance of some twenty-six miles, and could merit the designation of a "three days' walk."[3]

Other commentators have assumed that the designation of Nineveh's size as a "three days' walk" was not a reference to the circumference or diameter of the city, but that the city was so large that it would take three days to walk through all its streets (Ehrlich 1912: 269; Brichto 1992: 75). This interpretation has had particular appeal for those pulpit commentators who envisage Jonah going through the city preaching on every streetcorner (e.g., Keil 1874: 405). A typical comment is given by G. L. Archer (1964: 298–99): "after all, streetcorner preaching requires a fairly extended stop at each place the message is delivered."

The problems with this standard interpretation are primarily twofold. In the first place, no other city in the Bible or in any ancient Near Eastern literature is described either by the circuit of its walls or by its diameter.[4] In the Bible an important city such as Gibeon in Josh 10:2 or Jerusalem in Jer 22:8 is termed an עִיר גְּדוֹלָה ("a large city") just as Nineveh is described here. In the Akkadian annals, the capital or most important city of a region is invariably termed an *āl šarrūti* "a royal city." Neither literature uses the time taken to go around the city's walls as a means of indicating a city's dimensions.

The second, and more signficant, problem encountered with taking "a three days' walk" as referring to the size of Nineveh is the fact that this interpretation cannot adequately explain what happens at the beginning of the next verse. That verse, chapter three, verse four, reads וַיָּחֶל יוֹנָה לָבוֹא בָעִיר מַהֲלַךְ יוֹם אֶחָד. This sentence is usually taken to mean that Jonah, already at the city, walked through, or around, one third of the city before announcing his prophecy. This interpretation underlies some of the most recent translations of this sentence. Thus Sasson (1990: 224) in the Anchor Bible translates: "hardly had he gone into town a day," and Limburg (1993: 77) in the Old Testament Library renders: "and Jonah started to go through the city, walking for one day." But these translations do not properly render the phrase וַיָּחֶל יוֹנָה לָבוֹא בָעִיר, which means literally "Jonah began to enter the city."[5] If, as these translations assume, Jonah had already arrived at the city, then the expression "began to enter the city," which connotes arrival, is decidedly incongruous.[6] My view is that this phrase means what it says: Jonah had just arrived at Nineveh.[7] The following phrase,

מַהֲלַךְ יוֹם אֶחָד "a one day's walk" is an adverbial clause of time[8] and records the time it took for Jonah to reach Nineveh, not the time it took him to go through it. Similarly, the preceding phrase מַהֲלַךְ שְׁלֹשֶׁת יָמִים "a three days' walk" does not refer to the dimensions of Nineveh, but refers to the distance that one has to travel in order to reach Nineveh.[9] In Biblical Hebrew, distance between places may be described by the adjective רָחוֹק "far,"[10] but distance can also be described by the amount of territory one can travel in a day.[11] Nineveh is very far away: it is so distant that it requires a מַהֲלַךְ שְׁלֹשֶׁת יָמִים, "a three days' walk," to reach it. Notwithstanding this great distance, Jonah is able to reach the city in a very short period of time by a מַהֲלַךְ יוֹם אֶחָד "a one day's walk." Furthermore, I believe that the phrase מַהֲלַךְ שְׁלֹשֶׁת יָמִים, "a three days' walk," may be used figuratively to indicate a journey involving a long period of time, not necessarily a literal "three days." Likewise, the second phrase מַהֲלַךְ יוֹם אֶחָד "a one day's walk," may also be used figuratively to indicate a journey involving a short period of time, and not necessarily a literal one day's journey. Support for this interpretation is to be found in the usage of the cognate phrases in Hebrew and Akkadian.

Since in Biblical Hebrew the word מַהֲלָךְ in the meaning of journey reoccurs only in Neh 2:6,[12] we are obliged to turn to its identical synonym דֶּרֶךְ[13] to see how it is used in similar phrases when distance is calculated by the extent travelled in a day. The phrases used are דֶּרֶךְ שְׁלֹשֶׁת יָמִים and דֶּרֶךְ יוֹם, phrases that are virtually synonymous with מַהֲלַךְ יוֹם אֶחָד and מַהֲלַךְ שְׁלֹשֶׁת יָמִים. These phrases, דֶּרֶךְ שְׁלֹשֶׁת יָמִים, and מַהֲלַךְ יוֹם אֶחָד and מַהֲלַךְ שְׁלֹשֶׁת יָמִים, דֶּרֶךְ יוֹם, are used figuratively to indicate distances involving long and short periods of time. In violation of the spirit of his agreement with Jacob, Laban removed all the dark sheep and the speckled goats from his flock, and put between Jacob and himself a דֶּרֶךְ שְׁלֹשֶׁת יָמִים, "a three days' journey," that is, a very long distance (Gen 30:36). When the Israelites left Mount Sinai they marched דֶּרֶךְ שְׁלֹשֶׁת יָמִים, "a three days' journey" (Num 10:33 twice), a very long way; and at one stage in their wanderings in the wilderness the Israelites journey for such a long distance, that it is described as דֶּרֶךְ שְׁלֹשֶׁת יָמִים (Num 33:8). Thus, the phrase דֶּרֶךְ שְׁלֹשֶׁת יָמִים, "a three days' journey," can connote long distances, and not necessarily a journey that literally took three days.[14]

Similarly, and by contrast, יוֹם דֶּרֶךְ, "a day's journey" describes a very short distance, one that can be accomplished easily within one day. For example, the quails which were sent by God in response to the Israelites' request for a change of diet landed in such proximity to the camp that they were only יוֹם דֶּרֶךְ "a day's journey" on this side and יוֹם דֶּרֶךְ "a day's journey" on that side (Num 11:31 twice). That is, the quails fell so close to the camp that they were easily collected.

Further corroboration of the contention that the phrases מַהֲלַךְ שְׁלֹשֶׁת יָמִים, "a three days' walk" and מַהֲלַךְ יוֹם אֶחָד "a one day's walk" are used figuratively to connote long and short distances is to be found in Akkadian phrases that are practically identical in form and usage to the Hebrew phrases. Thus the Akkadian phrases *mālak sebet ūmi* "a seven day journey," or *mālak ḫamšat ūmi* "a five day journey," exhibit the same structure as Hebrew מַהֲלַךְ שְׁלֹשֶׁת יָמִים and מַהֲלַךְ יוֹם אֶחָד. Both languages use these units of time to express distance and faraway places. Sargon II, for example, describes the extraordinary distance of the island of Cyprus as being a veritable *mālak sebet ūmi* "seven-day journey" (Lyon 1883: 14.28–29), that is, very far away.[15] Such units of time express distance in a figurative sense. Thus, "a journey (*mālaku*) of five, seven, fifteen, or more days" (*ūmī*) connotes a long distance, but "a one day's journey" (*mālak ištēn ūmi*), connotes a short distance. For example, in the Epic of Gilgamesh, to reach the waters of death, Gilgamesh and Urshanabi, the boatman, are able to cover a considerable distance described as "a journey of one month and fifteen days" (*mālak arḫi u ḫamiššeret ūmi*).[16]

On the contrary, when a short distance is intended, Akkadian, like Hebrew, uses the expression "a one day's journey" (*mālak ištēn ūmi*). For example, Nebuchadnezzar II records that, in his campaign against the Elamite king, he pitched his camp along the bank of the Tigris but the distance between the two armies was only "a one day's journey" (*mālak ištēn ūmi*), that is, a very short distance (Wiseman 1961: 72, rev. 19). Apparently it was too close for comfort for the Elamite king, because he is said to have panicked with fear and fled back home to Elam.

The argument for the figurative use of the phrase מַהֲלַךְ שְׁלֹשֶׁת יָמִים is also supported by a similar use of the number three elsewhere in the Book of Jonah. Jonah is said to be in the belly of the great fish for "three days and three nights."[17] It is true that elsewhere in the Bible, the expression "three days" may indicate either a long period of time, like our English phrase "for days" (e.g., Josh 2:16; 2 Chr 20:25),[18] or a shorter time span, that is, three specific days (e.g., Gen 40:13, 40:19; Josh 1:11). However, when the phrase "three nights" is added to the "three days," then it always indicates a long period of time (e.g., 1 Sam 30:12 and Esth 4:16; Bauer 1958: 354–58, esp. 356). So Jonah was in the big fish a long time.

Finally, my interpretation admirably not only fits the context but also fits in with an overall reading of the book as a satire (Marcus 1995: 93–159). Everything in Jonah is hyperbole and larger than life. The legendary Nineveh, albeit full of sin, was *the* "great city" par excellence, the "Big Apple" of its time.[19] The city was thought not only to be colossally big but also to be very far away in the east. In actuality, it was over six hundred miles away (Porten 1981: 238), but in biblical terms, it was a מַהֲלַךְ שְׁלֹשֶׁת יָמִים, "a three days' walk." Nevertheless, in accordance with the exaggerated techniques of the satire, Jonah can cover this great distance "lickety split" in an exceptionally short amount of time, namely in a מַהֲלַךְ יוֹם אֶחָד "a one day's walk."

When read in a parodic mode, further support of my thesis comes from a consideration of some details in the stories related about Elijah. It has long been noted that there are many parallels between the Jonah and the Elijah stories. A number of commentators have proposed that Elijah, in particular, served as a model for Jonah (Feuillet 1947: 168–69; Lacocque and Lacocque 1990: 147–48)[20] and that Jonah is burlesqued by being presented as a caricature of the story of Elijah in Beersheba in 1 Kings 19 (Schildenberger 1962: 95; Magonet 1976: 102; Lacocque and Lacocque 1990: 150). In this episode, Elijah, like Jonah, makes a journey in a very short amount of time. Elijah, fleeing for his life from Jezebel, left his servant in Beersheba in Judah and quickly journeyed into the wilderness דֶּרֶךְ יוֹם "a day's journey" (1 Kgs 19:4). Elijah thus performed an extraordinary feat by covering a great distance within a short period of time. This is not the only athletic feat recorded about Elijah. Recall that he had run, like a jogger, in front of Ahab's chariot from Mount Carmel to Jezreel seventeen miles away: "The hand of the Lord had come upon Elijah. He readied himself (lit. tied up his skirts), and ran in front of Ahab all the way to Jezreel" (1 Kgs 18:46). In a parodic emulation of Elijah's feat, Jonah manages to cover over six hundred miles מַהֲלַךְ שְׁלֹשֶׁת יָמִים in just one day מַהֲלַךְ יוֹם אֶחָד.

To summarize this discussion. I have suggested that the phrase מַהֲלַךְ
שְׁלֹשֶׁת יָמִים, "a three days' walk," does not refer to the dimensions of
Nineveh but refers to the distance that Jonah has to travel in order to
reach Nineveh. The phrase is also figurative to indicate a journey involving a long period of time, not necessarily a literal "three days."
Similarly, I have suggested that the phrase מַהֲלַךְ יוֹם אֶחָד, "one day's
walk," is used figuratively to indicate a journey involving a short period of time. Support for this interpretation may be found in the usage
of cognate phrases in Hebrew and Akkadian, by the usage of the number three elsewhere in the book, and by the fact that this interpretation
helps elucidate not only the biblical text but also fits in nicely with a
reading of the Book of Jonah as a satire.

NOTES

1. Supporting texts are Deut 1:39, which describes young children not know-
    ing good and evil, and Isa 7:16, which foretells when Israel and Syria will
    be destroyed by Assyria. Destruction will come sooner than it will take
    an infant born to a young woman today to reach an age of discrimination
    (to understand between right and wrong), that is, in a matter of a few
    years, very soon.
2. Older estimates were that the city wall was about 12 km (7 miles) in
    circumference; see Madhloum (1967: 77).
3. Biblical support for this interpretation is said to be found in the genea-
    logical list of Gen 10:11–12, where four cities, Rehoboth-Ir, Calah, Resen,
    and Nineveh, appear to be collectively termed "the great city" (Watts
    1975: 76). But the usual interpretation is that the designation refers ei-
    ther to Calah or to Nineveh. Wiseman's suggestion (1979: 38) that the
    three days indicate three days of diplomatic activity, the first day indicat-
    ing the day of arrival, the second that of visiting, business, and rest, while
    the third that of departure, is purely speculative.
4. Herodotus' description of Babylon describes the walls only as part of its
    architectural features (Wiseman 1979: 37).
5. The *Peshitta* specifies that the city is Nineveh. It reads ושרי יונן למעל
    לנינוא "Jonah began to enter Nineveh."
6. Furthermore, if the phrase had to do with going through or around the
    city, a different verb of movement such as לָלֶכֶת "to go" instead of לָבוֹא
    "to come," would have been expected. Such a verb does actually occur at
    the beginning of the verse which states that Jonah, in compliance with
    God's command in vv. 1 & 2 of קוּם לֵךְ אֶל־נִינְוֵה ("Set out for Nineveh!")

did actually set out for Nineveh in accordance with God's instructions. The language indicating Jonah's compliance is formulated precisely like that of the command (קוּם לֵךְ אֶל־נִינְוֵה v. 1 // כִּדְבַר יְהוָה v. 3; דְּבַר־יְהוָה v. 2 // וַיָּקָם יוֹנָה וַיֵּלֶךְ אֶל־נִינְוֵה v. 3). The force of this statement of Jonah's departure to Nineveh is that of an anticipatory exposition common with descriptions of departure elsewhere in the Bible (e.g., Gen 22:3; 24:10; 28:5; 1 Kgs 17:10). These verses describe reports of departures to a place before the individual arrives there. For example, in Gen 22:3, Abraham is reported having gone to the specially commanded place (וַיָּקָם וַיֵּלֶךְ אֶל־הַמָּקוֹם אֲשֶׁר־אָמַר־לוֹ הָאֱלֹהִים), yet he does not actually see the place till three days later (v. 4); or in Gen 28:5, Jacob is reported having gone to Paddan-aram (וַיֵּלֶךְ פַּדֶּנָה אֲרָם), yet his adventures on the way remain to be related (Gen 28:10–29:2).

7. This is the standard usage of the phrase לְבֹא בְ. Other examples of לְבֹא בָעִיר meaning "entering in a city" are in 1 Sam 4:13; 23:7; and 1 Kgs 13:25.

8. Such constructions are so-called because they lack an expected preposition such as "on," "in," or "for." A parallel example to מַהֲלַךְ יוֹם אֶחָד of an adverbial accusative of time is וַיָּסֹבּוּ דֶּרֶךְ שִׁבְעַת יָמִים, "they circled about for seven days" (2 Kgs 3:9). Other examples are צָהֳרַיִם "at noon" וּשְׁלֹשׁ־עֶשְׂרֵה שָׁנָה; יוֹם אֶחָד "in one day"(Gen 27:45); בָּאֹפֶל // "in darkness"; מָרָדוּ "in the thirteenth year they rebelled" (Gen 14:4). See *GKC* §118i and Waltke and O'Connor (1990: §10.2.2c).

9. The only person I have found to have made this suggestion is Cohen (1987: 13). He uses this detail as part of his argument that Jonah delivered his own message (of doom) and not God's message (with a promise of mercy for repentance) to Nineveh. God was planning to give him a "carefully-worded message" on the three days journey, but Jonah preempted God by covering the distance in one day (1987, 14). Cohen, like all the other commentators, however, takes the time periods literally.

10. As, for example, עָרִים רְחֹקֹת "distant cities" in Deut 20:15, and רְחוֹקָה "distant" used to describe the city of Laish, which was so far away from Sidon (Judg 18:28).

11. A similar construction is observable in Akkadian, particularly in Sargon's description of Cyprus as being so far way: "a distance of seven days," see *infra*.

12. There the Persian king Artaxerxes asks Nehemiah how long he will be gone on his journey (מַהֲלָךְ) to Jerusalem. In Ezek 42:4 the word refers to an areaway in the new temple which was to be ten cubits wide. The plural form מַהְלְכִים in Zech 3:7 probably signifies "goings" or "free access."

13. It is not without significance that all the various Targumim consistently translate the Hebrew word דֶּרֶךְ by מַהֲלָךְ. See Gen 30:36; 31:23; Exod 3:18; Num 10:33; 33:8; 2 Kgs 3:9, etc.

14. The same phenomenon may be observed with the phrase דֶּרֶךְ שִׁבְעַת יָמִים, "a seven day journey." It too connotes long distance. Laban has to travel a long way דֶּרֶךְ שִׁבְעַת יָמִים , "a seven day journey," to catch Jacob, who had fled from him (Gen 31:23). To quell the revolt of Mesha, the king of Moab, Jehoram of Israel with his allies, Jehoshaphat of Judah and the king of Edom, march for such a long time in the wilderness, דֶּרֶךְ שִׁבְעַת יָמִים, "a seven day journey," that their water supplies were exhausted (2 Kgs 3:9).

15. Akkadian, like Hebrew, normally uses the adjective *rūqu* "far" to describe distant lands (*mātāti rūqêti*), see n. 10 *supra*.

16. *Gilg.* X iii:49. Schmökel (1966: 93) terms this "übermenschliches Tempo."

17. This phrase has been the subject of many allegorical interpretations; see Landes (1967: 446–50).

18. The number three is often used as a superlative; a thing is entirely what it is said to be (e.g., dead for 3 days = really dead; God thrice holy = perfectly holy). It is often associated with the perfection of God's being or action (Sorensen 1967: 569).

19. In the book of Judith (1:1), it is the capital city, the "great city" of Nebuchadnezzar II of Babylon, mistakenly called "king of the Assyria."

20. The connection with Elijah was made already by the Rabbis, who made Jonah the son of the widow of Sarepta whom Elijah revived (BT *Sukkah* 80:5; *Pirqei de Rabbi Eliezer* 33).

REFERENCES

Alexander, D.
    1988   *Jonah: An Introduction and Commentary*. Tyndale Old Testament Commentaries 23b. Downers Grove, IL: Inter-Varsity.

Allen, L. C.
    1976   *The Books of Joel, Obadiah, Jonah and Micah*. New International Commentary on the Old Testament. Grand Rapids, MI: Eerdmans.

Archer, G. L., Jr.
    1964   *Survey of Old Testament Introduction*. Chicago: Moody.

Bauer, J. H.
    1958   Drei Tage. *Biblica* 39: 354–58.

Bewer, J. A.
    1912   *A Critical and Exegetical Commentary on Jonah*. International Critical Commentary. Edinburgh: T. & T. Clark.

Brichto, H. C.
1992   Toward a Grammar of Biblical Poetics. New York: Oxford
        University.
CAD
1956–   The Assyrian Dictionary of the Oriental Institute of the Univer-
        sity of Chicago. Chicago: The Oriental Institute.
Cohen, J. M.
1987   Jonah's Race to Nineveh. Dor le Dor 16/1: 10–15.
Day, J.
1990   The Book of Jonah. Pp. 32-47 in In Quest of the Past: Studies on
        Israelite Religion, Literature and Prophetism, ed. A. Van der
        Woude. Oudtestamentische Stüdien 26. Leiden: Brill.
Ehrlich, A. B.
1912   Randglossen zur hebräischen Bibel. Vol. 5. Reprint 1968.
        Hildesheim: Georg Olms.
Feuillet, A.
1947   Les sources du livre de Jonas. Revue Biblique 54: 161–86.
Freedman, D. N.
1990   Did God Play a Dirty Trick on Jonah at the End? Bible Review
        6/4: 26–31.
Gilg = Campbell Thompson, R.
1929   The Epic of Gilgamish Text, Transliteration, and Notes. Oxford:
        Clarendon.
GKC = Cowley, A. E.
1910   Gesenius' Hebrew Grammar As Edited and Enlarged by the Late
        E. Kautzsch. Second English Edition Revised in Accordance with
        the Twenty-Eighth German Edition (1909). Reprinted 1960.
        Oxford: Clarendon.
Keil, C. F.
1874   The Twelve Minor Prophets. Vol. 1. Trans. J. Martin, from Ger-
        man. Biblical Commentary on the Old Testament. Edinburgh:
        T. & T. Clark.
Kimhi = David Kimhi or Radak (1160–1235)
1951   Commentary in Miqra’ot Gedolot. Rabbinic Bible containing
        commentaries by Rashi (Solomon ben Isaac), Radak (David
        Kimhi), Meṣudat David (Yeḥiel Hillel Altschuler). New York:
        Pardes ‹1524/5› [in Hebrew].
Lacocque, A., and Lacocque, P.-E.
1990   Jonah: A Psycho-Religious Approach to the Prophet. Studies
        on Personalities of the Old Testament. Columbus: University of
        South Carolina.
Landes, G. M.
1967   The "Three Days and Three Nights" Motif in Jonah 2:1. Journal
        of Biblical Literature 86: 446–50.

Limburg, J.
1993   *Jonah*. Old Testament Library. Louisville: Westminster/John
          Knox.
Lyon, D. G.
1883   *Keilschrifttexte Sargon's Königs von Assyrien (722–705 v. chr.)*.
          Leipzig: Hinrichs.
Madhloum, T.
1967   Excavations at Nineveh. *Sumer* 23: 76–82.
Magonet, J.
1976   *Form and Meaning: Studies in Literary Techniques in the Book
          of Jonah*. Bible and Literature Series 8. Reprint 1983. Sheffield:
          Almond.
Marcus, D.
1995   *From Balaam to Jonah: Anti-prophetic Satire in the Hebrew
          Bible*. Brown Judaic Studies 301. Atlanta: Scholars.
Parrot, A.
1955   *Nineveh and the Old Testament*. New York: Philosophical Li-
          brary.
Porten, B.
1981   Baalshamem and the Date of the Book of Jonah. Pp. 237–44 in
          *De la Torah au Messie. Etudes d'exegese et d'hermeneutique
          bibliques offertes a Henri CAZELLES pur ses 25 annees
          d'enseignement a l'Institut Catholique de Paris (Paris, 1979)*,
          eds. M. Carrez, J. Dore, and P. Grelot. Paris: Desclee.
Sasson, J. M.
1990   *Jonah: A New Translation with Introduction, Commentary, and
          Interpretation*. Anchor Bible 24B. Garden City, New York:
          Doubleday.
Schildenberger, J.
1962   Der Sinn des Buches Jona. *Erbe und Auftrag* 38: 93–102.
Schmökel, H.
1966   *Das Gilgamesch Epos. Eingeführt, rhythmisch übertragen und
          mit Anmerkungen versehen*. Stuttgart: W. Kohlhammer.
Sorensen, H. J.
1967   Numbers and Number Symbolism (in the Bible). Pp. 568–70 in
          New Catholic Encyclopedia. Vol. 10, ed. by the editorial staff at
          Catholic University of America. New York: McGraw Hill.
Stronach D., and Lumsden, S.
1992   UC Berkeley's Excavations at Nineveh. *Biblical Archeologist*
          55/4: 227–33.
Stuart, D.
1987   *Hosea-Jonah*. Word Biblical Commentary 31. Waco, Texas:
          Word Books.

Vawter, B.
1983   *Job and Jonah: Questioning the Hidden God.* New York/Ramsey: Paulist.
Waltke, B. K., and O'Connor, M. P.
1990   *An Introduction to Biblical Hebrew Syntax.* Winona Lake: Eisenbrauns.
Watts, J. D. W.
1975   *The Books of Joel, Obadiah, Jonah, Nahum, Habakkuk and Zephaniah.* Cambridge Bible Commentary. Cambridge: Cambridge University.
Winton Thomas, D.
1953   A Consideration of Some Unusual Ways of Expressing the Superlative in Hebrew. *Vetus Testamentum* 3: 209–24.
Wiseman, D. J.
1961   *Chronicles of Chaldaean Kings (626–556 B.C.) in the British Museum.* London: British Museum.
1979   Jonah's Nineveh. *Tyndale Bulletin* 30: 29–51.

5   Ruth Revisited

EDWARD F. CAMPBELL, JR.

*In the early 1970s, I spent a lot of time on the book of Ruth, start-
ing with a paper given at the Biblical Colloquium (published as
Campbell 1974). George Landes and I had been members of Colloquium for more than a decade by then, and have been ever since,
until his retirement last year and mine this year.*

*It is a privilege to join in felicitating George Landes. I hope that
Carol Landes will also be honored by this piece. It takes the form of
a paper updated from its presentation to the Biblical Colloquium in
1995. Perhaps there is no harm in picturing a study group George
and I both appreciate and to which we both owe so much as it hears
and critiques (some of the responses made for alterations) the product of one of its members as he revisits old precincts.*

My earlier work on Ruth (Campbell 1974; 1975) tried to feel
its way into a genre that had very few parallels in the literary records of the ancient Near East, but was frequent in the
Hebrew Bible. It sought comparative insight from certain of the stories of the patriarchs, from the Joseph cycle, the Judah-Tamar story,
the wooing of Rebekkah, and the prose frame of Job. Gunkel had written about the genre, specifically in connection with Ruth, and had provided the form-critical term *Novelle* (Eng.: novella); but, ground rules
for describing the genre were inarticulate, its *Sitz im Leben* unclear,
and its literary characteristics only beginning to be recognized. In the
mode of the time, Gunkel had speculated about precursor forms of the
genre, exploring the form and content of oral tales that may have lain
behind the finished product—adumbrating some of what more recent
folkloristic analyses would say. Luis Alonso-Schökel, Werner
Dommershausen, and Stephen Bertman, among others, had identified
construction techniques involving repetition of key words and
paranomasia that pointed to the playfulness and appeal of stories such
as Ruth. There was some speculation about who composed such sto-

ries in ancient Israel, but few of us were culling modern Hebrew research to any extent at the time, and no one I can spot from that time had noticed S. D. Goitein's *'Iyyunim ba-Miqra* (1957) with its striking essay on "Women as Creators of Biblical Genres," written about 1952, and finally brought to the attention of the English-speaking world by its publication in translation in *Prooftexts* in 1988—after having been injected into the discussion by various women. This happened notably in essays written throughout the 1980s published in Athalya Brenner's *A Feminist Companion to Ruth* (1993).

Meanwhile, I was being driven to address issues of the Bible and the life of women by seminary students, and I had a predisposition in that direction from my liberal heritage, though it was hard to see everything that was going on in the tumultuous 1960s and 1970s. In 1970, there were no women in the Biblical Colloquium. I am, however, married to one, and she had already begun the protracted and loving task of bringing me into recognition of dimensions of partnership that our culture of the time was beginning to see—a task that has decorated the major portion of our married life.

The Myers *Festschrift* paper (Campbell 1974) proposed to describe the short story genre while at the same time refusing to picture it as so discrete as to be isolated from illumination from other nearby genres. It claimed that the short story was a fictional-historical composition, probably typical of village life at least at inception, constructed of attention-grabbing moves that would appeal to a wide audience of experientially-sophisticated people. The short story by design entertained as well as instructed. It focused on life situations and thus had to wrestle with circumstances that often stretched custom and demanded ingenuity in resolving problems encountered on the home front. With Gunkel, it posited a group of (male) "professional" Hebrew storytellers. However, the paper rejected as unproductive the efforts to reconstruct literary precursors, whether oral or written, to the finished product, claiming on the analogy of Ben Edwin Perry's works on Latin romances that creativity passes through a zero point on the way from known motifs and schemas to new literary products, and that a piece of artistry, oral or written, needs to be appreciated on its own as a new composition.

When my *Anchor Bible: Ruth* appeared in 1975, it built on this paper, but proposed village women as possible candidates for professional Hebrew storytellers, elaborated on their artistry, and sought to press on to the social circumstances of the story, on the underlying assumption that the drama of the story had to do with the predicament of three women cast loose by a series of misfortunes into coping in a world insensitive to their circumstances and oblivious to the perspectives of their sex. Actually the commentary did not work on the premise that Israelite culture was oblivious to women's perspectives; latent in it was a suspicion that Israel was not as patriarchally problematic a society as it was currently being described and that the story could be rescued for all audiences, because some at least in Israel were not oblivious, even some men. Phyllis Trible and others—among them, I sense, Cynthia Ozick (1987)—have seen Israelite culture as not quite so patriarchal as it is now all but universally portrayed.

In revisiting Ruth, I turn first not to the issues of authorship or folklore style, but to what the story is saying happened to Ruth, Naomi, and Boaz—and to Orpah and Mr. So-and-So—in Bethlehem. There has been a lot of ink spilled on the subject. It seems, however, that the philological stage is still pretty much set for current inquiry by the immensely careful and provocative study of Jack Sasson, which appeared in 1979, and was reprinted with a very important four page foreword in 1989. Some of this book's fruitfulness emerges from its analysis, via Vladimir Propp, of the formalist-folklorist character of the story, but Sasson (see the 1989 foreword) arrived at most of his reconstruction of the drama in Bethlehem without using that style of analysis. I set out here two contrasting reconstructions of the plot, more or less Sasson versus Campbell. I shall structure the discussion in terms of nine "Divergences."

We start with the circumstance that all the male members of the immediate family of Elimelek are dead. Naomi takes the road back to Judah from Moab because God has seen to the needs of people there and there is food. If the storyteller has in mind better circumstances for coping back in Judah on other grounds than food, that point is not going to be made explicit now. The two younger women set out with their mother-in-law; along the way, she tries to talk them into going back each to their mother's house, there to make new marriages. Marriage is obviously a solution. Encountering resistance, she uses argument to persuade.

Divergence #1: The argument Naomi makes is either somehow related to levirate practice or it is not. Sasson here observes that what

Naomi proposes in her hyperbolic speculations is not levirate-based; any children in her womb now could hardly be sired by Elimelek's brother and that is the essential of levirate responsibility: "… [T]here is no question here of 'levirate' marriage—such marriages depending, as they do, on issues from the same *father*, not *mother*," says Sasson (1989: 24). No husband currently available to Naomi where she is could serve in a levirate role. Nor, as the sequel shows, do we have in Bethlehem a situation in which brothers live together in a *bêt- ʾāb*, brothers of Elimelek who could do for Naomi what Onan and Shelah were expected to do for their elder brother Er in Genesis 38. For Sasson, then, what Naomi is speaking of here is marriage, but not the kind of marriage that would "raise up a man's name on his inheritance." Marriage and issues of land-inheritance are not connected, as they would be in levirate.

What, then, is Naomi referring to? I grant that it is at some distance away from levirate as described in what we have in the Bible. Nevertheless, an alternative to Sasson's alternative is to see this as a distinct if hyperbolic reference to a responsibility of which what we know as levirate is one instance. That responsibility is to take care of widows and a way to do that is to sire a son, who both secures the wellbeing of the widow *and* sees to the family's future, including keeping the family's name related to family holdings. Marriage and care-giving are connected here in Ruth chapter 1, though it is to be granted that nothing speaks to continuation of property in a family line.[1]

Divergence #1 in a nutshell: We as audience are focused on the wellbeing of Orpah and Ruth, not on property rights, but is there an adumbration of a connection between the two or should we block that thought? On Sasson's reading, Naomi is focused not on herself but on the other two; there is a selflessness to her urging. Several women authors have recently explored this profound consideration and seen it as strong evidence of what the story has to say about characteristics of female companionship, in presumed contrast to male ways (more below).

On the other hand, Naomi is made to say more: that things behind and things ahead look grim for herself: "It is far more bitter for me than for you." The storyteller emphasizes that there are other issues in the picture, and Naomi is not about to suppress them. There is a hint that there should be systems, customs, opportunities back home that might help resolve the predicament she is in, or that it is deeply regrettable if there are not—things roughly in the same territory of custom as levirate marriage and its aims of care and continuance.

There is no divergence to speak of about the scene upon Naomi's arrival in Bethlehem. That scene is about the problem, not the solution. Naomi is in despair and speaks in the form of complaint/lament. She confronts deity with vehemence. Even having the town women sympathize with her brings no solace. If there is any hint of relief, it lies only with the touching way the storyteller pushes Ruth into the background of the visual field but keeps her forward in the audience's thought by naming her and reminding us that Ruth is a "returnee," using the guide verb of the first chapter.

Divergence #2: What is the nature of the sentence in the first verse of chapter 2? Sasson would have this verse be a part of the narrative, intrinsic to the events that follow and necessary for them. His conclusion is buttressed by his Proppian analysis, since 2:1 is flanked by the two elements in the story corresponding to the folklore step when the hero/heroine leaves home on a quest. In 1:18–22 the heroine must set out on a quest to overcome one lack, her need for marriage, while in 2:2 she must quest food for herself and the one to whom she has committed herself. Folklore analysis does not accept connective verses like 2:1 as being used for asides to the audience; everything is supposed to advance the story.

Sasson's translation of *ûlĕnoʿŏmî mĕyuddāʿ / môdaʿ lĕʾîšāh* is "Now Naomi knew of an acquaintance of her husband ...." (His use of the verb "knew" has nothing to do of course with the root *ydʿ* in the noun "acquaintance"; it simply supplies—without philological demonstration—the answer to the question whether Naomi knew about Boaz or was not aware of him.) To Sasson, Naomi knew.

The alternative here is to claim that the opening sentence of the chapter is addressed to the audience, like other sentences such as the explanation of the sandal exchange in 4:7, providing information that permits the audience to relish what is developing while the characters are still in the dark. The disjunctive syntax at the opening of the chapter can doubtless be explained as utilized only for shifting the scene, but I maintain it supports taking 2:1 as an explanation for the audience. It is not worded grammatically as an element of the story. Verse 2 will pick up with a conjunctive sequence, and it is hard to be sure just what it is conjunctive to, though one might take it as meaning "So (in light of it being harvest time), Ruth said ..." rather than "Now, Ruth said ...." Divergence #2 is over whether Naomi and Ruth know about Boaz or they do not, as the second chapter's action begins.

Divergence #3: The significance of *mĕyuddā'* / *môda'*, the *kethib/qere* alternatives in 2:1. On the matter of Sasson's translation of this vocable as "acquaintance" I have some quarrel. What is, in fact, the nature of the relationship expressed in the term? Sasson surely means more than a casual acquaintance, because Boaz is in the *mišpaḥâ* of Elimelek, and the fact that he is an *'îš gibbôr ḥayil* should mean that he is well-known in Bethlehem. The alternative I chose while staying with *kethib mĕyuddā'* (1975: 88–90), "covenant-brother," is venturesome, designed to suggest that there is a lot more to be learned about the customary *and* voluntary associations of people who can be expected to pick up responsibility for care-giving in Israelite social structure; my attempt (1975: 88–90) to find help in discerning this from the reflex of *mĕyuddā'* in the LXX Lucianic variant at 2 Kgs 10:11 did not impress Sasson (1989:39), but the question remains. Let me return to this later.

Divergence #3 in short: does describing Boaz as a *mĕyuddā'* / *môda'* signify anything about what Boaz might have been doing or should have been doing in relation to these widows or not? For that matter, who else stood in relation to these two widows who could or should have been involved?

Divergence #4: Did Ruth set out to find Boaz's field plot or did she set out to glean wherever she could find the opportunity? Sasson assumes she knew about Boaz and set out in expectation of finding Boaz's plot, intending to find favor in his eyes. Sasson accurately notes that the expression *limṣō' ḥēn bĕ'ênāyw* virtually never occurs with "the one whose favor is sought left undetermined." "In his eyes ..." should have a specific person in mind. This is one reason he needs to have verse 1 be a part of the storyline, rather than an aside to the audience; we need Boaz as antecedent. Sasson translates "in the hope of pleasing him (Boaz)." The syntax of the sentence is unusual, however, bordering on unique. We have prepositional *'aḥar* and an *'ăšer* clause with an imperfect verb and a resumptive pronominal suffix. Sasson notes only Ezek 40:1 as a parallel to *'aḥar 'ăšer* with anything like this meaning, and there "after which" is temporal, not local. The more common combination *ʾaḥărê ʾăšer* is construed elsewhere only with perfect-tense verbs, nowhere else as here with an imperfect. What do we do under such circumstances? The meaning is thoroughly ambiguous, and we cannot say. The choice rests completely on what one answers to the dilemma posed as divergence #2.

Divergence #5: Sasson reads the sequel with sensitivity, and there is reason to accept his general depiction of the plot line of Ruth and Boaz's first encounter. I think Sasson and those who follow him are quite right in charting the developing awareness in Boaz as the day goes along. Nobody seems to be able to figure out quite what 2:7 says, but the proposal that Ruth has asked for something more than gleaning and must wait for the owner's permission, because the overseer lacks or refuses to exercise authority to permit it, persuades most recent commentators. Divergence #5 comes with Sasson's motive for her doing this, namely that she has contrived a reason to be introduced to Boaz by the overseer, or at least to have Boaz take note of her—she has overstepped what custom permitted so as to engineer the need for an encounter.

An alternative understanding is to continue to see Ruth as artless throughout this scene, a position that governed my own reading in 1975 and one that I am ready to alter partially. Another helpful suggestion from Sasson is that Ruth's speech to Boaz in 2:13 is anything but artless, when she says "You have spoken to the heart (tenderly) to your *šipḥâ*. Yet I am not even considered one of your *šipḥôt*." Sasson appeals here to 2:1 where we have been introduced to Boaz as part of Elimelek's *mišpaḥâ*, and I believe he is right to insist we pay attention to the word play on the root. His conclusion: Ruth is, subtly but in a progression of less-and-less subtlety, working upon Boaz's sense of where she should belong. Sasson then builds a picture of Boaz mulling all this over before lunchtime, as the recognition grows in him that Ruth should be brought more nearly into the circle at the center of which he stands. With the meal-sharing and with his instruction to let her now do what she sought in 2:7, glean among the sheaves, and adding even more to that, he admits her into the *familia*. Divergences ##4 and 5 are connected: Does Ruth set out knowingly to intercept Boaz or does she not, and does she engineer Boaz's attention upon her or is he the initiator?

While granting partially Sasson's emphasis upon calculated movements, I prefer to see *both* participants developing step-by-step in their contact with one another, rather than seeing one setting a trap for the other (see Fewell and Gunn 1990, who explore with care and imagination the developing relationship).

I see no disagreement, in the reading of chapter 2, on the question of whether marriage for Ruth *and* relief for Naomi are both in the scene. In the background, they are growing in the fertile minds of the audience. How they are balanced and how they are related is unclear to a modern audience. The ancient audience probably had more to refer to in its collective experience, but the story is both managing the dawning awareness of the characters and tantalizing the audience by keeping the question of their connection under wraps. Little is explicit yet as to whether either Ruth or Boaz discerns what lies ahead. Sasson finds Ruth to have plotted the scene; the alternative would emphasize that the sequence of events is what the audience is enjoying, not the blossoming success of a crafty woman. When Ruth gets back to Naomi, it is Naomi's speech that first introduces the word *gō ʾēl*. If the scene in the field has seemed to focus more on Ruth's attractiveness to Boaz and the prospect of marriage, Naomi can be said to have shifted the focus to redemption.

Divergence #6: What happens in 3:9–10? We can now leap to what happened at the threshing floor. Now there is plotting. Few are in doubt that Ruth uncovered the lower half of Boaz's anatomy and that she has marriage in mind. It is probably true that her use of the word *ʾāmâ* of herself in identification to Boaz signals the step beyond *šipḥâ*-hood to marriageability.

Since Sasson and I agree that Ruth and Boaz did not consummate marriage at the threshing-floor, the problem shifts to understanding 3:9–10. Sasson's translation to the *athnah* in verse 10 is "'May you be blessed by the Lord, daughter,' said Boaz. 'You have acted in a worthier fashion in the last instance than in the first.'" The question is, what are the first and second instances? Nearly all interpreters have seen Ruth's care for Naomi to be the first and her "saving herself" for Boaz as the second. Hence her proposal in 3:9 is taken as of one piece, when she says "I am Ruth, your *ʾāmâ* so spread your wing over your *ʾāmâ* because you are redeemer." But Sasson has been developing step by step a distinction between what Ruth wants for herself and what she wants for Naomi. By removing levirate practice from the picture in chapter 1, by having that chapter be about Naomi's concern for Ruth and Orpah and not for herself, by having Ruth set out to glean with the intent to get to Boaz's field so that she can take advantage of Boaz's expected generous concern for Naomi while *on a parallel but not connected path* she steps closer to a personal relation to Boaz—by all these, Sasson has been keeping land redemption (*gĕʾullâ*) and marriage apart. Ruth is acting for Naomi's benefit; she is also acting for herself. Naomi has been acting for Ruth. And now the issue has become how these begin to conjoin. Sasson's translation of 3:9 is crucial to his answer: "'I am Ruth your handmaid,' she replied, adding: 'spread your robe over your handmaid; you are a redeemer.'" Sasson's semicolon is a full stop. The first segment is about marriage, the second is about redeeming. The first is for Ruth's benefit, the second for Naomi's. Boaz's reply responds to each part: your first instance of *ḥesed* is to ask for marriage; your second, even better, is to be thinking of the wellbeing of your mother-in-law. The first is an act of *ḥesed* for herself and him, the second for Naomi. Redeeming has nothing to do with marriage; marriage nothing to do with redeeming; neither has any connection to levirate practice. But Ruth wants both things. She can and does look after her own interests, and she does not want to be cut away from her beloved mother-in-law, for whom she wants to secure the future while keeping her "in the family."

To make this stand, Sasson then must indulge in a *tour de force* with respect to the grammar of what is said next about the redeeming process. We learn of the person nearer, who ought to do the redeeming responsibility. If he will do the redeeming, well and good; if he will not, Boaz will do it. The trouble is that the verbs expressing redeeming are suffixed with pronominal object suffixes: "if he will redeem you ... I will redeem you." Sasson renders instead "redeem *for* you" and "I myself will do so." For him, the redemption act is for Naomi's benefit, not Ruth's. Ruth has got what she wants, betrothal. Although she also wants Naomi's wellbeing secured, that does not constitute *gĕʾullâ* for Ruth, but rather *gĕʾullâ* for Naomi. By inserting "for" Sasson has preserved his distinction between what is for Ruth and what is for Naomi, but has violated the expected meaning of the verb or verbal noun constructions of *gʾl* with suffix. No other use of the root with suffix does that.

Divergence #6, then, is over whether Ruth has separated two actions in her request and Boaz responded separately to these two, or whether there is a natural connection between the two and Ruth is saying much the same thing in two different ways. There is no disagreement that Ruth asked for, and got, commitment from Boaz to marry her.

Divergence #7: This divergence is not between Sasson and Campbell, but between others who comment on the scene, notably for our purposes here the essay built closely on Sasson's reading of the story by Adrien Bledstein (1993): Did the two have intercourse there at the threshing floor? Did they marry there? This is pertinent to the understanding of 4:5 and the crucial moment in the scene at the city gate. Bledstein claims, with Cyrus Gordon, that they married, by the path to marriage afforded in Mishnah Qiddushin 1:1, but of course that must be kept secret until it is time to spring the news at the city gate. The question then shifts from marriage to whether a man-child will be conceived.

That will be, then, where the drama at the city gate will lie. Boaz will say to Mr. So-and-So, "... on this very day when you decide to redeem the field you should know that I have already married Ruth." Mr. So-and-So now needs to calculate the likelihood of a child being born and does so by concluding the chances are very good. If there is no child from their union, the "solution" which connects marriage to redeeming will not materialize. Bledstein has to take 4:13 as a summary sentence, retrospective to its position: So, dear audience, this is how it happened "that Boaz took Ruth, she became his wife, he had relations with her and YHWH allowed her to conceive." But that sentence should not be taken as retrospective because it is the one that conveys the news that YHWH gave conception and Ruth bore a son. Not until then is it clear to the audience that Boaz's risk worked, and Mr. So-and-So made the right decision, if protecting his inheritance is what he has uppermost in mind.

Bledstein provides us with more plot pieces to make all this even more dramatic: Mr. So-and-So was actually a no-good, very likely to act the way Onan had in Genesis 38, and therefore, if he could have married Ruth, would have still found a way to keep that field by interrupting impregnating her. Explanatory forays of this kind are intriguing but hardly persuasive.

Divergences ##8 and 9: How does one read 4:5? Two cruces are here, divergences ##8 and 9, but one now appears to be solved. It has to do with *ûmē ʾēt*. Francis Andersen's 1970 proposal that this is to be analyzed as disjunctive *w*, "and," plus enclitic *mem* plus direct object sign is now widely accepted (Gordon 1987; Rendsburg 1987; Wallace 1987). The syntax is bumpy, but there is a break, signalled, by the way, by the *athnah* between "On the day of your acquiring the field from Naomi's hand" and "Ruth the Moabitess, wife of the dead ...." There is clear disjunction and there is a nice touch of retardation as Boaz stretches out what he is about to say about Ruth, before getting to the crucial verb. Divergence #8 pertains to the reading of *wm 't*, but the practical difference in translation between Sasson's *wgm 't* and enclitic-*mem* on the conjunction is nil.

The second crux, divergence #9, is whether to read the *kethib* or *qere* on the following verb: *qānîtî* or *qānîtâ*. Sasson adopts the *kethib* and brings about the connection between the resolution of what Ruth the heroine lacks and needs and the resolution of what Naomi needs: "Know that on the very day you are purchasing the field from Naomi, I am acquiring Ruth of Moab, wife of the deceased, in order to perpetuate the memory of the deceased upon his estate." You do redemption, I do marrying, *but* they come together in that I hereby pledge that the first child Ruth and I have will be designated Mahlon's heir and the land you paid for will become his and through him Naomi's. It is easy for Sasson then to develop the possible scenario that will jeopardize Mr. So-and-So's inheritance not just once but perhaps regularly—every time Naomi and her pledged "son" may need to sell that field again.

I now find Sasson's decision about 4:5 compelling, though I did not risk it in 1975 nor in the minimal revision just completed for the revised *New American Bible*. For one thing, one can explain the shift from *kethib* to *qere* more effectively than one can explain the addition of the first person *mater yod* on the *kethib*. The story, whether it actually employs the concept of levirate as such or not, swarms with elements that would remind ancient readers of levirate, and as Sasson observes, the tradition would have been led by so many hints of it to connect land redemption with marriage and perpetuating the name of the dead. So a shift to the second person would represent the secondary adoption of a logical interpretive reading by the Masoretes. The first person is the *lectio difficilior*, and hence the reading to be adopted.

Sasson's resulting picture gives a plausible reason for Mr. So-and-So to change his first decision. The sandal act is not *halîṣâ*—symbolic release from levirate responsibility—but is an otherwise unattested ceremonial act, in need of an explanation by the storyteller. Divergence #9 ceases to be a disagreement, and divergence #8 really is not one.

Of the nine divergences described, I concede on the point of there being no levirate as technically known from explicit reference in the Bible (OT and NT) in chapter 1's conversation among the women (#1); I concede partially on the adroit way in which Ruth gains closer and closer proximity to Boaz (while still claiming that the story shows both parties developing the relationship) (#5); Sasson and I remain content with our sense of no "marriage" at the threshing floor (#7); I claim no problem on *wm˒t* (#8); and I take as a working hypothesis accepting the *kethib* at 4:5 (#9). On the others, here are three areas of questioning:

1. It is not essential to Sasson's understanding of the story that Ruth be seen as contriving the scene in chapter 2. The effort to read Ruth in that way causes Sasson to give a forced reading in 2:2, so that Ruth sets out to find Boaz's field in full knowledge that he is a person that Naomi knows can extend them help. The syntax of 2:2 is unparalleled; it is more strained by Sasson's reading than by the traditional one, that Ruth sets out on a venture not knowing how things will turn out.

In spite of the claim that an aside to the audience and interruption of the flow is not supposed to happen in typical folklore, verse 2:1 is best understood as just that. I have not tried to check this interpretation against other folklore, but I have watched village storytelling in Balâṭah village, at the site of ancient Shechem. At village gatherings, children and foreign visitors were supplied data during the recital of a traditional story (about village participation in major events outside the immediate vicinity of town). Also, I have tried to glean all I can from Parry and Lord's Serbian storytellers. Sasson's view of verse 2:1 just does not fit with my experience. I continue to think that Ruth set out for the field, on her own initiative, and without instigation from Naomi, who is pictured as immobilized in her self pity. Ruth did this almost at once; these widows needed food and there cannot have been much of a time lapse between the end of chapter 1 and the start of chapter 2 (compare Fewell and Gunn 1990: 34–35), in spite of my own and other's insistence that the last verse of chapter 1 brings the story to a *Stillstand*; it was not a long *Stillstand*, just a transition. The drama is that Ruth plunges forth to relieve need, and there has not been any time for planning things out. Indeed she may do so without knowing the practice and custom of the gleaning law very well.

This claim connects, of course, to the part divine intervention is seen to play. In having Ruth set out purposefully to find Boaz's field and seek to gain his favor, Sasson undercuts significantly the claim of theologians reading the Ruth book that the "hidden" God is a role player in the story (see again his foreword to the 1989 edition). The note in 2:3 that Ruth happened at once upon Boaz's field is taken by Sasson to be a mark of the sense of urgency the chapter is creating—an emphasis that Ruth must strike while the iron is hot. Good fortune it is, but it is coincidental, not providential. But there is no necessary conflict between the proposal of a playfully providential God, who is regularly invoked in the book as blessing what is going on, and the need for things to happen briskly. Indeed, the two themes are quite compatible. Sasson, who has his doubts about a Solomonic Enlightenment and a body of literature stemming from it that features a God working in the shadows, may not find such compatibility, but I do not see the problem.

On the other hand, the issue of divine activity is more integral to the book than Sasson's treatment suggests. It comes to explicit expression in the complaint/lament of Naomi at the end of the first chapter, as she cries out before the women in Bethlehem. One of the dramatic movements within the book is that of Naomi, from bereft widow to returner to outcrier to recipient to dispatcher again to recipient. For Sasson (1989: 201), Naomi is dispatcher according to the roles identified by Propp in standard folklore; the dispatcher is regularly the beneficiary of the hero/heroine's success in the quest.

But Naomi is more central to the story than that role suggests; as the one who changes, she is the one about whom the story is really told. She expresses her complaint by hurling accusations against God whom she finds to have falsely accused her. God is on trial in Naomi's words, in much the same way as God is on trial in Job, Jeremiah 12, and in lament psalms. Part of the genius of the Ruth story lies in the way it explores how deity answers tragedy and its attendant lament. Standard folklore may not regularly indulge in such God-problems, but it regularly explores inexplicable turns of difficulty and equally inexplicable turns of good fortune for its heroes, its dispatchers, and its donors. I see no need for a studied attempt to eliminate the motif of divine providence from Ruth in order to preserve the initiative of the human actors. The story is precisely about the compatibility of the two.

2. A second concern extends beyond interaction with Sasson's study to the work of several of the contributors to the Brenner volume, *A Feminist Companion to Ruth*, notably Mieke Bal, Adrien Bledstein, and Brenner herself, and to many other commentaries on Ruth. It has to do with the way the laws and customs of ancient Israel are used as guide posts for reading stories in the Bible. In the Anchor Bible Commentary, it was necessary repeatedly to ask whether customary law as we have it in the law collections can be taken as existing legislation, capable of being invoked and applied in specific situations that present themselves. For example, does the fact that we have an articulation of the levirate practice in Deut 25:5–10 mean that we thereby have *the* practice of kinship marriage that can be used to understand each instance where the problem it addressed arose? True, it seems to apply very well in understanding the Tamar-Judah story, or at least it serves to explain why Onan succeeded Er, and why Shelah was next in line. It does not serve to tell us whether Judah was an appropriate substitute. We do not know whether Onan was married or whether that matters. There is a gap between levirate practice as "codified" in Deuteronomy 25 and the general customary understanding that a widow is to remain in the *bêt- ʾāb* of her dead husband's family—especially since Tamar does not, but is sent to her own father's house to wait for Shelah. In short, as all would agree, the collections of customary law are replete with gaps. The rabbis repeatedly had to search out ways to meet these gaps, and the oral law tradition had to find ways to develop law, even to find permitted ways to circumvent it.

For this reason, I am uncomfortable with interpretations that apply textual law formulations as givens. It seems to me that Sasson and others are too neat in concluding a) that there is no pertinence in Ruth of the levirate scenario; b) that we know what the work of the *gō ʾēl* is from the law formulations and sporadic applications of it in cases such as that of Ruth or Jeremiah and his uncle's field; or c) that marriage and *gĕ ʾullâ* belong to separate legal domains. Sasson does in fact observe that clearly one of the goals that levirate sought to reach is present in Ruth even if levirate is not. Indeed, if we let comparative law formulations from Assyria and Hatti inform the picture, we could by analogy expand Israelite levirate law to at least explain why Judah might be fulfilling it and perhaps to explain why Boaz could be a levir candidate (Campbell 1975: 33).

My specific concern here is with Sasson's decision to remove levirate entirely from Ruth and to understand Ruth 3:9–10 as he does. On the face of it, I find it difficult to sustain the claim that the audience is not being invited to think, albeit in hyperbolic terms, about a levirate-like custom in the chapter 1 encounter between Naomi and the two daughters-in-law. I am even more dubious that Ruth asks for two separate things in 3:9 and receives two separate assurances from Boaz in response.

The circumstances these three women face in chapter 1 of Ruth, and later that the two women face in Bethlehem, are very complex. One of Sasson's reasons for not wanting levirate marriage in the picture is that if it were applicable, someone should have come up with it as a solution at once upon the return of the two women. True, and also true is that Naomi has been thoroughly described to us in her own words as beyond child-bearing. Is it clear, then, that Ruth is also a candidate for levirate marriage? Mahlon is dead and so is the only brother we know of, so on the "if brothers dwell together" criterion of Deuteronomy 25 that style of levirate is excluded. Does this mean that Ruth was free to marry anyone she wanted to, and that Boaz is surprised that she has not already chosen one of the younger (or older) people she has encountered in the harvesting? Or is it possible that Ruth is to be viewed as waiting for the whole system of custom to find its way through the complex scene and come up with a solution to a very knotty situation? I choose with Sasson to take the "men whether rich or poor" as merismus, but I take the verse to mean that Boaz is commending Ruth for having waited until the intent behind all the various customs that might have pertained is acted upon. There are a host of avenues to that intent. We have not yet even been told about one of them, namely that there seems to be a field over which Naomi has at least the right of disposal. That should have played a part in the solution-search by this time. The women could have had its produce, perhaps, upon their return. Has the land been taken over in their absence? How do they get it back? Whose is it?

The picture I mean to be drawing of Israelite society as depicted in Ruth is one in which principle guides practice. We cannot legitimately take specific laws and assume they apply in each scene. Judgment at the city gate involved the free play of principle and precedent. On that basis, I suspect that the storyteller, by having Naomi speak as she does to her two daughters-in-law on the road back, is indeed referring to levirate in the sense that she is expressing circumstances in the wider field of custom of which levirate is a specific exemplar. In telling Ruth in 2:20 that Boaz is *qārôb lānû* and that he is one of *gō ʾǎlēnû* she is exploring the connections between marriage for widows in the household and land redemption, not artificially juxtaposing them. And in 3:9, Ruth is intertwining two trajectories toward responsible behavior, not proposing one thing that will benefit her and another separate thing that will benefit Naomi. We simply do not have much of a picture of Israelite social practice explicit in the Bible. The fact that we do not even know from the Bible how people got married is cautionary, and *Qiddushin* 1:1 is evidence that there was a range of matters to think about in the oral law tradition. Athalya Brenner's attempt to find two separate stories lying behind Ruth, one premised on redemption and one on marriage, each taking as definitive the law constructions explicitly attested in the Bible, as a way to explain what seem to be departures from legal practice when the finished product is written, is an instance of expecting all to be explained by what has been made explicit.

3. Closely connected to this issue of law and custom is the question of social structure that functions to deliver on the society's ideology. This is the place to reintroduce a defence of taking *mĕyuddā ʿ* and **môda ʿat* as important contributions in the Ruth story. We may not know it from elsewhere, but it appears from Ruth 2:1 that *mĕyuddā ʿ* and its close synonym in 3:2 have significant meaning for the social structure of town and/or village life in Israel.[2] My 1975 term "covenant-circle" was informed, of course, by explorations in the area of treaty language (Huffmon 1966; Huffmon and Parker 1966). To Sasson, covenant belongs to the political-theological realm and frame of reference and ought not to be transported into folklore or even a folkloristic story.

My premise is that the lofty covenant ideology in Israel informed the ethos of ancient Israel from court to temple to village to countryside. Recent claims, portrayed effectively by Dever (1995), that such a theological perspective was a view of a late cultured elite and quite at odds with Israelite "popular" religion among the common people, have not persuaded me, even though I am predisposed to take archaeological evidence with great seriousness. The data Dever cites have not reached a critical mass. In any case, another task of archaeology and social history in conversation with the Bible is to keep exploring what village and town life might have looked like. The responsibilities of the *bêt-ʾāb* do not presumably end at the doorway of a housing compound for an extended family. What are the next circles out and what responsibilities do members of those circles have? What is a *mĕyuddāʿ* or a member of a *môda ʿat expected to do to further the common good? What is a *mišpāḥâ* supposed to deliver in terms of care? How complicated is it to know or discern a way toward resolution? Will it not frequently take a goad from someone to get things moving? That is what the drama of the Ruth book seems to depend upon. Getting the "process of delivery" of custom and law into gear is difficult; the gears do not always mesh, and there are people who do not want them to mesh if it means they will have to do something they do not want to do, let alone those who mean well but cannot afford to go beyond certain limits.

Two further and pertinent issues about Ruth bear mentioning as this revisit concludes. The first is: Can any of what has been said so far pertain to the issue of the process of authoring the Ruth story? Several articles in the *Feminist Companion to Ruth* address this issue, more than just the ones that are placed in Part II of the volume, addressed to "gendered authorship." And Goitein had entertained the idea that a woman was author of the story in his lost article now found (1988). In 1975 (21–23), I proposed it not because I had much of an idea how one would identify women's speech and women's writing but because Ruth was a story that sounded like the one the wise woman of Tekoah told to David (2 Sam 14:4–17, see NRSV)—replete with thorny questions that slip in among the holes in the pattern of custom (which, in this case, permitted unscrupulous "users of the law against the law" to maneuver to their own advantage).

The late Fokkelien van Dijk-Hemmes (1993) applies to Ruth criteria put forward by literary critic Elaine Showalter for identifying literary products of women's culture. Note, this is not quite the same as claiming a woman's authorship of the final product; it is to see the text as having a recognizable woman's voice that has not been suppressed by later scribal activity. The criteria are:

1. The text should contain traces of an intent that is less than normally androcentric;
2. There should be talk in the text of a definition or redefinition of reality from the female perspective;
3. The result of that definition or redefinition should show definable differences between the view of male and female figures.

Consider the second and third criteria first: reality seen from a female perspective, and discernible differences in view between male and female figures. Van Dijk-Hemmes finds that woman-perspective fills the conversations in chapter 1: the talk is of what pertains to the needs of women, not the needs of a male-oriented concern about inheritance of land. At the end of chapter 4, likewise, the chorus of women felicitate Naomi with emphasis upon the lad born to Naomi and upon the sheer joy it is giving her as she holds it to her bosom. Redemption here is for the sake of Naomi and her social security. Both of these scenes and exchanges have their counterpart in the male voice, in the negotiations at the city gate and in the chorus of witnesses who bless Boaz, and in the exchange between Boaz and his overseer in chapter 2.

Then too, van Dijk-Hemmes is impressed by the use of the term "mother's house" in Ruth 1:8, when the young women are encouraged to return. Carol Meyers, in a series of studies (e.g., Meyers 1993) has shown that the *bêt-ʾēm* need not be some special entity totally different from a *bêt-ʾāb*. It fits in the narrative in much the same position as Tamar's return to her *bêt-ʾāb* in Genesis 38, as well as with the usage in Gen 24:38–40 in the quest for a wife for Isaac, and in the Song of Songs. Meyers was kind enough to cite *AB: Ruth* as a notable exception to the efforts to explain away "mother's house" as a reference to a harem, or to "running home to mother," but I did not see it then as equivalent to a *bêt-ʾāb*. Now I believe that to be the case, and we need to reckon with houses headed by women. As a *bêt-ʾēm*, one can point to the household of Elisha's widow friend in 2 Kgs 8:1–6, who has land and produce restored to her ownership after a seven-year sojourn away. Here, be it noticed, it took intervention by the court to set things right. Principle was probably clear enough, in this case having to do with property and inheritance. We have no law recorded that would apply.

On Showalter's first criterion, about traces of intent less than normally androcentric, van Dijk-Hemmes reaches into controversial territory, of women's ways and men's ways. The male voice, she avers, is usually given to seeing things in terms of rivalry and competitiveness, and indeed that is the way many of the stories about women in the Bible are told: Sarah vs. Hagar, Hannah vs. Peninnah, Rachel vs. Leah. (Presumably competitiveness signifies that men told these episodes.) Woman-voice, on the other hand, deals with cooperation and avoids competition. Orpah in the Ruth story is not a rival, not even a foil. She chooses one of two wise ways; Ruth adds to wisdom a loyalty of staggering proportions. The women in this story all love each other.

As I suspect most are, I am suspicious of a neat distinction between a feminine voice and a masculine voice, but I am not nearly as suspicious of the distinction when it is described in terms of a tendency. What several recent women authors are proposing is that there is the expression of the feminine voice preserved in stories such as Ruth. So I'll risk a further proposal, drawn from the insights of Carol Gilligan (1982) after she reconducted some of Lawrence Kohlberg's tests on making moral decisions with a female population in contrast to a male one. Women, she ascertained, were not content to take up moral dilemmas, problems posed in dualistic terms, as givens: what would you do under these circumstances, this or that? Instead women often sought another way, a *tertium quid*, or a way to re-image the original scenario. What we gain by not looking for laws that tell us what to do and what not to do for each of the issues of custom in Ruth is something of that freedom. The problem is one of finding a generative and alternative way through. One has not done enough when one cites one law to govern this and another to govern that; one has to work out a generative solution that brings everyone out with at least enough justice to permit life to go on with some fruitfulness. If a story like Ruth, or like Judah-Tamar, or like the one the wise woman of Tekoah keeps evolving so as to tie David up in knots of moral decision making, deals with such a pattern of moral reasoning, is it not perhaps an indication of women-culture?

Notice that all this speculation does not prove woman "writership" of these stories in the final form we have them. I do not know just how to tackle the question of women composing the written form of biblical tales, let alone other texts. Woman writership does not seem very likely from what we know of Israelite male and female roles. But women as storytellers are now, I believe, as firmly entrenched in the social landscape of ancient Israel as are women singers of victory songs. Whether a male scribe, in recording the story, could silence the woman's voice in making the transition I seriously doubt. Van Dijk's category of double voicing, where male and female perspectives both appear as they do in Ruth, does not help much in determining who the author of the final product might have been. But I used the term "scribe" in the sentence before last on purpose. Hannah may not have written the Song of Hannah, but the scribe who did write it wrote down a woman's song. Somehow our sense of authorship is going to have to make room for these phenomena.

A last comment on the application of folkloristic analysis. Sasson has made a real contribution by applying a Proppian analysis to Ruth (note the foreword to the 1989 edition, where he enters his own caveats), so as to help us to see Ruth as hero and Naomi as dispatcher/recipient. As Mieke Bal has pointed out, however, there is some reason to see Boaz as both a donor and a dispatcher/recipient during the course of the story. He benefits, even if we do not go so far as the inventive Bal has gone in turning Boaz into a lonely and yearning old bachelor scared at the prospect of having no offspring a la Victor Hugo's *Booz endormi* (Bal 1993; cf. Fewell and Gunn 1990: passim). In fact, as always, a form serves about as well to underscore departures from the norm as it does to articulate the norm. In Ruth, for example, the simple schema of the folklore succession is doubled in its middle part, since there must be two quests for the hero, encountering two lacks. I prefer to stay with two firm and defensible claims: storytelling in a mode that folklore studies can illuminate was a feature of Israelite society, probably village and town society, and women often were folk stories' creators. Soon, if not already, we should have a more complete set of criteria to be able to tell a woman-story from a man-story, but in the final analysis we may never be able to do so, simply because there is too much feminine in too many men, and too much masculine in too many women to be sure, or, perhaps we can say, to matter.

NOTES

1. As is often noted, our information about inheritance for Israelite widows is disconcertingly small. A fascinating article by Martha Roth (1991–1993) has brought together a series of Neo-Babylonian laws and

legal documents that at the very least give a hint of what might be expected in the culture of Israel in the later monarchy period, if not throughout Israel's social history. 2 Kgs 8:1–6 gives a strong hint that structures for widow inheritance were in place in Israel, of which we get practically no other indications in the preserved text.

2.   There is a large agenda of discovery ahead for the social meaning of these terms. A starting place is the cluster of three uses of the expression *mudû šarri* in Ugaritic material and in older Akkadian materials, "a friend/friends of the king." This must have some pertinence to the list of royal retainers in the house of Ahab whom Jehu killed (2 Kgs 10:11); in that passage, *měyuddā ʿ* is the term used. But what would this term mean within a family or clan? Raymond Westbrook is exploring these terms as he pursues Old Babylonian uses of *mudû* along with two parallel terms *naptarum* and *ubarum* (1994), but the passages in this ancient period (the time of the Laws of Eshnunna) point more in the direction of "strangers" or "foreigners"—people who need the protection of the laws—than in the direction of proximity and responsibility. On the other hand, the fact that there are hospitality dimensions to something called a *bīt naptari* and that the root *paṭaru* relates to redeeming is tantalizing (1994: 41).

REFERENCES

Bal, M.
  1993   Heroism and Proper Names, or the Fruits of Analogy. Pp. 41–69 in *A Feminist Companion to Ruth*, ed. A. Brenner. Sheffield: Sheffield Academic.
Bledstein, A. J.
  1993   Female Companionships: If the Book of Ruth Were Written by a Woman …. Pp. 116–33 in *A Feminist Companion to Ruth*, ed. A. Brenner. Sheffield: Sheffield Academic.
Brenner, A.
  1983   Naomi and Ruth. *Vetus Testamentum* 33: 61–65, reprinted as pp. 70–84 in *A Feminist Companion to Ruth*, ed. A. Brenner. Sheffield: Sheffield Academic.
  1993   Naomi and Ruth: Further Reflections. Pp. 140–44 in *A Feminist Companion to Ruth*, ed. A. Brenner. Sheffield: Sheffield Academic.
Campbell, E. F.
  1974   The Hebrew Short Story: Its Form, Style and Provenance. Pp. 83–101 in *A Light Unto My Path: Old Testament Studies in Honor of Jacob M. Myers*, eds. H. Bream, R. Heim and C. Moore. Philadelphia: Temple University.

1975   *Ruth: A New Translation with Introduction and Commentary.* Anchor Bible 7A. Garden City: Doubleday.

Dever, W. G.
1995   "Will the Real Israel Please Stand Up?" Part II: Archaeology and the Religions of Ancient Israel. *Bulletin of the American Schools of Oriental Research* 298: 37–58.

Fewell, D. N., and Gunn, D. M.
1990   *Compromising Redemption: Relating Characters in the Book of Ruth.* Literary Currents in Biblical Interpretation, 1. Louisville: Westminster/John Knox.

Gilligan, C.
1982   *In a Different Voice: Psychological Theory and Women's Development.* Cambridge, MA: Harvard University.

Goitein, S. D.
1988   Women as Creators of Biblical Genres. Trans. M. Carasik from Hebrew. *Prooftexts* 8: 1–33.

Gordon, C. H.
1987   WM- "and" in Eblaite and Hebrew. Pp. 29-30 in *Eblaitica: Essays on the Ebla Archives and Eblaite Language. I*, ed. C. H. Gordon, G. A. Rendsburg and N. H. Winter. Winona Lake, IN: Eisenbrauns.

Gunkel, H.
1913   *Reden und Aufsätze.* Gottingen: Vandenhoeck and Ruprecht.

Huffmon, H. B.
1966   The Treaty Background of Hebrew *Yāda ͑. Bulletin of the American Schools of Oriental Research* 181: 31–37.

Huffmon, H. B., and Parker, S. B.
1966   A Further Note on the Treaty Background of Hebrew *Yāda ͑. Bulletin of the American Schools of Oriental Research* 184: 36–38.

Meyers, C.
1993   Returning Home: Ruth 1:8 and the Gendering of the Book of Ruth. Pp. 85–114 in *A Feminist Companion to Ruth*, ed. A. Brenner. Sheffield: Sheffield Academic.

Ozick, C.
1987   Ruth. Pp. 361–82 in *Congregation: Contemporary Writers Read the Jewish Bible*, ed. D. Rosenberg. New York: Harcourt Brace Jovanovich.

Rendsburg, G. A.
1987   Eblaite U-MA and Hebrew WM-. Pp. 34–41 in *Eblaitica: Essays on the Ebla Archives and Eblaite Language. I*, ed. C. H. Gordon, G. A. Rendsburg and N. H. Winter. Winona Lake, IN: Eisenbrauns.

Roth, M. T.
 1991–93 The Neo-Babylonian Widow. *Journal of Cuneiform Studies* 43–45: 1–26.

Sasson, J. M.
 1989 *Ruth: A New Translation with a Philological Commentary and a Formalist-Folklorist Interpretation.* 2nd. ed. Sheffield: Sheffield Academic.

van Dijk-Hemmes, F.
 1993 Ruth: A Product of Women's Culture? Pp. 134–39 in *A Feminist Companion to Ruth*, ed. A. Brenner. Sheffield: Sheffield Academic.

Wallace, C.
 1987 WM- in Nehemiah 5:11. P. 31 in *Eblaitica: Essays on the Ebla Archives and Eblaite Language. I*, ed. C. H. Gordon, G. A. Rendsburg and N. H. Winter. Winona Lake, IN: Eisenbrauns.

Waltke, B. K., and O'Connor, M.
 1990 *An Introduction to Biblical Hebrew Syntax.* Winona Lake, IN: Eisenbrauns.

Westbrook, R.
 1994 The Old Babylonian Term *napṭarum. Journal of Cuneiform Studies* 46: 41–46.

6 Holy War Ideology and the Rapid Shift of Mood in Psalm 3

EE KON KIM

Attention has long been directed to the phenomenon of reversal from complaint to confidence in the lament psalms. Thus, that no agreement has been reached concerning the real motivation of such a sudden change of mood in the lament psalms, in both the national laments and the individual laments, is remarkable. Explanations by students of the Psalter have pointed to: (1) a postulated priestly oracle of salvation, which intervened just before the rapid and radical transition of mood (cf. F. Küchler 1918; followed by Gunkel 1933: 246; Mowinckel, 1962, I: 217–18; Begrich 1964: 217–31); (2) a psychological dynamic in which the psalm's wholehearted outpouring of distress to God issues in a spontaneous surge of relief (cf. Heiler 1958; followed by Westermann 1981; and partially Gunkel 1892; *et al.*); (3) a cultic actualization (dramatization or recitation) of the tradition of the divine saving acts (cf. Weiser 1962: 43, 70, 79–82; Noth 1963: 80–81).

Previous studies attempting to account for the sudden shift of mood from cry of distress to assurance of salvation in the lament psalms can generally be classified according to one of these three explanations. However, the three hypothetical conjectures above are seriously flawed in that there is no internal evidence for them in the lament psalms themselves and in that they have failed to explore the traditio-historical roots of the motivation for the sudden change of mood of the lament psalms. The purpose of this study is to point out the striking inadequacy of the traditional explanations of the shifting phenomena in the lament psalms, and to give an example that strongly buttresses a suggested alternative.

I. INADEQUATE THEORIES WITHOUT
TEXTUAL EVIDENCE

1. In the early days of the form-critical study of the psalms, F. Küchler already offered a very plausible and classical theory. According to his theory, a priestly oracle of salvation had already occurred ahead of the certainty of having been heard in the lament psalms. The expression of having been heard is introduced through the notice of this oracle (Küchler 1918). However, the inadequacy of this theory is found not only in the fact that there is no extant example of any such postulated oracles among the lament psalms, but also in the fact that expressions of complaint, rather than expressions of confidence, are placed right after the announcement of the priestly *Heilsorakel*.

Remarkably, at verses of confidence such as Pss 6:9; 12:8; 27:13; 28:6; 55:23; 56:10; 57:7; 60:14; and 89:39, before which the postulated priestly oracle of salvation might be expected to appear (cf. Gunkel 1892: 22, 116, 228, 243, 246, 258, 595), there is never suggested any oracle of salvation, with the exception of Pss 12:8; 60:14; and 89:39. Indeed, even Ps 60:14 is not placed right after the oracle, Ps 60:8–10. That is, verses 11–13, which must be the expressions of a complicated mentality caused by complaint and petition (*Klage und Bitte*), are placed right after the proclaimed oracle of salvation. The contextual situations of Pss 12:8 and 89:39 are not different from those of Ps 60:14.

The excellent work of J. Begrich and S. Mowinckel, who have sought a precise cultic setting for the priestly oracle of salvation and have also attempted to relate it clearly to a sudden change of mood in the lament psalms, has produced only three Psalms, 12, 60, and 89, in which the exact oracular formula is preserved: the oracular passages Pss 12:6; 60:8; 89:20 are introduced or concluded by *yō'mar YHWH*, *'ĕlōhîm dibber*, and *'āz dibbartā*.

In the case of Psalm 12, the lamenter places his citation (v. 6) from the prophetic-oracular phrase in Isa 33:10, "Now I will arise!," right after his *lamentation* (v. 5). Accordingly, the confidence expressed in vv. 7–8, which suddenly occurs, has long been recognized as a reaction to the oracle in v. 6. What matters here, however, seems to be how to interpret v. 9 (the concluding verse): "On every side the wicked prowl, as vileness is exalted among the sons of humanity." This sentence must be a complaint verse. That is to say, even after a salvation oracle a complaint occurs. Most interpreters, however, want to add a conjunction ("though" or "even though") to the head of the verse in question: "Even though the wicked prowl on every side ..." (see Gunkel 1892: 44; Kraus 1978: I, 238; Briggs 1906: I, 97; Weiser 1962: 158, 161; Leslie 1982: 224). This interpretation appears to serve the artificial intention of letting the psalm end not with complaint but with confidence. However, there are no grammatical or textual reasons to add a conjunction to the verse! We see in this verse evidence that even after a priestly oracle of salvation, a complaint can occur.

Psalm 60, as well as Psalm 12, places a complaint (vv. 12–13) after the oracle (vv. 8–10). Even though the last verse (v. 14) ends with confidence in accordance with the promise of the oracle, the salvation oracle (vv. 8–10) does not change the psalm's mood of lamentation (vv. 3ff.) into that of confidence (cf. the complaint in vv. 12–13): "the fog [of complaint] has not all disappeared immediately" (Weiser 1962: 441). If there is a good explanation for the complaint after a salvation oracle, it must be that "strangely enough," the psalmist is not wholly reassured by the "oracle" (Oesterley 1953: 229).

In Psalm 89 the mood of complaint (vv. 39ff.) after the royal oracle, which is given to the Davidic dynasty (vv. 20–38), is very strikingly presented. The studies of Sarna (1963) and Mullen (1983) on Psalm 89 come to the conclusion that the oracle (originally Nathan's oracle in 2 Samuel 7) that the Davidic dynasty will prosper, whether it is assured by the divine promise (Sarna) or by the heavenly witness (Mullen), was freely adapted by the psalmist in order to point out *the contrast between the ancient oracle (concerning Davidic victories) and the present distress of the psalmist's own day.*

In light of the above observations, it is clear that the lament psalmists *freely adapted* ancient oracles and other salvation traditions to their new situations in distress. That is to say, it is obvious that they have not depended upon a cultic act such as the oracle of salvation. The two articles of Sarna and Mullen seem to give a reasonable answer to the question of why the above three lament psalms (Pss. 12, 60, and 89) place their complaints after the salvation oracle: they do it in order to emphasize their present situation in need of salvation by contrasting the present distress with the past victories formulated in oracular form. This characteristic of the lament psalms seems to tell us that the salvation oracle as such is not a sufficient explanation of the sudden transition from complaint to confidence.

2. Heiler (1958: 236), who holds that words of prayer are not borrowed from a formula but are a spontaneous creation, argues that prayer essentially goes forth through both the experience of need and trust in the divine promise. Accordingly, Heiler believes that self-forgetful surrender to the highest God, namely, dependence upon God's will, creates the sudden change of mood in the lament psalms. Even though Heiler comments that the effective force of prayer does not exclude the adoption of a traditional formula, he admirably emphasizes the abruptness of the order of thought in the prayer, an abruptness that springs from emotion (Heiler 1958: 236–38). For Heiler, the essential nature of "biblical prayer" is the unrestricted expression of compelling emotion.

Thus the main components of the biblical prayer, such as "complaint," "petition," "confession of sinfulness," "expression of trust," "thanksgiving," "praise," according to Heiler, spontaneously arise from the consciousness of dependence upon God, the strong will to live, and the desire for self-assurance. As a result, "prayer" is recognized as a product of the ambivalence of two emotions, "fear and hope." Consequently, the rapid change in mood in the lament psalms seems to be recognized by Heiler as a spontaneously and inwardly rising process of the soul in prayer. The sudden change of mood in the lament psalms also can be recognized as issuing from "the psychic struggle," in which hope asserts itself against all the feelings of fear and rises to unshakable confidence.

Heiler writes, "A wonderful metamorphosis takes place in the prayer itself, unconsciously, involuntarily, often quite suddenly …. The petitioner carries on an internal conflict between doubt and certainty, hesitation and assurance, until finally faith and trust break through with victorious power" (Heiler 1958: 263). "A great number of the psalms … show the same conflict between fearful uncertainty and hopeful courage, the violent alternation of feeling from trembling anxiety to bold confidence" (Heiler 1958: 261).

In general, in Heiler's psychological approach, biblical prayer seems to parallel the "general" circumstances of religious prayer. Such a model for the creation of prayer, in which prayer takes place on the summit of a generalized religious experience (Heiler 1958: 228), might make it possible to put the lament psalms into a category of purely non-cultic prayer. But we must consider the fact that the lament psalms, whether individual or national, have been transmitted through a cult, which is widely defined as a religious life of experience where various traditions converge and diverge.[1] Of course, it is not easy to determine whether the greater part of the psalms were cultic (cf. Mowinckel 1962), private imitations of old cult songs (cf. Gunkel 1892, 1933; Begrich 1964), or older than any cult, that is, independent of cult (cf. Heiler 1958). Neither is it possible, on the other hand, to argue that lament psalms written outside of the cult would have been uninfluenced by it; we see, for example, imitations of the style of the cultic psalms in Jeremiah and Deutero-Isaiah. Indeed, Israelite piety in the lament psalms must have grown under the influence of historical and cultic traditions. Heiler's psychological approach to the Israelite prayers largely ignores the particular relationship of the Israelite prayers with their traditio-historical background.

C. Westermann, who, to his astonishment found that there are no psalms which do not progress beyond petition and lament, convincingly relates the sudden transition of mood in the lament psalms to a psychological approach to the function of the "vow of praise" in these psalms (Westermann 1981: 74). The vow of praise, according to Westermann (1981: 222), has the psychological motivation of a striving for "continuity," in which lamenters bind together the present moment of lament with a moment, in the past, of deliverance and a moment, in the future, that is spoken about in the vow of praise. Accordingly, the sudden transition from lamentation to joy in the lament psalms has been anticipated from the beginning of each psalm.

The psychological approach to the lament psalms provides a better explanation for their shift of mood than does the postulation of a priestly oracle of salvation, since the great majority of these psalms contain no reference to such an oracle. However, it does not seem possible to regard the sudden change of mood in the Israelite lament psalms as a purely psychological phenomenon of private prayer without any association with the influence of the cult and in defiance of their traditio-historical background.

As Weiser (1962: 81, 348) suggests, even the psalms that have been composed far away from the temple, such as Psalms 42, 43 and 137 are related inwardly to the sanctuary and its cultic tradition, because their authors long for the time when they once were privileged to be in the house of God. Indeed, the Hebrew psychology of faith, as is well-known, cannot be considered as a purely psychological phenomenon in isolation from the influence of its traditio-historical background. As Childs (1976: 17–30; cf. Pedersen 1926: 128) argues, Hebrew psychology, with its recognition of the historical dimension of the external world, did not generally exhibit a "mentality" in which an "event" was conceived of merely as a "manifestation of the soul," independent of external factors. In the light of these things, a "purely" psychological process of the inner soul also is not a sufficient explanation for the rapid change of mood in the lament psalms. Therefore, what is important in the study of the lament psalms is to clarify an external impulse that is over and above the purely psychological inner resources of the lament psalmists themselves.

3. A. Weiser, who believes that the lament psalms were firmly established in the cult of the covenant festival, where the renewal of divine salvation was understood to be celebrated by the cultic actualization of the *magnalia Dei* in the form of a verbal representation, rejects the above two explanations of the rapid change of mood in the lament psalms. He further argues that the great majority of laments do not refer to an oracle cast into a rigid mold, and that the inner certainty reached after the lamenter's soul had passed through severe struggle does not represent the only means that will enable the petitioner to overcome every kind of suffering.

More concretely, Weiser (1962: 82) asserts that the inner certainty of the lament psalmists belongs to an expression of thanksgiving after their participation in the traditional actualization of salvation in the cult, in which the experiences of salvation were incorporated. That is to say, the change of mood in the lament psalms is understood to have taken place after the lamenter's participation in the actualization of *Heilsgeschichte* tradition in the cult. In this sense, Weiser's basic argument, even though he leans toward a cultic interpretation, seems to be based on a synthesis between the cultic and the non-cultic interpretations. Nevertheless, Weiser's fundamental argument is that the rapid change of mood in the lament psalms results from participation in the traditional actualization of salvation in the cult (Weiser 1962: 79–83).

What matters here, however, is that Weiser does not show how the results of participation in the actualization of *Heilsgeschichte* in the cult have shifted to the writing down of the lament psalms. That is, he does not present any evidence that the lament psalmists combined their cultic experiences with their lament songs. As Childs has pointed out (Childs 1976: 62), Weiser does not present any clear indications of a shift from the psychological to the cultic.

Furthermore, the recapitulation of *Heilsgeschichte* in the cult, whether it has been performed in the form of a cult drama (Mowinckel 1962, *et al.*) or in the form of a verbal representation (Noth 1963; von Rad 1951; Westermann 1981; Kraus 1978; *et al.*), has as its own unique function the presentation of "a *contrast* between what God had done earlier and is now doing," and, moreover, is followed not by an expression of confidence but of complaint! The following passages reflect the function of the cultic recapitulation of *Heilsgeschichte* in the lament psalms more clearly:[2]

> *Example 1*
> Ps 22:5–6, *recapitulation*
> Ps 22:7–9, *complaint* (not confidence)
> > But I am a worm, and no man any more;
> > Scorned by men and despised by the people.

> *Example 2*
> Ps 44:2–9, *recapitulation*
> Ps 44:10–17, *complaint* (not confidence)
> > But you have cast us off and abased us;
> > You do not go out with our armies.

The above examples strongly bear witness to the fact that by contrasting God's earlier acts of salvation (*Deus revelatus*) with his present absence (*Deus absconditus*), that is, by recapitulating the earlier history of salvation, the lament psalms attempt to emphasize the present distress and military humiliation (cf. Sarna 1963; Mullen 1983). Therefore, it can be concluded that the re-presentation of the *Heilsgeschichte* in the lament psalms must have a fundamentally different context from that of the rapid change of mood in the lament psalms: The re-telling of the past history in the lament psalms must be characterized as an exhibition of the ground of complaint through the *contrast* between the present situation of distress and God's earlier acts of victory.

To sum up: the above arguments indicate that among the lament psalms we have no evidence that either a "priestly (or cult prophetic) oracle of salvation" or a "cultic actualization of the *Heilsgeschichte*" provided "objective motivation" for the sudden change of mood of the psalm. This means that the rapid shift of mood in the lament psalms is never schematically limited to a cultic act. This is not to say that the sudden change of mood in Israelite lament psalms is a purely psychological occurrence, totally dissociated from cult and tradition-history. Accordingly, the task that remains is the examination of where this change of mood is rooted. My thesis is that the rapid change of mood in the lament psalms can be regarded as being derived from a free combination of two factors: (1) the traditionally typical Israelite faith of the lament psalmists and (2) the aftereffect that resulted from the recapitulation of the salvation tradition in the cult.

II. THE IMPETUS OF HOLY WAR IDEOLOGIES AS A MOTIVATION OF THE RAPID SHIFT OF MOOD IN PSALM 3

My arguments so far have shown that agreement has not been reached concerning the proper motivation for the abrupt change of mood in the lament psalms, nor has a comprehensive explanation been provided for it. This means that we need to explore a different, more convincing explanation.

Psalm 3 provides us with a key to the mystery of the sudden shift of mood in the lament psalm:

Psalm 3 is a typical psalm of lament, which exhibits all of the lament's basic components, including *"Anrufung"* (v. 2a), *"Klage"* (vv. 2–3), *"Vertrauen"* (vv. 4–7), *"Bitte"* (v. 8a), *"Gewissheit der Erhoerung"* (v. 8b), and *"Bekenntnis"* (v. 9) (see Gunkel 1892: 13).

These components of the lament songs in Psalm 3 are well-organized to mark clearly the sudden shift of mood right after *"Klage"* (vv. 2–3) and *"Bitte"* (v. 8a): the psalm begins with a complaint against the innumerable enemies arrayed against the lamenter, but abruptly moves to confidence of salvation.

Psalm 3 is an example in which an individual experience becomes an expression of the national (or communal) experience, although the language is left in its individual form: the lament singer combines his personal experience of salvation with the liturgical confession of the community.

Psalm 3 is structured as follows:

Anrufung (v. 2a)
O Yahweh,

Klage (vv. 2–3)
O Yahweh, how many are my adversaries! How many rise
up against me!
How many are saying of me: "There is no salvation for him
in God!" (Selah)

Rapid Change of Mood
Vertrauen (vv. 4–5, 6–7)
But you, O Yahweh, are a shield round me, my glory, and
One who holds up my head.
When I cry out my voice to Yahweh, he answers me from
His holy mountain. (Selah)

I lay down. Then I fell asleep. I awakened, because
Yahweh sustains me.
I fear not the multitudes of people, who have deployed
against me on every side.

Bitte (v. 8a)
Rise up, O Yahweh! Give me victory, O my God!

Rapid Change of Mood
Gewissheit der Erhörung (v. 8b)
Surely[3] you smote all my enemies on the cheek! You
smashed the teeth of the wicked!

Bekenntnis (v. 9)
Salvation belongs to Yahweh!
Your blessing is upon your people. (Selah)

Psalm 3, which is typically well-structured as a psalm of lament,
seems to respond to our long-pending question about the motivation
for the rapid shift of mood in the lament psalms with the following
three decisive indications.

1. *Indication one.* Psalm 3 makes efficient use of abundant military
terminology, as is often the case in the lament psalms where the extensive war imagery figures prominently as one of their features:

1a. The primary examples of the usage of military terminology are *māgēn* ("shield") in verse 4, *mēribbôt* ("from multitudes") in verse 7, and *šātû* ("they deployed") in verse 7.

The word *māgēn* ("shield") refers to a military weapon that was used for protection; this word is parallel to "sword" in Deut 33:29 and "buckler" in Ps 91:4. Even if one were to follow Dahood (1966: 16–17) and translate *māgēn* as "Suzerain" on the basis of the Punic *māgōn*, *mgn* would still have a military sense, since Punic *māgōn* is used for Carthaginian generals.

The word *rĕbābôt* ("multitudes") also occurs elsewhere in military contexts (e.g., Deut 32:20; Judg 20:10). Although Dahood translates the word as "shafts," deriving it from a root *rbb*, "to shoot arrows," it seems that the psalmist here has emphasized the numerousness of his enemies by means of employing the root *rbb* I ("be numerous"): the psalmist has already employed the same root three times in verses 2–3 with respect to his enemies.

The term *šātû* ("they deployed") refers to a military act, which indicates that an army composed of myriads is set or put in battle array. The form recurs in Isa 22:7, and there its military sense emerges definitely.

1b. This short psalm, which comprises only eight verses plus a superscription, seems to attest that military imagery plays an important role in the formation of the psalmist's poetic spirit. The psalm's other examples of the usage of military terminology can add more conviction about the role of military imagery in the formation of the lament psalms: (a) the frequent mention of the "enemy" (and its synonyms), whose identity in the Book of Psalms is always uncertain (vv. 2, 7, 8), (b) the expressions of confidence, such as "I fear not," which seems to be a poetic adaptation of the priestly oracular formula *ʾal-tîrāʾ* ("Fear not!," v. 7),[4] and (c) the sudden appearance of the expression "Rise up! O Yahweh!" (v. 8), which is parallel to the war-cry (Humbert 1946) spoken when the Ark is carried into war (Num 10:35; cf. Judg 5:12; 7:15). This extensive war imagery used in this lament psalm seems to indicate that the definite impact of holy war ideology on Israelite faith has also had an important influence upon the formation of the lament psalms.

2. *Indication two.* In this context, the placement of the holy war ideologies in Psalm 3 helps us to understand the faith-motivation for the abrupt shift of mood in the lament psalms:

2a. The hyperbolic contrast of number and strength between the pious lamenter and his numerous enemies in verses 2–3 seems to be stimulated by the Israelite basic ideology of holy war. This ideology was armed with a faith that Yahweh saves His people, not by sword and spear, great army and strong warrior, and warhorses and their great strength, but by [their calling on] the name of Yahweh of hosts (cf. 1 Sam 17:47a; Ps 33:16–17). A good example of such a holy war ideology is provided by the account of the holy war led by Gideon, where the hyperbolic contrast between the small number of Israelite troops ("like a barley cake rolling through the Midianite camp") and the many Midianite soldiers ("like a swarm of locusts lying along the valley") is very highly dramatized (cf. Judges 7). So it is natural for Psalm 3 to be concluded with a *Bekenntnis*, "salvation belongs to Yahweh" (v. 9).

2b. The most important tenet of the holy war ideology (von Rad 1951: 57) is that only strong, "fearless trust" in Yahweh the Divine Warrior is required for the one who hopes for salvation. Such an ideology has explicit overtones in Ps 3:4–5, 6–7. Striking parallels occur in the earlier source of the Pentateuchal traditions (J; Exod 14:13–14), the prophets of the eighth century (Isa 7:4; 30:15; 31:1ff.; Hos 14:3), the Deuteronomic law of war (Deut 20:1–9), and in the historico-theological statements of later historians (the Deuteronomist and the Chronicler) concerning holy wars led by Gideon (Judges 7), David (1 Samuel 17), and Jehoshaphat (2 Chronicles 20).

2c. Another important motif of the holy war tradition in Psalm 3 is found in an urgent petition (shout), which is followed immediately by a sudden statement of victory over the enemies. This is shown in verse 8: at the very moment when the psalmist shouted "Rise up, O Yahweh!" (v. 8a) the enemies have *already* been destroyed (v. 8b).

> *v. 8a: Urgent Short Petition*
> Rise up, O Yahweh! Deliver me, O God!

> *v. 8b: Abrupt Confidence in Victory*
> Surely you *have smitten* (Hebrew perfect tense) all my enemies on the cheek!
> You *have smashed* (Hebrew perfect tense) the teeth of the wicked!

The expression "Rise up, O Yahweh!" right before the abrupt confidence in victory surely is parallel to the "war cry" (*tĕrû ʿâ*) shouted on the departure of the Ark for war (cf. Num 10:35),[5] where Yahweh as a "Warrior" is addressed directly (cf. Exod 15:3), as is Deborah in the Song of Deborah in Judg 5:12 (see Schwally 1901: 25–28). The lament psalmist's confidence in the sudden defeat of enemies (vv. 8a and 8b), therefore, must be derived from a tradition of holy war faith that assumes that at the very moment of war-cry (*tĕrû ʿâ*) the enemies will be struck down suddenly with God's terror and dread. This suddenness of confidence must be related to an ideology of holy war that has its origins in a faith in divine intervention eliminating any human accomplishment and effort. Accordingly, such confidence expressed in the form of the *tĕrû ʿâ* can be argued to provide an explanation for the rapid change of mood in the lament psalms, whose patterned expression can now be seen in the following structure: war cry —⟩ victory shout.

In addition to this verse-structure, there also appears another expression "Salvation (or Victory) belongs to Yahweh" (v. 9) right after the above verse (v. 8), which also sounds like a war-cry (*tĕrû ʿâ*) and with which the whole Psalm 3 ends. This expression is closely related to the tenet of the holy war ideology that the defeat of the enemy by Yahweh means the very salvation of Yahweh, as evidenced by such songs as Judg 5:31, Exod 15:1b–2a, and Exod 14:13 (J). Also, this expression, as is shown in 1 Sam 17:47 and 2 Chr 20:15, 17 is tied closely to the expression, "The war is Yahweh's," which also sounds like a war-cry signaling victory (Craigie 1983: 71).

In concluding my above argument about the motivation for the sudden shift of mood in the lament psalms, I cannot close without noting the fact that the lamenters very strikingly tend to stress a complaint against the "enemy" and a petition for the destruction of the "enemy." As is well-known, the concept of enemy in the war narratives of the Old Testament seems to be best understood from within the framework of the ideology of the holy war, in which the enemy of the "oppressed" (Israel) always and uniformly coincides with the enemy of Yahweh (cf. Judg 5:31; 1 Sam 25:26; 30:26). Although the concept of the "enemy" in the lament psalms cannot be pressed into such a single narrow conception as, e.g., "sorcerer," "gentile," "political opponent," "accuser," or a metaphor of "death" or "disease,"[6] it is noteworthy that all the concepts of enemy in the lament psalms are monotonously stylized in conformity to the strict dichotomy between the afflicted (the lament psalmists) and the wicked (*rĕšā ʿîm*), which framework is strongly imprinted upon the literature of the holy war narratives. Accordingly, the dichotomized concept of enemy in the lament psalms can be argued to be derived from that of the holy war tradition, since the dichotomized antagonism between the lament psalmists as the afflicted and the enemy as the one who afflicts permeates all parts of the lament psalms. Psalm 3 is an exemplary lament psalm, in which the idea of Yahweh's warfare against enemies forms a basic framework of the process of sudden shift in mood.

3. *Indication three.* The more striking evidence for solving the great riddle of the abrupt change in mood in the lament psalms is that the holy war ideologies accompanied with war imagery are placed almost everywhere that the mood-transition occurs. Psalm 3 is a good example of this.

3a. The first abrupt change of mood in Psalm 3 occurs in verse 4, right after the complaints in verses 2 and 3, which is characterized by the complaint against the numerousness and the mockery of enemies. The expression in verse 4 that changes the mood of complaint into confidence in Yahweh's protection is introduced by the confessional faith in Yahweh as a shield, a metaphorical term from the military sphere. This dimension of trust in God the Warrior armed with the shield must have its root in the tradition of the holy war. The faith of Abraham in his confession of God as a shield in Gen 15:1 also seems to have its root in the holy war tradition, in view of the fact that Abraham was concerned with the ideology of the war of Yahweh (Westermann 1985: 218; *pace* P. D. Miller, Jr. 1987: 88). This idea is also found in Deut 33:29; Pss 18:3, 31; 28:7; 33:20; 84:10; 144:2. Thus it is a faith rooted in holy war tradition that carries the lament psalmist over the obstacles that have been deployed against him.

The mood transition effected by the confessional faith in Yahweh as a shield in verses 4–5 is more importantly extended to the "fearless trust" of the lamenter in Yahweh in verses 6–7, whose faith-motif is spread throughout the holy war tradition: the exhortative address "Fear not!" at the beginning of the holy war can be found in Exod 14:13 (J); Deut 20:3; Josh 8:1; and 10:8–11; Judg 7:3; 1 Sam 23:16, 17; 2 Sam 10:12; etc.

3b. The second abrupt change of mood in Psalm 3 occurs in verse 8b right after the petition in verse 8a. The phenomenon in which a petitionary shout (v. 8a), spoken in the form of war-cry (*tĕrû ʿâ*), abruptly transforms into confidence (v. 8b) of victory over enemies appears very often at the conclusion of holy wars, where the terror (*ḥāmam, mĕhûmâ* or *ḥărādâ*) of God happens suddenly in the enemies' encampment.[7] The emphasis upon the abrupt defeat of the enemy right after the shout of the short petition in Psalm 3, therefore, bears witness to the holy war ideology that salvation (victory) is Yahweh's alone, debarring human merit. Accordingly, expressions of confidence preceded by such short petitions (similar to war-cries) as "Rise up, O Yahweh!" (cf. "Awake, Deborah!" in Judg 5:12) in the lament psalms can be understood as resulting from the influence of the holy war faith, in which Yahweh's military intervention itself is the very assurance of salvation (victory).

In conclusion, in so far as there appear expressions of *complaint* right after both announcements of the priestly (or cultic prophet's) oracle of salvation and the recollections of Yahweh's past acts of salvation in history in the lament psalms, and since the purely psychological metamorphosis of the prayer's inner soul is not a proper explanation for the sudden shift of mood in the lament psalms, we have no alternative but to yield to a proposal that the rapid change of mood in the lament psalms is best accounted for in the context of the holy war faith in Yahweh as a Warrior.

Indeed, the discovery of this function of holy war ideologies in the lament psalms is sure to produce an excellent matrix for the establishment of an Old Testament theology, where we can hope to develop the hermeneutical task of witnessing to the *heilsgeschichtliche* kerygma in the Old Testament.

NOTES

1. Cf. Mowinckel's dialogue with Gunkel (Mowinckel 1962: I, 13–14).
2. Cf. Pss 74:12–17; 77:11–21; 80:9–15; 83:10–12; 85:2–4; 126:1–3.
3. For the translation of the Hebrew term *kî*, see Dahood (1966: 19), Craigie (1983: 70–71), Muilenburg (1961: 135–59, esp. 136), Pedersen (1926: 118–19).
4. For the exhortative address at the beginning of the holy war, see, e.g., Exod 14:13; Deut 20:3; Josh 8:1; 10:8–25; Judg 7:3; 1 Sam 23:16, 17; 2 Sam 10:12.

5. This psalm can be said to be a liturgical fragment rooted in holy war ideology used in the reenactment of the wars of Yahweh (Cross 1966: 28–29).
6. Cf. Mowinckel (1921: chaps. 1–4; 1962: I, 242; II, 6–8), Pedersen (1926: 320–22), Schmidt (1934: 7; 1928: 26), Birkeland (1955), Anderson (1965/66: 18–19), Westermann (1981: 194).
7. Cf. Exod 15:14–16; 23:27–28; Deut 2:25; 11:25; Josh 2:24; 5:1; 10:2; 24:12. See von Rad (1951: 10–13).

REFERENCES

Anderson, G. W.
1965/66   Enemies and Evildoers in the Book of Psalms. *Bulletin of the John Rylands Library* 48: 18–19.

Begrich, J.
1964   Das Priesterliche Heilsorakel. Pp. 217–31 in *Gesammelte Studien zum Alten Testament*. München: Chr. Kaiser.

Birkeland, H.
1955   *The Evildoers in the Book of Psalms*. Oslo: I Kommisjon Hos Jacob Dybwad.

Briggs, C. A.
1906   *A Critical and Exegetical Commentary on the Book of Psalms*. 2 vols. Edinburgh: T. & T. Clark.

Childs, B. S.
1976   *Memory and Tradition in Israel*. Studies in Biblical Theology 37. London: SCM.

Craigie, P.C.
1983   *Psalms 1–50*. Word Biblical Commentary 19. Texas: Word.

Cross, F. M.
1966   The Divine Warrior in Israel's Early Cult. Pp. 11–30 in *Biblical Motifs: Origins and Transformations*, ed. A. Altmann. Cambridge, MA: Harvard University.

Dahood, M.
1966   *Psalms 1–50*. Anchor Bible 16. New York: Doubleday.

Gunkel, H.
1892   *Psalmen*. Göttingen: Vandenhoeck & Ruprecht.
1933   *Einleitung in die Psalmen*. Göttingen: Vandenhoeck & Ruprecht.

Heiler, F.
1958   *Prayer: A Study in the History and Psychology of Religion*. New York: Oxford University.

Humbert, P.
1946   *La "Terou'a."* Neuchatel: Secrétariat de L'université.

Küchler, F.
1918   Das Priesterliche Orakel in Israel und Judah. *Beihefte zur Zeitschrift für die alttestamentliche Wissenschaft* 33: 285–301.
Kraus, H. J.
1978   *Psalmen*. 2 vols. Neukirchen-Vluyn: Neukirchener.
Leslie, E. A.
1982   *The Book of Psalms*. Michigan: Baker.
Miller, P. D., Jr.
1987   Review of *The Rapid Change of Mood in the Lament Psalms*, by E. K. Kim. *Interpretation* 41: 88–89.
Mowinckel, S.
1921–24   *Psalmenstudien*. 6 volumes. Kriestiania: In Kommision bei Jacob Dybwad.
1962   *The Psalms in Israel's Worship*. 2 vols. Nashville: Abingdon.
Muilenburg, J.
1961   The Linguistic and Rhetorical Usages of the Particle *kî* in the Old Testament. *Hebrew Union College Annual* 32: 132–59.
Mullen, E. T., Jr.
1983   The Divine Witness and the Davidic Royal Grant: Psalm 89: 37–38. *Journal of Biblical Literature* 102: 207–18.
Noth, M.
1963   The "Re-presentation" of the Old Testament in Proclamation. Pp. 76–88 in *Essays on Old Testament Hermeneutics*, ed. C. Westermann. Atlanta: John Knox.
Oesterley, W. O. E.
1953   *The Psalms*. London: S. P. C. K.
Pedersen, J.
1926   *Israel: Its Life and Culture*. 2 vols. London: Oxford University.
Rad, G. von
1951   *Der Heilige Krieg im alten Israel*. Zürich: Zwingli.
Sarna, N. M.
1963   Psalm 89: A Study in Inner Biblical Exegesis. Pp. 29–46 in *Biblical and Other Studies. Vol. I*, ed. A. Altmann. Cambridge: Harvard University.
Schmidt, H.
1928   *Das Gebet der Angeklagten im Alten Testament*. Giessen: Alfred Topelmann.
1934   *Psalmen*. Tubingen: Mohr.
Schwally, F.
1901   *Semitische Kriegsaltertümer: I, Der heilige Krieg im alten Israel*. Leipzig: Dieterich.

Weiser, A.

1962   *The Psalms*. Philadelphia: Westminster.

Westermann, C.

1981   *Praise and Lament in the Psalms*. Atlanta: John Knox.

1985   *Genesis 12–36*. Minneapolis: Augsburg.

7 The Song of the Sea and Salvation History

THOMAS B. DOZEMAN

he Song of the Sea and salvation history have become closely
interwoven in contemporary scholarship. Noth and von Rad
set the stage with their interpretation of the exodus within the
perspective of salvation history. Von Rad characterized salvation history as a "canonical history"—a mixture of historical experience and
cultic legend recounting divine acts of salvation that formed the nation
of Israel (1962: 126, 129). Salvation history emerges from tribal cel-
ebrations of the exodus, according to von Rad, and is fully developed
already in the early monarchical period. Its central themes grew to
include the promise of land to the ancestors, exodus, wilderness wandering, and life in the land of Canaan.[1] Noth provided a bridge to the
poetry of the exodus, when he concluded that Exod 15:21b preserved
the nucleus of salvation history, since it implied the conquest of the
land (1981: 46–62; 1962: 104–105, 121–23). But he judged the Song
of the Sea (Exod 15:1–18) to be a late composition.

The Song of the Sea became the cornerstone of salvation history for
the Albright School. Comparison with Ugaritic literature provided the
basis to isolate a corpus of archaic poetry, of which Exod 15:1–18 was
considered a central example. This approach to the origin of Israelite
literature positioned early representatives of the school, such as Cross
and Freedman (1975: 45–65), over against Noth in arguing that the
complete version of the Song of the Sea (rather than just the couplet in
15:21b) constituted the earliest account of the exodus. They also concluded that the song was part of an epic of salvation history, forming
the basis for all subsequent pentateuchal tradition (Cross and Freedman 1955: 237–50; Cross, 1973: 112–44; Freedman 1980: 77–129,
167–227). Their thesis presented a strong counter-argument to von

Rad and Noth concerning the literary character of early Israelite tradition. Yet it reinforced the broader thesis that the exodus was an event of salvation history from its inception. Now the entire sequence of exodus, wilderness, and conquest could be shown to be embedded in an archaic poem. One result of intensifying a hermeneutic of salvation history was that the original unity of the Song of the Sea emerged as an important feature in arguing for its antiquity.

Comparison with Ugaritic mythology was used to strengthen both the antiquity and the original unity of the Song of the Sea. Cross argued that the poem preserved in a historicized form an old mythic pattern: (1) the combat of the divine Warrior and his victory at the Sea, (2) the building of a sanctuary on the "mount of possession" won in battle, and (3) the god's manifestation of "eternal" kingship. He concluded that "although Israel's early religious evolution was neither simple nor unilinear," nevertheless, "the power of the mythic pattern was enormous." The Song of the Sea illustrates this power by using the mythic pattern "to mythologize historical episodes to reveal their transcendent meaning" (1973: 112–44, esp. 142–44).

This brief overview illustrates that salvation history has influenced the interpretation of the Song of the Sea. The antiquity of the poem is often dependent on arguments for its original unity, reinforced by comparison with Ugaritic mythology. I wish to reevaluate the role of salvation history in the Song of the Sea through a study of the poem's original unity. I will argue that the earliest form of the Song of the Sea is ancient poetry. But it lacks the wilderness and conquest motifs, and thus is not a celebration of salvation history. The study will separate into two parts. The first part will trace the transmission history of the Song of the Sea in two parts. An original version of the hymn celebrates Yahweh's victory at the sea (vv. 1–12, 18). Deuteronomistic writers refashion this hymn into an event of salvation history, with the addition of the wilderness wandering and conquest motifs (vv. 13–17). The literary study will provide background for a comparison between the Song of the Sea and the Baal-Yamm/Nahar myth in the second section.

I. THE PROBLEMS OF UNITY

The Song of the Sea presents a variety of tradition-historical problems. Zenger notes debate concerning the poetic meter, organization, genre, *Sitz im Leben*, date of composition (both with regard to the history of traditions and to the problems associated with archaic Hebrew morphology and comparative Semitic linguistics), the unity of Exod 15:1–18, and its relationship with Exod 15:21b (1980: 452–53).[2] Our task is more narrow—to determine whether the poem in Exod 15:1–18 is an original unity. There are several indications that it is not. An examination of the content; genre, linguistic features, and meter; and specific motifs suggests that the Song of the Sea has gone through a history of composition.

First, content. The most striking contrast within the hymn is the content of vv. 1–12, 18 and vv. 13–17. As Jeremias (1987: 99) has recently noted, the first half of the poem focuses on (1) Yahweh alone, (2) in a battle event, (3) where the enemy is destroyed in the sea, (4) culminating in Yahweh's victory and kingship. This sequence of events contrasts with vv. 13–17, where the focus is on (1) Israel, (2) being lead on a journey by Yahweh, (3) through nations that are specifically named, (4) culminating in their arrival at the cult. The change of content raises questions concerning the relationship of the two parts. But content by itself is not a reliable indicator of a history of composition.[3] A series of additional problems suggests that the strophe concerning the wilderness and conquest in vv. 13–17 is a later addition.

Second: genre, linguistic features, and meter. The genre of the present form of Exod 15:1–18 is unclear.[4] Problems include a mixture of hymnic phrases and ballad.[5] References to God also shift between third and second person.[6] Most problematic is that a hymn of the individual celebrating Yahweh's past victory at the sea (vv. 1–12) shifts both in topic and in time (vv. 13–17) to describe Israel's wilderness journey and eventual arrival at Yahweh's cult. Zenger (1980: 468–69) writes: "If v. 1b is thought of as the summary or as the title of a hymn that follows, then vv. 13–17 could scarcely have been original to the stated theme."

Scholars have sought to maintain the unity of the poem in spite of the problem of genre. Schmidt and Muilenburg, for example, account for the diverse parts by arguing that the poem is a liturgy (Schmidt 1931: 63–64; Muilenburg 1966: 153). Alter (1985: 53–54) suggests that the change of topic is "meant to project out of the stunning experience of the Reed Sea a larger pattern of God's powerful ... acts in history."[7] Cross (1973: 121–32) addresses the problem of time by arguing that

vv. 1b–18 is an archaic victory song, and that all the prefixed forms of the verbs in vv. 13–17, including the refrain in v. 16b and the approach to the sanctuary in v. 17, must be read as preterits on analogy to Ugaritic *yaqtul* forms. He concludes that the poet wrote "from the point of view of one re-enacting the Conquest, including both the episode of the sea and the passing over into the land to a Palestinian sanctuary" (Cross 1973: 128 n. 59). Brenner (1991: 36–39) takes yet another approach by arguing that vv. 13–17 are future in their orientation, but that "the defeat of the future enemies and the security of the friends of God" is a developed form of the victory song.

Brenner's conclusion that references to the future are characteristic of the victory song is based on the concluding half verse in the song of Deborah (Judg 5:31a), where the poet writes, "So (כֵּן) perish all your enemies, O Yahweh! But his loved ones be like the rising (כְּצֵאת) of the sun in its might" (1991: 39). But the syntax does not support the reading. The construction כֵּן + כְּ indicates comparison between a past and present situation (Waltke and O'Connor 1990: 641 Par. 38.5.a). And, in view of this, Hauser's more limited conclusions concerning the elements within a victory song are to be preferred: focus on specific names for God, application of specific terms to God, description of God's use of the forces of nature, mocking of the enemy, and a description of the enemy's fall (1987: 265–84). References to the future are not part of such a genre.

Cross' reading of the wilderness and conquest as past events also creates problems. A consistent reading of the *yaqtul* verb forms as preterits in vv. 13–17 runs into difficulty already in vv. 14–16a, where the fear of Israel's neighbors need not be read as a singular past event.[8] And it becomes even more difficult to maintain in the refrain of v. 16b. The syntactical construction of עַד with imperfect nearly always has future meaning, requiring that the opening couplet of v. 17 also be read as a statement about the future.[9] Coats (1969: 9) saw the problem and employed Westermann's (1981: 150–64) language of declarative and descriptive praise to account for the different styles of speech. He concluded that there was a transition in genre between the event at the sea and the wilderness-conquest material. The former is declarative praise (praise of God for a specific deed) and the latter descriptive (more general praise of God in all times and in all places).

Study of genre leads to the following conclusions. The arguments of Schmidt, Muilenburg and Alter are helpful in accounting for the present form of the hymn, but they by-pass the problem of genre that is stated by Zenger. Cross may be correct in his assessment of the Song of the Sea as being a victory song, but such a form-critical assessment would only apply to the first part, where Yahweh destroys the Egyptians (vv. 1b, 4a) with the use of his right hand (vv. 6b, 12). Other motifs supporting this conclusion include images of Yahweh as a warrior (v. 3a), God's fierce anger (vv. 7, 8a) and destroying breath (v. 10), as well as the contrasting imagery of the enemies' anticipation of victory and the sudden reversal brought about by Yahweh (v. 9). All of these images envision a past event, which, upon comparison with other similar songs (e.g., the Song of Deborah in Judges 5), appears to be a common trait in the victory song (Hauser 1987: 265–84). Such a conclusion, however, argues against the inclusion of vv. 13–17 within the genre by definition.

The problems of content and genre posed by the insertion of vv. 13–17 carry over to poetic structure. The 2 + 2 meter that predominates in vv. 1–12 is difficult to maintain in vv. 14–16a, prompting some scholars to scan lines in 3 + 4 (v. 14) and 4 + 4 (vv. 15a and 16a) meter.[10] Zenger and Jeremias go so far as to conclude that v. 15b is prose rather than poetry (Zenger 1980: 464; Jeremias 1987: 99).

Third, motifs and diction. A final point of contrast between vv. 1–12, 18 and vv. 13–17 is the lack of verbal contact between the two sections. This contrast may simply be the result of the difference in subject matter, as some scholars have argued (Brenner 1991: 28–29). Those taking this position note that there is repetition of certain motifs (e.g., כאבן, in vv. 5, 16; יד in vv. 9, 17; עז in vv. 2, 13; and קדש in vv. 11, 13, 17), which weave the two sections together (Muilenburg 1966: 155–56; Freedman 1980: 187–89; Brenner 1991: 30–31). The distinctive deuteronomistic language within the limited boundaries of vv. 13–17 suggests, however, that the points of contact between the two sections are the result of redaction and not an original unity.

The clearest signs of deuteronomistic interpretation of the sea tradition are the words יבשה, to indicate Yahweh's drying up of the sea, and עבר (e.g., Jos 2:10; 4:23; 5:1), to describe the people's crossing of the Red Sea and the Jordan River (Butler 1971: 107–49; Coats 1969: 1–31; Norin 1977: 77–107; Jeremias 1987: 93–106; Spieckermann 1989:

96–115; Foresti 1982: 41–69). Neither motif occurs in vv. 1–12, suggesting those verses of the hymn are not of deuteronomistic origin. The motif of Israel "crossing over" is central in vv. 13–17 (see the refrain in v. 16b). Other motifs strengthen the ties to deuteronomistic tradition. Divine leading of Israel dominates the strophe (vv. 13, 17, נהל, נחה, and especially בוא), and it is also prominent in deuteronomistic tradition. בוא is used frequently in deuteronomistic tradition to describe Yahweh's promise of land (Boorer 1992: 133–35) and Israel's possession of it (Braulik 1978: 95; McConville 1984: 33–35; Butler 1971: 156–62; Jenni 1970: 251–61; and Preuss 1975: 20–49). The fear of the nations in vv. 14–16a (e.g., פחד, אימה, מוג, חיל, רגז) also repeats language from deuteronomistic tradition (Butler 1971: 162–99; Norin 1977: 96–97; Zenger 1980: 475; Jeremias 1987: 99; Foresti, 1982: 48–50; and Moran 1963: 333–42). מוג and אימה (Jos 2:9, 24) describe the fear of nations at the approach of Israel, while רגז, חיל, and פחד characterize their fear during the Israelite conquest (Deut 2:25). Repetition of the relative זו is likely archaizing. Brenner has argued that the description of salvation in vv. 13–17 as a divine act of redemption (גאל in v. 13) and purchase (קנה in v. 16) with the syntactical construction עם־זו points to exilic reinterpretations of the exodus (1991: 127–30).[11]

The imagery of temple building and parallels to Canaanite mythology in v. 17 raise questions concerning its relationship to vv. 13–16.[12] Cross (1973: 112–42) used the parallels to Canaanite mythology to argue that v. 17 is part of a pre-monarchical version of the Song of the Sea. The syntax and imagery of the verse, however, encourage its reading with the deuteronomistic addition in vv. 13–16. It contrasts to the third person speech of v. 18 in referring to God, employing instead the more direct second person speech characteristic of the body of the hymn. Verse 17 repeats language from v. 13 to describe Yahweh's holy abode (אל־נוה קדשך in v. 13 and מקדש אדני in v. 17), framing the strophe (Blenkinsopp 1992: 159). The suffixes on the initial verbs (ותטעמו, תבאמו) refer to Israel not Pharaoh or the Egyptians, continuing the imagery of Yahweh leading Israel in vv. 13–16. Also the tense of the verbs in v. 17 fits the future orientation of vv. 13–16 (see especially v. 16b).[13] Finally Mettinger (1982: 27) has argued that the imagery of Yahweh's dwelling place (מכון לשבתך) presupposes the influence of

Zion tradition. This insight does not argue for deuteronomistic author-ship, but it does preclude a pre-monarchical date.[14]

Interpretation suggests that the Song of the Sea is not an originally unified poem. A celebration of Yahweh's past battle at the sea (vv. 1–12, 18) is supplemented with the pastoral leading of Israel and the future conquest of the land (vv. 13–17). Exod 15:1–12, 18 is a victory hymn, separating into three parts: an introduction (vv. 1–3), the body (vv. 4–11), and a conclusion (vv. 12, 18). Clear divisions concerning the structure must remain tentative. As Coats (1969: 2) noted, "sug-gested patterns of bicola or tricola as strophic units produce no satis-factory results, no consensus." Although there is debate whether vv. 2, 12, and 18 fit the context of the hymn, I retain each. First person praise is carried through both v. 1b and v. 2, and vv. 2–3 work in concert to provide elaboration on the divine name (Muilenburg 1966: 157).[15] The meaning of "earth" as "underworld" in v. 12 and the repetition of ימינך ("your arm") from v. 6b provide a coda to Yahweh's victory at the Sea (Cross 1973: 129),[16] while the exclamation of Yahweh's kingship in v. 18 has durative meaning as a conclusion to vv. 1–12.[17]

Exod 15:1–12, 18 is a celebration of Yahweh's salvific power con-ceived as a holy war event. The two refrains (vv. 6 and 11a) indicate that victory is over earthly (v. 6) and cosmic (v. 11a) forces. Verses 4–5 and 7 describe the defeat of Pharaoh and the Egyptian army, ac-centuated by the first refrain: "Your right hand, Yahweh, glorious in power; Your right hand, Yahweh, shattered the enemy" (v. 6). Verses 8–10 indicate Yahweh's power over the sea (מים and ים in v. 8 and ים and מים in v. 10), prompting the second refrain, "Who is like you among the gods, Yahweh?" (v. 11a).[18] The conclusion returns to the histori-cal enemy, describing the destruction of the Egyptian army (v. 12), and ends with the proclamation of Yahweh's enduring kingship (v. 18). Kingship indicates that victory is celebrated from the perspective of the land. Verses 13–17 represent a reinterpretation of the victory hymn within the perspective of salvation history. The land becomes a future hope, not a present reality. Triumph at the sea inaugurates di-vine leading in the wilderness and the future conquest of the land.

The deuteronomistic reinterpretation of the Song of the Sea is likely exilic, certainly not earlier than the late monarchical period.[19] The vic-tory hymn is pre-exilic. Past study, moreover, suggests that it is ar-chaic poetry, perhaps originating already in the pre-monarchical period. Norin (1977: 77–107) argues for a pre-monarchical core to the psalm, which underwent significant expansion. Few have followed his lead, but nearly all concede redactional additions in vv. 1–12, 18. The arguments for the archaic character of the hymn by Cross and Freedman (1955: 243) emphasize morphology and comparison to Ugaritic prosody. Their research is supported by Robertson (1972: 28–31), who concludes that the strongest examples of genuinely archaic forms occur in vv. 1–12.[20] The archaic victory hymn celebrates Yahweh's victory at the sea. Deuteronomistic editors reinterpret the victory hymn as salvation history either at the close of the monarchical period or during the exile.

II. MYTHIC PATTERNS IN THE SONG OF THE SEA

Many scholars have explored the mythological background to the Song of the Sea, especially with regard to the conflicts of Baal in the Canaanite mythology.[21] Comparison often includes all of the Song of the Sea (Exod 15:1–18) and at least the conflict between Baal and Yamm/Nahar (CTA 2, 3 and at times also 4), regardless of whether an author suspects a history of tradition in the development of the Song of the Sea or senses problems in the sequencing of the Ugaritic tablets.[22] In contrast to past studies, the present comparison will attend strictly to the tradition-historical development of the Song of the Sea outlined in the first section. Such an approach, it is hoped, will provide insight into the early cultic history of the exodus. Comparison will illustrate that Exod 15:1–12, 18 parallels only CTA 2, where the focus is on divine combat and victory. The deuteronomistic addition in Exod 15:13–17 incorporates the motifs of temple construction and divine enthronement from CTA 3–4.

The structure of CTA 2 can be summarized in three parts: (1) Baal's conflict with the enthroned god Yamm/Nahar; (2) Baal's victory over Yamm/Nahar; and (3) Baal's proclamation of kingship. CTA 2 begins with a description of Yamm's enthronement in his newly built temple (CTA 2.I and III), prompting a conflict with Baal (CTA 2.IV). Baal initially loses this conflict (CTA 2.IV.1–7). But after encouragement from the god Kothar-wa-Khasis, who entreats Baal to seize his eternal kingship (*tqh.mlk. 'lmk. drkt.dt.drdrk*, CTA 2.IV.10–11), he defeats Yamm (CTA 2.IV.7–27). CTA 2 ends with Baal proclaiming

the death of Yamm and his kingship (*ym.lmt.b 'lm yml*[*k*], CTA 2.IV.32).
Baal's proclamation of kingship at the close of CTA 2 should not be
interpreted as an enthronement. Baal has no temple (*hkl*), throne (*ksu.
ṯbt*), dominion (*drkt*), or land of possession (*arṣ.nḥlt*). All appear necessary to complete a god's enthronement.[23]

CTA 3 and 4 complete the process of Baal's enthronement. The
tablets indicate his need for a temple, accentuating the motifs of enthronement (*ksu. ṯbt*), dominion (*drkt*), and a land that Baal can possess (*arṣ.nḥlt*). Twice in CTA 3 and 4 Baal's kingship is proclaimed
in the context of his not yet having a temple. The implication is that a
temple must be built to complete his enthronement (CTA 3.E.40–47;
4.IV.43–62).[24] The plot structure of CTA 4 describes the construction
of the temple and the sequence of events resulting in Baal's enthronement. First, the construction of a temple leads to a feast (CTA 4.I–VI).
Next, Baal marches into the surrounding area seizing cities and towns,
thus building an empire (CTA 4.VII.7–12). Finally, he returns to his
temple, sits on his throne (CTA 4.VII.13–52), and concludes that no
one could challenge his kingship or take over the land of his possession (*umlk.ubl.mlk*//*arṣ.drkty.yštkn*, CTA 4.VII.43–44).[25]

The literary development of the Song of the Sea echoes the separation between conflict and temple construction evident in CTA 2 and
3–4. Exod 15:1–12, 18 follows the three-part structure of CTA 2: conflict, victory, and proclamation of Yahweh's kingship. The proclamation of an eternal kingship at the end of each liturgy, moreover, is identical (Hebrew: יהוה ימלך = Ugaritic: *b 'lm ymlk*).[26] Yet the parallels
end abruptly at this point. Exod 15:1–12, 18 does not include motifs of
temple construction, conquest, or the establishment of a kingdom necessary for divine enthronement in CTA 3–4.

Exod 15:13–17, conversely, includes motifs that are central to CTA
3–4: temple building (vv. 13, 17),[27] conquest of surrounding peoples
(vv. 14–16), and divine enthronement in an established kingdom (v.
17). Once again the verbal parallels are striking. Particularly noteworthy is Exod 15:17, where Yahweh's temple is located בהר נחלתך
(= *bg̀r.nḥlty* in CTA 3.C.27; 3.D.64), and where Yahweh's enthronement is described as taking place מכון לשבתך (=*ksu ṯbt* in CTA 1.III.1;
3.F.16; 4.VIII.14; 5.II.16). The two motifs are part of a larger network
of related terms in the Ugaritic mythology, describing a god's enthronement as including not only a mountain of possession (*bg̀r. nḥlt*) won in

battle (*bgd ʿlbg̱r tliyt*) and the establishment of a throne (*ksu t̪bt*), but also a land of possession (*arṣ nḥlt*) and a domain or kingdom (*drkt*).[28]

Comparison between the Song of the Sea and the mythology of Baal reinforces indirectly the earlier literary study of this essay. Exod 15:1–12, 18 and 13–17 not only contrast with each other in content, genre, and language but they also explore distinct aspects of Canaanite mythology. Exod 15:1–12, 18 is a celebration of divine victory over chaos or evil and a proclamation of Yahweh's rule. The hymn refrains from describing kingship with the more monarchical imagery associated with temple construction and enthronement in CTA 3–4. The cultic ideology envisions salvation as divine victory over the kind of social structures that make enthronement possible. The anti-monarchical *Tendenz* supports an early date and aids in accounting for social tension concerning the monarchy that lingers in later tradition. Israel plays no role in their salvation either by participating in the conflict or by journeying with Yahweh through a wilderness march. Instead, the destruction of Pharaoh and the kingship of Yahweh are a singular event, as Baal's conflict with Yamm/Nahar, where the death of Yamm and the kingship of Baal are proclaimed simultaneously (CTA 2.IV.32). The absence of journeying with God suggests that the land is a present reality for Israel and that the content of Yahweh's victory is life in the land. Whether this hymn served as a liturgy at Shiloh in conjunction with the ark (Spieckerman 1989: 88; Otto 1967: 65–77) or at another cultic center, such as Gilgal (Cross 1973: 137), is difficult to confirm.

The deuteronomistic addition to the Song of the Sea in Exod 15:13–17 is not a free literary creation. It expands the early version of the victory hymn by including the imagery of temple building, conquest, and enthronement from CTA 3–4. As Mettinger (1982: 27) has demonstrated, the deuteronomistic additions presuppose Zion tradition. But Exod 15:17 is not simply an affirmation of Zion tradition, where Yahweh's enthronement was celebrated as a present reality.[29] The enthronement of Yahweh is placed in the future, as the end result of salvation history. Deuteronomistic tradents achieve this by thoroughly historicizing the mythology of Baal's conflict with Yamm/Nahar. In their version, Yahweh's initial victory at the sea is no longer part of a single event resulting in kingship. Instead victory at the sea propels Israel on a journey with God (v. 13) through other nations (vv. 14–16a), which eventually leads to the crossing of the river (v.16b), before the people arrive at Yahweh's cult and celebrate divine enthronement (vv. 17–18).[30] The emergence of salvation history is an innovation by deuteronomistic tradents, perhaps as late as the exilic period.

NOTES

It is with great pleasure that I dedicate the following article to my professor, George Landes, whose love of language and willingness to share it freely with students has modeled teaching for myself and many others.

1. For more extended discussion of salvation history, see Gnuse (1988) and Thompson (1992: 209–10).

2. The antiquity of the poetic couplet in Exod 15:21b is not a central concern, since it lacks the wilderness and conquest motifs. Thus a decision in favor of its antiquity would only support the arguments being advanced in this article. For arguments in favor of the antiquity of this couplet, see Crüsemann (1969: 19–38), who anchors the tradition-historical development of the hymn form in Exod 15:21.

3. Scholars who note the abrupt change of topic, but favor an essentially unified poem (at least with regard to the joining of exodus and wilderness-conquest traditions) include Cross (1973: 121–44), Muilenburg (1966: 151–69), Freedman (1980: 187–227), Childs (1974: 251–52), Strauss (1985: 106–107), Rozelaar (1952: 221–28), Alter (1985: 50–54), Howell (1989: 9, 34–35, 42), Tournay (1988: 68), and most recently Brenner (1991: 26–34). Those suggesting some form of tradition-historical development in the joining of the two parts of the poem include Watts (1957: 371–80), Coats (1969: 1–17), Zenger (1980: 452–82), Butler (1971: 102–99), Norin (1977: 77–107), and Spieckermann (1989: 96–115).

4. Form-critical assessments include: hymn (Rozalaar, Watts, Fohrer), victory song (Cross, Freedman, Cassuto, Brenner), enthronement hymn (Mowinckel), liturgy (Schmidt, Muilenburg), thanksgiving (Noth), hymn of praise (Rylaarsdam), hymn of an individual (Crüsemann, who describes this form as a mixed type), and simply mixed (Westermann, Coats). For a review of scholarship on genre, see Butler (1971: 4–60, 79–101); and more recently Strauss (1985: 103–109).

5. See already Schmidt (1931: 61), who speaks of hymnic (vv. 6, 7, 11) and ballad (3–5, 8–10, 12–13, 14–17) styles; or Beer (1939: 80), who distinguishes between hymn (vv. 2, 3, 6, 7, 11, 12) and ballad (vv. 4, 5, 8–10, 13–17). Compare Muilenburg (1966: 155), who adds further distinctions between hymnic refrains (vv. 6, 11, 16cd), hymnic confessional speech (vv. 2–3, 7–8, 12–14), and epic narrative (vv. 4–5, 9–10, 15–16b), and is followed by Freedman (1980: 188 et passim). Howell (1989:

1–34) distinguishes between declarative (vv. 6–7, 11) and descriptive (vv. 4–5, 8–10, 12) praise in the first part of the song, while noting that the personal proclamation of praise in vv. 2–3 fits neither category. For still additional discussion, see Crüsemann 1969: 193–94; Jeremias 1987: 96; and Spieckermann 1989: 104.

6. Verses 1–5, 18 refer to God in the third person, while vv. 6–17 change to the second person in referring God. For discussion of the "you–form" in addressing God within the hymn form, see Crüsemann (1969: 193–94) and Jeremias (1987: 96).

7. See Childs (1974: 251–52), who also concludes that "whenever Israel's tradition [of] the redemption at the sea is recounted, the subsequent leading of the redeemed people into the land is invariably included."

8. For discussion, see Robertson (1972: 28–31), Michel (1960: 21–26), Crüsemann (1969: 191–92); and Spieckermann (1989: 111–12).

9. The use of the imperfect with עַד occurs three times in the Pentateuch, all with future meaning. There are two occurrences in the Deuteronomistic History: Joshua 10:13, where the meaning is past, and 2 Sam 10:5, where the meaning is future. The construction occurs five times in the poetry of Isaiah (22:14; 26:20; 32:15; 42:4; 61:1, 7) always with future meaning. Still other occurrences throughout the Hebrew Bible reinforce the future meaning of this construction (Hos 10:12; Pss 57:1; 94:13; 110:1; 132:5; 141:10). Only in Ps 73:17 could past meaning possibly be attributed to the construction (עַד־אָבוֹא), but even here a frequentive meaning is probably more appropriate (the psalmist understands the way of the wicked every time he enters the sanctuary).

10. Watts (1957: 376–77) scans vv. 14–16a: 3:4; 4:4; 4:4; Muilenburg (1966: 155, 163) notes the problems of meter, but fails to provide an analysis. Cross and Freedman (1955: 242) read vv. 14–16a: 3:3; and then 2:2 throughout (followed latter by Cross [1973: 126], but changed by Freedman [1980: 211–12] to 3:4 in v. 14, while vv. 15 and 16ab could be either 2:2 or 4:4). Finally, Howell (1989: 34–35) scans v. 14 (3:3), v. 15 (3:3:3 or 2:2/2:2/2:2) and v. 16a (2:2/2:2/2:2).

11. The syntax, according to Brenner, finds its clearest parallels in Second Isaiah (e.g., Isa 43:1, 21; 44:24). Compare Cross and Freedman 1955: 249.

12. Parallels include "the mountain of your inheritance" (בְּהַר־נַחֲלָתְךָ) = "mount of possession" (ǵr nḥlt, CTA 3.C.27; 3.D.64) and "the place that you made your abode" (מָכוֹן לְשִׁבְתְּךָ) = "sitting on his throne" (ksu ṯbt, CTA 1.III.1; 3.VI.15; 4.VIII.13; 5.II.16).

13. There is some ambiguity concerning the meaning of "the mountain of your inheritance" (בְּהַר־נַחֲלָתְךָ)—is it the temple, the land, or both? For discussion see Wijngaards (1969: 82–84). Brenner (1991: 141) argues

that the reference designates the land, and that such use is late, occurring first in Jer 2:7; 16:18; and 50:11. Whether the usage is deuteronomistic is difficult to confirm, even though the use of נחלה is frequent in deuteronomistic tradition (both in the dtr history [e.g., 1 Sam 26:19; 2 Sam 14:16; 20:19; 21:3] and in Jeremiah [e.g., Jer 12:7–9; 50:11]). For a complete listing, see Horst (1961: 140).

14. Blenkinsopp (1992: 159–60) also concludes that both מכון לשבתך in v. 17a (see 1 Kgs 8:13 and also Isa 4:5; Dan 8:11) and מקדש אדני in v. 17b (see Ps 48:9; 87:5) presuppose Zion tradition.

15. Verse 2 presents a variety of problems for interpretation, including: (1) the shortened form יה (Cross and Freedman 1955: 243); (2) the lack of a first person suffix on זמרת (Cross and Freedman 1955: 243; Spieckermann 1989: 96 n. 2); (3) the meaning of זמרת as "glory" or "music"? (Loewenstamm 1969: 464–70); "protection" (Parker 1971: 373–79); or the designation of Yahweh as a protective deity (Barré 1992: 623–37); (4) the meaning and etymology of the *hapax legomenon* אנוהו (Dahood 1978: 260–61); and (5) the meaning of the phrase אלהי אבי as a specific reference to the ancestors (Miller 1973: 114) or as an apostrophic reference to God (Spieckermann 1989: 96 n. 2).

    Decisions about language impact larger questions of genre. Schmidt (1931: 63–64) argued that v. 2 was the key for interpreting the hymn as a liturgy of the individual. Watts (1957: 374) concluded that the confession of personal faith was out of place in the larger context of vv. 1b, 3b–5. Cross and Freedman (1955: 243) note problems with the context and also add arguments concerning poetic meter as a reason for eliminating the verse from an original form of the hymn. Muilenburg (1966: 157) argued that v. 2 fits in its present context, because of the first person praise in vv. 1b and 2, and the focus on the divine name in vv. 2–3 (so also Hauser 1987: 282 n. 5).

16. Scholars have argued that v. 12 is connected with the Korah rebellion in Num 16:30–31 because of the imagery and the alliteration (נחית, נטית, נהלת) created when vv. 12–13 are read together (Muilenburg 1966: 164). The poetic devices more likely enter the text through redaction. See here Alter (1985: 53–54) on the ambiguity created when v. 12 is read both in the context of what precedes and follows. Alter's reading of the present form of the hymn is helpful, but it is difficult to see how the reference to the earth swallowing an opponent of Yahweh can mean anything other than the Egyptians. See especially Cross and Freedman (1955: 247 n. 39) and Cross (1973: 129) for an interpretation of v. 12 as a coda to the previous description of the sea event.

17. The prefixed form of the verb "to rule" (ימלך) refers to the future in the present form of Exod 15:1–18, following the future orientation of vv.

16–17. But v. 18 likely provided the conclusion to vv. 1–12, where a durative meaning would better fit the context. The clearest parallel to Exod 15:18 is Ps 146:10. See Kraus (1989: 550–53), who translates the psalm verse, "Yahweh rules as king forever."

18. Sea is not simply a passive instrument of Yahweh (Cross 1973: 31). It maintains a partially independent status in the hymn, suggesting that it is personified, but under Yahweh's control. Note, in particular, how sea functions as the subject of verbs in v. 8 (נערמו מים and קפאו תהמת) and in v. 10 (כסמו ים), but again only to provide a gauge for measuring Yahweh's strength. For similar conclusions, see Ollenburger (1987: 58–59) and Spieckermann (1989: 110–11).

19. See Mettinger (1982: 38–79) for discussion of the date of deuteronomistic tradition in the Pentateuch.

20. Robertson concluded that the clearest examples of *yaqtul* forms with preterit force occur in vv. 1–12 (see יכסימו in v. 5 and תבלעמו in v. 12).

21. Cross (1973: 112–20 et passim), Jeremias (1987: 93–106), Kaiser (1962: 40–77), Spieckermann (1989: 88–113), Norin (1977: 42–77), Mettinger (1982: 27, 67–75), Coats (1967: 253–65; and 1969: 1–17), Craige (1971: 3–31), Kloos (1986: 127–212), Smith (1990: 41–79).

22. See Clifford (1984: 183–201 esp. 188–93) for a review of the problems.

23. Baal is encouraged in CTA 2.IV.10 to seize his throne and to take over his rightful kingdom (*tqh.mlk. ʿlmk//drkt.dt.drkrk*), but the fulfillment of the second part of this statement, where Baal must take over his kingdom, does not occur in CTA 2. There are a number of examples suggesting a god's rule must be accompanied by the possession of a kingdom (*arṣ nhlt*) or a domain (*drkt*). Note, for example, how the descriptions of enthroned gods tends to mention both their possession of a throne (*ksu ṯbt*) and the description of the land over which they rule (*arṣ nhlt*). See, here, the description of Yamm in CTA 1.III.1, the description of Kothar-wa-Khasis in Memphis (CTA 3.C.27 and 3.F.16), of Mot in his underworld palace (CTA 4.VIII.14 and 5.II.16), or of Keret (CTA 16.VI.22–24). In other instances, when a god is overthrown, the loss of his throne (*ksu.mlk*) is accompanied by the description of the loss of his domain (*kht.drkt*). Examples include Baal's overthrowing of Yamm (CTA 2.IV.13, 20) or Anat's recounting of her victories (CTA 3.D.47). The same language is used at other places in the mythology of Baal (CTA 1.IV.24–25), in the Keret Epic (CTA 14.I.42–43) and in the description of Baal's enthronement over Mot (CTA 6.V.6).

24. In both CTA 3.E.40–45 and 4.IV.43–62 Baal's rule is affirmed (*mlkn.aliyn.bʿl // ṯpṭn. in.dʿlnh*), providing the basis for the proclamation that he needs a temple (*wn.in.bt[.]lbʿt.km.ilm* in CTA 3.E.46–47 or *ybn.bt.lbʿl* in CTA 4.IV.62).

25. See Mann (1977: 99), who describes in this material traces of a motif about the divine warrior with his vanguard.

26. See Cross (1973: 112–20), Jeremias (1987: 99–100, 103), and Spieckermann (1989: 110).

27. The deuteronomistic addition in Exod 15:13–17 is framed with images of temple construction in v. 13 (אל־נוה קדשך) and in v. 17 (בהר נחלתך, מקדש אדני, מכון לשבתך). See Norin (1977: 84–92) for discussion of אל־נוה קדשך in v. 13 within the larger context of Canaanite mythology.

28. *nḥlt* occurs six times. *arṣ nḥlt* occurs four times in combination with *ksu ṯbt* (CTA 1.III.1; 3.E.16; 4.VIII.14; 5.II.16), while the two additional occurrences are associated with Baal's holy mountain, *bgr nḥlt* (CTA 3.C.27; 3.D.64). Forms of *drkt* occur frequently in the context of enthronement (CTA 1.IV.25[?]; 2.IV.10, 13, 20; 3.D.47; 4.VII.44; 6.V.6; 14.I.42; 16.VI.24, 38, 53).

29. See Mettinger (1982: 1–19), for discussion of the permanent presence of Yahweh in the Zion cult tradition. See also Spieckermann 1989: 110–11.

30. See Jeremias (1987: 100–106) for discussion of the historicizing tendency in the deuteronomistic form of the Song of the Sea.

REFERENCES

Albright, W. F.
    1968   *Yahweh and the Gods of Canaan: A Historical Analysis of Two Contrasting Faiths.* The Jordan Lectures 1965. London: The School of Oriental and African Studies, University of London.

Alter, R.
    1985   *The Art of Biblical Poetry.* New York: Basic Books.

Barré, M. L.
    1992   My Strength and my Song in Exod 15:2. *Catholic Biblical Quarterly* 54: 623–37.

Batto, B.
    1983   The Reed Sea: Requiescat in Pace. *Journal of Biblical Literature* 102: 27–35.

Beer, G.
    1939   *Exodus.* Handbuck zum Alten Testament, 3. Tübingen: Mohr.

Blenkinsopp, J.
    1992   *The Pentateuch: An Introduction to the First Five Books of the Bible.* New York: Doubleday.

Boorer, S.
    1992   *The Promise of Land as Oath: A Key to the Formation of the Pentateuch.* Beihefte zur Zeitschrift für die alttestamentliche Wissenschaft 205. Berlin: de Gruyter.

Braulik, G.
1978   *Die Mittel deuteronomischer Rhetorik-erhoben aus Deuteronomium 4,1–40.* Analecta biblica 68. Rome: Pontifical Biblical Institute.

Brenner, M. L.
1991   *The Song of the Sea: Ex 15:1–21.* Beihefte zur Zeitschrift für die alttestamentliche Wissenschaft 195. Berlin: de Gruyter.

Butler, T. C.
1971   "The Song of the Sea": Exodus 15:1–18. A Study in the Exegesis of Hebrew Poetry. Unpublished Ph.D. Dissertation; Vanderbilt University.

Childs, B. S.
1974   *The Book of Exodus.* Old Testament Library. Philadelphia: Westminster.

Clifford, R. J.
1984   Cosmogonies in the Ugaritic Texts and in the Bible. *Orientalia* 53: 183–201.

Coats, G. W.
1967   The Traditio-Historical Character of the Reed Sea Motif. *Vetus Testamentum* 17: 253–65.
1969   The Song of the Sea. *Catholic Biblical Quarterly* 31: 1–17.

Craige, P. C.
1971   The Poetry of Ugarit and Israel. *Tyndale Bulletin* 22: 3–31.

Cross, F. M.
1973   *Canaanite Myth and Hebrew Epic: Essays in the History of the Religion of Israel.* Cambridge: Harvard University.

Cross, F. M., and Freedman, D. N.
1955   The Song of Miriam. *Journal of Near Eastern Studies* 14: 237–50.
1975   *Studies in Ancient Yahwistic Poetry.* Society of Biblical Literature Dissertation Series 21. Missoula, MT: Scholars.

Crüsemann, F.
1969   *Studien zur Formgeschichte von Hymnus und Danklied in Israel.* Wissenschaftliche Monographien zum Alten and Neuen Testament 32. Neukirchener-Vluyn: Neukirchener Verlag.

Dahood, M.
1978   Exodus 15,2 *ʾanwēhû* and Ugaritic *šnwt*. *Biblica* 59: 260–61.

Day, J.
1985   *God's Conflict with the Dragon and the Sea: Echoes of a Canaanite Myth in the Old Testament.* University of Cambridge Oriental Studies 35. Cambridge: Cambridge University.

Foresti, C. F.
1982   Composizione e redazione deuternomistica in Ex 15,1–18. *Lateranum* 48: 41–69.

Freedman, D. N.
1980   *Pottery, Poetry, and Prophecy: Studies in Early Hebrew Po-*
            etry. Winona Lake, IN: Eisenbrauns.

Gnuse, R.
1988   *"Heilsgeschichte" as a Model for Biblical Theology: The De-*
            bate Concerning the Uniqueness and Significance of Israel's
            Worldview. College Theology Society Studies in Religion 4.
            Lanham: University Press of America.

Goodwin, D. W.
1969   *Text-Restoration Methods in Contemporary U. S. A. Biblical*
            Scholarship. Publicazioni del Seminario di Semitistica 5.
            Naples: Istituto Orientale de Napoli.

Hauser, A. J.
1987   Two Songs of Victory: A Comparison of Exodus 15 and Judges
            5. Pp. 265–84 in *Directions in Biblical Hebrew Poetry*, ed. E.
            R. Follis. JSOT Supplement Series 40. Sheffield: Sheffield Aca-
            demic.

Horst, F.
1961   Zwei Begriffe für Eigentum (Besitz). Pp. 141–56 in *Verbannung*
            und Heimkehr: Festschrift für Wilhelm Rudolph. Tübingen:
            Mohr.

Howell, M.
1989   Exodus 15,1b–18. A Poetic Analysis. *Ephemerides theologicae*
            lovanienses 65: 5–42.

Jenni, E.
1970   "Kommen" im theologishen Sprachgebrauch des Alten Testa-
            ments. Pp. 251–61 in *Wort-Gebot-Glaube: Beiträge zur*
            Theologie des Alten Testaments: Festschrift für W. Eichrodt.
            Abhandlungen zur Theologie des Alten und Neuen Testaments
            59. Zürich: Zwingli.

Jeremias, J.
1987   *Das Königtum Gottes in den Psalmen: Israels Begegnung mit*
            dem kanaanäischen Mythos in den Jahwe-König-Psalmen.
            Forschungen zur Religion und Literatur des Alten und Neuen
            Testaments 141. Göttingen: Vandenhoeck und Ruprecht.

Kaiser, O.
1962   *Die Mythische Bedeutung des Meeres in Ägypten, Ugarit und*
            Israel. Second Edition. Beihefte zur Zeitschrift für die
            alttestamentliche Wissenschaft 78. Berlin: Töpelmann.

Kloos, C.
1986   *Yhwh's Combat with the Sea: A Canaanite Tradition in the Re-*
            ligion of Ancient Israel. Leiden: Brill.

Kraus, H. -J.
1988   *Psalms 60–150.* Trans. H. C. Oswald, from German. Minneapolis, MN: Augsburg.
Loewenstamm, E.
1969   The Lord is my Strength and my Glory. *Vetus Testamentum* 19: 464–70.
Mann, T. W.
1977   *Divine Presence and Guidance in Israelite Traditions: The Typology of Exaltation.* Johns Hopkins Near Eastern Studies. Baltimore: Johns Hopkins University.
McConville, J. G.
1984   *Law and Theology in Deuteronomy.* JSOT Supplement Series 33. Sheffield: JSOT.
Mettinger, T. D. N.
1982   *Dethronement of Sabaoth: Studies in the Shem and Kabod Theologies.* Coniectanea biblica, Old Testament 18. Lund: Gleerup.
Michel, D.
1960   *Tempora und Satzstellung in den Psalmen.* Abhandlungen zur Evangelischen Theologie I. Bonn: Bouvier.
Miller, Jr., P. D.
1973   *Divine Warrior In Early Israel.* Harvard Semitic Monographs 5. Cambridge: Harvard University.
Moor, J. C. de
1971   *The Seasonal Pattern in Ugaritic Myth of Baʿlu.* Alter Orient und Altes Testament 16. Neukirchen-Vluyn: Neukirchener.
Mowinckel, S.
1962   *The Psalms in Israel's Worship. Vol. 1.* Trans. D. R. Ap-Thomas, from Norwegian. Nashville: Abingdon.
Muilenburg, J.
1966   A Liturgy of the Triumphs of Yahweh. Pp. 233–51 in *Studia Biblica et Semitica*, eds. W. C. van Unnik and A. S. van der Woude. Wageningen: H. Veenman en Zonen.
Norin, S. I. L.
1977   *Er Spaltete das Meer: Die Auszugsüberlieferung in Psalmen und Kult des Alten Israel.* Coniectanea biblica, Old Testament 9. Lund: CWK Gleerup.
Noth, M.
1962   *Exodus.* Old Testament Library. Trans. J. S. Bowden, from German. Philadelphia: Westminster.
1981   *A History of Pentateuchal Traditions.* Trans. B. W. Anderson, from German. Chico: Scholars.

Ollenburger, B.
1987   *Zion, the City of the Great King: A Theological Symbol for the Jerusalem Cult.* JSOT Supplement Series 41. Sheffield: JSOT.

Otto, E.
1967   Silo und Jerusalem. *Theologische Zeitschrift* 32: 65–77.

Parker, S. B.
1971   Exodus XV 2 Again. *Vetus Testamentum* 21: 373–79.

Preuss, H. D.
1975   בוא. Pp. 20–49 in *Theological Dictionary of the Old Testament.* Vol. 2, eds. G. J. Botterweck and H. Ringgren. Grand Rapids: Eerdmans.

Rad, G. von
1962   *Old Testament Theology.* Vol. 1, trans. D. M. G. Stalker, from German. New York: Harper and Row.

Robertson, A.
1972   *Linguistic Evidence in Dating Early Hebrew Poetry.* SBL Dissertation Series 3. Missoula, MT: Scholars.

Rozelaar, M.
1952   The Song of the Sea. Exodus XV,1b–18. *Vetus Testamentum* 2: 221–28.

Rylaarsdam, J. C.
1952   Exodus. *Interpreter's Bible.* Vol. 1, ed. G. A. Buttrick. Nashville: Abingdon.

Schmidt, H.
1931   Das Meerlied. Ex 15 2–19. *Zeitschrift für die alttestamentliche Wissenschaft* 49: 59–66.

Smith, M. S.
1990   *The Early History of God: Yahweh and the Other Deities in Ancient Israel.* San Francisco: Harper and Row.

Snaith, N. H.
1965   ים סוף: The Sea of Reeds: The Red Sea. *Vetus Testamentum* 5: 395–98.

Spieckermann, H.
1989   *Heilsgegenwart: Eine Theologie der Psalmen.* Forschungen zur Religion und Literatur des Alten und Neuen Testaments 148. Göttingen: Vandenhoeck und Ruprecht.

Strauss, H.
1985   Das Meerlied des Mose—ein Siegeslied Israels? *Zeitschrift für die alttestamentliche Wissenschaft* 97: 106–107.

Thompson, T. L.
1992   Historiography [Israelite]. Pp. 206–12 in *The Anchor Bible Dictionary.* Vol. 3, ed. D. N. Freedman. New York: Doubleday.

Tournay, R. J.
  1988   *Voir et entendre Dieu avec les Psaumes ou la liturgie prophétique du second temple à Jérusalem.* Cahiers de la Revue Biblique 24. Paris: J. Gabalda.
  1995   Le chant de victoire d'Exode 15. *Revue biblique* 102: 522–31.
Waltke, B. K., and O'Connor, M.
  1990   *An Introduction to Biblical Hebrew Syntax.* Winona Lake, IN: Eisenbrauns.
Watts, J. D. W.
  1957   The Song of the Sea—Ex. XV. *Vetus Testamentum* 7: 371–80.
Westermann, C.
  1981   *Praise and Lament in the Psalms.* Trans. K. R. Crim and R. N. Soulen, from German. Atlanta: John Knox.
Wijngaards, M.
  1969   *The Dramatization of Salvific History in the Deuteronomic Schools.* Oudtestamentische Studiën 16. Leiden: Brill.
Zenger, E.
  1980   Tradition und Interpretation in Exodus XV 1–21. Pp. 452–83 in *Congress Volume: Vienna 1980*, ed. J. A. Emerton. Supplements to Vetus Testamentum, 32. Leiden: Brill.

8   The Problem of Human Sacrifice in War: An Analysis of Judges 11

NAOMI STEINBERG

INTRODUCTION

Despite significant textual and archaeological evidence for the existence of human sacrifice in biblical Israel (Hackett 1987; Levenson 1993; cf. Mosca 1975; J. Day 1989), comprehensive and up-to-date assessments of sacrificial offering and the sacrificial system in the Hebrew Bible rarely make mention of this ritual (e.g., Anderson 1992). One reason for this omission is that the Priestly writer did not consider to be a normative Israelite ritual practice. Another is its repulsive character to contemporary believers. Yet is difficult to deny in its actual historical context within ancient Israel and in its lingering effects on later tradition. A. Green (1975) has convincingly demonstrated that took place in the ancient Near East and in ancient Israel. And, as J. Levenson has recently noted (1993: ix, 52), even after the practice of human sacrifice would appear to have stopped, the idea behind it continued on in biblical tradition (e.g., Ezek 20: 25–31).[1]

My aim in this paper is not to provide further documentation for the existence of human sacrifice in ancient Israel. Rather, it is to understand what such a ritual might mean within the social organization of early Israel. To that end, Judges 11 will serve as my case study on . The first section of my paper will explore the problems that must be addressed in order to recover the meaning of sacrifice from the perspective of social anthropology. The second part will pay particular attention to the function of sacrifice within the context of early Israelite social structure. This methodological perspective sets the analysis

of within the wider framework of comparative studies, which interrelate social structure and religious culture, as well as social organization and ritual practice. In order to bring the latter topic into sharper focus, thirdly I will examine the biblical perspective on war with a brief survey of relevant biblical data. The final section of this study will discuss the pre-Deuteronomistic account of the sacrifice of Jephthah's daughter.[2] I will demonstrate that the pre-Deuteronomistic account of Judges 11 is a story of human sacrifice and that such practice had a connection to patrilineal kinship in ancient Israelite society.

I. PROBLEMS OF INTERPRETATION

In the past, theorists who have addressed the problem of sacrifice often reached conclusions that were determined by their evolutionary perspective on the nature of sacrifice or by their assumption of a unified cross-cultural meaning for this ritual practice.[3] At the very outset of this study, I believe we must recognize that the answer to the problem of interpreting the meaning of sacrifice may lie in the realization that the logic of sacrifice is culturally determined, and though this logic may have cross-cultural linkage, no theory of sacrifice can provide a universal explanation of the significance of this ritual practice.

A second issue to be addressed concerns the lack of terminological precision in scholarly discussion of sacrifice, due to the range of meanings given to the term sacrifice in contemporary English language. To take but one example, while I personally sympathize with the feminist assessment that full literary depiction of women in the Hebrew Bible as characters is sacrificed to the androcentric perspective of the biblical writers, and while I clearly understand how the word sacrifice is used in the sentence, this metaphorical usage of the term sacrifice does not refer to the ritual practice under discussion in this study. An awareness of the looseness with which sacrifice language is found in contemporary English requires that we address the problem of terminology (Strenski 1996: 10–20). In order to avoid any imprecision in this study, I will apply the term sacrifice to translate the Hebrew word ʿôlâ, which will be discussed later in this paper, and use this English word in its original Latin sense of "to make holy."[4]

The third issue relevant to understanding the meaning of sacrifice in Judges 11 concerns the necessity of methodological self-consciousness on the part of the interpreter to the fact that the sacrificial system

outlined in the Hebrew Bible is the product of editing by the Priestly
writer who aimed to routinize and formalize ancient Israelite ritual. In
what follows, I will demonstrate that the principle interest of the Priestly
source was to maintain the purity of the Israelite people in their relationship to Yahweh. From the perspective of the Priestly writer, sacrifice was intended to remove impurities from the community of
Yahweh's followers. This would suggest that sacrifice functions as a
means of vertical connection between the human and the divine levels.
Clearly then, read in its present canonical context, Judges 11 suggests
the removal of the impurity of the land occasioned by bloodshed of
warfare; moreover, the abominations of the local inhabitants pollute
the land and provide the rationale for Yahweh turning control of it over
to Jephthah. Of course, the latter perspective is the general viewpoint
of both the Priestly writer (Leach 1985; Katz 1990)[5] and the
Deuteronomistic redactor (Deut 9:4–5; 18:9–12).

Moreover, one should note that cultic impurity, viz. pollution, and
moral impurity, viz. wrongdoing, are equated in the final form of the
biblical text. Consider, for example, the account in Numbers 12 of the
punishment Miriam receives for the moral error of challenging Moses'
authority. The latter action becomes the occasion for Miriam to be
afflicted with leprosy and for her to be sent outside the Israelite camp
due to her state of cultic pollution. In order to avoid any methodological confusion, I will maintain the distinction between cleanliness and
impurity (the cultic) and sin and guilt (the ethical) in the following
study of Judges 11.

In order to proceed, we must also distinguish past theological study
from the anthropological analysis intended here. On the distinction
between the two approaches to the biblical narratives that recount stories of sacrifice, Rogerson maintains:

> The anthropologist would presumably concentrate upon the
> structure and function of a sacrifice: insofar as he looks at
> the story it is only to elucidate a coherent system of sym-
> bols. The theologian would concentrate upon sacrifice as
> seen in terms of the story, and the insight into eternal reality
> which that story might contain (Rogerson 1980: 58).

What is more, the Jewish-Christian theological approaches rely on a
synchronic reading of the final form of the text, whereas an anthropological analysis goes behind the final context in order to interpret the

symbolic significance of sacrifice in the culture. Also, our study of in Judges 11 investigates the ancient theoretical framework that required the ritual murder of a human being rather than the historical veracity of the killing itself, which lies beyond reconstruction anyway. We must acknowledge that the information available in Judges 11 does not permit a reconstruction of the actual act of human sacrifice. Further, Judges 11 is an example of what Levine (1965) labels as "a descriptive text." In other words, it describes in narrative form what happened when Jephthah vowed a vow,[6] rather than prescribing the correct order of ritual detail for offering .

Finally, despite the differences between the theological and anthropological perspectives, there is some overlap, e.g., the need for rituals such as sacrifice, between the two approaches to the biblical data.

II. SACRIFICE AND SOCIAL STRUCTURE

One of the most celebrated theoretical perspectives for beginning to interpret human sacrifice in Judges 11 is found in the study by Hubert and Mauss (1964) of the structure and function of Vedic and Hebrew sacrificial rituals. Their analysis of the comparative evidence of these two societies led them to conclude that a sacrificial offering functioned as a gift linking the sacred and the profane realms; a sacrificed victim bridges these two domains because its body belongs to the profane physical world whereas its life belongs to the sacred divine world. The sacrifice serves as a means of transformation of the condition of the individual, or the group, who offers the sacrifice. Thus, the sacrificer and the sacrificial victim identify with each other through the process of sacrifice, and the performance of the ritual connects human and divine. In order to explain better the nature of this communion, Hubert and Mauss remark:

> The sacred things in relation to which sacrifice functions, are social things. And this is enough to explain sacrifice. For sacrifice to be truly justified, two conditions are necessary. First of all, there must exist outside the sacrificer things that cause him to go outside himself, and to which he owes what he sacrifices. Next, these things must be close to him so that he can enter into relationship with them, find in them the strength and assurance he needs, and obtain from con-

tact with them the benefits he expects from this rite. Now
this character and intimate penetration and separation, of
immanence and transcendence, is distinctive of social matters to the highest degree .... We understand then what the
function of sacrifice can be .... It is a social function because sacrifice is concerned with social matters (Hubert and
Mauss 1964: 101–102).

The obvious inference from Hubert and Mauss is that sacrificial ritual
is a symbolic action which communicates information concerning the
social construction of reality (cf. Berger and Luckman 1967). This
social information conveyed through sacrifice is culturally determined;
the meaning of sacrifice must be related to its function of maintaining
a particular social structure. This study will test the Hubert and Mauss
perspective by way of an exegesis of Judges 11.

We begin by noting that in the case of premonarchic Israel, social
organization was kinship based. The elemental unit of social organization was the *bêt ʾāb*, a family household, an extended family, i.e., a
descent group or lineage. The next level of social organization is the
mišpāḥâ, "the maximal lineage (or possibly, the clan)" (Lemche 1985:
269), which is an enlargement of the lineage group to include kinship
relationships formed through marriage. Finally, there is the *šēbeṭ*, the
tribe.[7]

The relationship between the humans, who lived in this intertribal
society, and their God Yahweh was expressed in terms that were an
extension of this kinship structure: theirs was a religious ideology that
linked social organization on the human and divine levels in terms of
kinship. Thus, the appropriateness of the communion sacrifice as understood by Hubert and Mauss for interpreting Judges 11 is based upon
the sacred understanding of social organization in premonarchical Israel.

It appears that sacrifice serves a social function in Judges 11 as it
symbolically communicates information about the relationship between
the judge as a representative of social structure in premonarchic Israel
and Yahweh. More specifically, the ideological framework of holy
war,[8] which serves as the backdrop for the events recounted in Judges
11, requires awareness of the importance of categories of kinship in
shaping social organization in early Israel; on the human level, kinship
relationships determine social boundaries through patrilineal descent lines.

This interpretation of the data on social structure as reflected in the biblical narratives follows anthropological perspectives that recognize both sacrifice and kinship as determinants of social boundaries, though these boundaries are often not determined solely by biology (Jay 1992: 30–60). In the Hebrew Bible, it is Yahweh alone who gives life and land. Therefore, for purposes of understanding the relationship between Yahweh the divine warrior/father and the judge Jephthah, the human warrior/father, the distinction between the biological father, the *genitor*, and the descent line father, the *pater* is helpful. A *genitor* fathers children while a *pater* may be an individual different from the father, the one to whose lineage these children are attached (Jay 1992: 54–55). In the contemporary Western world, an example of the separation between *genitor* and *pater* may be seen in the case of the adoption of a child by an individual, the *pater*, who is a different person than the one who fathered the child biologically, the *genitor*. In speaking of one such biblical example that distinguishes between the *genitor* and the *pater*, Levenson (1993: 41) remarks of Isaac, "Abraham is his biological father, but it is God who sets aside the laws of biology that have prevented his conception for year upon painful year." In the birth of Isaac, procreation comes from Yahweh rather than from Abraham.

The author of Judges 11 reports further information concerning the relationship between the divine warrior and the human representative of Yahweh by stating that God's spirit has come upon the judge (v. 29). The "spirit of Yahweh" may be understood in sociological terms as referring to the charismatic endowment in Israel's judges (Malamat 1976: 152–68). While the spirit of Yahweh may communicate to the reader the authority of Jephthah to act in the capacity of commander (*qāṣîn*) of the troops, possession of that spirit also becomes an occasion for Jephthah's feelings of communion with God to find verbalization in his vow.

Commentators have remarked on the "unfaithfulness" of Jephthah's vow (Trible 1984: 97), given the fact that the reader knows that the spirit of Yahweh has already come upon Jephthah, and that, in the context of the stories of the judges, this information provides a means by which to anticipate the success of Jephthah in battle. Although reference to the effects of the spirit of Yahweh upon an individual's future actions provides a theological interpretation of the course of events, it does not satisfy social scientific aims to analyze the actions of the judge. It is not inconsistent for one who is a charismatic leader to request help from God. Thus, a judge might request all available help. While theology seeks to understand the relationship between divine and human, social science investigates interactions among human beings.

As discussed above, war, like kinship, provides a means for creating boundaries among peoples and their gods. War in Judges focuses on land issues. Judg 11:21–24 makes clear that land possession is a gift from the deity one worships. Victory comes to Jephthah through the agency of Yahweh. The passage presupposes an ideology of battle between deities that sets the frame for justifying land-possession claims: one group of people receives a particular piece of land because their deity has fought against another deity and won that land as spoil. Gods, not people, grant land. The Hebrew Bible, in general, and Judges 11, specifically, emphasizes that Yahweh the warrior is the God of Israel, but that Yahweh also recognizes the existence of other deities. Moreover, Judg 11:23–24 affirms that Israel deserves the land she claims because the Israelites had previously been victorious over the Amorites (Num 21:21–24); the Amorites surrendered it to the triumphant deity of the Israelites, Yahweh.[9] The results of battle are determined by Yahweh, who grants or denies land on the basis of those results.

This interpretation of Judges 11 in the context of ancient war ideology is reinforced by the close parallel between it and 2 Kings 3, a story of in the Transjordanian region by the king of Moab. In 2 Kgs 3:26–27, we learn that the king of Moab (who dwells in land contiguous with that of the threatening Ammonites) sacrificed "his eldest son who was to reign in his stead" as a sacrifice, in the hopes of reversing the course of a siege and achieving military victory against Israel. In both texts, a sacrifice is offered (or at least vowed) on the occasion of a military crisis. Interestingly, both Judges 11 and 2 Kings 3 are geographically set in the Transjordan.[10] Moreover, in both texts the offering of the next-of-kin is labeled an *ʿōlâ*.

III. THE BIBLICAL PERSPECTIVE ON WAR

We move now to the topic of pollution in the biblical text. An analysis of Numbers 31 provides us with insight into the Priestly view that battle pollutes the Israelite soldier and his war camp. The battle in this example is between the Israelites and the Midianites, and it is occasioned by the apostasy to Baal of Peor (Numbers 25). In Numbers 31, after a successful battle against the Midianites, the soldiers fail to follow proper victory rituals, which require that they murder their captives as a sacrifice to Yahweh. Specifically, the lives of the enemy women are spared: those who are responsible for the cultic defilement of the Israelites are not removed from Israel and Yahweh's presence. Numbers 31:19 commands, "Encamp outside the camp seven days; whoever of you has killed any person, and whoever has touched any slain, purify yourselves and your captives on the third day and on the seventh day." The verses following report the Priestly instructions for the purification of the battle area. This ancient view regarding the effects of exposure to the dead in battle makes it clear that the act of war itself defiles.[11] Thus, ceremonial purification is required for the Israelite warriors whose contact with the dead in battle had left them ritually defiled.

From the perspective of Numbers 31, it is evident that the Priestly writer understood military conflict to be defiling. This understanding of battle by P will now be compared with the Deuteronomistic ideology on the same subject. In this case, we will analyze 2 Samuel 11, which addresses a different kind of military impurity.

Unlike Numbers 31, which primarily concerns issues of purity at the conclusion of battle, 2 Samuel 11 provides information on the purity expected of soldiers during battle. Second Samuel 11 reveals that Uriah the Hittite has a deeper commitment to the battle consecration of soldiers in the Israelite army than does David, commander-in-chief of the army. The context, of course, is the situation of David having impregnated Uriah's wife Bathsheba, and of the former's attempt to arrange for Uriah to spend the night with his wife, in order that her legal husband could be mistaken for the father of the child.

While the battle against the Ammonites rages, David arranges for Uriah to return home to his wife. David repeatedly encourages Uriah to have sexual relations with Bathsheba his wife, but Uriah understands that the act of sexual intercourse jeopardizes his purity as a soldier. Ever faithful to the cultic consecration of battle, Uriah replies to David,

> The ark and Israel and Judah dwell in booths; and my lord Joab and the servants of my lord are camping in the open field. Shall I then go to my house, to eat and to drink, and to lie with my wife? As you live, and as your soul lives, I will not do this thing (v. 11).

Even after David gets Uriah drunk, the former fails in his attempts to convince Uriah to have sexual intercourse with his wife and thereby have him think that he is actually the man who has impregnated Bathsheba.

Numbers 31 and 2 Samuel 11 reflect two different editorial perspectives that make up the final form of the Hebrew Bible. Moreover, these two texts focus on different stages in the behavior becoming a soldier, one during war and the other after battle. Thus, it is all the more significant that the two traditions agree in their common ideology of war as an act requiring and endangering purity. Initial purity, inevitable pollution in battle, and subsequent purification are the stages in a military rite of passage according to the final form of the biblical texts.

IV. JUDGES 11

Judges 11 does not reflect either the Priestly or Deuteronomistic perspectives on ritual purity. Rather, Judges 11 understands war and the role of sacrifice to be sacred, creating a communion between Yahweh and the army leader as representative of the social order. One element that appears in Judges 11 but in neither of the other two previously discussed texts is crucial: the vow that Jephthah makes prior to entering into battle against the Ammonites. To be sure, a vow to God spoken in times of trouble is hardly unique to Judges 11, as Gen 28:20–22, for example, shows (Parker 1979: 693–700). Yet, the vow made in Gen 28:20–22 occurs prior to the individual actually confronting his personal challenge, rather than in the midst of distress as in the case of Judges 11. The sequence is significant, as another war text, Numbers 21, demonstrates.

Num 21:1–3 concerns conflict between Israel and the Canaanite king of Arad, ruler in the Negeb. After the Canaanite ruler captures a group of Israelites, the remaining Israelites vow that if Yahweh makes them victorious against the Canaanites, the Israelite soldiers would "put them [the Canaanites] under the *ḥerem*" (v. 2). The vow is a sacred promise made in the form of an oath to annihilate the Canaanites and their city, i.e., to offer them up as that which is dedicated to Yahweh (Milgrom 1990: 428–30).

The vow of the Israelites in Numbers 21 parallels Jephthah's vow to Yahweh in Judges 11:

Num 21:2 "Israel vowed a vow (*wayyiddar neder*) to Yahweh and said,

Judg 11:30 "Jephthah vowed a vow (*wayyiddar neder*) to Yahweh and said,

Num 21:2 'If you will indeed give this people into my hand,

Judg 11:30 'If you will indeed give the Ammonites into my hand,

Num 21:2 'I will totally destroy (*wĕhăḥăramtî*) their cities.'"

Judg 11:31 '... I will offer it up for a sacrifice (*wĕhăʿălîtihû ʿôlâ*).'"

In each example, the vow is constructed as a statement of conditions and consequences. But despite the verbal correspondences between the two vows, and the fact that both occur before battle but are only offered after the war has been won, and that both are prayers that involve sacrifice (as is the case at Ugarit; Miller 1988: 139–55), one important distinction separates the two texts. The sacrifice offered up to Yahweh after battle in Judges 11 comes not from the spoils of victory, as is the case in Numbers 21, and as is expected after war (whether or not a vow is made; cf. Numbers 31 above); rather, the sacrifice is Jephthah's own daughter.

The divergence between Judges 11 and Numbers 21 can be explained in light of recent study that argues that the depiction of schematized battle practices argued for by earlier biblical scholarship (von Rad 1951) comes from the Deuteronomistic editing of the biblical text. The textual data indicates a variety of war practices. Within the range of practices was a vow before battle, a vow whose very giving was occasional, as was the exact content of the vow (Gottwald 1976: 942).

Parallels between the vows of Judges 11 and Numbers 21, and prayers in the Psalter, and certain Ugaritic texts suggest that vows be interpreted form-critically as prayers. One prays to, or petitions, God for help by making a vow of a sacrificial offering. Then, in response to the deity's answering of the prayer, the sacrifice mentioned earlier is carried out (Miller 1988: 147–53).

Thus, a vow functioned as a petition for help and reinforced the ideology outlined above that the people depend on Yahweh to grant military success. The vow/prayer is an acknowledgement of God's control of battle and land and of Israel's relationship with God in this context.

When Jephthah vowed to offer up an *ʿôlâ* ("sacrifice") to Yahweh,
literally he promised to sacrifice as holy "an offering of ascent" or to
make holy "an ascending offering" (Levine 1974: 6) as a gift to God in
gratitude for the divine gift of battle success, i.e., land. Typically, the
ʿôlâ was an animal sacrifice, so named because upon being burnt its
smoke rose to God above who could consume its aroma (Gen 8:20–21).
This sacrifice was a gift to God, one that solidified the relationship
between Yahweh above and the individual offering the sacrifice below
(Anderson 1992: 877–78).

The key to unlocking the internal logic of the vow and its related
sacrifice in Judges 11 is the emphasis placed on Jephthah's family household, his *bêt ʾāb* in the material framing the battle tradition. The
pericope introduces Jephthah with information that brings prestige to
him—he is a mighty warrior, a man of valor—yet it notes that he does
not come from the primary descent line of his father; he is the son of a
zônâ a word that refers to a woman who functions as a secondary wife
to her husband (Bird 1989: 119–39).[12]   Kinship structure in ancient
Israel is such that the offspring of a woman who holds the status of the
primary wife to her husband function as his heirs: they receive both his
name, i.e., they serve as next of kin in the family descent structure, and
they inherit from him. These primary heirs displace other children
borne by a secondary wife to her husband in the settlement of inheritance claims (Steinberg 1993: 35–86). Thus family issues frame Judges
11. The introductory sentences in the chapter make clear Jephthah's
position in his father's house vis-à-vis his brothers' through Gilead's
primary wife, "You shall not inherit in our father's house for you are
the son of another wife" (v. 2).[13]

As was discussed earlier in this study, the *bêt ʾāb*, "father's house,"
referred to in v. 2 is the basic social unit in ancient Israelite social
organization. In pre-exilic Israel, this term can refer both to a residential unit—a family dwelling together—or to a descent group. Significantly, the word *bayit* occurs several times in Judges 11. Jephthah
vows to Yahweh, "If you will give the Ammonites into my hand, then
whoever comes out first from the door of my house to meet me when I
return victorious from the Ammonites, shall be Yahweh's and I will
offer that being up as a sacrifice" (vv. 30–31). The ambiguity of the
bayit as both Jephthah's descent line and his residence[14] requires our
attention.

Commentators have noted that biblical custom would suggest women routinely come out to meet victorious soldiers returning home from battle (Boling 1975: 208; Setel 1992: 31). Thus it is no surprise to read in v. 34 that Jephthah's daughter comes out to meet her father "with timbrels and with dances" when he returns to Mizpah. Jephthah might have expected his daughter to be the one to come forth from his house—in both a physical and a kinship sense—upon his return from fighting the Ammonites. In that case, Jephthah could have expected his daughter to greet him as part of the traditional ritual of dancing/singing women coming out to meet warriors upon their return from victory.[15] However, the ambiguity between the *bayit* as both a kinship unit and a residential unit heightens the tension in the story. The dramatic effect would be lost in the text if Jephthah had known that his daughter specifically would be the one to greet him upon his return. Moreover, there is the verbal ambiguity of his vow: if Jephthah had intended to sacrifice his daughter one might expect him to refer to her directly by name. In light of Jephthah's grief (v. 35) when he realizes that his daughter must be sacrificed, we should consider that Jephthah might have expected one of his daughter's companions, who are by her side without introduction in vv. 37–38, to be the first to meet him when he returned home from battle. While the text does not provide enough information for the modern reader to determine who these female companions are, social scientists include servants and others who attach themselves to a household to be members of a family household. It is conceivable then that Jephthah had these other household members in mind when he made his vow. Tragically, however, Jephthah's daughter met him after his return. This being the case, "the one coming out of my house" (11:31) might now be better translated as "the fruit of my loins," or "my only child, my next of kin, i.e., my primary heir" (11:34b).[16] Notably, to speak of an animal as the one who would come out to greet Jephthah upon his return to battle would be an anthropomorphizing of animals in a way not typical of biblical narratives (Thompson 1963: 90).[17]

Stager's study of the social organization of the family in premonarchic Israel provides further data for interpreting the consequences of Jephthah's vow (Stager 1985: 1–35). We have seen already that Jephthah is an outsider to his lineage and, as Stager convincingly argues, the offspring excluded from his father's patrimony turned to other forms of employment for economic survival. The excess of young men who would not expect to inherit from their father's estate sought their livelihood in occupations such as military service and the priesthood. We are to understand that because his mother was a *zônâ* to Gilead, Jephthah will not inherit with Gilead's other sons (v. 2) and must seek his fortune elsewhere—in this case as a man of war. Thus Jephthah became a mercenary who gathered around him other mercenaries (Boling 1975: 197). The end result of this situation is that Jephthah's daughter is the only individual to continue on his descent line, in as much as these mercenaries are not part of his descent line.[18]

Feminist interpreters, who are interested in remembering the young woman and the sacrifice she made for her father in order that they might recover her memory (Bal 1988: 41–68; 1989: 211–31; Exum 1992: 65–69; Tapp 1989: 157–74), remind us that the name of Jephthah's daughter has not been preserved in the text. It may not be, as some commentators maintain, that the woman's name is lost due to the fact that she is a woman. I contend that Jephthah's daughter is nameless not because she is unimportant as a female, a daughter in the absence of a son, but because to have a name is to have a place in the lineage—something the circumstances will not allow her to have. Jephthah, a man without a lineage, saves his people who do have a lineage, paradoxically by giving up his own chance for a lineage through his daughter. This loss of descent line and the same namelessness characterize the son of the king of Moab who is sacrificed in the name of war. Second Kings 3, like Judges 11, makes clear that the one sacrificed was to continue in his father's place. The battle is won because the son gave his life, and his place in his father's lineage, i.e., he lost his name. To have a name is to have a place in the lineage. The rescue of Isaac from sacrifice in Genesis 22, and his place in the lineage of Terah, through his father Abraham, is an exception that proves the rule.

Moreover, although a few commentators would argue that *bĕtûlâ* (cf. 11:37) means that Jephthah's daughter "had not known a man" (11:39), most agree that the term is not synonymous with "virgin." In light of that distinction, I argue that *bĕtûlâ* marks the pubescent age (before the daughter has borne children; Wenham 1972: 326–48; Bal 1988: 46–48; P. L. Day 1989: 59). References to Anat as *btlt 'nt* confirm that *bĕtûlâ* does not mean virginity, but refers to a woman who has not yet borne children (Exum 1992: 67). Consequently, a woman can be a *bĕtûlâ* and not be a virgin, e.g., she may not yet have experienced her first menstrual period but may already have married and have had sexual intercourse with her husband. Given the early age of marriage for women in antiquity, this discovery should come as no surprise. Joel 1:8 speaks of a married woman who is a *bĕtûlâ*, lending strong support to the argument that a woman could be a *bĕtûlâ* and not be a virgin; in the case of Jephthah's daughter, she is both a *bĕtûlâ* and a virgin.[19]

Following out this linguistic and biological distinction, the daughter goes off not "to bewail her virginity," but to attend a rite of passage from one stage of life to another—a ritual marking the life stage of having reached the age of puberty. Cross–cultural data indicate that this rite of passage is a time for celebration of the beginning of a new stage in life, and also a time to lament the loss of childhood (Richards 1956: 20; van Gennep 1960). The evidence of Judges 11, limited as it may be, is extremely valuable because it gives a glimpse at a women's ritual in ancient Israel, and it suggests that ancient Israelite women participated in their own gender-segregated life-cycle rituals. Thus, Jephthah's daughter expresses sadness that her sacrificial death comes at a time when she had just reached the age of puberty, i.e., she is now biologically able to bear children but will be prevented from ever doing so in light of her impending death.[20]

I contend that the emphasis on the notice that Jephthah's daughter is a *bĕtûlâ* ties the information on the female ritual attended by the daughter back to the story of the war vow. Both halves of the text reflect an underlying concern with membership in a *bayit*. The first part of the story brings this theme to the forefront through the emphasis on "the father's house," while the second section extends this theme with the repeated references to the daughter as a *bĕtûlâ*. That Jephthah's daughter had reached puberty but had not yet been given the opportunity to reproduce means that she was not yet able to bear an heir to continue her father's line, that indeed she was the last member of his line, and that with her death his line would end. By virtue of being a *bĕtûlâ*, her father's line ends upon her death. By virtue of dying a *bĕtûlâ*, there is neither the promise nor hope of future fertility.

V. CONCLUSION

Past studies of sacrifice in early Israel have focused on the conditions of pollution and purity remedied by this ritual act. These analyses of the function of sacrifice operate on the level of the canonical perspective of the relevant texts. However, they fail to satisfy our questioning of the religious and symbolic function of Jephthah's sacrifice in the pre-Deuteronomistic account of Judges 11. The sacrifice of his next-of-kin appears to be the supreme gift/sacrifice Jephthah can offer to Yahweh; paradoxically, Jephthah maintains the social structure of the wider society through the death of his daughter, with the result that there will be no one left to inherit from him. The society continues on, even though Jephthah's line does not.

We may conclude then that the example of Judges 11 supports the thesis of Hubert and Mauss presented earlier in this work. We have demonstrated in our analysis that sacrifice serves "a social function because sacrifice is concerned with social matters" (Hubert and Mauss 1964: 102). Through his sacrificial offering of his only offspring, Jephthah brings about a bond that unites the divine warrior/father the grantor of land to the human warrior/father. This sacrifice creates and maintains the descent line between Yahweh and Israel, symbolized through the immolation of the battle leader's next-of-kin. Jephthah sacrifices and "makes holy" what is ritually profane, his family's future, because war is a sacred act. The logic of such an exchange is that the sacrificer identifies with the sacrificed. In order to receive one must give. In so doing, heaven and earth connect. From death comes life; one is needed in order to obtain the other.[21]

NOTES

To my teacher, George M. Landes, who helped me during graduate school to acquire the intellectual skills needed in order to make the journey to Nineveh and back. In honor of his retirement, this article is offered as one stop along that journey.

1. Recent study suggests that as late as the sixth century B.C.E., a small minority of citizens in the Southern Kingdom continued to practice child sacrifice (Ackerman 1992: 217).
2. In its present context "the device of narrating negotiations between the two warring parties in 11:12–28 allows Dtr once again to recapitulate the

sacred history of the exodus and conquest and to fully integrate the exploits of Jephthah into this history" (van Seters 1983: 345). Noth (1981: 118, 120) also regards vv. 12–28 as later Dtr material.

3. Some theorists held both presuppositions. E.g., in the nineteenth century, Tylor (1971, 2: 1–87) connected religion with "soul-ghosts" who populated the world. Tylor thus believed that when a human was sacrificed its "soul-ghost" was set free as a gift offered to deceased ancestors, or in honor of a deity. Smith (1889) viewed sacrifice in terms of totemism. He argued that sacrifice was a communal meal between a people and its deity, who was both their totemic representation in animal form and their kin. Frazer (1951), who also connected sacrifice with a theory of totemism, specifically addressed the subject of human killing.

More recently, Girard (1977) has attempted to bring together anthropological and psychoanalytic theories on sacrifice. According to him, sacrifice is a safety valve for the violence that would otherwise bring complete chaos to society. The work of Jay (1992) introduced the subject of gender into discussions of . She located the performance of sacrifice in societies organized by patrilineal kinship systems. From her perspective, sacrifice by men reverses childbirth by women. Jay mystifies women in their common role as childbearers. She universalizes motherhood but says the construction of manhood and fatherhood is unique to each context.

4. That which is presented but not actually burnt should be called an offering (Anderson 1992: 873).

5. On the place of blood in the P source, see Geller (1992).

6. On the intent and form of the vow, see Marcus (1986: 13–27).

7. For an introduction to social structure in premonarchical Israel, see Gottwald (1979: 237–92), Lemche (1985: 245–90).

8. Due to limitations of space, in this study I have singled out only those issues that have direct bearing on Judges 11. On Yahweh as divine warrior, see von Rad (1951). Reviews of the history of the study of the divine warrior and holy war can be found in Cross (1973: 79–144), and Gottwald (1976: 942–44).

9. The enemy in Judges 11 is the Ammonites, though Jephthah recites the past history of Israel's struggles with the Transjordanian nation of Moab, whose deity was Chemosh, and the Amorites (11:12–28). In Num 21:21–24 the details of Israel's struggle with and victory over the Amorites are recounted. There we learn that the Amorite land Israel obtained had previously been Moabite territory, until the Amorites captured it. Scholarly consensus on the confusion between the Amorites and Moabites of Numbers 21 and the Ammonite struggle in Judges 11 maintains that Jephthah's explanation of Israel's right to possess the land is a

Deuteronomistic addition to an earlier pre-Deuteronomistic text. For a full discussion of scholarly views on the redaction of the Jephthah story, see Richter (1966).

10. On child sacrifice as a Transjordanian religious ritual, see Hackett (1987).

11. On the requirement for the purity of the warriors while they are encamped in the wilderness, see Num 5:1–4 and Deut 23:10–15. For a discussion of the diverse subjects treated in this classic text on war, see Noth (1968: 228–33).

12. Bal (1988: 202) argues that the term refers to residence patterns after marriage; specifically, she contends that a zônâ is a woman who does not live with her husband's father after her marriage. According to Bal, from the perspective of the editors of the text this is improper.

13. Marcus (1990) argues that before his death Gilead had adopted and therefore legitimated Jephthah as his son. Marcus further contends that after the death of their father, Gilead's other sons demanded that the city elders reverse Jephthah's status as a full son of Gilead. Having acceded to this demand the elders were pressured by Jephthah to reinstate him as a legitimate son of Gilead before he would agree to serve as their military leader. For the most recent discussion of this topic and related issues, see Willis (1997).

14. Some argue that the physical layout of the ancient Israelite home was such that an animal might likely have been the first being to "greet" Jephthah upon his return. For a discussion of the physical arrangement of an ancient Israelite home, and the placement of both humans and animals within it, see Boling (1975: 208).

15. See Exod 15:20–21; 1 Sam 18:6–7. Cf. Judg 5:28–30 as well as the role of Deborah as singer (along with Barak) of this song.

16. Judg 11:34b reads yĕḥîdâ just as Isaac is Abraham's yāḥîd and the child sacrificed in the Philo of Byblos account is reported to be the firstborn. I do not believe that either the sex or age of the child sacrificed as an 'ôlâ was relevant; cf. Jer 3:24. The evidence from Carthage of child sacrifice supports this position (Heider 1985: 202) regarding a child offered as a payment in exchange for victory from the deity at a time of personal/national emergency. The sex of the offering is important, however, in the case of the zebaḥ bĕkôr who must be a male child.

17. There are, of course, talking animals, such as the serpent in the Garden of Eden and Balaam's ass.

18. Possibly the final redactor attempted to minimize the occurrence of in biblical Israel by attributing its practice to a man who ultimately had no chance to live on through his patrilineage. Verse 35 should be translated as "you are the source of my grief," meaning that the daughter's death ends the line of Jephthah. This does not mean that Jephthah blames his

daughter for meeting him upon his return, only that he realizes the consequences of his vow.

19. P. L. Day (1989: 59) explains, "It seems, therefore, reasonable to surmise that *bĕtûlâ* does not mean virgin. Thus, *bĕtûlîm*, which in Judg 11:37 means the state or condition of being a *bĕtûlâ*, should not be translated 'virginity.' Rather, it refers to a particular stage in the female life cycle, and like the word 'adolescence,' is best understood as a social recognition of puberty. More precisely, I would define a *bĕtûlâ* as a female who had reached puberty and was therefore potentially fertile, but who had not yet given birth to her first child."

20. Similarly, Day (1989: 59–60) explains: "When we are told in v. 39 that Jephthah's daughter had not known a man, it is our first indication that she was a virgin, and it is noted *not* in connection with her retreat to the hill country but rather as a condition pertaining at the time she was sacrificed. In other words, it is her status as a *bĕtûlâ*, not her virginity, that is the focus of attention when she and her companions go off to the hills. We should expect, therefore, that the ritual observance her story explains would have the same focus."

21. The Transjordanian setting of Judges 11 may, of course, reflect a local ritual that was not shared by all of Israel. Hackett (1987: 125–36) argues that the P source did not accept the Transjordan and its traditions.

REFERENCES

Ackerman, S.
   1992   *Under Every Green Tree. Popular Religion in Sixth-Century Judah.* Harvard Semitic Monographs 46. Atlanta: Scholars.
Anderson, G. A.
   1992   Sacrifice and Sacrificial Offerings (OT). Pp. 870–86 in *Anchor Bible Dictionary*, vol. 5, ed. D. N. Freedman. New York: Doubleday.
Bal, M.
   1988   *Death and Dissymmetry: The Politics of Coherence in the Book of Judges.* Chicago: University of Chicago.
Berger, P., and Luckman, T.
   1967   *The Social Construction of Reality.* New York: Doubleday.
Bird, P.
   1989   The Harlot as Heroine in Biblical Texts: Narrative Art and Social Presupposition. *Semeia* 46: 119–39.
Boling, R. G.
   1975   *Judges.* Anchor Bible 6A. Garden City, NY: Doubleday.

Cross, F. M.
1973   *Canaanite Myth and Hebrew Epic: Essays in the History of the Religion of Israel.* Cambridge: Harvard University.

Day, J.
1989   *Molech.* University of Cambridge Oriental Publications 41. Cambridge: Cambridge University.

Day, P. L.
1989   From the Child is Born the Woman: The Story of Jephthah's Daughter. Pp. 58–74 in *Gender and Difference*, ed. by P. L. Day. Minneapolis: Fortress.

Exum, J. C.
1992   Jephthah: the Absence of God. Pp. 45–69 in *Tragedy and Biblical Narrative: Arrows of the Almighty.* Cambridge: Cambridge University.

Frazer, J. G
1951   *The Golden Bough: A Study in Magic and Religion.* Abridged edition. New York: Macmillan.

Geller, S. A.
1992   Blood Cult: Toward a Literary Theology of the Priestly Work of the Pentateuch. *Prooftexts* 12: 97–124.

Girard, R.
1977   *Violence and the Sacred.* Baltimore: Johns Hopkins University.

Gottwald, N. K.
1976   War, Holy. Pp. 942–44 in *The Interpreter's Dictionary of the Bible*, Supplementary volume, ed. K. Crim. Nashville: Abingdon.
1979   *The Tribes of Yahweh: A Sociology of the Religion of Liberated Israel, 1250–1050* B.C.E. Maryknoll, NY: Orbis.

Green, R. W.
1975   *The Role of Human Sacrifice in the Ancient Near East.* American Schools of Oriental Research Dissertation Series 1. Missoula, MT: Scholars.

Hackett, J. A.
1987   Religious Traditions in Israelite Transjordan. Pp. 125–36 in *Ancient Israelite Religion: Essays in Honor of Frank Moore Cross*, eds. P. D Miller, P. D. Hanson and S. D. McBride. Philadelphia: Fortress.

Heider, G. C.
1985   *The Cult of Molek: A Reassessment.* JSOT Supplement Series 43. Sheffield: JSOT.

Hubert, H., and Mauss, M.
1964   *Sacrifice: Its Nature and Function.* Chicago: University of Chicago. Original 1898.

Jay, N.
1992   *Throughout Your Generations Forever: Sacrifice, Religion, and Paternity*. Chicago: University of Chicago.

Katz, M. A.
1990   Problems of Sacrifice in Ancient Cultures. Pp. 89–201 in *The Bible in the Light of Cuneiform Literature: Scripture in Context III*, eds. W. W. Hallo, B. W. Jones and G. L. Mattingly. Lewiston: Edwin Mellen.

Leach, E.
1985   The Logic of Sacrifice. Pp. 136–50 in *Anthropological Approaches to the Old Testament*, ed. B. Lang. Philadelphia: Fortress.

Lemche, N. P.
1985   *Early Israel*. Vetus Testamentum Supplements 37. Leiden: Brill.

Levenson, J. D.
1993   *The Death and Resurrection of the Beloved Son: The Transformation of Child Sacrifice in Judaism and Christianity*. New Haven: Yale University.

Levine, B.
1965   The Descriptive Tabernacle Texts of the Pentateuch. *Journal of the American Oriental Society* 85:307–18.
1974   *In the Presence of the Lord*. Leiden: Brill.

Malamat, A.
1976   Charismatic Leadership in the Book of Judges. Pp. 152–68 in *Magnalia Dei: The Mighty Acts of God*, eds. F. M. Cross, W. E. Lemche, and P. D. Miller. Garden City, NY: Doubleday.

Marcus, D.
1986   *Jephthah and His Vow*. Lubbock, TX: Texas Tech.
1990   The Legal Dispute Between Jephthah and the Elders. *Hebrew Annual Review* 12: 105–14.

Milgrom, J.
1990   *Numbers*. Philadelphia: The Jewish Publication Society.

Miller, P. D.
1988   Prayer and Sacrifice in Ugarit and Israel. Pp. 139–55 in *Text and Context*, ed. W. Classen. JSOT Supplement Series 48. Sheffield: JSOT.

Mosca, P. G.
1975   Child Sacrifice in Canaanite and Israelite Religion: A Study in *Mulk* and *mlk*. Unpublished Ph.D. Dissertation. Harvard University.

Noth, M.
1968   *Numbers*. Old Testament Library. Philadelphia: Westminster.

1981   *The Deuteronomistic History.* JSOT Supplement Series 15.
            Sheffield: JSOT; German original 1943.

Parker, S. B.
1979   The Vow in Ugaritic and Israelite Narrative Literature. *Ugarit-
            Forschungen* 11: 693–700.

Rad, G. von
1951   *Der Heilige Krieg im alten Israel.* Zürich: Zwingli.

Richards, A. I.
1956   *Chisungu: A Girls' Initiation Ceremony Among the Bemba of
            Northern Rhodesia.* London: Faber and Faber.

Richter, W.
1966   Die Überlieferungen um Jephtah, Ri 10:17–12:6. *Biblica* 47:
            485–556.

Rogerson, J. W.
1980   Sacrifice in the Old Testament: Problems of Method and Ap-
            proach. Pp. 45–59 in *Sacrifice*, eds. M. F. C. Bourdillon and M.
            Fortes. New York: Academic.

Setel, D. O'Donnell
1992   Exodus. Pp. 26–35 in The *Women's Bible Commentary*, eds. C.
            A. Newsom and S. H. Ringe. Louisville: Westminster/John Knox.

Smith, W. R.
1889   *Lectures on the Religion of the Semites: The Fundamental Insti-
            tutions.* 2nd ed. London: A. and C. Black.

Stager, L. E
1985   The Archaeology of the Family in Ancient Israel. *Bulletin of the
            American Schools of Oriental Research* 260: 1–35.

Steinberg, N.
1993   *Kinship and Marriage in Genesis: A Household Economics
            Perspective.* Minneapolis: Fortress.

Strenski, I.
1996   Between Theory and Speciality: Sacrifice in the 90s. *Religious
            Studies Review* 22: 10–20.

Tapp, A. M.
1989   An Ideology of Expendability: Virgin Daughter Sacrifice in
            Genesis 19.1–11, Judges 11.30–39 and 19.22–26. Pp. 157–74
            in *Anti-Covenant: Counter-Reading Women's Lives in the He-
            brew Bible*, ed. M. Bal. Sheffield: Almond.

Thompson, R. J.
1963   *Penitence and Sacrifice in Early Israel Outside the Levitical Law:
            An Examination of the Fellowship Theory of Early Israelite Sac-
            rifice.* Leiden: Brill.

Trible, P.
  1984   *Texts of Terror: Literary-Feminist Readings of Biblical Narratives*. Philadelphia: Fortress.

Tylor, E. B.
  1971   *Religion in Primitive Culture. Researches into the Development of Mythology, Philosophy, Religion, Art and Custom*, 2 vols. London: J. Murray. Original 1871.

Van Gennep, A.
  1960   *The Rites of Passage*. Chicago: University of Chicago.

Van Seters, J.
  1983   *In Search of History: Historiography in the Ancient World and the Origins of Biblical History*. New Haven: Yale University.

Wenham, G. J.
  1972   *Bĕtûlâ* "A Girl of Marriageable Age." *Vetus Testamentum* 22: 326–48.

Willis, T. M.
  1997   The Nature of Jephthah's Authority. *Catholic Biblical Quarterly* 59: 33–44.

9 Historicizing the Prophets: History and Literature in the Book of Jeremiah

ROBERT R. WILSON

Throughout his long and distinguished career, George Landes has focused his teaching and scholarship on three areas that he always insisted were integrally related to each other: the study of Biblical Hebrew and its cognate languages, the reconstruction of Israel's history and that of its neighbors, and the close reading of large blocks of biblical literature. The first of these interests is represented by his many years of refining his already effective techniques for teaching elementary Biblical Hebrew, by his Hebrew word frequency list, and by his scholarly work on Ammonite. On the historical side, he has been a career-long member of the American Schools of Oriental Research and contributed much to its archaeological programs. Finally, his literary and theological interests are readily apparent in his long-time fascination with the Book of Jonah and in his studies of the Priestly Writer.

In and of themselves these areas of interest are hardly unusual in the biblical guild, where large numbers of scholars continue to study languages, collect and interpret historical data, and produce literary studies of texts. However, George Landes's insistence on the interrelatedness of all of these things is rapidly becoming a minority position in contemporary biblical scholarship. While most scholars continue to believe that a thorough knowledge of Hebrew is necessary for credible literary studies, there is much less certainty about the way in which the Hebrew Bible ought to inform historical research. Similarly, literary interpretations are increasingly being done without any effort to provide the texts with a historical context, and indeed an impressively large number of scholars now argue that historical studies are irrelevant for literary readings of the Bible (Perdue 1994: 231–62). Even scholars with interests in biblical theology, who thirty years ago might have blended history and literature in order to arrive at an account of Israel's "salvation history," are now suggesting that historical references in the Hebrew Bible have been deliberately obscured or omitted altogether in order to free the text to speak to new situations (Perdue 1994: 153–96). In short, the biblical field is becoming fragmented, with students of language, history, and text no longer clear about how they should relate to each other.

Illustrations of this growing fragmentation could be drawn from a number of recent publications, but two rather different examples will suffice. In his monograph on the study of Israel's history, Philip R. Davies helpfully distinguishes three different Israels represented in current scholarly discussion. The first, which he designates "biblical Israel," is the Israel of the biblical writers, whose literary efforts created a history reflecting their own interests and beliefs. The second is "historical Israel," an entity based principally on archaeological research into the peoples and events in Palestine during the biblical period. Finally, there is "ancient Israel," which is a scholarly construct based on a selective appropriation of the other two Israels (Davies 1992: 11–21). While Davies recognizes that all three Israels are historical reconstructions by human authors and therefore subject to their particular interests and biases, he clearly believes that "historical Israel" is a more accurate representation of the way things were during the biblical period than either "biblical Israel" or "ancient Israel." In his view "biblical Israel" as it is represented in the texts is neither unified nor consistent and clearly reflects the particular concerns of the relatively small groups that produced the biblical writings. These groups were concerned primarily with the problems and ideologies of their own time and retrojected these concerns into earlier historical periods. Because Davies believes that the biblical writers lived and worked in the Persian period or later, their actual knowledge of the time of their ancestors was at best fragmentary and distorted. Their accounts of early Israel and its history are accordingly unreliable historiographic sources. Modern historians should therefore take them for what they are: reflections of the perceptions, ideals, and problems of the writers' own situations and not of the earlier period with which they deal. Given

Davies's view of "biblical Israel," it is not difficult to understand why he feels that the modern scholarly chroniclers of "ancient Israel" have created an entity that in fact never existed (Davies 1992: 94–133, 155–61).

While Davies's reminder that the biblical writers had their own particular interests that helped to shape their literature has been generally accepted in the modern debate, his efforts to relate those interests to the late postexilic period have been much more controversial. Many of the problems to which the texts seem to speak were not unique to the late Second Temple period but were a perennial concern in earlier times as well. No matter how one conceives of the early monarchy or the events surrounding the fall of Jerusalem, it is likely that these events would have raised questions about national identity, the nature and legitimacy of particular religious practices and beliefs, and the structure of legitimate political authority. It would therefore not be surprising to find texts created in these earlier periods dealing with some of the same problems that plagued Israelites later in their national life. Furthermore, as Davies's own analysis of "biblical Israel" demonstrates, the Bible's historiographic texts provide modern readers with valuable insights into how Israel's writers perceived their world and its problems. Such texts should therefore not be neglected but studied carefully to determine if possible why they were created in the first place and how they function in their present biblical context.

Precisely this sort of concern with literary context and function is reflected in the work of Brevard S. Childs, whose "canonical approach" to scripture pays a great deal of attention to overall literary shape and whose work might therefore be expected to take seriously the way in which the Bible's historiographic texts work in their present literary settings. However, Childs feels in general that Israel's actual history can be reconstructed only with a great deal of uncertainty and that this sort of material in any case has not been particularly helpful in uncovering the real theological interests of the Bible's writers and editors (Perdue 1994: 153–55). Furthermore, in treating individual biblical books, Childs often argues that the final shapers of the texts have removed or de-emphasized historical details, presumably in order to free the texts to function more generally for later communities of faith.

This tendency toward dehistoricizing is particularly clear, according to Childs, in the way that the major prophetic books have been shaped.

The best example is provided by Isaiah. Here Childs follows the scholarly consensus in dating Isa 40–55, Second Isaiah, to the exilic period; but he notes, correctly, that the writers of this material made no effort to provide a new historical context for these chapters. Introductory date formulas are lacking, and, outside of references to Cyrus, there are few obvious signs of the text's original exilic setting. The effect of incorporating Second Isaiah into the Isaianic corpus in this subtle way is to set this exilic literature in the time of the eighth century prophet First Isaiah. This move in turn encourages the reader to interpret Second Isaiah as a collection of prophecies of Israel's future salvation rather than as a divine word spoken much later to the exilic community. Furthermore, the earlier First Isaiah material has been reworked to incorporate words of promise to Israel, so that the overall impression of the edited work is that Isaiah spoke both words of judgment and words of promise (Childs 1979: 325–34).

More challenging to Childs's approach is the Book of Ezekiel, which seems throughout to reflect the historical period of its composition and which supplies specific dates for many of its oracles (Ezek 1:1–3; 3:16; 8:1; 20:1; 24:1; 26:1; 29:1; 29:17; 30:20; 31:1; 32:1; 32:17; 33:21; 40:1). This amount of historical grounding would seem to invite interpretations that are set against the historical background of the times, the traumatic years between July 593 (the prophet's call) and April 571 (the book's last dated oracle, occasioned by the ending of Nebuchadnezzar's siege of Tyre) (Greenberg 1983: 8). Yet here too Childs suggests that the historical references in the book have been muted. In his view, the book's account of actual events and people has been given such a heavy theological interpretation that historical reality has faded into the background. Even the explicit dates have a theological purpose: to mark off the time between the prophet's call (Ezek 1:1–3) and the fall of Jerusalem (24:1; 33:21) as a period of unrelenting judgment for the people and the city and similarly to designate the period after the fall as a time of promise and restoration (33:21; 40:1) (Childs 1979: 361–67).

Finally, Childs faces what in some ways is the greatest challenge to his theory that the prophets have been dehistoricized, the Book of Jeremiah. The difficulty here is caused by the fact that since the seminal commentary of Bernhard Duhm at the beginning of the century, scholars have agreed that the Book of Jeremiah contains a great deal of material that appears to be biographical in form. Found primarily in chapters 26–45, it narrates the prophet's conflicts with a number of individuals and groups (chaps. 26–36) and then provides a more-or-less continuous narrative of events leading up to the fall of the city and the prophet's journey to Egypt (37–45). In the present Hebrew text this narrative is followed by a collection of oracles against foreign nations, and the book concludes with a historical retrospective on the fall of Jerusalem, apparently based on or at least related to 2 Kgs 24:18–25:30 (Jeremiah 52). Duhm suggested that this biographical material was produced by the scribe Baruch and then added to a collection of Jeremiah's poetic oracles now found in Jer 1–25. To this growing corpus later editors added units of didactic prose at various points throughout the book (Duhm 1901: XII–XXII).

Duhm's account of the growth of the book was refined by Sigmund Mowinckel, whose work set the terms for much of the modern debate. Following Duhm, Mowinckel isolated within the book a core collection of poetic oracles, which go back to the prophet himself and which now make up much of chapters 1–25. This "A" poetic material was later supplemented by biographical narratives ("B") composed by an anonymous author. In Mowinckel's view, this new material was simply added to the oracle collection and is now found in a single block in chapters 26–45. Finally, didactic prose speeches ("C") containing a good bit of Deuteronomistic language and theology were added to both the "A" and the "B" material, and a small collection of promise oracles ("D") was incorporated (Jer 30–31) (Mowinckel 1914: 20–45; cf. Mowinckel 1946).

Since Mowinckel's time, there has been much scholarly debate about the origins of the "B" and "C" passages, about their literary history, and about their relation to "A" and to each other. This debate, which is helpfully summarized by a number of recent studies, need not concern us here (Perdue 1984: 14–28; Nicholson 1970: 1–19; Collins 1993: 104–121; Seitz 1989: 1–6; and Holladay 1989: 10–24). However, for our purposes it is important to note that the commonly accepted account of the editorial history of Jeremiah suggests that at some point following the collection of the prophet's poetic oracles the book was historicized through the addition of narratives about the prophet and the people around him (Mowinckel's "B"). Childs recognizes the importance of this large block of historiographic material and suggests that it must have been created fairly shortly after the lifetime of the prophet. However, he also notes, correctly, that "B" cannot be considered an independent, straight-forward account of historical events, since recent research has shown that it already reflects to a certain extent Deuteronomistic influences, a characteristic which it also shares with the didactic speeches (Mowinckel's "C"). Furthermore, the "B" material may not be a single coherent block but may itself be the result of several editorial operations, each of which may have had a slightly different purpose (Wanke 1971; cf. Pohlmann 1978 and Seitz 1989, both of which were published after Childs's study). All of these observations suggest to Childs that the large block of historiographic material must have a theological function (or several theological functions) within the book.

In order to uncover the theological meaning of these history-like narratives, Childs first focuses on chapter 36, a "B" narrative recounting Jeremiah's preparation of a scroll containing all of his words up to this point, the fourth year of King Jehoiakim (Jer 36:1). This, says Childs, is a recognition by the tradition that Jeremiah gave his oracles in two forms: oral and written. The writing of the scroll marks the transition from one form of prophecy to another. Childs concludes that Jeremiah's prophecies from the thirteenth year of King Josiah to the fourth year of Jehoiakim were in oral form (Jer 25:1–3), while the prophet's words after that time were in writing. In traditional scholarly terms, the earlier oral prophecies are preserved in the present book's "A" poetic passages, while the later written prophecies make up the didactic prose "C" passages. Jeremiah 25, a chapter usually assigned to "C," immediately precedes the beginning of the large block of "B" material and in Deuteronomistic terms places Jeremiah in the line of prophets "like Moses," thus linking Jeremiah to the larger canon, and particularly to the Law. Jeremiah's written prophecies ("C") should be considered summaries of his earlier oracles ("A") (Childs 1979: 345–47).

This argument would seem to suggest that the "B" material (or at least Jeremiah 36) is intended in some way to legitimate the "C" didactic prose speeches as authentic Jeremiah prophecies and might imply that "C" preceded "B" in the editorial history of the book, although Childs does not make this claim. Instead, when he turns to the question of the function of "B," he makes the important observation that the Book of Jeremiah in fact contains two types of material dealing with the life of the prophet. In addition to the extensive collection of biographical prose narratives ("B"), the book also contains several "A" poetic passages sometimes called complaints, laments, or confessions (Jer 11:18–12:6; 15:10–21; 17:14–18; 18:18–23; 20:7–18). Both kinds of material, however, function in much the same way. Following Nicholson (1970: 55), Childs argues that the purpose of all of the historiographic passages is to dramatize in concrete form Israel's rejection of God's word as it was mediated by the prophets. This theme clearly underlies the scroll story in chapter 36, where the king's rejection of Jeremiah's written words is graphically portrayed. The same point is made by a number of other stories and can be seen particularly in Jeremiah 26, the so-called second temple-sermon. This passage places Jeremiah within a line of Judahite prophets whose oral messages were rejected by both king and people. By preserving these stories about Jeremiah, the biblical writers also provided a reminder that his message to Israel consisted not simply of words but of actions as well. He not only spoke of divine judgment but in a sense lived in that judgment as a result of the people's persecution (Childs 1979: 348–50).

The great strength of Childs's treatment of the historical material in the Major Prophets is that he makes a genuine attempt to take it seriously within its present literary context. At the same time, his arguments in support of the proposition that the final editors of the text have subordinated historical material in the interests of making theological points often fail to appreciate fully the complexity and force of the historical references. In many cases, the large number of specific details that the editors have allowed to survive in the present text suggests that more is at stake in these passages than Childs envisions. To take the case of Isaiah, the final form of the text does not simply link chapters 40–55 generally with the fairly long time during which the First Isaiah was active. Rather Isaiah 40 is prefaced by three historical narratives that seem to be designed to function literarily and theologically as links between the two halves of the book. Isaiah 39 recounts a visit to King Hezekiah by the messengers of the Babylonian king Merodach-baladan. While the visit may have had a basis in reality in a Babylonian attempt to organize opposition to Assyria, it here becomes the occasion for a judgment oracle by Isaiah that predicts the exile and thus marks the transition from the oppressive era of the Assyrians (Isa 1–39) to the oppressive era of the Babylonians (Isa 40–55). The word of judgment to Hezekiah becomes the backdrop against which the exilic promises of chapter 40 are to be heard. In a similar way, the narrative of Hezekiah's illness in chapter 38 also seems to be shaped to underscore theological points made elsewhere in the book. Hezekiah's illness leads Isaiah to announce the king's death, and this announcement is perhaps intended to adumbrate Israel's eventual suffering and exile. However, the king's petition causes God to add fifteen years to Hezekiah's life and to promise Jerusalem's rescue from the Assyrians. This linking of the king's temporary reprieve and the fate of the city, though out of place chronologically in the narrative sequence (see Isa 37:33–35), suggests a parallel between the two. Just as Hezekiah will eventually die, in spite of any pious deeds that he may have done, so too will the reprieve of the city narrated in Isa 36–37 be temporary. The Assyrians may not be the agents of God's judgment, but the Babylonians are waiting in the wings (Isaiah 39). Finally, Isa 36–37, the famous story of the miraculous deliverance of Jerusalem during the Assyrian invasion of 701, graphically illustrates God's power over foreign rulers and thus in a way strengthens God's promises of return from exile in chapters 40–55. However, at the same time the historical reality of the invasion shines through the text. During this campaign the Assyrians did a good bit of damage outside of Jerusalem, a fact which leads Isaiah to speak of the invasion as an event of judgment as well as salvation. This judgment motif points ahead to the eventual Babylonian invasion, which will finally bring the judgment which the city deserves; but it also points backward to other political upheavals that combined judgment and salvation in a similar way. It is no accident, then, that the other major block of historical narrative in Isaiah deals with an earlier threat of invasion from Syria and Ephraim (Isa 7–9). This narrative is similar in structure to the account of the Assyrian invasion, and the two stories are probably intended to be read typologically as a pair. Certainly the reader of Isaiah is being invited to compare the faithful Hezekiah with the unfaithful Ahaz, but it is worth noting that in spite of the different reactions of the kings involved, both stories lead to the same outcome. Just as Jerusalem was saved during Hezekiah's time, so also the city was spared during the reign of Ahaz. In both cases, however, salvation was set in the context of judgment (Ackroyd 1974; Seitz 1991: 119–191; Mathews 1995: 157–79).

Just as Childs's treatment of the historical narratives in Isaiah does not fully deal with their detail and complexity, so also his suggestion that the explicit dates in Ezekiel simply mark the book's theological turning points seems to understate the case. Although in this instance the evidence is not so clear, several scholars have argued that all of the dates had some significance for the exiles and were intended to provide historical background against which Ezekiel's visions and oracles were to be understood. Ezek 1:2–3 and 3:16 (July 593) date the prophet's call to approximately the time of the anti-Babylonian gathering held in Jerusalem by Zedekiah (Jeremiah 27). According to Jeremiah, it was on this same occasion that the prophet Hananiah predicted that within two years the exiled king Jehoiachin and the rest of the exiles of 597 would return to Jerusalem (Jeremiah 28). The temple vision in Ezek 8:1 (September 592) is dated to the same year that the Egyptian Pharaoh Psammetichus II toured Palestine and Phoenicia, apparently in an effort to encourage an anti-Babylonian coalition. In 20:1 the prophet's long history of Israel's rebellion is dated to August 591, the end of the two-year period after which Hananiah had predicted the exile would end. Ezek 24:1 (January 588) marks the beginning of Jerusalem's siege. An oracle of Tyre's destruction is dated in 26:1 to March/April 587–586, the beginning of the Babylonian siege of Tyre. Predictions of Egypt's destruction are dated in 29:1 to January 587, the time of Pharaoh Hophra's unsuccessful attempt to break the siege of Jerusalem. An oracle beginning in 29:17 and dated to April 571 correlates with the failure of the Babylonian siege of Tyre and promises that the Babylonians will capture Egypt instead. Ezek 33:21 (March 585), of course, marks the fall of the city and the exile of its inhabitants. Although the remaining dates in the book cannot presently be correlated with significant events, the evidence on the ones cited above is sufficient to suggest that all of the dates in the book are intended to supply a historical backdrop of some sort for Ezekiel's oracles and that these historical references are intended to be guides for the interpretation of the book (Greenberg 1983: 8–11).

Finally, the biographical narratives in Jeremiah also seem to be much more complex and full of detail than would seem necessary if Childs were correct in describing their function. For example, in the "B" material preserved in Jer 26–45, forty-six individuals are mentioned by name, and eighteen different titles are assigned to them. In the stories themselves, a number of details concerning the physical surroundings of the characters have been preserved, and in general a great deal of attention has been given to providing the stories with a feeling of historical reality. This level of detail suggests that the writer or writers are not simply interested in describing generic characters. Rather the intent seems to be to create historical portraits that would have been recognizable to the original audience (Seitz 1989: 8–13). Of course, it might be possible to argue that this wealth of detail was simply a feature of the stories before they were incorporated into the present book, and that the editors chose to leave the narratives intact even though they contained material that was extraneous to the editors' interests. However, some attention ought to be given to another possibility: that these details are part of a more complex set of functions that need to be explored more fully.

A fruitful point of departure for this exploration might be Childs's perceptive remark that materials concerning the life of Jeremiah occur in the book in two forms: the biographical narratives of chapters 26–45 and the so-called laments found in 11:18–12:6; 15:10–21; 17:14–18; 18:18–23; and 20:7–18. This latter group of texts has received a great deal of attention in recent Jeremiah research and is often thought to provide insight into the prophet's psychological state. Although the texts have frequently been studied in their immediate literary contexts, little attention has been given to their possible functions within the book as a whole (Skinner 1922; Polk 1984: 127–62; Diamond 1987; O'Connor 1988; Smith 1990). Yet the very placement of these texts is suggestive. They all appear within the context of the "A" poetry in the first part of the book and thus could be thought of as a sort of prelude to the biographical narratives that begin in chapter 25. Whether this sequence is intentional or simply an accident having to do with the way in which the book came together is now impossible to determine, but when the laments are read together with the biographical narratives, some interesting interpretive possibilities begin to emerge. In order to explore all of these possibilities in detail, it would be necessary to do a thorough study of the laments together with a careful examination of all of the biographical narratives, a task that far exceeds the amount of space available here. Nevertheless, even a brief look at the laments will suggest what the contours of a more extensive study might be.

The first lament appears in Jer 11:18–21 and, as scholars have often noted, contains elements reminiscent of the biblical psalms of lament. Still, in spite of the generic character of Jeremiah's complaint, specific personal experiences seem to lie behind it, even though they are not clearly defined. The prophet complains of *their* evil deeds, even though *they* are not identified (11:18). Unspecified plans are referred to, and these seem to threaten the prophet's life (11:19). Finally, in legal language the prophet invokes God as the divine judge who is entreated to declare Jeremiah innocent and to punish his enemies (11:20), who are by implication guilty. This use of legal language raises for the first time issues of guilt, innocence, and justification that will also appear elsewhere in the laments. However, Jeremiah's lament does not end with a statement of faith or an assurance of being heard, which might normally be expected to appear as the final element of a complaint psalm. Rather, the prophet receives an immediate reply from God. This reply is in prose, in contrast to the poetry of the complaint, although it is not usually identified with the Deuteronomistic "C" prose found elsewhere in the "A" oracle collection. Nevertheless this prose reply, whatever its origin, shares one important feature with the "C" prose: it seems to be intended to clarify or disambiguate the poetic material with which it is associated. In this case, God's reply clearly identifies the anonymous enemies of the complaint: they are the people of Anathoth, who are quoted as threatening the life of the prophet if he will not stop delivering divine oracles. God interprets this attempt at restraint as a crime and pronounces a severe judgment against the opponents, an action that presumably vindicates the prophet and provides the just judgment called for in the complaint.

The concern with vindication and the wrongful suffering of the innocent is taken up again in general terms in 12:1–6. Like Job, Jeremiah suggests that bringing charges against God is always a fruitless endeavor, but the prophet nevertheless questions God's justice when the guilty thrive (12:1–2). In contrast, the innocent seem to be ignored by God and allowed to suffer. Against the background of this double accusation concerning divine justice, Jeremiah renews his plea that God punish the prophet's unnamed guilty enemies and that the suffering of the (innocent?) land be brought to an end (12:3–4). But in this lament, God's response to Jeremiah's petition is neither the customary assurance of being heard nor an oracle of judgment against the opponents, as was the case in 11:21–23. Instead, in a poetic response God suggests that the prophet's request is inappropriate and that his problems will become even worse. Even his own family will turn against him, and the prophet is exhorted to prepare himself for that event. In any case, God does not release the prophet from his task, even though, from Jeremiah's perspective, the result of continuing to prophesy is likely to be certain suffering and death. This sense of divine tyranny over the prophet will appear in the later laments as well.

It is interesting that this lament is followed in the present text by another (12:7–13), which is sometimes taken to be a renewal of Jeremiah's complaint. In this case, however, the "I" of the complaint is better interpreted as referring to God, who has, like Jeremiah, also suffered separation from house and beloved family and watched the family land suffer destruction. The juxtaposition of these two laments seems to be intended to draw an analogy between Jeremiah's situation and God's situation in this crucial time in Israelite history. Just as the prophet is threatened and rejected by his family, so also Israel has rejected God, with the result that both suffer without the possibility of relief. Similarly, just as the prophet must persist in his task in spite of the personal consequences, so also God seems destined to pursue the punishment and destruction of Israel in spite of the personal pain that is involved. The way in which these passages have been juxtaposed may thus introduce the theme of the inevitability of judgment, a theme which is also the subject of the "C" didactic prose passages in the surrounding units (11:14–17; 14:11–12; cf. the ambiguous poetic oracle in 8:22–9:2 [English 8:22–9:3], and the divine warning to the prophet not to trust his neighbors that follows it).

The next lament in the sequence (15:10–21) begins with a somewhat obscure prose dialog, which seems to begin with Jeremiah's wish that he had not been born (and therefore not had to fulfill his prophetic commission, which occurred in the womb of his mother [1:5]) but which seems to end with a divine judgment speech referring to the exile (15:10–14). This is followed by a poetic lament, in which the prophet again complains of the persecution that comes when he delivers God's word and asks God to destroy the unnamed opponents. The prophet questions God's justice and implies that God has deserted him. However, God's response to Jeremiah's pleas follows the same pattern as the complaint in 12:1–6. No word of assurance is given; no relief from enemies is promised. Rather God urges Jeremiah to change his current behavior and to resume the job of being God's prophet. In return, God does promise that Jeremiah will be able to stand up to the opposition, although the opposition itself will be formidable and cause the prophet much pain. The opponents will continue to fight but will not prevail (15:19–21).

Jer 17:14–18 also follows the by now familiar pattern. God is reminded of the prophet's faithfulness to his task and urged to punish the opposition and not to play a direct role in persecuting the prophet. In this instance there is no divine reply of any sort, although the prose insertion in 17:19–27 and the "C" prose unit in 18:1–12 may be intended to supply God's answer.

In 18:18–23 a prose introduction in verse 18 supplies at least a minimal context for the complaint that follows in 18:19–23. The origin of this prose unit is unknown, but like the similarly anonymous prose of 11:21–23, it seems to interpret the "A" poetic unit with which it is associated. In this case the complaint is to be set against the historical background of a plot to bring unspecified charges against Jeremiah because of his prophetic activities ("the word will not perish from the prophet"). The lament itself follows the typical form. The prophet maintains his innocence and wonders why he is being persecuted. Then in a speech that evokes images of military defeat he urges God to punish the plotters (18:19–23). As in the previous complaint, no divine response is given in the poetic unit itself, although the immediately following prose narrative of a sign act involving a broken jug may be intended as a later attempt to supply a response.

The final complaint in 20:7–18 is both the most complex in the series and the one which follows most closely the pattern of the psalm of lament. The prophet begins by accusing God of seducing him and forcing him to deliver only oracles of judgment and destruction. The prophet has no control over the situation but must deliver the divine word that he has been given (20:7–9). Even though Jeremiah recognizes the danger to which his task exposes him, he cannot relent. But in this case, as in the typical complaint psalm, the prophet realizes that the same divine warrior who overpowers the prophet is also a source of strength against the prophet's enemies. Maintaining his righteousness, Jeremiah calls for retribution on his persecutors (20:10–13). In 20:14, for the only time in the corpus, a fragment of a psalm praising God expresses the assurance that God will hear and act on Jeremiah's behalf. Yet immediately the mood of gloom returns. In 20:14–18 the prophet, like Job, curses the day of his birth and all of those associated with it. The general character of this complaint and its strong associations with Job 3 have led some scholars to question its originality here (Polk 1984: 152–62). However, the motif of challenging God's justice and complaining about divine tyranny appears elsewhere in Jeremiah's laments, so if influence from Job 3 is present here it extends only to the literary form and not the content of the unit. In the context of Jeremiah, a curse on the day of birth must be connected with the prophet's prenatal call in 1:5 (cf. 15:10–21).

This quick review of Jeremiah's complaints shows that they share a number of characteristics and motifs, and the concentration of these motifs in this ten-chapter section of the book has the effect of reinforcing them just before the beginning of the biographical narratives in chapters 26–45. Among the characteristics and motifs of the laments are the following: (1) The reasons for the prophet's distress are often unclear, and there are no references to specific enemies, at least within the poetic units themselves. Where specifics are given, they are in prose units of unknown origin (11:21–23; 18:18). (2) God's justice is often questioned, either in general terms or with specific reference to Jeremiah's situation. The only explanation ever given for the prophet's suffering is related to the exercise of his prophetic duties. In addition, the complaints make other charges against God, including desertion and coercion. (3) Several of God's replies to Jeremiah indicate that there will be no change in the prophet's situation, in spite of his requests, and that things will get worse before they get better. (4) At least in the poetic units, the question of whether or not God will punish Jeremiah's evil opponents is left open. (5) God however does promise the prophet protection from death at the hands of his enemies, as well as the strength to persist in the face of continued opposition (15:19–21).

Against the background of the complaints, the biographical narratives take on a greater range of meanings than is sometimes associated with them. Rather than being simply an account of Jeremiah's silent suffering to be emulated by later Jewish communities, or a record of Israel's rejection of the divine prophetic word, the narratives seem to function on a number of levels to answer questions raised by the preceding, concentrated collection of prophetic complaints. First, expanding on the prose interpretation in 11:21–23, the biographical narratives make clear who Jeremiah's opponents were, both in terms of group identity (the priests, the prophets, all the people) and in terms of specific, named individuals (for example, chapter 26). At the same time, the texts explicitly identify supporters of Jeremiah who protect him and who by implication have heard his prophetic warnings and repented. It is the identification of this group of supporters, who by implication will survive the judgment of exile, which prevents the narratives from being interpreted simply as a record of Israel's rejection of Jeremiah's message. In contrast to the complaints, the narratives suggest that Jeremiah's words did have some effect and that some Israelites did listen. The specificity of the narratives at this point suggests that this issue was of some interest in the exilic community, where group identity may have been based on perceptions of what the exiles' ancestors did during the crucial years before Jerusalem's fall.

Second, the ways in which the biographical narratives sometimes seem to duplicate material in Jer 1–25 (Jeremiah 26 // Jeremiah 7, for example) may be a subtle attempt by the authors of the narrative material to imply historical contexts for all of the poetic material and not just for the complaints. Some modern scholars have in fact tried to read the book in this way, using the biographical narratives to reconstruct a history of Jeremiah's activities and then trying to fit individual oracles into that history. However, the biographical narratives probably do not contain enough specific material to permit such a retroactive reading.

Third, the narratives address the questions about God's justice that the complaints raise. With respect to the people, the narratives indicate that at least certain people who think that they are innocent are in fact guilty because they have rejected the prophet's divine word. The trauma of exile, recounted in great detail, is thus an appropriate punishment for them. In contrast, the narratives suggest the existence of another group of people who hear the divine word and survive, thus reaping the reward of their faithfulness. The narratives are not just about faithful sufferers but also about guilty evil doers who are punished. Included in this latter group are presumably Jeremiah's opponents, who are duly destroyed, thus resolving the ambiguity about their fate that is present in the complaints (see, for example, Jeremiah 28 and the later narratives detailing the fate of Zedekiah).

With respect to Jeremiah, who raised the question of God's justice in his complaints, the biographical narratives provide a different solution to the problem. In this case the narratives elaborate a suggestion already made in the complaints themselves. Jeremiah's suffering is due solely to his prophetic activities, and his fate has nothing to do with his personal guilt or innocence. This point is made sharply in chapter 26, which narrates three examples of prophets who faithfully deliver similar messages but who suffer different fates. The focus of the narrative is clearly Jeremiah himself, who is told to stand in the temple court and to deliver a conditional message of judgment: If the people will not listen to God and the prophets who speak the divine word, then the temple and city will be destroyed (26:1–6). The people, however, do not hear the prophet's speech conditionally—which would require them to take action one way or the other—but instead hear Jeremiah's words as an unconditional prediction of judgment deserving the death penalty. When the officials of Judah are summoned to preside over a trial, Jeremiah defends himself by pointing out that he has no control over his actions and is simply delivering the message that God has given him. The story up to this point thus illustrates precisely the state of affairs about which Jeremiah complained in his laments. He cannot resist God's command to prophesy about the threat of impending disaster, but when he does so his opponents threaten his life. The officials and "all the people," however, accept Jeremiah's defense and tell the priests and prophets that because he speaks a divine word he does not deserve the death penalty (26:7–16). Some unnamed elders then appear and cite two precedents from earlier cases. In the days of King Hezekiah, Micah of Moresheth prophesied in words like those of Jeremiah, and the king and people listened and repented, with the result that God relented, and the prophet, presumably, remained safe. In a second case, however, in the time of the present king, Jehoiakim, the prophet Uriah spoke words similar to those of Jeremiah, and the king and people did not listen. Rather the king sent a delegation to Egypt to capture the fleeing prophet, who was subsequently killed (26:17–23). In both of these cases, as in the case of Jeremiah, the fate of the prophet does not depend on his righteousness or unrighteousness, which is the Deuteronomistic assumption underlying Jeremiah's complaints, but rather on the reaction of the people to the divine word. At the end of this story, Jeremiah too escapes, although not because of his own righteousness. Instead, Ahikam the son of Shaphan, who is presumably one of the individuals who listened to Jeremiah, protected the prophet from the threats of the people (26:24). In the end, the issues raised by the case remain unresolved, and Jeremiah is saved to prophesy another day. Lying behind the narrative seems to be the assumption that while the fate of ordinary people may correlate with their righteousness or unrighteousness, the situation with prophets is rather different. Because they have no control over what they do and say when they represent God, there is no necessary connection between their behavior and their fate. They seem to fall outside of the normal expectations regarding reward and punishment, and as a result Jeremiah's earlier charges about God's injustice are beside the point.

Finally, when the biographical narratives are read in the light of the laments, it becomes clear that in the end God was faithful to the promises of protection and support made in the complaint sections. Jeremiah's charges that God has deserted him turn out not to be true. Although the prophet suffers, he is not killed, even though he does have several narrow escapes. In the end, he simply drops out of the narrative. No report of his death is recorded, perhaps because such a report might be interpreted as a failure of God's protection.

The above exploration of the way in which history-like material functions in Jeremiah suggests that at some point in the book's development historical narratives were added to an already existing collection of oracles in order to aid in the interpretation of this earlier material. The interests of these historicizing materials seem to extend far beyond the simple recitation of historical data, and they seem to have a complex set of functions in relationship to the earlier texts to which they have been joined. Yet in spite of these functions, which appear to be both theological and sociological, the narratives remain clearly in the form of an historical account, even though we may no longer be in a position to test their accuracy. In the case of Jeremiah, then, it appears that the best approach to the material is the one that George Landes has so long advocated. History and literature must be taken together as dialog partners within the book, and neither can safely be subordinated to the other.

REFERENCES

Ackroyd, P. R.
    1974   An Interpretation of the Babylonian Exile: A Study of 2 Kings 20, Isaiah 36–39. *Scottish Journal of Theology* 27: 329–53.

Childs, B. S.
  1979   *Introduction to the Old Testament as Scripture.* Philadelphia: Fortress.
Collins, T.
  1993   *The Mantle of Elijah: The Redaction Criticism of the Prophetical Books.* Sheffield: JSOT.
Davies, P. R.
  1992   *In Search of "Ancient Israel."* Sheffield: JSOT.
Diamond, A. R.
  1987   *The Confessions of Jeremiah in Context.* Sheffield: JSOT.
Duhm, B.
  1901   *Das Buch Jeremiah.* Tübingen and Leipzig: Mohr.
Greenberg, M.
  1983   *Ezekiel 1–20.* Anchor Bible 22. Garden City, N.Y.: Doubleday.
Holladay, W. L.
  1989   *Jeremiah 2: A Commentary on the Book of the Prophet Jeremiah Chapters 26–52.* Hermeneia. Minneapolis: Fortress.
Mathews, C. R.
  1995   *Defending Zion.* Berlin: Walter de Gruyter.
Mowinckel, S.
  1914   *Zur Komposition des Buches Jeremia.* Kristiania: Jacob Dybwad.
  1946   *Prophecy and Tradition.* Oslo: Jacob Dybwad.
Nicholson, E. W.
  1970   *Preaching to the Exiles: A Study of the Prose Tradition in the Book of Jeremiah.* New York: Schocken.
O'Connor, K. M.
  1988   *The Confessions of Jeremiah: Their Interpretation and Role in Chapters 1–25.* Atlanta: Scholars.
Perdue, L. G.
  1984   Jeremiah in Modern Research: Approaches and Issues. Pp. 1–32 in *A Prophet to the Nations: Essays in Jeremiah Studies*, ed. L. G. Perdue and B. W. Kovacs. Winona Lake, IN: Eisenbrauns.
  1994   *The Collapse of History.* Minneapolis: Fortress.
Pohlmann, K.-F.
  1978   *Studien zum Jeremiabuch.* Göttingen: Vandenhoeck & Ruprecht.
Polk, T.
  1984   *The Prophetic Persona.* Sheffield: JSOT.
Seitz, C. R.
  1989   *Theology in Conflict: Reactions to the Exile in the Book of Jeremiah.* Berlin: Walter de Gruyter.
  1991   *Zion's Final Destiny.* Minneapolis: Fortress.

Skinner, J.
   1922   *Prophecy and Religion: Studies in the Life of Jeremiah.* London: Cambridge University.
Smith, M. S.
   1990   *The Laments of Jeremiah and their Contexts.* Atlanta: Scholars.
Wanke, G.
   1971   *Untersuchungen zur sogenannten Baruchschrift.* Berlin: Walter de Gruyter.

10 Jethro's Wit: An Interpretation of Wordplay in Exodus 18

EDWARD L. GREENSTEIN

I. INTRODUCTION

After the exodus, when the Israelites are encamped at the "mountain of God" (Exod 18:5),[1] Moses is paid a visit by his father-in-law, called here Jethro.[2] Jethro is, from the outset, the focal character of the episode. The narrative opens with the phrase "Jethro heard" (v. 1) and continues to feature Jethro as the subject of (most of) the verbs in main clauses ("Jethro took," v. 2; "Jethro came," v. 5; "He [viz., Jethro] spoke," v. 6; "Jethro rejoiced," v. 9; etc.). It is Jethro who officiates at the communal sacrifice (v. 12), and it is he who expresses dismay at Moses' inefficient handling of legal disputes and advises his son-in-law as to how he might do it better (vv. 14–23). Most strikingly, it is he, a non-Israelite, who blesses YHWH for having delivered the Israelites from Egypt, rehearsing in that context a piece of the Hebrew *Heilsgeschichte*, which Moses had recounted for him (vv. 8–11). The episode ends with a picture of Jethro alone, going back "to his (own) country" (v. 27).

Scholarly discussion of the episode has been preoccupied with mostly historical concerns. Debate has revolved around the questions of whether there is more than one tradition embedded here, and whether in at least one of the putative early traditions the god YHWH was worshipped among the Midianites, or Kenites, before YHWH was adopted as god by the Israelites (cf. the discussion in, e.g., Childs 1974: 321–25).

The present discussion is concerned with the canonical form of Jethro's visit, with its place in the larger story of the exodus, and, even more, with certain significations within the episode itself. This is, therefore, in contrast to the diachronically oriented studies alluded to in the preceding paragraph, a synchronic investigation. Yet, not all synchronic studies are the same. As a synchronic study, the present discussion may be distinguished from alternative ones by the focus of its hermeneutical approach, an approach that has been selected for two reasons, one of which follows from the other.

The approach is to seek out instances of wordplay, especially punning. The search for puns emerged out of some observations I made on the language of Jethro's dialogue in the course of writing annotations to Exodus for the *HarperCollins Study Bible* (Greenstein 1993); and from the fact that when I did that project, I had wordplay on the mind, having not very long before written an article on Hebrew wordplay for a reference work (Greenstein 1992b). For me, however, it is not enough to make observations on a certain rhetorical phenomenon, to point out instances of wordplay and leave them at that. In spite of my occasional inclinations to perform interpretive readings that highlight discontinuities and incompatabilities in scripture (Greenstein 1989), I have on this occasion chosen to organize the various puns I have found into a coherent web of data, as the pieces of a design. Coherence, as I have maintained elsewhere (Greenstein 1995), is not an inherent property of texts but rather the result of a hermeneutical effort (see, e.g., Rabinowitz 1987: 141–69). Texts, in this view, do not come organized in any uniquely defined manner; they are made to cohere in a certain way through the process of reading. I make the effort to produce a certain textual coherence here both to incorporate my observations into a more global view of the theme and thrust of the exodus narrative, and to call attention to the puns that I find. After all, the puns, like other textual features, only take on significance once they are made into an instrument of interpretation.

Specifically, I shall suggest that the language of Jethro's discourse is peppered with wordplay, and that the wit that his paronomasia may be taken to bespeak may be understood to shore up his image as a sage. The fact that Jethro is characterized as wise is, I shall suggest, crucial to his major role in the episode at hand and in the story at large.

II. WORDPLAY AS AN INDICATOR OF WIT

In the Hebrew Bible, clever speech is often open to interpretation as an index of intelligence. The concept is, to my way of understanding,

given explicit expression in Prov 16:21. The verse is typically translated as it is in the RSV:

> The wise of heart is called a man of discernment,
> And pleasant speech increases persuasiveness.

The first line is rather redundant, unless one takes the second line as
an explication of it. C. H. Toy (1916: 329), accordingly, explains that
the "discernment" that figures in the first line takes the form of the
prudent use of language that is the subject of the second line. However, in light of the fact that *lēb*, ordinarily "heart," in the Bible is, as
Ginsberg (1967: 80) has demonstrated, more than occasionally an organ of speech,[3] I would interpret Prov 16:21 to mean:

> One clever with language is called discerning,
> As one sweet of speech enhances a message.

This sense may be corroborated by citing a similar couplet, two verses
below, in Prov 16:23, where *lēb*, "heart," is certainly the source, if not
the actual organ, of speech:

> A clever heart uses his mouth wisely,
> Enhancing the message with his lips.

In any event, biblical narrative provides several practical occasions
for drawing the conventional nexus between wisdom and wit. Perhaps
the best-known example is that of Abigail, praised by modern commentators as "a master of rhetoric" (Garsiel 1990: 167; cf. Hertzberg
1964: 203; Gunn 1980: 99; Levenson 1982: 230; Fokkelman 1986:
496–511),[4] whose eloquence prevents David from slaying her parsi-
monious husband and whose selective reportage, again to her good
fortune, leads to her husband's fatal heart attack (cf. Miscall 1986:
156; Biale 1992: 19). Abigail is introduced explicitly as a particularly
intelligent woman (*ṭôbat śekel*; 1 Sam 25:3), and her intelligence is
evident in her wordplay (Garsiel 1985: 126–33; 1990; Levenson 1982:
221–23, 226–27; Fokkelman 1986: 495, 500). Her verbal wit is widely
noted in the following, rather obvious, example, where the word *nābāl*,
"rogue, fool," appears in diverse permutations and puns:

> Let my lord not pay mind (*libbô*) to this scoundrel
> (*habbĕliyyaʿal*), to Nabal (*nābāl*), for like his name, so is
> he: Nabal (*nābāl*) is his name, and he is full of heinous
> folly (*nĕbālâ*) (1 Sam 25:25).

A number of subtler and less elaborate paronomastic chains have also
been noted in the episode: "wineskins" (*niblê yayin*; v. 18) and "when
the wine had left Nabal" (*hayyayin minnābāl*; v. 37); "till the light of
daybreak (*habbōqer*; v. 22)—"urinator at the wall" (*bĕqîr*; v. 34)—
"in the morning (*babbōqer*) ... within him (*bĕqirbô*; v. 37)"; "when at
daybreak the wine had left Nabal (*minnābāl*), ... his heart (*libbô*) died
within him and he turned to stone (*lĕʾāben*; v. 37)."

The next most famous rhetorician in biblical narrative would seem
to be the anonymous woman of Tekoa, whose powers of persuasion
are employed by David's general, Joab, in order to return Absalom to
Jerusalem, following his banishment for fratricide (2 Samuel 14). She
is introduced as "a wise woman" (v. 2), and her vocation as a professional speaker would appear to be adumbrated throughout her discourse,
where the *Leitwort dābār*, both as a verb *dabbēr*, "speak," and a noun
dābār, "word," appears sixteen times in eight verses (vv. 13–20). Her
dialogue has been compared to Abigail's (Segal 1968: 317; Gunn 1978:
42–43; McCarter 1984: 345), and her speech, too, has been called "a
masterpiece" (Fokkelman 1981: 141).[5] Within her discourse in vv.
6–7 one finds, for example, wordplay between *šiphâ*, "handmaid," and
mišpāhâ, "family"; between *šĕnê bānîm*, "two sons," and *šĕnêhem ...
bênêhem*, "the two of them ... between them"; and between *yôrēš*,
"heir," and *nišʾārâ*, "remained." Similarly, in vv. 16–17 one finds
wordplay between *nahălâ*, "estate," and *mĕnûhâ*, "repose." That the
wise woman's wordplay is deliberate may be deduced from the fact
that in vv. 15–16 she refers to herself as "handmaid" using the term
ʾāmâ as well as its synonym *šiphâ*. The fact that she calls herself only
šiphâ in vv. 6–7 may be understood to have been motivated by the
resultant pun on *mišpāhâ*.

Yet another female master of the rhetorical arts is the "wise woman"
of Abel, Beth-ha-Maʿacah (2 Sam 20:16–19). Following Joab's as-
sassination of Amasa, in the war for David against Sheba ben Bichri,
Joab found himself besieging the northern town of Abel. When it appears that the city wall is about to be breached, a certain wise woman,
who takes it upon herself to speak on behalf of the inhabitants of the

town, appeals to Joab to spare the people of Abel. She weaves into her relatively brief dialogue what strike me as two large puns. Her invitation to "draw near" to listen, *qĕrab* (v. 16), connotes "combat" (2 Sam 17:11; Zech 14:3; Ps 78:9; Job 38:23) and the "approach" to battle (e.g., Deut 2:19, 37; 20:10). The woman nevertheless explains to Joab the general that Abel is proverbially famous as a peace-loving town and then asks plaintively: "Why would you annihilate (*tĕballaʿ*) a territory of YHWH's?" (v. 19). The pun on Abel (*ʾābēl*), with metathesis (cf. Tur-Sinai 1959), lest you missed it, is reinforced in Joab's reply: "Heaven forbid, forbid, that I might annihilate (*ʾăballaʿ*), that I might destroy!" (v. 20).

One of the Bible's greatest punsters is generally not remembered for his wit, and even less for his intelligence. Nevertheless, credit for sophisticated verbal play of various types must be given to Samson. Samson's problems result, it will be recalled, not from a lack of intellectual capacity but from a surfeit of emotional passion. Perhaps his skills as a wordsmith may be attributed to the same divine spirit that imbued his every act with superhuman dimensions. In any case, Samson's verbal faculties are manifested in several forms—in riddles (Judg 14:14, 18a; 18b), in puns (esp. 15:16), in proposals (14:2; and chaps. 15–16 passim), and in prayers (15:18; 16:28, 30).

Most of Samson's wordplay has been discussed in some detail by Crenshaw (1978) and Segert (1984; cf. Zakovitch 1982: 143–44; Kim 1993: 414–15), so we shall content ourselves here with only a few outstanding illustrations. Samson's riddle (Judg 14:14)—"From the feeder out came food, from the strong out came sweet"—it has long been observed (references in Kim 1993: 244), is not only intriguing in and of itself, it contains a double entendre in the fact that the noun-stem that lies behind the mysterious "strong feeder," *ʾary-* (vv. 5, 18), denotes both a lion and honey (cf. Arabic *ʾary*, "honey"). The "feeder" (*ʾōkēl*) and the "food" (*ma ʾăkāl*) are therefore, on one level of the Hebrew lexicon, homonymous; the riddle is thus also a pun. In the same vein, Samson's angry response to the Philistines' ill-gotten solution to his riddle is rife with structural repetitions and rhyme (e.g., Zakovitch 1982: 116):

> If with my heifer you did not plow,
> You'd not have got my riddle now (Judg 14:18b).

When Samson kills a thousand men with the jawbone of an ass, and commemorates the event by naming the site of the massacre, he heaps pun upon pun.

> With the jawbone of an ass, mass upon mass,
> With the jawbone of an ass I have slain a thousand men (Judg 15:16).

First, he plays on the two senses of *ḥămôr*, "ass" and "heap," or "mass." Next, he names the site *Rāmat leḥî*, "Jawbone Height" (v. 17), in which the term *leḥî* both describes the "cheek," or "ridge," where he performed his feat and evokes the instrument by whose means he performed it. Then, by calling the place by its chief topographical trait— it is a "height," *rāmâ*—he puns on the last thing he did before naming the site: he threw down the ass' jawbone. The word for "height," *rāmâ*, is homonymous with a poetic synonym of the verb employed here, *hašlîk*, "to throw down" (e.g., Exod 15:1; so Zakovitch 1982: 144).

III. WORDPLAY IN JETHRO'S DISCOURSE

The language of Jethro, too, contains a number of plays, which, in line with the theory we have adopted above, function as an index of his wit and sagacity. It may be noted, not altogether parenthetically, that the language of the entire chapter of Exodus 18, and of Jethro in particular, is somewhat peculiar. Benno Jacob (1992: 501) enumerates the following rare or unusual words and forms: the verb *ḥādōh* (v. 9), "to rejoice," the usage of *nābōl* (v. 18), "to wilt" (more on which below), the verb *zîd* (v. 11), "to scheme," the usage of *ḥāzōh* (v. 21), "to see," in the sense of "select," the third masc. pl. accusative pronoun form *ʾethem* (v. 20), and others. Some of these usages or forms have parallels in the so-called Covenant Code of Exodus 21–23.[6] In any event, a competent reader of Exodus 18 will be struck by a variety of unusual words.[7] One should also be on one's toes to notice wordplays.

One of the key terms that repeatedly occurs in Exodus 18 is the noun *dābār*. It is first presented in the curious, ambiguous phrase *kî baddābār ʾăšer zādû ʿălêhem* (v. 11), which is linguistically difficult and is translated (and emended!) variously. Targum Onkelos takes it to refer to the affliction that Egypt had perpetrated against Israel, which would become the affliction by which God, in retribution, would punish Egypt:

"by the (same) thing that they (viz., the Egyptians) had plotted against them (viz., the Israelites)."[8] Be that as it may, the word *dābār* is soon picked up again, but this time it is used by Jethro to ask Moses what "thing" (*dābār*) he thinks he's doing, trying to hear and resolve all legal disputes among the Israelites by himself (v. 14):

> What is this thing (*dābār*) that you are doing to the people?
> Why do you sit (in judgment) all by yourself? (Exod 18:14).

Note that the verb *yāšōb* appears here as an elliptical idiom, "to sit (in judgment)," as we know from within (e.g., 1 Kgs 7:7; Isa 16:15; cf. Gemser 1955: 123) and without the Bible (e.g., the Ugaritic epic of Aqhat; KTU 17.5.4–8) that judges would sit to listen to cases.

Moses replies to Jethro, using the word *dābār* in its technical, juridical sense of "a legal case" (e.g., Paul 1970: 89 n. 6):

> When there be a legal dispute (*dābār*), it comes before me
> (v. 16).

The ancient versions, and many later commentators and translators, take the referent of "it" and the subject of "comes before me" to be not "a legal dispute" but rather "the people," mentioned in the preceding verse. However, the verb *bō ʾ*, "come," is specifically used of a legal dispute being presented, as in, for example, the nearby passage, Exod 22:8: "the case (*dābār*) of the two (parties) comes before the divine oracle (for adjudication)."[9]

Hearing Moses use *dābār* in its technical sense, and realizing that this answer is no answer at all, Jethro returns to his usage of *dābār* in its more ordinary sense: "The thing (*dābār*) you are doing is no good" (v. 17). Indeed, says Jethro forcefully, the "thing" you are trying to do is "too heavy for you" (v. 18). This phrase carries an extra measure of censure because, in its context following the story of the plagues and the exodus, where the root *k-b-d*, "heavy," is a *Leitwort* (Greenstein 1993: 85a), the words *kî kābēd mimměkā haddābār*, "for the thing is too heavy for you," echo the announcement of the fifth plague, cattle disease, called *deber kābēd mě ʾ ōd*, "very heavy pestilence" (Exod 9:3). In fact, the same wordplay is used in announcing and relating the plague of pestilence (*deber*): "Tomorrow will YHWH do this thing (*dābār*) in the land … YHWH did this thing (*dābār*) on the morrow" (9:5).

In the present passage, Jethro does not simply throw out words. The image of Moses' burden being too heavy for him to bear, he resumes below in Exod 18:22: "you must lighten up your own load, letting (the appointed magistrates; see v. 21) bear the burden (together) with you."

In the balance of the passage, the key word *dābār* is used and reused, both in the technical sense of "legal case," as in v. 19—"you shall bring cases (*dĕbārîm*) to the divine oracle"—and again, twice, in v. 22, and in the simple sense of a "thing" that Moses should be doing (v. 23)—as opposed to the "thing" that he should not have been doing.

In fact, if Moses will do the right thing, then, says Jethro, he will be able to endure (v. 23). The verb Jethro chooses to convey "endure"—*ʿāmōd*, literally, "to stand"—is a rich pun. For when the old priest had been asking Moses the rhetorical question, "What are you doing?" (v. 14), he reiterated his question and asked, "Why do you *sit* (*yōšēb*) all by yourself?" Only if Moses stops sitting alone will he be able to stand, Jethro wittily explains.[10]

It is possible to trace the pun even further, by observing Jethro's next choice of words. If Moses will follow his advice, he "will be able to stand," and "all the people will be able to return home in peace." The phrase for "home" is *māqôm*, the regular word for "place." It is derived from *qûm*, a close synonym of the verb Jethro had applied to Moses, *ʿāmōd*, "to stand." In fact, the Aramaic targum, Targum Onkelos, translates Hebrew *ʿāmōd* in v. 23 with the cognate of Hebrew *qûm*, namely, as *limqām*.

Jethro pulls off another, more minor, pun in v. 19. When Jethro says to Moses, "May God be with you (*ʿimmāk*)," first, the word *ʿimmāk*, "with you," echoes the same word in the preceding verse, where it plays on the word *ʿām*, "people" (so Hakham 1991: 248): "this people (*hā ʿām hazzeh*) that is with you (*ʿimmāk*)." More poignantly, Jethro may well be using the word for "God"—*ʾĕlōhîm*—in both its senses, within the exodus narrative in general and within this episode in particular, as both the generic name for God and as the designation of "the oracle" from which Moses receives instruction.[11] Moses, Jethro tells him, will need both divine support *and* the help of the oracle, which will adjudicate difficult cases for him. Interestingly, one finds both interpretations among the traditional Jewish commentators. Thus, Rashi understands *ʾĕlōhîm* here to represent the counsel that Moses receives from God in the process of adjudication; whereas Rashi's grandson

Samuel ben Meir understands *ʾĕlōhîm* here as a show of divine support for the overworked leader.

One of the oddest usages that one finds in Jethro's discourse is, as we noted above, that of the verb *ḥāzōh*, "to see," in the sense of "to find, to select." The more common synonym of *ḥāzōh*, the verb *rāʾōh*, "to see," is attested quite a number of times in the secondary sense of "seeking" or "selecting" (cf. Brown, Driver, Briggs 1907: 907b). The most famous instance is in the Akedah narrative, where Isaac asks Abraham where the animal for the offering is, and Abraham replies that God will "find" or "select" (*yirʾeh*) the animal (Gen 22:8). Only here, in Exod 18:21, however, is the verb *ḥāzōh* attested in this meaning. Indeed, in the performance part of the command-fulfillment sequence, when Moses actually chooses men to be magistrates, the verb *bāḥōr*, the common locution for selection, is used (v. 25). It is hard to deny the proposal, made already in the early rabbinic midrash on Exodus, the Mekhilta, that Jethro's choice of the verb *ḥāzōh* is occasioned by its other, more common use, as a term for prophetic vision.[12] Moses is to use his prophetic powers in making good choices in naming magistrates. The denotation may be "to select/find," but the connotation is "to divine."

The next of Jethro's puns we will look at is found in another of the peculiar linguistic usages in Exodus 18. Jethro warns Moses that if he continues to perform all adjudication of disputes alone he will—*nābōl tibbōl* (v. 18). Most modern commentators take the verb to be *nābōl*, "to wilt," usually said of plants (Brown, Driver, Briggs 1907: 615).[13] Medieval Jewish exegetes are divided. Some, like Rashi, follow the Targum and understand the verb the same way: Moses will be wilted, that is, wasted, exhausted, by trying to handle disputes from morning till night. Others, however, like Samuel ben Meir, relate *nābōl* here to the verb *bālōl*, "to confuse, confound," induced by the irregular verb form in the Tower of Babel story where God says: "Come, let us go down and confound (*nābĕlâ*) there their language." Rather than make sense of our passage in either one way or the other, I would prefer, especially in light of Jethro's other puns in the episode, to understand *nābōl tibbōl* as double entendre: Moses will be both confused and exhausted if he attempts to handle all legal matters by himself. One might even propose, though not without playfulness, that the doubled form of the verb—infinitive absolute plus finite form—suggests that both senses of *nābōl tibbōl* are to be heard.

That Jethro is an able punster and pundit is indicated perhaps by the narrator in what may be a somewhat subtle play on his name. The name Jethro, from the root *y-t-r*, is most readily explained to mean "one who is preeminent" (e.g., Radday 1990: 67). The Akkadian cognate, (*w*)*atru*(*m*) is used especially in the phrase *atra-ḫasīsa*, "exceedingly wise," which is also the name given to the Old Babylonian Noah, Atra-ḫasīs. Jethro, too, may make a play on his name. Moshe Garsiel (1991) has argued that in Numbers 10, where Moses' father-in-law is called not Jethro but Hobab, there is an implicit wordplay (e.g., Zakovitch 1980) not on the name Hobab but rather on the, shall we say, hidden name, Jethro. Moses begs his father-in-law to remain with the Israelites in order to guide them through the wilderness. A term that is used in that chapter for scouting for rest stops is *tûr*, "to reconnoiter, to scout." Garsiel suggests that the use of *tûr* in Numbers 10 evokes the name *yitrô*, "Jethro," with which it shares two consonants in the same sequence.

Bearing in mind this possible midrashic name derivation—as Garsiel calls the literary etymologies in the Bible—Jethro may be playing on his name when, in Exod 18:20, he directs Moses to "instruct the people in the route on which they should go." The verb *tûr* is not used, but the concept is there. I wonder if there is an implicit play here on *tûr*.

In any case, even without the possible paronomasia just mentioned, Jethro's record as a punning rhetorician is strong.

IV. JETHRO'S WISDOM

If Jethro is indeed being characterized in Exodus 18 as a witty and, by implication, wise man, one may then ask what function that plays in the narrative. To put it differently, what sense might we make of the fact that Jethro is depicted as an extraordinarily knowing person?

I would suggest both a general and a context-specific understanding of Jethro's wit and wisdom. Jethro is one of a number of non-Israelites who is said to recognize the greatness of God and appreciate the power in the mighty acts of God. The language of Jethro's so-called confession of faith—"Blessed is YHWH who has rescued you from the hand of Egypt and from the hand of Pharaoh"—(Exod 18:10)—recalls the first instance of the gentile recognition of YHWH, by Melchizedek, who affirmed, in the presence of Abram: "And blessed is El Elyon who has delivered your enemies into your hands" (Gen 14:20; cf. Buber 1958: 96). Indeed, the word used there for "your enemies"—*ṣārêkâ*—is echoed here in the name of Egypt—*miṣrayim*.

Other well-known gentiles who come to recognize Israel's god are Balaam the prophet (Num 22–24); Rahab, the woman of Jericho who, in Josh 2:9–11, appears actually to quote from the Song at the Sea and other Torah passages connected with the exodus (e.g., Kaufmann 1966: 96; Eslinger 1989: 33–40; cf. Soggin 1972: 41); the Queen of Sheba (1 Kgs 10:9); the Aramean army officer, Naaman (2 Kgs 5:15); Ruth the Moabite (Ruth 1:16–17); and the sailors taking Jonah to Tarshish (Jon 1:16). It is a biblical topos (e.g., Sarna 1966: 117).

Rahab and Naaman each employ a similar formula of acknowledging the supreme power of Israel's God. They each say "Here: I know" (or the like) that God is greater than all others, or is incomparable in greatness (Josh 2:9, 11; 2 Kgs. 5:15; cf. Labuschagne 1966). Jethro does the same: "Now I know that YHWH is greater than all gods" (Exod 18:11; cf. e.g., Childs 1974: 328–29).

In the context of the exodus narrative, Jethro forms an ideal contrast to the arch-enemy of both Israel and God—Pharaoh, king of Egypt (Buber 1958: 94–95). When Moses and Aaron had first confronted Pharaoh about releasing the Hebrew slaves for a pilgrimage to their God in the wilderness, the king scornfully replied: "Who is YHWH that I should heed his voice and release the Israelites? I do not recognize YHWH, and so will I not release Israel" (Exod 5:2). One of the chief purposes of the plagues, as many commentators have observed, is to show Pharaoh, Egypt, and even Israel that YHWH is God and must be recognized and worshipped (references and discussion in Greenstein 1995: 564). Jethro is doing now, after hearing of what God did in Egypt, what Pharaoh should have done immediately, or at the very first opportunity. The connection between Jethro's positive behavior and its contrast with the experience of Israel in Egypt is underscored in Jethro's several allusions to the deliverance of Israel from Egypt. Jethro, in antithesis to Pharaoh, can see right away what God has wrought, and he's ready to pay appropriate tribute in words.

In view of the way that Jethro's wisdom, as seen in his wit, may function within the exodus narrative, one may explain in a similar manner the placement here of Jethro's establishment of the Israelite judiciary. Curiously, and significantly, this achievement of Jethro's is not accredited to him in Deuteronomy, where Moses himself claims to have taken this initiative (Deut 1:9–15). The fact that Deuteronomy passes over Jethro's role may say less about Deuteronomy's agenda than it does about Exodus'. It is important in the context of Exodus to highlight Jethro's wisdom. Setting up the system of magistrates for Moses is, like Jethro's verbal wit, an index of his intellectual powers. Jethro is wise, and his wisdom is exemplary. What does the sagacious Jethro do with his smarts? He establishes a system of magistrates *and* he recognizes the unique powers of YHWH.

Jethro, a gentile, can see the power and grandeur of Israel's god. Such recognition carries special weight precisely because Jethro is a distinctively wise man. Acknowledging the supremacy of God, we may infer from this and from so many biblical texts, would be a wise move for Israel as well. How does the wise man put it? "Reverence of the Lord is the beginning of knowing" (Prov 1:7a).

NOTES

A version of this article was presented at the Columbia University Seminar for the Study of the Hebrew Bible, 19 October 1994; I am grateful to the several colleagues in attendance who made helpful comments. For nearly twenty years I enjoyed seeing our cherished colleague, George Landes, at the monthly meetings of the seminar, as well as on other occasions. I am honored and pleased to publish this paper in tribute to him. It should be noted that the transcriptions of Hebrew follow the stipulated conventions for this volume; they should not be taken to represent the phonology of ancient and/or Tiberian Biblical Hebrew (see Greenstein 1992a). Verbal roots are cited in the infinitive absolute form. Ugaritic texts are referenced according to the standard abbreviation KTU (= M. Dietrich, O. Loretz & J. Sanmartín, *The Cuneiform Alphabetic Texts from Ugarit, Ras Ibn Hani and Other Places*. 2nd enlarged ed. Münster: Ugarit-Verlag, 1995).

1. The phrase echoes Moses' initial visit to this mountain (Exod 3:1). It has long been noted that Exodus 18 is chronologically out of sequence; see the extensive comment by Abraham Ibn Ezra at v. 1, and see further Glatt (1991: 152–57).
2. For a summary of the problem of the various names of Moses' father-in-law, see Slayton (1992).
3. Cf., e.g., Ps 27:8; Prov 23:33; Qoh 5:1.
4. For a broader discussion of Abigail's "verbal power," see Bach (1989: 41–58).

5. For analysis of the rhetoric, see Fokkelman (1981: 126–47) and Hoftijzer (1970: 419–44).

6. Cf., e.g., *ʾethen* in Exod 20:21 (Dotan ed.); *yāzîd* in 21:14; compare also *šillûaḥ* in Exod 18:2 with *šalleaḥ* in 22:4.

7. The distinctive language of Exodus 18 is obliquely reflected in the fact that the Dead Sea Scrolls draw precisely on that chapter for halakhic terminology that differs from traditional usage; cf. Qimron and Strugnell (1994: 139).

8. אֲרֵי בְּפִתְגָמָא דַחֲשִׁיבוּ מִצְרָאֵי לְמִדָּן יָת יִשְׂרָאֵל בֵּיהּ דְּנִינוּן.

9. See also Isa 1:23b, where *bōʾ*, "come," serves as the predicate of *rîb*, "legal case"; cf. Luzzatto (1965 [1871]: 307); Ehrlich (1970 [1899]: 168).

10. In the present example, the inevitable tension between a diachronic and a synchronic approach can easily be illustrated. Although some source critics attribute the entire chapter, Exodus 18, to E (e.g., Driver 1911: xxvi), others divide it between two once autonomous strands (e.g., Auerbach 1975: 90–92). According to the latter, vv. 14 and 23, between which we have found wordplay, belong to different sources. In a synchronic perspective, however, the two verses are part of a single text, regardless of their historical origins. Similarly, Auerbach's source division separates vv. 14, 17, and 18 from v. 16, among which we, taking a synchronic view, find punning on the different senses of *dābār*, "thing, word, legal case."

11. For *ʾĕlōhîm* as a divine "oracle," cf., e.g., Gen 25:22; Exod 4:14–16; 21:6; 22:7. For the understanding of *ʾĕlōhîm* in such passages as "household gods," see the discussion in Paul (1970: 50–51, 90, with 90–91 n. 6).

12. See also the commentary printed in large rabbinic Bibles, the Keli Yaqar, to Exod 18:21.

13. For another application to human subjects, see 2 Sam 22:46a.

REFERENCES

Auerbach, E.
  1975   *Moses.* Trans. and ed. R. A. Barclay and I. O. Lehman, from German. Detroit: Wayne State University.

Bach, A.
  1989   The Pleasure of Her Text. *Union Seminary Quarterly Review* 43: 41–58.

Biale, D.
  1992   *Eros and the Jews.* New York: Basic Books.

Brown, F.; Driver, S. R.; Briggs, C. A.
1907   *A Hebrew and English Lexicon of the Old Testament*. Oxford: Clarendon.

Buber, M.
1958   *Moses*. New York: Harper.

Childs, B. S.
1974   *The Book of Exodus*. Old Testament Library. Philadelphia: Westminster.

Crenshaw, J. L.
1978   *Samson: A Secret Betrayed, A Vow Ignored*. Atlanta: John Knox.

Driver, S. R.
1911   *The Book of Exodus*. Cambridge Bible. Cambridge: Cambridge University.

Ehrlich, A. B.
1969   *Mikra Ki-Pheschutô*. Vol. 1. The Library of Biblical Studies. New York: Ktav. [Original printing: 1899].

Eslinger, L.
1989   *Into the Hands of the Living God*. JSOT Supplement Series 84. Sheffield: Almond.

Fokkelman, J. P.
1981   *Narrative Art and Poetry in the Books of Samuel, Volume I: King David*. Assen: Van Gorcum.
1986   *Narrative Art and Poetry in the Books of Samuel, Volume II: The Crossing Fates*. Assen: Van Gorcum.

Garsiel, M.
1985   *The First Book of Samuel*. Ramat Gan: Revivim Publishing (Hebrew).
1990   Wit, Words, and a Woman: 1 Samuel 25. Pp. 161–68 in *On Humour and the Comic in the Hebrew Bible*, ed. Y. T. Radday and A. Brenner. Sheffield: Almond.
1991   *Biblical Names: A Literary Study of Midrashic Derivations and Puns*. Ramat-Gan: Bar-Ilan University.

Gemser, B.
1955   The RÎB- or Controversy-Pattern in Hebrew Mentality. Pp. 120–37 in *Wisdom in Israel and in the Ancient Near East Presented to Professor Harold Henry Rowley*, ed. M. Noth and D. W. Thomas. Supplements to Vetus Testamentum 3. Leiden: Brill.

Ginsberg, H. L.
1967   Lexicographical Notes. Pp. 71–82 in *Hebräische Wortforschung: Festschrift zum 80. Geburtstag von Walter Baumgartner*. Supplements to Vetus Testamentum 16. Leiden: Brill.

Glatt, D. A.

1991   *Chronological Displacement in Biblical and Related Literatures.*
            Society of Biblical Literature Dissertation Series 139. Atlanta:
            Scholars.

Greenstein, E. L.

1989   Deconstruction and Biblical Narrative. *Prooftexts* 9: 43–71.
            Repr.: pp. 21–54 in *Interpreting Judaism in a Postmodern Age*,
            ed. S. Kepnes. New York: New York University, 1996.

1992a   An Introduction to a Generative Phonology of Biblical Hebrew.
            Pp. 29–40 in *Linguistics and Biblical Hebrew*, ed. W. R. Bodine.
            Winona Lake: Eisenbrauns.

1992b   Wordplay (Hebrew). Pp. 968–71 in *Anchor Bible Dictionary*,
            vol. 6, ed. D. N. Freedman. Garden City, New York: Doubleday.

1993   The Book of Exodus. Pp. 77–150 in *The HarperCollins Study
            Bible*, ed. W. Meeks. San Francisco: HarperCollins.

1995   The Firstborn Plague and the Reading Process. Pp. 555–68 in
            *Pomegranates and Golden Bells: Studies in Biblical, Jewish,
            and Near Eastern Ritual, Law, and Literature in Honor of Jacob
            Milgrom*, ed. D. P. Wright et al. Winona Lake: Eisenbrauns.

Gunn, D. M.

1978   *The Story of King David.* JSOT Supplement Series 6. Sheffield:
            JSOT.

1980   *The Fate of King Saul.* JSOT Supplement Series 14. Sheffield:
            JSOT.

Hakham, A.

1991   *The Book of Exodus. Da ʿat Miqraʾ.* 2 vols. Jerusalem: Mossad
            Ha-Rav Kook (Hebrew).

Hertzberg, H. W.

1964   *I & II Samuel: A Commentary.* Trans. J. S. Bowden, from Ger-
            man. Old Testament Library. Philadelphia: Westminster Press.

Hoftijzer, J.

1970   David and the Tekoite Woman. *Vetus Testamentum* 20: 419–44.

Jacob, B.

1992   *The Second Book of the Bible: Exodus.* Trans. W. Jacob with Y.
            Elman, from German. Hoboken, NJ: Ktav.

Kaufmann, Y.

1966   *The Book of Joshua.* Jerusalem: Kiriath Sepher (Hebrew).

Kim, J.

1993   *The Structure of the Samson Cycle.* Kampen: Kok Pharos.

Labuschagne, C. J.

1966   *The Incomparability of Yahweh in the Old Testament.* Pretoria
            Oriental Series 5. Leiden: Brill.

Levenson, J. D.
   1982   I Samuel 25 as Literature and History. Pp. 220–42 and 317–19
            in *Literary Interpretations of Biblical Narratives, Volume II*, ed.
            K. R. R. Gros Louis with J. S. Ackerman. Nashville: Abingdon.
Luzzatto, S. D.
   1965   *Commentary on the Five Books of the Torah*, ed. P. Schlesinger.
            Tel Aviv: Dvir Publishing (Hebrew). [Original printing: 1871.]
McCarter, P. K., Jr.
   1984   *II Samuel.* Anchor Bible 9. Garden City: Doubleday.
Miscall, P. D.
   1986   *1 Samuel: A Reading.* Bloomington: Indiana University.
Paul, S. M.
   1970   *Studies in the Book of the Covenant in the Light of Cuneiform
            and Biblical Law.* Supplements to Vetus Testamentum 18.
            Leiden: Brill.
Qimron, E., and Strugnell, J.
   1994   *Qumran Cave 4, V: Miqṣat Maʿaśe Ha-Torah.* Discoveries in
            the Judaean Desert 10. Oxford: Clarendon.
Rabinowitz, P.
   1987   *Before Reading: Narrative Conventions and the Politics of In-
            terpretation.* Ithaca: Cornell University.
Radday, Y. T.
   1990   Humour in Names. Pp. 59–97 in *On Humour and the Comic in
            the Hebrew Bible.* JSOT Supplement Series 92. Sheffield: Al-
            mond.
Sarna, N. M.
   1966   *Understanding Genesis.* New York: Jewish Theological Semi-
            nary of America/McGraw-Hill.
Segal, M. Z.
   1968   *The Books of Samuel.* Jerusalem: Kiriath Sepher (Hebrew).
Segert, S.
   1984   Paronomasia in the Samson Narrative in Judges XIII–XVI. *Vetus
            Testamentum* 34: 454–61.
Slayton, J. C.
   1992   Jethro. P. 821 in *Anchor Bible Dictionary*, vol. 3, ed. D. N. Freed-
            man. Garden City, New York: Doubleday.
Soggin, J. A.
   1972   *Joshua: A Commentary.* Trans. R. A. Wilson. Old Testament
            Library. Philadelphia: Westminster.
Toy, C. H.
   1916   *The Book of Proverbs.* International Critical Commentary. New
            York: Scribner's.

Tur-Sinai, N. H.
  1959   Metathesis in the Biblical Text. Pp. 106–49 in *The Language and the Book*, vol. 2. Jerusalem: Kiriath Sepher (Hebrew).
Zakovitch, Y.
  1980   Explicit and Implicit Name-Derivations. *Hebrew Annual Review* 4: 167–80.
  1982   *The Life of Samson*. Jerusalem: Magnes (Hebrew).

11 The Impossible: God's Words of Assurance in Jer 31:35–37

HERBERT B. HUFFMON

I. INTRODUCTION AND TEXTUAL QUESTIONS

E asily the most popular passage in Jer 30–31 (30–33), widely referred to as "The Book of Consolation," is the new covenant passage in Jer 31:31–34. The bibliography on this passage is very extensive. Comparatively neglected, or even denigrated, however, is the following section, 31:35–37—in some editions of the Hebrew text, 31:34–36—with its words of assurance.[1] These verses also call for some special attention. A first question is the textual character of these words themselves. Following the reference to the new covenant in Jer 31:31–34, the *torah* as written on the heart such that all the people will "know" the Lord, who in turn will forgive them and remember their sin no more, there comes hymnic reference to God as the Lord of creation (31:35). (The latter part of this hymnic praise has an exact parallel in Isa 51:15b.) This hymn notes the wonders and regularities of the heavens and the sea, which themselves are the model for understanding God's new relationship with Israel. The "impossible words of assurance" then follow.

The text reads (with citation of both the Masoretic text and the hypothetical *Vorlage* of the Septuagint text, as retroverted from the text as reconstructed by Joseph Ziegler [1976]):

1. Textual Reconstruction

MT 31:35 / כה אמר יהוה נתן שמש לאור יומם חקת ירח וכוכבים לאור לילה

LXX 38:36 / כה אמר יהוה נתן שמש לאור יומם   ירח וכוכבים לאור לילה

רגע הים ויהמו גליו יהוה צבאות שמו /	MT
רגע הים ויהמו גליו יהוה צבאות שמו /	LXX
רגע הים ויהמו גליו יהוה צבאות שמו /	Isa 51:15b

Thus says the Lord, who provides the sun as light by day, the moon and the stars as light by night; who stirs up (or *quells*)[2] the sea, whose waves roar; the Lord of hosts is his name.

אם־ימשו החקים האלה מלפני נאם־יהוה /	MT 31:36
אם־ימשו החקים האלה מלפני נאם־יהוה /	LXX 38:37

גם זרע ישראל ישבתו מהיות גוי לפני כל־הימים /	MT
גם זרע ישראל ישבתו מהיות גוי לפני כל־הימים /	LXX

If (אם) these (natural) laws could depart from me (and they cannot)—oracle of the Lord—then (גם) the "seed" of Israel could cease being a nation for me for all time (and it cannot).

כה אמר יהוה /	MT 31:37
zero /	LXX 38:35

	אם־ימדו שמים מלמעלה ויחקרו מוסדי־ארץ למטה /	MT
אם־ירמו שמים למעלה נאם יהוה ואם ישפלו מוסדי־ארץ למטה /		LXX

	גם־אני אמאס בכל־זרע ישראל על־כל־אשר עשו נאם־יהוה /	MT
ואני לא אמאס בזרע ישראל נאם יהוה על־כל־אשר עשו /		LXX

If (אם) the heavens above could be measured (and they cannot), or the foundations of the earth beneath be explored (and they cannot), then I could repudiate (גם אני אמאס) all the "seed" of Israel for all that they have done—oracle of the Lord. (MT)

2. Notes on the Text

In Jer 31:35b the LXX "zero variant" for חקת seems the better and smoother text; note the possible intrusion from v. 36 (MT).[3] For the final assurance in Jer 31:37 the LXX *Vorlage*—whose sense is a bit elusive but does include an alternative impossibility—apparently read:

> If (אם) one could elevate the heavens above (and one cannot)—oracle of the Lord—and if (ואם) one could lower the foundations of the earth beneath (and one cannot), (so [responding to the unspoken answer]) I can not (ואני לא אמאס) repudiate the "seed" of Israel—oracle of the Lord—for all that they have done.[4]

In Jer 31:37a the LXX presumably read ירמו, which may involve a metathesis and a confusion of ד / ר (Becking 1994: 166–67), although the second part of the line seems to reflect a different text—perhaps following the logic of the alternative reading of the first part of the line. For the "elevate"/"lower" parallel, note Ps 75:8 and 1 Sam 2:7. In Jer 31:37c the LXX apparently read a contrastive negative, perhaps misreading *lû(ʾ)* as *lōʾ*—"But I can not reject ...." The Hebrew *Vorlage* of the LXX may have read, "If ..., then I indeed could reject ..." or "then I shall *not* reject the offspring of Israel" (Becking 1994: 167). The Greek text is difficult to account for as it stands (McKane 1996: 831).

Although the LXX *Vorlage* seems to have a superior text at points, the sequence in the LXX does not make as much sense as that in the MT. With a sequence corresponding to MT vv. 36, 37, 35, the hymnic verse occurs in the middle of the "impossible" verses. Although this preserves the proper sequence for vv. 35–36 (MT) / vv. 36–37 (LXX), providing a context for the reference to the cosmic regularities, the overall LXX sequence seems wrong. This different sequence may have resulted from a marginal correction that was incorporated in the wrong place. The scribe's eye could have skipped from the כה אמר יהוה at the beginning of MT v. 35 to the כה אמר יהוה at the beginning of MT v. 37 (though lacking in the LXX v. 35!). MT vv. 35–36 were thereby omitted, and they were subsequently reintroduced in the wrong place. But this seems a desperate solution. Whatever the process underlying the LXX, the MT sequence seems the correct one.[5]

II. THE IMPOSSIBLE AS ASSURANCE

The striking and carefully crafted words of assurance do not concern aspects of the natural world impossible for people to comprehend, such as those featured in the many rhetorical questions in Job 38–39 that point to the transcendence of God. Instead, the words draw upon the unchanging world or the limits of human achievement in order to emphasize the comparable impossibility of God's turning aside from Israel. These words take the form of a "protasis–apodosis sequence in which an impossible (or inconceivable) circumstance negatively reinforces the assurance: 'if [אם] ... (then) also [גם]'" (Holladay 1989: 171). The words have but three close biblical parallels:

1) Jer 33:20–21:

כה אמר יהוה
אם־תפרו את־בריתי היום ואת־בריתי הלילה
ולבלתי היות יומם־ולילה בעתם
גם־בריתי תפר את־דוד עבדי מהיות־לו בן...

If (אם) you (pl.) could break my covenant with day and my covenant with night, such that there will not be day and night in their time (and you cannot), then (גם) my covenant with my servant David could be broken—that he would not have a son reigning on his throne—and (my covenant) with the Levitical priests, my servants.[6]

2) Jer 33:25–26:

כה אמר יהוה
אם־לא בריתי יומם ולילה חקות שמים וארץ לא־שמתי
גם־זרע יעקוב ודוד עבדי אמאס מקחת ...

If (אם־לא) I have not established (לא־שמתי) my covenant of day and night, the regularities of heaven and earth (but I have), then I could repudiate (גם...אמאס) the seed of Jacob and David, my servant, (not) taking from his seed rulers over the seed of Abraham, Isaac and Jacob. But (כי) I will restore their captivity and have compassion on them.

3) Gen 13:16:

(ושמתי את־זרעך כעפר הארץ אשר)
אם־יוכל איש למנות את־עפר הארץ
גם־זרעך ימנה

(I will make your seed as the dust of the earth; so that) if (אם) anyone can number the dust of the earth (and no one can), then (גם) your seed could also be numbered.

A close parallel in form, but with the impossible condition followed by words of divine judgment rather than assurance, also occurs:

4) Jer 5:1:

‎... אם־תמצאו איש אם־יש עשׂה משׁפט מבקשׁ אמונה ואסלח לה

(Roam the streets of Jerusalem and look carefully, and search in its broad places.) If (אם) you (pl.) can find anyone—if (אם) there is someone who does justice, someone who seeks truth (but there are no such persons), (then) I can pardon (ואסלח) her/Jerusalem (but I can't pardon her).

III. EVALUATION

Scholars differ as to whether or not these words of assurance are ideologically correct for (the Book of) Jeremiah. Among recent commentators, McKane (1996: 829) notes the rhetorical artistry of the "subtlety of the understatement," with the simple grammar of "if *this* then *that*," underscoring the assurance. Alternatively, Carroll (1981: 214) emphasizes the contrast with the early oracles of Jeremiah, with their theme of judgment, observing that "the irony of the developed tradition carrying views so antagonistic to his spirit should not be overlooked by the modern analyst of the book of Jeremiah." More specifically, Rudolph, Weiser and Leslie emphasize the support that these verses of assurance provide for Israel. In Rudolph's words (1958: 186), the "promised eternal duration of the proclaimed salvation ... is valid not merely for the new covenant (37), but also for the political future of the people (36)."[7] Other scholars are more in agreement with Carroll. Raitt (1974: 168 n. 2) finds the "argument from nature to history utterly unlike and contradictory to Jeremiah elsewhere," and Hyatt (1956: 1040) and Streane (1913: 196–97) label the verses as too nationalistic for Jeremiah.[8]

1. Role

In the Book of Jeremiah as it stands, the purpose of Jer 31:35–37 is to reinforce the announcement of the new covenant of 31:31–34, the internal transformation effected by God, the covenant written on the

heart. The assurance is that the new relationship will prevail, that God
will indeed "pardon their (Israel's) iniquity and remember their sin no
more." In the context of the Book of Jeremiah, the earlier chapters
repeatedly point out the difficulties the people face and the likelihood
of divine judgment. The formal parallel—but ideological contrast—in
Jer 5:1, already cited—"Roam the streets of Jerusalem and look carefully, and search in its broad places, if you (pl.) can find anyone—if
there is someone who does justice, someone who seeks truth, (then) I
can pardon Jerusalem (but there isn't and I can't)," points to the need
for some effective persuasion. Using an argument from the natural
world, the rhetorical question posed in the divine speech in Jer 13:23
points to the same need:

היהפך כושי עורו ונמר חברברתיו
גם־אתם תוכלו להיטיב למדי הרע

Can the Kushite change (היהפך כושי) his skin, or the leop-
ard his spots? (Of course not.) Then (גם) you (pl.) may
also do good who are adept at evil.

A similar rhetorical question drawing upon human custom is presented
in Jer 2:32:

Can a girl forget her ornaments (התשכח בתולה עדיה), or a
bride her attire? Yet my people (ועמי) have forgotten me,
days without number.

The same ideological point is found in the unflattering comparison
with the behavior of birds presented in Jer 8:7:[9]

Even the stork (גם־חסידה) in the heavens knows its times;
and the turtledove, swallow, and crane observe the time of
their coming; but my people do not know the order of the
Lord (משפט יהוה).

In the sections of the Book of Jeremiah dominated by the threat of
the coming judgment, various arguments are put forward to persuade
the people. Central is the linkage of cause and effect—lack of faithfulness leading to punishment. In Jeremiah 30–31, whether viewed as

reflecting a time prior to 609 or a time after 587—and I would prefer the later date, but date is not the present issue—the context is one of a clear emphasis on hope (or at least the prominence of hope, not so one-sidedly threat and judgment). This context suggests that one might find rather different rhetorical flourishes, rather different kinds of persuasion, so as to sustain a perception of the people's situation as something other than threat and judgment. Especially following the new covenant passage, with its transformative perception of Israel, one need not expect ideological consistency with contrary themes. The perceptions are different. As expressed by Thomas Raitt (1977: 178), the announcement in Jer 31: 31–34 is that "God creates both salvation and the preconditions for it, both repentance and the preconditions for it, both forgiveness and the preconditions for it, both a new election relationship and the preconditions for it." The "discontinuity" of the new covenant passage—i.e., discontinuity in the way of Israel, setting aside the former covenant, which Israel broke—is countered by the *continuity* of God, whose affirmation of Israel is as continuous as the cosmic regularity of day and night.[10]

This different situation calls forth new arguments. Utilizing a distinctive style—the words of "impossible assurance" in which an impossible protasis prepares for an apodosis expressing the reliability and endurability of God's favor—the theme of the new covenant is reinforced. The appeal is not to the unevenness of historical existence, with its oscillating judgment and salvation, but to the regularities and imponderabilities of the natural world. Other passages in the Book of Jeremiah, some of which have been mentioned, helped to prepare the way for this new rhetoric. Note, for example, the remarkable parallel and contrast in Jer 5:22–24:

> I placed the sand (חוֹל) as a boundary for the sea (as) a
> perpetual ordinance (חׇק־עוֹלׇם).... Though the waves toss,
> they cannot prevail .... But this people has a stubborn and
> rebellious heart ....They do not say in their hearts, "Let us
> fear the Lord our God, who gives the rain in its season, the
> autumn rain and the spring rain, and keeps for us the weeks
> appointed for the harvest (שׇׁבֻעוֹת חֻקּוֹת קׇצִיר)."

2. Background

The rhetoric in 31:35–37 has few precise parallels. The appeal to the sun, moon and stars, which are so predictable, and to the extent of the heavens and the depths of the earth, which are so beyond our count or our reach, provides the basis for the divine assurance that Israel cannot "cease" or be "repudiated" by God. In a similar way, the durability of the sun and the moon underscores the perpetuation of the line of David (Ps 89:36–38), and the immeasurableness of the stars, of the dust of the earth, or the sand of the seashore can reinforce the promise of un-countable descendants to Abraham, Sarah, Isaac, and Jacob (Gen 13:16; 15:5; 16:10; 22:17; 26:4; 28:14; 32:13), a promise reiterated in Hos 2:1 [ET 1:10]. Yet this comparison, a well-known *topos* in the ancient Near East, has its limitations, in that at times it represents a realized number, even if somewhat of a hyperbole. Israel is described as being in actuality "as many as the sand on the seashore for multitude" (2 Kgs 4:20), and the same characterization is used of enemies (e.g., Josh 11:4; Judg 7:12).

Our text's only precise parallel outside the Book of Jeremiah, as noted, is Gen 13:16: "I will make your seed as the dust of the earth; so that if anyone can number the dust of the earth, then your seed can also be numbered." And the independence of the close parallels within Jeremiah is suspect. These parallels in 33:20–21 and 33:25–26 form parts of the problematic passage 33:14–26. Not only is this passage lacking in the LXX, but its language, its references to David and the Levitical priests, and the presence of what Janzen (1973: 123) identifies as "post-Jeremianic elements in the eschatological expectation," all point to its being a later, expansionist incorporation. (To be sure, this is done in such a way as to provide an appealing literary framework in Jeremiah 30–33, as pointed out by Biddle [1988: 409–13], with the two sets of promises "assured by ordinances of nature.") The parallels in Jeremiah 33 thus end up seeming secondary and dependent on Jer 31:35–37. A striking paucity of independent parallel texts, therefore, helps us to see the special character of Jer 31:35–37.

As to the Jeremianic authorship of Jer 31:31–34 and 35–37, that ques-tion will be settled the same day that all the stars are counted and all the sand of the seashore is weighed, but let us note only that there is prepa-ration in the previous portions of the Book of Jeremiah for the new supportive arguments represented in 31:35–37.

3. Near Eastern Parallels and Biblical Connections

The background of such argumentation is not restricted to emphasis on the incomprehensibility of the wonders of the natural world in literature such as the Book of Job or Babylonian wisdom texts such as "The Dialog of Pessimism."[11] This kind of argumentation is ancient, though it is presented somewhat differently in Jer 31:35–37. Precise parallels are but few in the biblical texts, and they are also rather difficult to find in ancient Near Eastern literature. Note the similar rhetoric based on regularities and impossibilities in the natural world in some of the Amarna texts recently gathered by William Murnane:

1) From the *Hymn to the Rising Sun*, from the tomb of the "Greatest of the Seers" of the Aten, Meryre (I)

> Give him (the king) very many Sed Festivals with peaceful years. Give to him with the love of your heart—like the multitudes of sand of the shore, like the scales of fish upon the river, and the hairs of cattle. Keep him (the king) here until the swan turns black, until the crow turns white, until the mountains stand up to go, and until the flood flows backwards ... (Murnane 1995: 157, § 70.7).[12]

> So long as heaven exists, so will you (Akhenaten) exist! You shall achieve many years and myriads of jubilees, being here continually forever (a commonplace for the king and queen at Amarna)....You are born like the Aten is born: your lifetime is eternity, the lifetime of Re as king of the Two Lands, the years of Aten in heaven, while you dwell in Akhet-Aten, the beautiful place which you made for Re, to which all come (Murnane 1995: 159, § 70.9).[13]

2) From the tomb of the "Overseer of the Royal Quarters," Meryre (II):

> (As for) ..., they raise an outcry [to] the height of heaven at seeing Akhet-Aten, which Re made to be given to his son, ..., while he (=Aten) causes him (=king) to plunder every foreign country on which he shines, and he bequeaths the whole circuit to him in order to slake his heart with them [and to do what pleases his Ka], for they are under the feet of Waenre (Akhenaten), the one beloved like the [Aten], [until] the sea [gets up] on legs, until the mountains stand up to go, until water flows backwards (Murnane 1995: 164, § 71.3).[14]

Jer 31:35–37 does not seem to derive from Isa 40–66 either, as has been at least implied (Holladay 1989: 166). The Jeremiah verses, as powerfully expressed as they are, do not match the even greater power of the rhetoric in Isa 40–66, which presses further. Instead of arguing from the immutability of human conditions, such as changing one's skin, we find a different argument in the rhetorical question of Isa 49:15:

> Can a woman forget (התשכח אשה) her nursing child, (her) compassion for the son of her womb? (The expected answer—of course not!—gives way to granting the seeming impossibility! The text continues:) Even (גם) these (women) may forget, but I cannot forget you (O Zion).

Isa 54:10—as also Isa 51:6—expresses a similar point even more strongly. The enduring mountains and the "eternal hills" do not provide the model for maximal assurance:

> For the mountains may depart (כי ההרים ימושו) and the hills may be removed, but my love shall not depart (לא־ימוש) and my covenant of peace shall not be removed.

In Third Isaiah, the argument from impossibility is developed even more dramatically than in Second Isaiah. Isa 60:19–20 advises:

> The sun shall no more be your (f. sg. throughout) light by day; nor for brightness will the moon give light to you; but the Lord will be for you an everlasting light, and your God will be your glory. Your sun will no more go down; nor will your moon withdraw itself: for the Lord will be your everlasting light, and the days of your mourning will be ended.

A similarly dramatic argument is presented in Isa 66:22:

> For as (כי כאשר) the new heavens and the new earth, which I will make, will endure before me, says the Lord, so (כן) will your seed and your name endure before me.

4. Conclusion

Jer 31:35–37 is a powerful and innovative argument used as assurance for the amazing, transformational affirmation of Jer 31:31–34. It need not derive from "Wisdom" influence (with its emphasis on what people cannot do as opposed to what God will do) in some redactional process, nor does it derive from similar—but even stronger and surely later—arguments in Second and Third Isaiah.[15] It itself gave rise to a similarly strong—but less elegant and surely secondary—argument in Jer 33:20–21, 25–26. Its ideological home is most likely the new situation Jeremiah sought to convey—presumably late in his life—in a time of exile. But the time during which consensus on these matters will not be reached will endure "until the swan turns black, until the crow turns white, until the mountains stand up to go, and until the flood flows backwards." But note that there *are* black swans.

NOTES

1. Discussion of these verses, when offered, commonly focuses on the issue of authenticity or their connection with creation (Brongers 1945; Weippert 1981) or land theology (Brueggemann 1980), rather than their rhetorical role in the larger context.

2. Pope (1973: 185, s.v. Job 26:12a). Note that the Old Greek translators apparently read נער for the MT רגע (Becking 1994: 166, following a suggestion of J. Day), which could well be a misreading by the Greek translator (and so I reconstruct the MT text).

3. For discussion, see D. Barthélemy (1986: 689–90), who, however, favors the MT.

4. For the unexpected לא see the comments of Barthélemy (1986: 690–91, 628) in favor of the LXX adding the לא, citing Jer 5:2; 7:10; and 9:4.

5. Becking (1994: 167–68) judges it "impossible to decide which of the different orders is more authentic."

6. Cf. Ps 89:35–38.

7. Rudolph (1958: 186) writes: "The section concludes the whole, great prophecy of salvation for Ephraim. Yahweh crowns his graciousness with promised eternal duration of the proclaimed salvation, which is valid not merely for the new covenant (37), but also for the political future of the people (36); it is as clearly guaranteed as the change of day and night (Gen 8:22) or as the fact that the quiet of the sea is again and again dis-

turbed by storms (35b ...; cf. 5:22, 24; 8:7), and a new rejection of Israel is as unthinkable as the possibility of measuring the heaven (Isa 40:12, etc.) or penetrating the secrets of the depths of the earth." See also Weiser (1969: 289): "The future salvation is based in the unfathomable grace of God, through which this salvation is also constantly vouched for"; Leslie (1954: 107): "a majestic rhetorical climax to Jeremiah's prophecy of salvation for Ephraim." Bright (1965: 287) and Thompson (1980: 582), though not praising the eloquence of Jer 31:35–37, find these verses consistent with Jeremiah's message.

8. Streane nonetheless allows that the verses might be "a genuine fragment inserted here from another context." Duhm (1901: 258–59) is similar to Hyatt.

9. Cf. Isa 1:2–3 and Jer 18:14–15a, though the latter text has textual difficulties. An Egyptian parallel to this group, noticed by Crenshaw (1980: 26–27) in another connection, is found in "The Eloquent Peasant," B1 179–183 (new count). Lichtheim (1973: 175–76) translates the text: "Does the hand-balance deflect? Does the stand-balance tilt? Does Thoth show favor So that you may do wrong? Be the equal of these three: If the three show favor, Then may you show favor! Answer not good with evil, put not one thing in place of another!"

10. Contrast Brueggemann (1992, esp. 197–200), who sets discontinuity over against continuity (for Israel) without noting the continuity of God who punishes but sustains.

11. Lambert (1960: 148–49, lines 83–84): "Who is so tall as to ascend to the heavens? Who is so broad as to compass the underworld."

12. See also Murnane (1995: 122, § 59.4). Note also the discussion by Barucq (1962: 406–7).

13. Note also the similar motif in Tutu's praise of Akhenaten: "So long as the Aten exists, you (Akhenaten) shall be alive and rejuvenated continually" (Murnane 1995: 195, §89.9); "So long as he (the Aten) exists you shall exist continually" (Murnane 1995: 197, § 89.11).

14. On the motif of the strangely-acting sea, mountains, and water, see Barucq (1962: 235–36), and note the partial parallel in Murnane (1995, §70.7), cited above.

15. Note the comments of Unterman (1987: 102–106); see also Keown, Scalise and Smothers (1995: 136–37). Brueggemann (1992: 197–98) apparently views Isa 54:10 as representing cosmic discontinuity as opposed to the cosmic continuity of Jer 31:35–37, whereas the fundamental point seems to be the divine continuity, buttressed in Jer 31:35–37 by reference to cosmic order but buttressed even more strongly in Isa 54:10 (and Isa 51:6) by the affirmation that God's continuity with Israel is *more reliable* than the cosmic order itself.

REFERENCES

Barthélemy, D.
1986   *Critique textuelle de l'Ancien Testament.* Orbis Biblicus et
        Orientalis 50/2. Freiburg: Universitätsverlag / Göttingen:
        Vandenhoeck & Ruprecht.

Barucq, A.
1962   *L'expression de la louange divine et de la prière dans la Bible et
        en Égypte.* Institut Français d'archéologie orientale, Bibliothèque
        d'Étude 33. Cairo: Institut Français d'archéologie orientale.

Becking, B.
1994   Jeremiah's Book of Consolation: A Textual Comparison: Notes
        on the Massoretic Text and the Old Greek Version of Jeremiah
        xxx–xxxi. *Vetus Testamentum* 44: 145–69.

Biddle, M. E.
1988   The Literary Frame Surrounding Jeremiah 30,1–33,26.
        Zeitschrift für die alttestamentliche Wissenschaft 100: 409–13.

Bright, J.
1965   *Jeremiah.* Anchor Bible 21. Garden City, NY: Doubleday.

Brongers, H. A.
1945   *De Scheppingstradities bij de Profeten.* Amsterdam: H. J. Paris.

Brueggemann, W.
1980   On Land-Losing and Land-Receiving. *Dialog* 19: 166–73.
1992   A Shattered Transcendence? Exile and Restoration. Pp. 183–203
        in *Old Testament Theology. Essays on Structure, Theme, and
        Text*, by W. Brueggemann, ed. P. D. Miller. Minneapolis: For-
        tress.

Carroll, R. P.
1981   *From Chaos to Covenant. Prophecy in the Book of Jeremiah.*
        New York: Crossroad.

Crenshaw, J. L.
1980   Impossible Questions, Sayings, and Tasks. *Semeia* 17: 19–34.

Duhm, B.
1901   *Das Buch Jeremia.* Kurzer Hand-Commentar zum Alten Testa-
        ment 11. Tübingen: Mohr.

Holladay, W. L.
1989   *Jeremiah 2. A Commentary on the Book of the Prophet Jeremiah
        Chapters 26–52.* Hermeneia. Minneapolis: Fortress.

Hyatt, J. P.
1956   The Book of Jeremiah. Pp. 775–1142 in *The Interpreter's Bible,*
        Vol. 5, ed. G. A. Buttrick, et al. Nashville: Abingdon.

Janzen, J. G.
1973   *Studies in the Text of Jeremiah.* Harvard Semitic Monographs 6. Cambridge: Harvard University.

Keown, G. L.; Scalise, P. J.; and Smothers, T. G.
1995   *Jeremiah 26–52.* Word Biblical Commentary 27. Dallas: Word.

Lambert, W. G.
1960   *Babylonian Wisdom Literature.* Oxford: Clarendon.

Leslie, E. A.
1954   *Jeremiah.* Nashville: Abingdon.

Lichtheim, M.
1973   *Ancient Egyptian Literature. Volume 1: The Old and Middle Kingdoms.* Berkeley: University of California.

McKane, W.
1986–96 *Jeremiah.* International Critical Commentary. 2 vols. Edinburgh: T & T Clark.

Murnane, W. J.
1995   *Texts from the Amarna Period in Egypt.* Writings from the Ancient World 5. Atlanta: Scholars.

Pope, M.
1973   *Job.* Anchor Bible 15. Third edition. Garden City, NY: Doubleday.

Raitt, T. M.
1974   Jeremiah's Deliverance Message to Judah. Pp. 166–85 in *Rhetorical Criticism: Essays in Honor of James Muilenburg*, eds. J. J. Jackson and M. Kessler. Pittsburgh Theological Monograph Series 1. Pittsburgh: Pickwick.
1977   *A Theology of Exile. Judgment/Deliverance in Jeremiah and Ezekiel.* Philadelphia: Fortress.

Rudolph, W.
1958   *Jeremia.* Handbuch zum Alten Testament I/12. Second edition. Tübingen: Mohr.

Streane, A. W.
1913   *The Book of the Prophet Jeremiah together with The Lamentations.* Revised edition. Cambridge Bible for Schools and Colleges. Cambridge: University.

Thompson, J. A.
1980   *The Book of Jeremiah.* The New International Commentary on the Old Testament. Grand Rapids: Eerdmans.

Unterman, J.
1987   *From Repentance to Redemption. Jeremiah's Thought in Transition.* JSOT Supplement Series 54. Sheffield: JSOT.

Weippert, H.
1981   *Schöpfer des Himmels und der Erde. Ein Beitrag zur Theologie des Jeremiabuches.* Stuttgarter Bibelstudien 102. Stuttgart: Katholisches Bibelwerk.

Weiser, A.
1969   *Das Buch Jeremia, Kap. 25,15–52,34.* Das Alte Testament Deutsch 21. Göttingen: Vandenhoeck & Ruprecht.

Ziegler, J.
1976   *Ieremias, Baruch, Threni, Epistula Ieremiae.* Septuaginta. Vetus Testamentum Graecum Auctoritate Academiae Scientiarum Gottingensis 15. Second edition. Göttingen: Vandenhoeck & Ruprecht.

12 A Tempest in a Text: Ecological Soundings in the Book of Jonah

PHYLLIS TRIBLE

While a doctoral student at Union Theological Seminary, I wrote a dissertation on the Book of Jonah, under the supervision of Professor James Muilenburg. When time came for the oral defense, George Landes, then a junior member of the faculty, was asked to participate. In preparing for the event, he fell under the spell of Jonah. Years later, upon my return to teach at Union, Landes and I had innumerable animated conversations about the little book. So rich are its treasures that we never came close to exhausting them—though sometimes we exhausted ourselves. The following essay, interpreting Jonah from an ecological perspective, offers my colleague and friend yet another topic for our continuing discussions.

I. INTRODUCTION

For centuries storms of controversy have swirled around the Book of Jonah, all forty-eight verses. Scholars have hurled their questions at it, arguing voluminously about date, authorship, composition, setting, genre, purpose, theme, and point of view, and never coming to consensus. Unbowed by this battering from without, the book has survived for intrinsic readings. Yet the one offered here finds in the text a tempest more threatening than all the scholarly storms that have surrounded it.[1]

The tempest envelops Creator, creation, and chaos: the God of the heavens who made the sea and the dry land (Jon 1:9); the people, plants, and animals who inhabit them; and the netherworld whose bars close forever upon the dead (2:6). From the divine command that sets the plot in motion (1:2), "Arise, go to Nineveh," to the divine question that leaves the plot unfinished (4:11), "Shall I not pity Nineveh?," theology and ecology converge to stir up trouble.

II. A STORM AT SEA

The trouble begins when the divine command receives a disobedient response (1:1–3). Jonah arises not to go to Nineveh but to flee to Tarshish. Two cities compete for the scene of action: great Nineveh in the east, focus of God's interest, and unmodified Tarshish in the west, destination of Jonah's defiance. Along the way Jonah involves a third city, the seaport of Joppa where land meets water. There he finds the ship that will carry him from the presence of Yahweh—except that it does not.[2]

Yahweh pursues Jonah. The pursuit comes not in measured response but in violent extravagance, when the deity hurls a great wind to the sea (1:4). God acts first in the story as the subject of a verb whose object is nature. In turn, the wind produces a storm so great that the inanimate ship thinks itself about to splinter, and the animated sailors fill with fear. Cognizant of the divine source of the violence, the sailors cry out, each to his god (1:5). They also seek to appease the sea-god through sacrifices. All the wares on the ship they hurl to the sea even as Yahweh has hurled a great wind to the sea. A single divine act has terrified the entire world that Jonah inhabits.

Yet Jonah himself lies sound asleep in the womb-like recesses below the deck of the ship. Nature fierce in wind and storm neither frightens nor stirs him. He knows how to escape a hostile environment. He snores. In effect, he has reduced himself to an object, replacing the wares thrown overboard. Unlike the ship, he thinks not at all. The inanimate and the animate have reversed. Even when the desperate captain awakens Jonah, beseeching him to pray for deliverance, he makes no response (1:6). This human creature appears unaffected by the volatility of nature unleashed by the God whom he has disobeyed. Divine wrath misses its target, and the innocent suffer. Issues of theodicy flood the narrative.

Through the casting of lots the sailors identify Jonah as the culprit.[3] They ply him with questions; this time he answers. He proclaims his Hebrew identity and the identity of his god: "Yahweh God of the heavens I am fearing, the one who made the sea and the dry land" (1:9). Theological language is ecological language. "God of the heavens" indicates transcendent power; "the one who made the sea and the dry land," imminent power. Together these conventional phrases depict Yahweh as god of the cosmos. But Jonah uses them in an unconventional way. Placing the words "I am fearing" between the "God of the heavens" and " the one who made the sea and the dry land," Jonah puts himself in the center of the universe that Yahweh creates and controls. Ironically, the structure and substance of his sentence entrap him between divine power and divine presence. The God he flees surrounds him.

The sailors understand the terror. Their fear increases (cf. 1:5 with 1:10), and their plight intensifies, "for the sea is ranting and raving." With a seeming altruism that masks the ulterior motive to flee from God, Jonah recommends that the sailors toss him overboard (1:12). After delay and with reluctance (1:13–14), they do as he instructs (1:15). They throw him to the sea even as earlier they tossed their wares. The sailors give to nature one of their own. Thereupon the storyteller reports, without reference to Yahweh or to the wind, that "the sea ceased from its raging." Unaffected earlier by inanimate wares, the sea responds now to human sacrifice. Jonah as culprit holds power over nature, and fearful sailors use that power. Concerted human actions bring harmony to a hostile environment. But the sailors themselves take no credit for restoring the balance. Instead, they worship Yahweh (1:16).

III. A MAN OVERBOARD

Leaving the sailors behind, the story follows Jonah into troubled waters. "Yahweh appoints a great fish to swallow Jonah" (1:17). As the first action of this deity was to hurl a great wind, so the second action is similarly a verb whose object is nature. The God whom Jonah has disobeyed feeds him to a fish. The human creature becomes potential fodder for the animal creature, and the animal creature becomes appointed mediator between the human creature and the divine creator.

Whether the fish performs a benign or malignant function remains a moot question. From Jonah's perspective drowning would be his salvation, and the raging sea his rescuer. As a substitute for Tarshish, the sea would have taken him from the presence of Yahweh. But the fish thwarts his wish. This animal, the instrument of Yahweh, defies the human, first to save him from the sea and then to return him to dry land.

The verbs "swallow" (*bālaᶜ*) and "vomit" (*qîʾ*) report the ichthyic actions. Both carry negative meanings in the Hebrew Bible. By the work of Yahweh at the Exodus, the earth "swallowed" the enemies of Israel (Exod 15:12). By the work of Yahweh in the wilderness, the earth "swallowed" those who revolted against Moses; they went down alive into Sheol as they perished from the assembly (Num 16:30, 32, 34). So the fish appointed by Yahweh swallows Jonah. He descends alive into its belly. With reference to the second verb, "vomit," the book of Proverbs avers that to eat the bread of the stingy is like a hair in the throat: "you will vomit up the little you have eaten" (Prov 23:6–8). Another proverb declares that if one over indulges in the eating of honey, "that one will vomit it" (Prov 25:16). So at the word of Yahweh the fish vomits Jonah. If the verb "swallow" suggests that the fish is a hostile environment for Jonah, the verb "vomit" suggests that Jonah is a hostile substance for the fish. The food it consumes it cannot stomach. In a bulimic exercise the animal of the sea rejects human fodder.

Between these negative actions of swallowing and vomiting, Jonah prays a psalm from the belly of the fish. Similar to the inner recesses of the animated ship (1:5), this enclosure is womb-like. Within it Jonah recalls a cry that he claims to have made earlier to Yahweh from the womb (*beṭen*) of Sheol, the abode of the dead (2:2). That experience subjected him to ecological dangers far surpassing the horrors of land and sea. In the great deep, the floods, the waves, and the billows surrounded and overwhelmed him (2:3); the weeds wrapped around his head as he descended to the roots of the primeval mountains (2:5); and the netherworld closed in upon him forever (2:6). In Melville's words, Jonah saw "the opening maw of hell with endless pain and sorrows there" (Melville 1961: 57). Nature as chaos and chaos as nature enclosed him. Yet God brought up his life from the Pit, and to this God he rendered thanks.

Recalling the cry he made to Yahweh from the womb of Sheol, Jonah now prays from the womb of the sea creature. Dissonances between the psalm and the setting highlight his skewed perceptions and exacerbate theological tensions in the story. Jonah prays to the God from whose presence he seeks to flee, to the God who has fed him to the fish, and to the God who continues to manipulate him. That God he describes as his deliverer. The destroyer and the savior are one.

Far from being an entertaining scene with a happy ending, chapters 1 and 2 of Jonah abound in terror. Yahweh, God of the heavens, who made the sea and the dry land, exercises crushing power. Bending nature to the divine will, the deity stalks disobedient Jonah and in that pursuit endangers the lives of innocent sailors. Ecology and theology conspire to yield a tale of violence and vindictiveness. Soundings in the text but suggest the depths of the tempest.

IV. A CITY IN CRISIS

The tempest continues in chapters 3 and 4, though with marked differences. This time the divine command to go to Nineveh receives an obedient response. Jonah enters the great city. The narrative environment switches from the uncharted waters of storm to the settled terrain of *civitas*. But the civil is a community of unspecified evil (1:2; 3:10) and violence (3:8) and so a community under judgment. "Yet forty days and Nineveh will be overturned," announces Jonah (3:4). He neither names the agent of the overturning nor interprets the sense of the verb. Perhaps he knows not what he says, for the Hebrew word "overturn" (*hāpak*) holds the opposite meanings of destruction and deliverance. The verb and its passive voice fit well a city in crisis. In what way will Nineveh be overturned, and who will do the turning?

Immediately, with no explanation from the narrator or the characters, the citizens of Nineveh initiate the change (3:5). The first response comes then from the grass roots, not from the authorities. The people, "from the greatest to the least," believe in God; they call a fast; and they clothe themselves in sackcloth, the traditional garb of mourning and repentance. The merism "from the greatest to the least" suggests the riches of inclusivity: male and female, noble and peasant, rich and poor, age and youth—indeed, all sorts and conditions of people. In other words, the body politic takes responsibility to save the city. Corporate and social actions seek to overturn the urban crisis.

When the popular response reaches the king of Nineveh, he emulates the people's penitential practices (3:6). He leaves his throne to sit in ashes, and he removes his robe to cover himself in sackcloth. As the single individual of consummate power, he follows the lead of the citizens, "from the greatest to the least." Only then, after his individual response, does he assert the authority of his position. He issues a decree that institutionalizes what the Ninevites have already done in spontaneity (3:7–9). This entire passage (3:5–9) offers a democratic model for governing in which leader and followers interchange roles.

From salutation through instructions to conclusion, the decree of the king abounds in ecological motifs. The salutation addresses "the human and the animal" (3:7). The Hebrew word translated "the human," *hā-ʾādām*, echoes the word *hā-ʾādāmâ*, the earth (cf. Gen 2:7), and so grounds the people of Nineveh in the soil common to all humankind. Even in their particularity, they are the earthling. Moreover, they share with "the animal" syntactic and social equality. Addressing the two groups in tandem, the decree departs strikingly from those biblical passages in which human beings rank above animals (cf., e.g., Gen 1:26; 2:19–20; Ps 8:3–8).

The second line of the salutation, "the herd and the flock," reinforces the status of the animals. Through the emphasis of specificity, a part represents the whole. Unlike the fish of the sea that swallowed and vomited Jonah, these domestic animals are not instruments for divine purposes. Like the earthlings of the city, they bear responsibility for the outcome of the crisis. The royal decree posits a high theology for the animal world, and in this marvelous story the animals are equal to the task.

Three negative instructions order "the human and the animal" not to taste anything, not to graze, and not to drink water. They are to unite in fasting. Similarly, three positive instructions unite "the human and the animal" (3:8) in additional acts of penance. They are to dress in the sackcloth of mourning; they are to call to God with strength; and they are to turn from their evil and their violence. "The animal" shares, then, not only the status but also the sin of "the human." A high theology for the animal world cuts both ways.

The conclusion expresses tentative hope based on human and animal repentance. "Who knows," it says, "God may repent … and we will not perish" (3:9). Overturning by Nineveh may effect overturning by God, but there is no guarantee.

In all its parts, salutation, instruction, and conclusion, the royal decree treats animals on a par with human beings. Contrary to critics who deem these descriptions humorous or satiric (e.g., Marcus 1995: 121–22; Miles 1975), this reader hears the words as respect, not ridicule, and as pathos, not parody. Nineveh cares for its nonhuman population even as it cares for its people. Positing so close a link between the earthling and the animal, the city symbolizes the society of the cultivated earth. This urban environment seeks the well-being of all its creatures.

The outcome is salutary. "When God saw their deeds"—the deeds of the human and the animal—"how they turned from their way of evil, God repented of the evil that he said he would do to them, and he did not do it" (3:10). Nineveh overturned; God overturned.

Unlike the situation in chapters 1 and 2, in chapter 3 ecology and theology conspire to yield a tale of repentance and salvation. Although at the beginning Yahweh is again the divine power that commands Jonah, this time Jonah appears to change. Externally he obeys. He goes to Nineveh and there utters an ambiguous pronouncement that threatens destruction. Like the sailors, the Ninevites are god-oriented; unlike the sailors, they are not innocent. They are people and animals of evil and violence. Nonetheless, they understand repentance, including its lack of guarantee. So they turn. When God sees their turning, then God turns. Nineveh is saved.

New to the story, this theology of repentance works on a *quid pro quo* basis, an equal exchange between the city and the deity. Mutuality and reciprocity eliminate evil to yield salvation. God never punishes Nineveh; repentance supersedes retribution. But this theology of repentance carries disturbing irony, indeed its own terror, especially in juxtaposition to the theology of violence in chapter 1. There innocent sailors experienced the life-threatening fury of Yahweh; here guilty Ninevites experience the redemptive power of God. On the one hand, how can Yahweh move so easily to the destruction of the innocent? On the other, how can God move so easily to the salvation of the guilty? The issue of theodicy that flooded the sea likewise saturates the city.

V. A RHETORICAL GOD

Angry Jonah. The last chapter of the book offers no tidy resolution of these matters. To the contrary, the dissonances that have been gathering within the story explode through the character Jonah. Literally the Hebrew reads, "And it was evil to Jonah an evil great, and it burned to him" (4:1). Filled with the evil from which the Ninevites have turned, Jonah blazes with anger. He lashes out in a prayer that explains why at the beginning he sought flight to Tarshish. The explanation lies in the ancient confession that God is "merciful and gracious, slow to anger, abounding in steadfast love and repenting of evil" (cf. Exod 34:6–7).

Although the terrifying behavior of Yahweh in chapters 1 and 2 might well challenge this text, Jonah does not so apply it. Instead, he uses the ancient confession both to account for the salvation of Nineveh and to justify himself. In the process he subverts divine love into accusation, condemns compassion, and demands vindication from the merciful God who coerced obedience from him. With his existential environment ablaze, Jonah concludes his prayer by asking Yahweh to take away his life. "Better my death," he says, "than my life." Ecologically out of joint, Jonah seeks not to set things right but to confirm himself through theological manipulation. The death he desires he asks God to enact.

The divine reply further complicates the story. Yahweh, who has not spoken to Jonah since twice ordering him to go to Nineveh (1:2; 3:2), reemerges with a different kind of rhetoric that signals a different mode of being. Command yields to question. Playing off the narrated description that "it burned" to Jonah, Yahweh counters, "Is it good it burns to you?" But the rhetorical maneuver appears not to work. Jonah leaves town without replying. He spurns the divine question, letting the storyteller report his exit (4:5). Outside the city he sits under a booth that he has constructed as he waits to see what will happen within the city.

Jonah's diversionary tactics are self-defeating. To go out from the city leaves the place where the divine question was asked; yet previous geographical efforts to escape Yahweh's word have failed Jonah. To make a booth secures a shelter; yet in the past neither the innards of the ship nor the waters of the sea nor the belly of the fish has secured Jonah from Yahweh. To sit down entrenches Jonah's position; yet past efforts at entrenchment have resulted in expulsion (cf. 1:6). To see what will happen in the city resists what has already happened; yet from the beginning resistance has not succeeded. All Jonah's efforts to change his environment result in his defeat. In other words, ecological distancing will not bring him theological victory.

Divine Appointments. From an urban setting in Nineveh, the story has returned to a natural locale. Yahweh meets Jonah where he is, this time not at sea but on land east of the city. Both venues yield divine appointments: at sea, a fish, and now on land, a plant (4:6), a worm (4:7), and a wind (4:8).

The plant has two purposes: to shade Jonah and to deliver him from his evil (cf. 4:1). The first purpose comes to pass; Jonah delights in the plant. But the second remains unfulfilled. Neither Jonah nor the narrator nor God reports that the plant delivers Jonah from evil. Shaded by botanical mercy, Jonah may well mask his evil through his delight.

But his delight is short-lived. With the coming of dawn (a natural event not attributed to divine activity), a worm attacks the plant and it withers. Nature assaults nature. In Hebrew the sound of the verb "wither" (*wayyîbāš*) echoes the sound of the noun "dry land" (*hayyabbāšâ*), thereby producing a wordplay that evokes association with the fish episode (2:10). Like the fish of the sea, the worm of the earth is God's instrument. Unlike the fish, the worm mediates not between Yahweh and Jonah but between God and the plant. It shields the deity from directly perpetrating botanical death. Moreover, unlike the fish, whose role is ambiguous, both devouring and saving, the worm has only a negative function. It kills. Yet, as the story unfolds, this destructive act fits Yahweh's larger purpose of saving Jonah from himself. Such associations between the fish and the worm suggest the interrelation of the created order.

How Jonah responds to the demise of the plant as plant is not immediately known. A gap opens in the story. Recognition of it becomes crucial for understanding the movement and meaning of the events unfolding. Meanwhile, the narrative reports that the sun beats upon Jonah and that God sends a strong east wind on the land, even as Yahweh once hurled a great wind to the sea (1:4). On this occasion, the sun, rather than the divinely appointed wind, depletes Jonah. As the worm attacked (*nākâ*) the plant, the sun attacks (*nākâ*) his head. The botanical creature and the human creature experience similar assaults, which lead to parallel consequences. The plant withered; Jonah faints and asks to die.

From the natural rhythms of the cosmos, the coming of dawn and the rising of the sun, through the divine wind that blows where God wills, to particularities of the earth, a shade-giving plant and an attacking worm, nature benevolent and malevolent instructs Jonah. At times it works on its own; at other times God manipulates it. Either way, once the lessons are completed, Jonah remains untutored. Not even all the energies focused on him by Creator, creatures, and creation have made a difference. He holds fast, insisting as he did after the salvation of Nineveh, "Better my death than my life" (4:8ef).

Dialogue. God, however, is not persuaded. Having earlier interpreted Jonah's death wish as an expression of anger, the divine teacher and rhetorician returns to the subject. The interrogative mode focuses on a specific object: "Is it good it burns to you about the plant?" (4:9a). Coming after the sun has smote Jonah, the question is not about the plant as plant but about its withered effect upon him. This time around, unlike his former reaction to God's question about his anger, Jonah does not exit, and he does not change the subject. He stays put and he answers. First, he turns the divine interrogative into his own indicative. "It is good it burns to me." Next he escalates the value of his anger to match his wish, declaring that anger is good "unto death." These are Jonah's last words.

But his last words neither settle the matter nor end the story. Yahweh persists with a third question. Its meaning and efficacy depend upon the declarative sentence that prefaces it (4:10). The sentence begins with an independent clause reporting what was previously omitted, namely, the response of Jonah to the demise of the plant as plant. "You, you pitied the plant," says Yahweh. New to the story, the verb "pity" (*hûs*) connotes sympathy toward another. In the Hebrew Bible, the range of meanings for *hûs* includes compassion, benevolence, and mercy.[4]

The report of Jonah's pity differs tellingly from its surroundings. On the first occasion (4:6), when Yahweh appointed the plant, Jonah delighted in it because it provided him shade. That response was self-serving. On the third occasion (4:8), when the sun beat upon his head, Jonah became angry about the plant because it no longer provided him shade. That response was also self-serving. In between these two self-referential occasions, when a worm killed the plant, the response of Jonah was not recorded (4:7). Now at the end of the story, Yahweh supplies the missing information: "You, you pitied the plant ...." The gap in the story closes.

The delayed information enlarges the character portrayal of Jonah to suggest that there is more to him than a stereotype of disobedience and self-interest. Unlike the responses of delight and anger, his "pity" for the plant is not self-serving. It is disinterested compassion. Moreover, it indicates a view of nature that is not utilitarian but intrinsic. Jonah showed sympathy for the withered plant apart from the effect of the withering upon him. He acknowledged the integrity of the botanical creature.

The valuing of the plant as plant continues in the two relative clauses of Yahweh's declarative sentence. First, Yahweh reminds Jonah that he did not cause the plant to be great: "which you did not cause to be great." Jonah neither created nor nurtured it. Rather, it grew up independently of human ministrations. Second, Yahweh gives a poignant characterization of its miraculous yet short life: "which a child of the night became and a child of the night perished." To call the plant a "child" (*bin*) accords it the status of human creatures, a status already accorded the animals of Nineveh. Further, to link the childhood of the plant to the night bespeaks the mysteries of its origin and destiny. Night is both its cradle and its coffin. That time gives the plant a habitat apart from the dawn with its killer worm.

In the ecology of the story, the utilitarian plant acquires intrinsic worth. For a brief while, Jonah himself acknowledged the worth. He pitied the plant. Though subsequently he abandoned that understanding as he suffered from the beating sun, Yahweh now claims it to instruct him.

A Third Question. By supplying new information and articulating a new stance toward nature, Yahweh's declarative sentence forms the premise for the third divine question to Jonah (4:11). It bears the same structure as the declarative, an independent clause followed by two relative clauses. The argument moves from the small to the large: from the plant, a natural setting, to Nineveh, an urban environment, and from Jonah's response, human pity, to Yahweh's response, divine pity.

In the independent clause Yahweh argues, "And I, shall not I pity Nineveh the great city …?" The verb that is new for Jonah is likewise new for Yahweh. Nowhere else has the deity shown pity (*ḥûs*), for Nineveh or for anything. And nowhere else has the deity been characterized as the God who pities. In a *quid pro quo* arrangement, God repented because Nineveh repented (3:10). But here the language shifts to a theology not dependent upon deeds of repentance. "Shall not I pity Nineveh, the great city …?" Having just reminded Jonah that he did not cause the plant to become "great," Yahweh uses the adjectival form of the verb "become great" for Nineveh, which, throughout the story, has indeed been "the great city" (cf. 1:2; 3:2). Greatness links the ephemeral plant and the perdurable city.

In the relative clauses that follow, Yahweh continues to build analogies between the plant and Nineveh. The first clause, about the population of the city "which has many more than 120,000 humans (*'ādām*)," stands in parallel to the great size of the plant. The use of the Hebrew word *'ādām* for the people of Nineveh repeats the word used in the salutation of the royal decree (3:7–8). There "the earthling" connected with the animal; here "the earthling" connects with the plant. Similarly, the second clause, about the ignorant population of the city "who do not know their right hand from their left," stands in parallel to the childlike plant. With structural and analogous precision, Yahweh builds an argument for divine pity toward Nineveh that is based on Jonah's human pity for the plant: "And I, shall not I pity Nineveh the great city which has in it many more than 120,000 earthlings (*'ādām*) who do not know their right hand from their left ...?"

Outside this balanced structure, a coda completes the analogy with an ecological note. It extends Yahweh's pity to animals: "... many more than 120,000 earthlings who do not know their right hand from their left and animals many?" In the divine vocabulary, Nineveh is a socionatural setting with humans by the thousands and animals galore. The urban environment embraces the natural environment. After all, the animals had once joined the humans to repent and turn from violence (3:7b–9). Now Yahweh confirms what the king of Nineveh knew: that in issues of life and death animals matter alongside people. They matter so much that they receive the end-stress of the story. Its last words are "animals many."

Yahweh's rhetoric of pity departs, however, from the reasoning of the king who proposed a theology of human repentance tied to the possibility of divine repentance. Yahweh's rhetoric of pity also departs from the theology of violence that shaped the narrative of the sea. These departures relate to a change in recalcitrant Jonah, a change that signals the integrity of creation. He pitied the plant as plant, thereby becoming the model for Yahweh to pity Nineveh. Jonah's sensibility toward the natural world is the premise for divine sensibility toward the urban environment. At its close, a book replete with miraculous happenings surprisingly argues from natural rather than revealed theology. An ecology of pity becomes the paradigm for a theology of pity.

But is this pity also a theology of caprice? (see Cooper 1993). If, at the close, Yahweh shows compassion on Nineveh not because it has repented but simply because Yahweh chooses to show compassion, then what assurance is offered that on another occasion the deity might not respond with destruction? If the plant is pitied only after it withers, then what does pity for Nineveh imply about the future of the city? The questions become even more threatening when one recalls that the premise for divine pity is Jonah's pity. And how reliable is Jonah?

VI. CONCLUSION

To sound the depths of the book of Jonah is to find a tempest in the text more threatening than all the scholarly storms that have surrounded it. The story does not lend itself to gentle themes, facile summaries, and tidy resolutions. In it the divine character vacillates between weal and woe, the creation groans and travails, and the outcome for Nineveh remains questionable. Sovereignty, freedom, retribution, vindictiveness, violence, repentance, mercy, pity, and caprice sound major dissonances. Theologically and ecologically the book stirs up unsettling matters only to leave them unsettled. It does not conclude but rather stops with the rhetoric of the divine interrogative. Therein lies its terror and our hope. After all, we are Jonah outside the text, and we hold the power of an answer to Yahweh's question.

NOTES

1. This study first appeared as P. Trible, "A Tempest in a Text: Ecological Soundings in the Book of Jonah," *Theology Digest* 43/4 (Winter, 1996) 303–12 and is used by permission. Unless documented otherwise, this study draws upon research in Trible (1994: 107–225; 1996: 461–529).
2. On the cities Nineveh, Tarshish, and Joppa, see Sasson (1990: 70–71, 78–80).
3. For an interpretation of this incident in reference to violence and its resolution, see Girard (1977: 312–15).
4. E.g., Gen 45:16–20; Ezek 16:5; 20:17; cf. Fretheim (1977: 49–50), Wagner (1980).

REFERENCES

Cooper, A.
  1993   In Praise of Divine Caprice: The Significance of the Book of
              Jonah. Pp. 144–63 in *Among the Prophets: Language, Image
              and Structure in the Prophetic Writings,* eds. P. R. Davies and
              D. J. A. Clines. Sheffield: JSOT.

Fretheim, T. E.
  1977   *The Message of Jonah: A Theological Commentary.* Minne-
              apolis: Augsburg.

Girard, R.
  1977   *Violence and the Sacred.* Trans. P. Gregory, from French. Bal-
              timore: The Johns Hopkins University.

Marcus, D.
  1995   *From Balaam to Jonah: Anti-prophetic Satire in the Hebrew
              Bible.* Atlanta: Scholars.

Melville, H.
  1961   *Moby Dick or The White Whale.* New York: The New Ameri-
              can Library.

Miles, J. A.
  1975   Laughing at the Bible: Jonah as Parody. *Jewish Quarterly Re-
              view* 65: 168–81.

Sasson, J. M.
  1990   *Jonah: A New Translation with Introduction, Commentary, and
              Interpretations.* Anchor Bible 24B. New York: Doubleday.

Trible, P.
  1994   *Rhetorical Criticism: Context, Method, and the Book of Jonah.*
              Minneapolis: Fortress.
  1996   The Book of Jonah: Introduction, Commentary, and Reflections.
              Pp. 461–529 in *The New Interpreter's Bible.* Vol. 7, ed. L. Keck
              et al. Nashville: Abingdon.

Wagner, S.
  1980   *chûs.* Pp. 271–77 in *Theological Dictionary of the Old Testa-
              ment.* Vol. 4, eds. G. J. Botterweck and H. Ringgren. Grand
              Rapids, MI: Eerdmans.

13 The Place of Jonah in the History of Biblical Ideas

BARUCH A. LEVINE

E ach year, the entire Book of Jonah is read aloud in Jewish synagogues as part of the afternoon service of the Day of Atonement, Yom Kippur. The story of Jonah epitomizes the power of repentance, and serves to reassure the worshipers that God's arm is extended to receive them. Even the cruelest of Israel's ancient enemies, the Assyrians of Nineveh, were spared by God when they and their king heeded the admonitions of the Israelite prophet, Jonah, and turned back from their evil ways.

Since late antiquity, certain questions about the story of Jonah have puzzled commentators, who, like George Landes, the persistent scholar being honored here, have struggled to find the key to its interpretation.[1] What will follow are some reflections on certain themes in the book of Jonah that have crystallized in my thinking over many Days of Atonement and semesters of teaching, and through dialogue with learned colleagues. Recent studies have reawakened interest in this fascinating composition, replete as it is with wisdom themes, and brimming with intertextual allusions.[2]

I. THE EDUCATION OF A PROPHET

Among the several themes informing the Book of Jonah there is a pedagogic, or therapeutic message directed to the reader (or listener), one of psychological and moral import. The tale of Jonah dramatizes the contrast between self-awareness and self-denial. The role of God is that of the divine pedagogue, one often attributed to him in biblical literature and even more so in post-biblical Midrash. God's actions become meaningful not only for themselves, but because they teach humans his ways; they serve as object-lessons. God's behavior, always to be emulated, emerges as a model of the highest capacities of the human spirit, the best that is in us. For humans to be aware of the best in themselves requires, however, overcoming what we, these days, refer to simply as "denial." So long as we continue to deny that we have done wrong, repentance is impossible. But we must also cease to deny our innate goodness, our capacity to change for the better. It is this capacity to change that makes repentance at all possible. To promote such self-awareness, to jog humans out of their complex denials, biblical wisdom literature places God in the role of the experimental mentor who subjects certain of his creatures to intense, often painful experiences that force them to confront their inner feelings. This is what happened to Jonah, and recounting his experience is intended to encourage us to see in ourselves the capacity for love and human kindness that makes it possible to change course, to return to the right path. We are to learn from Jonah's experience.

The central enigma of the story comes at the end of chapter three, where we read that God spared Nineveh, relenting about the destruction he had decreed for the city. Inevitably, the key to the Jonah story is to account for the prophet's overwhelming distress at this news. This is, in fact, the burden of the fourth chapter, whose literary analysis is admittedly complicated. Notwithstanding, there can be no misreading Jonah's own interpretation of his distress as the author attributes it to his leading character. Jon 4:2 paraphrases Exod 34:6–7 on the subject of God's attributes of mercy and forbearance, a resonance already present in Jon 3:9–10, and which strongly recalls Joel 2:13–14. God is *ḥannûn wĕraḥûm ʾerek ʾappayim wĕrab-ḥesed wĕniḥām ʿal-hārāʿâ* ("gracious and merciful, slow to anger and abundant in lovingkindness, who relents of doing harm"). Being aware of these attributes of God, the prophet becomes incredibly angry and depressed, wishing for his own death. What he had always known had now been realized: Because the God of Israel is merciful and forgiving he had allowed Nineveh to be spared.

One of several, traditional Jewish interpretations explains that Jonah foresaw what the Assyrians would do to his own people, Israel, in days to come and was distressed that he was making God's mercy available to these potential enemies through the fulfillment of his prophetic mission. This apprehension would account for his attempted flight in the first instance: He could not bear to bring a message of repentance to perhaps the cruelest of Israel's future enemies.[3]

This interpretation bears the stamp of homiletical hindsight, and would require us to assign an unrealistically early date to the book of Jonah, one which I doubt can withstand critical examination. In a related manner, Yehezkel Kaufmann's modern espousal of an early date for the composition of Jonah, one preceding the rise of the Neo-Assyrian empire, and before its threat to northern Israel and Judah became real, is contradicted by linguistic and cultural considerations (Kaufmann 1967: 279–87). But, leaving aside the predictive theme in the traditional interpretation we must admit that its major thrust is symmetrical. It is an effort to answer both of the reader's (or listener's) queries on the same basis, and it reinforces the statement of Jon 4:2 that from the outset Jonah knew what to expect and for this reason had sought flight to Tarshish. That Jonah should have been distressed at the sparing of Israel's enemies is taken by the later tradition as an indication of his love for his people and his land. The prophet was angry with God for failing to prevent an outcome devastating to his own people by mercifully allowing the Assyrians to avert divine punishment.

In such terms, how are we to understand the lesson of the gourd (Jon 4:6–11)? The final didactic words of the book of Jonah make the point that just as human beings are innately compassionate so is God, and that the prophet was wrong to have been distressed over the sparing of Nineveh. The lesson of the gourd teaches that the people of Nineveh are also God's creatures, men, women and small children too young to know their right hand from their left, and that the gates of repentance are open to them. Proverbially, the most wicked of humans are capable of changing for the better. That being so, it would not have been insightful, or morally proper for the prophet to have evaded his mission even out of concern for his own people. Jonah's attitude had been based on a misunderstanding of God's true posture with respect to his creatures, and on a misunderstanding of human nature, as well. He required painful education, and this would not be long in coming.

Despite the persuasiveness of this traditional interpretation in illuminating Jonah's lesson, a hypothetical argument against it can still be raised along the following lines. If, indeed, the Assyrians had repented at an early period, they might never have become an evil empire and would not have later constituted a danger to Israel. Should not the prophet have hoped, therefore, in anticipation, that his admonitions would be effective? But, the Jewish sages may have been more skeptical than we realize. Perhaps their message was, precisely, that the message of the book of Jonah is naive; that repentance may work for a time under immediate threats, but that people who are wicked at the core usually revert to their former state once they are spared, that the lasting lessons of experience are not easily learned or applied. In fact, a Midrashic tradition has it that after forty days the people of Nineveh actually reverted to their wicked ways (see Ginzberg 1913: 246–53). It was typical of the Jewish sages to doubt the sincerity of repentance. To quote their own words: "One who says: 'I will sin and then repent, sin and then repent,' is never afforded sufficient opportunity to achieve repentance'" (see the Babylonian Talmud, *Yômā* ʾ85b). Moreover, such skepticism is not limited to post-biblical thinking. Ezekiel also speaks of similar recidivism (Ezek 3:20–21; 18:21–23). Nevertheless, such attitudes directly clash with the tenor of the book of Jonah, itself, which, whether we judge it to be naive or not, clearly thinks well of people, including non-Israelite people.   And so, we are left with our original queries.

In the search for answers we return to the scene on the ship, narrated in the first chapter. This scene has more to do with the message of repentance than has usually been assumed. I have found no comparable set of human attitudes expressed anywhere in the Hebrew Bible. Here we have people of diverse nationalities who are literally "in the same boat." They share a common belief in divine power, which overrides their differing religious and national identities. They do not doubt that the deity worshiped by any of them had the power to cause a storm at sea. Their initial complaint against Jonah was, precisely, that he was not doing his part in appeasing his god, who might, for all they knew, be the one responsible for their perilous situation. When prayer failed, those aboard turned to an acknowledged strategy of ancient peoples: The expiation of an offense through the surrender of the offender to the proper divine power. There can be no expiation until the offender has been punished and the deity appeased. The offender was identified, or trapped, if you will, by casting lots, and the lot revealed that Jonah was the offender, and that his God had whipped up the storm.

Some of what happened next is unusual to find in a biblical tale. True, it is not unusual in the biblical literary tradition for gentiles to acknowledge the awesome power of Israel's God, *in extremis* (though their pronouncement of sacrificial vows stretches matters a bit!), but it is exceptional to find people of different nations making such efforts to save a Hebrew from death, at great risk to themselves, after his guilt had been established, and after he, himself, had come clean in acknowledging it. The reader is impressed that these are good people; the author of Jonah leaves no doubt on that score. One could even say that the people on the ship, by hesitating to act on the result of their oracular determinations, were deviating from the accepted predicates of religious behavior. After all, they weren't pleading for the life of an innocent man, and yet, in Jon 1:14, they say that his death at their hands would constitute *dām nāqî*ʾ "innocent blood," a characterization elsewhere reserved for the death of the truly innocent. Could it be that the author of Jonah wants the reader (or listener), at this early point in the story, to regard Jonah's confession of his own guilt and his acknowledgment of God's power (Jon 1:9, 12) as acts of repentance that should have entitled him to be spared? And further: Could this be Jonah's first lesson by the divine pedagogue; was the prophet supposed to learn something about himself from the extraordinary demonstration of human compassion by those aboard ship? Did he learn something from this experience, after all?

A piece of Jewish folklore I first heard in my youth, and for which I do not know the source, goes something like this: "What a strange story Jonah is! Throughout our history, the nations of the world have repeatedly caused us suffering on account of our religious beliefs and our national identity; they have expelled us from many lands and cast us into the sea. We pleaded with them to spare us, but they would not heed our voice. But listen to Jonah and consider his gentile shipmates! He identifies himself as a Hebrew who worships the God of heaven, fully acknowledges his guilt, and pleads with the passengers and crew to cast him overboard so as to save themselves. What do these gentiles do? They call upon Jonah's God to spare him, try bravely to reach the shore, and finally, in desperation, ask forgiveness for doing what they had to do!"

Jonah is spared for the while; God assigns the great fish the task of swallowing him. One could say that God spared Jonah because his job was not done, because words pronounced by God do not return unless they have attained their mark (Isa 55:11). Or, without opposing this notion, one could suggest that God had accepted Jonah's repentance. But, did Jonah understand the power of human repentance at this point in the story?

Whoever deserves our thanks for composing the psalm of chapter two, or for inserting it as an available psalm, or for adapting the same, left us subtle clues: Jonah had sought to flee from God's presence (Jon 1:3), but now, crying out to God from the belly of the fish, he longed for that very presence (Jon 2:5). So, the prophet did learn something about God from his near-death experience: He now realized that escape from God's reach was impossible. As one who had tried to get beyond the range of God's voice he now hoped that God would hear his voice from Sheol (Jon 2:3). Significantly missing from the psalm, however, is any clue that Jonah had learned something about the power of human repentance, or that his perception of his role as a prophet had changed. He had been spared by a merciful God for reasons unclear to him, so that when God reiterated his charge, Jonah knew better than to disobey a second time.

Although we are left up in the air as the story of Jonah ends, it seems that its author wanted us to conclude that the parable of the gourd got through to Jonah. It is often the case that biblical narratives conclude with an unanswered query, or leave a situation unresolved. The absence of any indication to the contrary is taken to imply that the closing statement was meant to stand. A classic example is the dialogue between Moses and his Midianite father-in-law, Hobab (Num 10:29–36). Moses urged his father-in-law to join up with the Israelites on their journey to Canaan, stressing his need of Hobab's familiarity with the desert, and promising to deal generously with him in the new land. Hobab declines, but Moses persists, repeating his offer in Num 10:32. But the very next verse, Num 10:33, merely relates that "they" journeyed on for three days, leaving it unresolved whether or not Hobab had, indeed, decided to join up with them. The reader is to assume that this is what occurred, although nothing that follows makes this outcome explicit.

Jonah was now a different man. He had failed to respond to the kindness of others, or to God's kindness, but he finally responded to his own inner feelings of compassion. But, we are getting ahead of the story!

Had Jonah indeed responded on the first two counts, he would not have been so upset at the expectation of Nineveh's repentance; he would have rather welcomed it. It is clear, therefore, that as chapter three of Jonah begins, Jonah is the same man that he was before, except that he is now more realistic about his own position. He knows that he must carry out his prophetic charge. In Jon 4:3 we read that the prophet beseeches God to take his life, for it would be better to be dead. The key verb is Hebrew *ḥ-r-ḥ* (v.1), which may be merely an alternate realization of geminate *ḥ-r-r* "to be heated, to flare up." Idiomatic *lāmmâ ḥārâ lĕkā*, "Why have you become so agitated?," and variations of the same occur several times outside of Jonah (Gen 4:6; 2 Sam 19:43; 22:8// Ps 18:8, and so forth). The image seems to be that of flared nostrils, as indicated by the frequent idiom *ḥārâ ʾap* "the nostrils flared up." This idiom describes reactions to a complex of related emotions, though rejection seems to be at the core of them. Thus, Cain felt severely rejected after his offerings had been rejected by God (Gen 4:5–6). Rejection also accounts for the angry response of the northern Israelites when they felt that David and the Judeans had slighted them (2 Sam 19:21–44). David speculates that Saul might become enraged at the thought that he was plotting against him, and for this reason failed to appear at the New Moon feast (1 Sam 20:5–8).

If rejection, or abandonment by God was Jonah's dominant response as he monitored the actions of the people of Nineveh and their king, then we may characterize his understanding of his prophetic role and of his relationship to God in the following terms: The true prophet is one sent by God bearing a reliable message, and when what he or she has predicted actually happens, all recognize the legitimacy of the prophet through whom God has spoken, and all acknowledge God's power. If, however, a prophet was disproved by unfolding events, it is a sign either that the spirit of prophecy had left him or her, or that the person claiming to be a true prophet was a charlatan. A Midrashic tradition has it that Jonah actually suffered from a bad reputation; that he had once predicted the destruction of Jerusalem only to be discredited by the people after Jerusalem's repentance. He then became known as "the false prophet" (Ginzberg 1913: 246–53). In effect, this Midrash imputes to the people the same perception as it does to Jonah, himself.

This view of prophecy is not unknown in biblical thinking. Thus, Deut 18:21–22 states: "And should you say to yourself: 'How shall we recognize the oracle (as one) which YHWH has not spoken?' What the prophet speaks in the name of YHWH but does not happen, nor does it come about, that is the oracle that YHWH has not spoken. The prophet spoke it brazenly; you need not be in fear of him." Beyond this pragmatic test, meant to apply between the Israelites and their would-be prophets, there is the further consideration that Jonah was sent to a foreign city as a prophet of doom. This might explain how it is that as chapter four begins, we find Jonah dejected and angry as he observes the people of Nineveh acting effectively to avert God's decree. The fact that his unreliability had been exposed among a gentile population might have added to his depression, as well as the likelihood that he may have been less willing to save the Ninevites than he would have been to be of help to his own people. To put it bluntly: Jonah felt that God had "set him up."

This raises the question as to whether we ever encounter in biblical literature, in the genre usually referred to as "oracles against the nations," an Israelite prophet of doom who holds forth the prospect of repentance to foreign nations and peoples, those whose sins and crimes, and often their acts against Israel, specifically, would have expectedly sealed their doom. One searches hard for such mitigation of the divine decree in oracles against the nations. It would, therefore, be reasonable for an Israelite prophet to be angry over a rescue mission to Nineveh. In fact, there were occasions when Israelite prophets were angry even when called upon to offer rescue to their own people! Moses initially resisted the mission of liberating the Israelites from Egypt with repeated objections (Exod 3:10–11, 13; 4:13), and he was subsequently distressed over it (Exod 5:22–23). Jeremiah was very frightened initially when called, so that strong assurances were necessary (Jer 1:6–9, 17–19). What is more, he cried out continually, accusing God of having seduced him into submission, rendering him unable to resist the fire burning within him (Jer 20:7–10). He cursed the day of his birth (Jer 20:14–18).

In this connection, it is striking how dramatically the oration against Nineveh preserved in Nahum, chapter 1, contrasts in tone with the story of Jonah. There, the God of Israel is characterized as wrathful and destructive, and there is no thought of his ever forgiving Nineveh. What is most suggestive is the resonance of Exod 34:6–7 in Nah 1:2–3. Above, we saw how Jon 4:2 had resonated the same version of divine attributes so as to dramatize God's willingness to forgive. In contrast, Nahum's horrendous oracle of doom is construed to produce the opposite characterization: "A passionate and vengeful deity is YHWH (*ʾēl qannôʾ wĕnōqēm YHWH*); YHWH is vengeful and possessed of wrath (*ûba ʿal ḥēmâ*); YHWH is vengeful towards his foes and he retains his anger towards his enemies. YHWH is slow to anger and forbearing in power (*YHWH ʾerek ʾappayim ûgĕdol kōaḥ*), but he will surely not exonerate (*wĕnaqqēh lōʾ yĕnaqqeh*).

To put it bluntly: God allowed the Assyrians to gain enormous power and domination; he took his time bringing them down, being, as we know, long forbearing. But now, the time had finally come, and at this point, there was no escaping God's terrible punishment. The deferral of punishment, viewed as a sign of divine mercy in Exodus, here becomes a liability. Seizing on the "down side" of Exod 34:6–7, and picking up the theme of passion from the continuation of Exod 34:14, the author of Nahum rather invidiously turned on the attribute of divine patience, which, as regards Nineveh, worked to the ultimate ruin of that imperial capital. Whereas the inevitable consequence expressed as *wĕnaqqēh lōʾ yĕnaqqeh* in Exod 34:7 meant, originally, that notwithstanding God's mercifulness, there could be no escape from accountability for transgression, the author of Nahum voiced that caveat with extreme emphasis. Although extreme even for an oracle against the nations, Nahum, chapter 1, produces more of what we would expect in terms of likely attitudes toward the Neo-Assyrian empire in biblical literature.

Perhaps the closest we come to the vision of penitent gentiles is in the late prophecies preserved in Isaiah 19. This chapter presents several interpretive and historical problems, and yet its oracles progress in a recognizable pattern: Egypt's doom is predicted (Isa 19:1–15), as is the hegemony of Israel over Egypt, and the acknowledgment of the power of Israel's God among the Egyptians (Isa 19:16–21). Among other things, Egyptians will worship the God of Israel sacrificially and pronounce vows that they will duly fulfill. After the Egyptians will be alternately battered by Israel's God and granted respite by him (an echo of the saga of the ten plagues), they will finally "turn back to YHWH" (*wĕšābû ʿad-YHWH*), who will hear their entreaty and bring them well being (Isa 19:22). Then we read the following:

> On that day, there will be a highway leading from Egypt to Assyria; Assyrians will come into Egypt, and Egyptians into Assyria, but the Egyptians will be tributary to Assyria.
> On that day, Israel will constitute the third party alongside Egypt and Assyria. A blessing shall be pronounced by

YHWH of the Heavenly Hosts in the midst of the earth, as
follows: "Blessed is my people, Egypt, and the work of my
hands, the Assyrians, and my possession, Israel" (Isa
19:23–25).

Without attempting to identify the *Sitz-im-Leben* of these oracles
precisely, which, even if it were possible, would take us far afield, it is
obvious that they have something in common with the perceptions that
inform the book of Jonah. The Egyptians will repent sincerely only
after many beatings, whereas the people of Nineveh will repent as an
immediate response to Jonah's oracle of doom. A telling link with Jonah
comes in the characterization: *ûma ʿăśēh yāday ʾaššûr*, "and my creatures, the Assyrians" (Isa 19:25), which recalls God's explanation of
the parable of the gourd: "You would have spared (*ʾattâ ḥastā ʿal-*)
the gourd, over which you did not toil (*ʾăšer lōʾ- ʿāmaltā bô*), nor did
you raise it; which came into being in a night and perished in a night.
Should I not spare Nineveh, that populous town where many more
then twelve myriads of human beings reside, who cannot tell between
their right arm and their left, and much cattle?" (Jon 4:10–11).

It is precisely the factor of repentance, so dominant in the late prophecies in Isaiah 19, which helps explain why Jonah would not have understood initially how an Israelite prophet might be the instrument of
rescue for the gentiles. Jonah's conversion to a belief in repentance
occurred only after the lesson of the gourd, as we shall see presently.
When he arrived at Nineveh, Jonah was still the traditional prophet of
doom, so that when his prediction of Nineveh's destruction did not
come true, he was devastated.

The divine pedagogue then staged a situation that aroused in Jonah
strong feelings of loss. The gourd that had given him shade from the
scorching sun and brought him pleasure withered away as fast as it had
grown. His pain at this loss was too real to deny. In the mode of a
caring teacher, God verbalized Jonah's own feelings. The care that
others, probably strangers, had shown toward him aboard the ship, and
the care that God had shown toward him in the depths of the sea had
failed to induce compassion in Jonah. What did get through to Jonah
was the awareness that he, himself, had felt intense loss, and he was
given to understand that God also experiences loss at the death of his
creatures. The choice of a withering plant by the author of Jonah to

epitomize the transitory character of human life was not incidental; it is a frequent simile in biblical wisdom literature. Like grass and aftergrowth, the human creature withers away before we know it, as if in a single day (Pss 37:2; 90:5; 103:15). Jonah's gourd vanished in a single night!

This is as much as can be said for now about Jonah's education as a prophet, about his inner development. I realize that I have not adequately accounted for the issues at stake in his relationship with God. This will require us to explore the premises of biblical prophecy further, and to examine the theme of repentance itself. Beyond both human and divine compassion is the dynamism of human behavior and its effect on God.

II. REPENTANCE AS EMPOWERMENT: A VARIABLE IN THE HUMAN-DIVINE RELATIONSHIP

Yehezkel Kaufmann (1967: 279–87), whose literary-historical assignment of the book of Jonah to an early date must be rejected on critical grounds, is the very scholar who has clarified for me how consequentially the theme of repentance functions in certain biblical sources, while it is conspicuously absent from others. He does so, in the first instance, by contrasting the story of Jonah with the narrative preserved in Gen 18:20–32 on the overturning of Sodom and Gomorrah. In utter contrast to Jonah, who seeks to evade a mission of mercy, Abram, unsolicited, petitions God to spare the twin towns of wickedness if only a few righteous citizens could be found residing in them.

The dictional link between the two narratives is localized in the verb h-p-k "to overturn." Significantly, destruction depicted as "overturning" (Hebrew hăpēkâ, mahpēkâ) and conveyed by forms of the verb h-p-k is said chiefly with reference to Sodom and Gomorrah (Gen 19:25, 29, Deut 29:22; Isa 1:6–7; 13:19; Jer 49:18; 50:40; Amos 4:11) and Nineveh: "Forty days from now Nineveh is to be overturned (wĕnînĕwēh nehpāket)"(Jonah 3:4).[4] By innuendo, Sodom and Gomorrah are probably the indefinite referents in Jer 20:16, as well. The thematic, or intertextual link between the Book of Jonah and Genesis 18 is in the expression kî-ʿālĕtâ rāʿātām lĕpānāy, "for their evildoing has ascended to me" (Jon 1:2). Compare Gen 18:20–21: "Then YHWH said: 'The outcry of Sodom and Gomorrah has truly become great, and their offense is grievous. I must descend in order to ascertain whether they have irreversibly committed what their outcry reaching me (*habbā ᵓâ ᵓēlay*) [indicates they have], and if not, I will know [that as well].'" (Also see Gen 19:13.)

What this means is that the wickedness of Nineveh, like that of Sodom and Gomorrah, was an internal matter primarily affecting the people of these towns themselves. There is no indication of hostility on the part of the Ninevites toward Israel; in fact, no relationship with Israel is ever intimated. As is the case with the oracle of Nahum, in the book of Jonah the people of Nineveh are never identified as Assyrians, nor is Nineveh ever referred to as the capital of the Assyrian state, or empire, although in Nahum there are clear allusions to conquest and imperial domination that are suggestive in this regard. In a similar vein, there is no indication in the narratives of Sodom and Gomorrah of hostility between the Canaanites of these towns and the clan of Abram, who was actually allied with their kings in the war against the invading forces (Genesis 14). The aggressive xenophobia exhibited by the Sodomites toward strangers, like that of the residents of Gibeah (Judges 19), was clearly a reflection of the perverseness and demoralization of their own community, and the same was undoubtedly true of the crimes of the Ninevites.

In this connection, it is significant that the greatest crime of all that a king can commit is one against his own land and people. In the dramatic *māšāl* against the king of Babylon (Isa 14:3–20), historically the king of Assyria, of course, he is charged with vast destruction of other lands, of turning the known world into a desert. But his most horrendous crime is what he brought upon his own land and people: " You shall not be united with them (= with all the kings of the earth) in burial for you have destroyed your own land; you have slain your own people" (Isa 14:20). Once again, we are talking about Assyrians.

Kaufmann notes two differences between the story of Jonah and the narratives of Sodom and Gomorrah. The first may be referred to as the "terms of engagement" between the human and the divine, and the second as the presence, or absence of repentance as a dynamic factor. According to Kaufmann, Abram appealed to God's justice when the latter was moved by wrath, whereas Jonah demanded justice from God when the latter was moved by compassion. Thus Abram: "Shall the judge of all the earth fail to act justly?" (Gen 18:25). And thus Jonah:

"For I know that you are a gracious and compassionate God, slow to anger and abundant in steadfast love, who relents of doing harm" (Jon 4:2).

But this difference, in and of itself, falls short of yielding an understanding of the story of Jonah as it is told, and is mild compared with the second difference discussed by Kaufmann. He correctly focuses on repentance as the crucial variable in the human divine relationship. The Sodom and Gomorrah narratives project only limited human options. They belong with a genre of encounter narratives where the disposition of the appeal is left to God. Humans may beseech God for mercy on any number of grounds, or outdo themselves in appeasing him by prayer and sacrifice. They may appeal to his justice, as did Abram, or, like Moses on several occasions, they may appeal to God's good name, to his wish to be acknowledged by the nations as reliable and all powerful, or as merciful and forgiving. But there is no suggestion that the people of Sodom and Gomorrah might be spared if they repented and turned back from evil. It is never suggested that humans are empowered with the means to annul a divine decree in this way, and if sincerely repentant, that they could count on God's merciful response. Even the "call" of Jonah to the people of Nineveh (Jon 2:4) merely announces a prediction of doom, but says nothing about a way to avert such an outcome through repentance. The reader may be a little surprised to read that the wicked people of Nineveh placed credence in the prediction, but one is even less prepared for the surprise of their repentance.

The author of Jonah introduces the theme of repentance through three key words that define the human-divine relationship. The first is the noun *rāʿâ*, which enjoys a range of connotations including "evildoing, harm, suffering." The second is the verb *šûb*, "to return, turn back." The third applies only to God and is conveyed by the verb *n-ḥ-m*, " to relent, have a change of heart." As the story begins, the *rāʿâ* "evildoing" of the Ninevites had reached God (Jon 1:2). Later, they were to renounce their *rāʿâ* and "turn back" (*šûb*) to the true path: The text of Jon 3:5–4:1 warrants a close reading:

> The citizens of Nineveh placed their trust in God, and proclaimed a fast, and donned sackcloth from their smallest to their greatest. The matter reached the king of Nineveh, who arose from his throne and removed his robe, and covered

himself with sackcloth and he sat upon ashes. He issued a
loud call in Nineveh by order of the king and his lords as
follows: 'Neither man nor beast, herds or flocks may eat
anything; they may not graze or drink. Let them cover themselves with sackcloth and call out to God vociferously. Let
them turn back (*wĕyāšūbû*), each one, from his evil path
(*middarkô hārā'â*) and from the violence that is in their
palms. Who knows but that God will turn back (*yāšûb*) and
relent (*wĕniḥḥam*), and turn back (*wĕšāb*) from his rage,
so that we shall not perish.' Then God observed their deeds,
that they had turned back (*kî-šābû*) from their evil path,
and God relented of the harm (*wayyinnāḥem hā'ĕlōhîm 'al-
hārā'â*) that he had commanded to do to them, and did not
do it. Then Jonah experienced great suffering (*wayyēra'
'el-yônâ rā'â gĕdôlâ*), and he became agitated.

As represented, the people of Nineveh and their king were experi-
menting with God; they were uncertain, initially, whether their con-
trite acknowledgment of wrongdoing and their return to the true path
would induce God to relent, but it did. This is a way of saying that
humans can rely on the efficacy of repentance. The author of Jonah
undoubtedly regarded repentance as a dispensation deriving from God's
love for his creatures and for the world he created. It is a function of
divine mercy, but it goes beyond that. When humans repent they become entitled to divine mercy and forgiveness. Repentance is an empowerment of humankind. In its dynamic, repentance shares the bind-
ing force of vows and of the covenantal relationship. It is a type of
contractual assurance offered by God through his spokesmen, the prophets, that if humans return to the true path, God has undertaken to cancel
their liabilities.

It is not difficult to trace the diction of repentance as expressed in the
passage from Jonah cited above. In addition to the themes already
noted, we have the frequent image of the "path" (Hebrew *derek*). Life
is a path, and people often stray from the right path, or choose the
wrong road on which to continue their journey through life. If, however, at any point they turn back to the right path, they are again headed
in the right direction, and will avert the punishments meted out to those
who have left the right path but who fail to return to it.

The idiom *šûb midderek rā'â*, "turn back from an evil path," is characteristic of Jeremiah (18:11; 25:5; 35:15; 36:3, 7), and it is picked up

by Ezekiel (3:18; 13:22; 33:8–9, 11) and First Zechariah (1:4). (Compare 1 Kgs 13:33; 2 Kgs 17:13, both late redactional passages.) It would not be inaccurate to conclude that it was introduced in the near-exilic or early-exilic period. The role in which Jonah is eventually instructed, and which he initially had failed to comprehend, is very close to that projected for the true prophet in Ezek 3:17–19, where the factor of repentance is likewise crucial:

> Son of man, I have appointed you as a lookout for the House of Israel. When you hear a word from my mouth, you must forewarn them on my behalf. When I announce to the wicked person: 'You shall surely die!'—but you do not forewarn him, and do not speak in order to warn the wicked person away from his wicked path and thereby enable him to live— he, as a wicked person, shall die as punishment for his own sin, but I will requite his blood from you. But, if you did forewarn the wicked person, and yet he did not turn back from his wickedness and from his wicked path, he shall die as punishment for his sin, and you will have saved your own life.

The crucial power of repentance, of true and lasting repentance without reversion to sinfulness, is repeated in Ezekiel 18 in a similar manner. Whereas Ezekiel is defining the role of the Israelite prophet sent by God to his own people, the author of Jonah extends the same prophetic responsibility to prophets on a mission to the nations. This means, among other things, that God was being exceptionally merciful in granting Jonah a second chance, and it also means that God strongly sought to avoid the destruction of Nineveh. Abram's God was not as compassionate!

III. CONCLUSION

The inner agenda of Jonah, and its most insightful idea is that repentance and denial cannot co-exist in human experience. Beyond that, we learn that repentance requires the belief that just as God is capable of overcoming his anger, human beings can do the same; that like God, humans can relent of the harm they intended to do, and if they succeed in this, God will answer "Amen." In a sense, all that happened to Nineveh happened to Jonah, and all that happened to both Nineveh and

Jonah happened to God, or, shall we say, with respect to the conception of God as presented by the author of the book of Jonah.

That Nineveh should be the object of divine compassion is hardly incidental. Again one is reminded of the utopian visions of Isaiah 19, canonically attributed to the Isaiah of eighth century B.C.E. Jerusalem, but which actually derive from a later time. That earlier prophet, Isaiah of Jerusalem, had been most concerned with the role of Jerusalem in an age of world peace. Perhaps the author of Jonah, not unlike those who gave us the late prophecies of Isaiah 19, understood how important would be the role of Nineveh, the capital of the gentiles, in a redeemed world.

NOTES

1. I have profited greatly from George Landes' scholarly work on Jonah, especially his careful examination of linguistic criteria published in the H. M. Orlinsky Volume (Landes 1976). It is a source of personal pleasure to me that the two of us were "bound together" in that volume, where one of my Hebrew studies deals with similar linguistic criteria used in dating the priestly source of the Pentateuch. Over the years, George's addresses to the Columbia Seminar on the Hebrew Bible dealing with the interpretation of Jonah have been particularly enlightening to me.
2. The reader is referred to the expansive commentary by Sasson (1990) for a recent discussion.
3. See Ginzberg (1928: 349 n. 27), for the relevant Midrashic sources.
4. The verb *h-p-k* is used with reference to a destruction but without obvious reference to Sodom and Gomorrah in 2 Sam 10:3; 1 Chr 19:3; Prov 12:7; and Hag 2:22.

REFERENCES

Ginzberg, L.
   1913   *The Legends of the Jews.* Vol. IV. Philadelphia, PA: Jewish Publication Society.
   1928   *The Legends of the Jews.* Vol. VI. Philadelphia, PA: Jewish Publication Society.
Kaufmann, Y.
   1967   *History of the Religion of Israel.* Vol. 2. Jerusalem: Bialik Institute, and Tel-Aviv: Dvir.

Landes, G. M.

1976   Linguistic Criteria and the Date of the Book of Jonah. Pp. 147–70 in *Eretz-Israel* 16 (H. M. Orlinsky Volume). Jerusalem: Israel Exploration Society.

Sasson, J. M.

1990   *Jonah: A New Translation with Introduction, Commentary, and Interpretations.* Anchor Bible 24B. New York: Doubleday.

14 No Small Thing: The "Overturning" of Nineveh in the Third Chapter of Jonah[1]

JOHANNA W. H. VAN WIJK-BOS

I. JONAH AMONG THE INTERPRETERS

The story of Jonah, acknowledged by most commentators today to be a paradigmatic narrative that renders meaning most readily when questions of its historicity are put aside, may be analyzed as a theological lesson. When the question is raised as to the content of this lesson, three main lines of interpretation are discernible in Christian circles. For the first and most traditional understanding, the didactic purpose of Jonah is that it teaches about a God who cares for the entire world, rather than about only the one people, Israel. Universalism versus particularism is the message of Jonah. Frequently assumed to have its setting in the postexilic restoration period, this universalistic message would then stand in stark contrast to the more inward looking, exclusivist attitudes and practices of some circles, such as those of Ezra and Nehemiah, for example. Jonah, in this view, provides a counterpoint to the point made in the restoration period by groups who circled the wagons tightly around the insiders, keeping out the ones who did not belong to the covenant people, who were viewed with hostility as a threat to their well-being.

Within this schema, Jonah as a prophet generally receives a negative judgment from the interpreters. Even for those who acknowledge that the salvation of a city such as Nineveh might be difficult to accept for those who had suffered most from its cruelties, Jonah remains the bigoted representative of a bigoted people: in fact, he is seen as typical in that regard.[2]

This judgment is congruent with a Christian perspective on the restoration period of postexilic Judah that pervaded Christian interpretations of the Bible for a long time. Until very recently, a Wellhausanian view of biblical religion dominated Christian biblical interpretation. In this view, the religion of ancient Israel reached its zenith with the pre-exilic prophets, only to founder on the rocks of a postexilic narrow understanding of religious identity and a rigid conception of the law. According to such a reading, Christianity became the true successor to the religion of ancient Israel, as it had found its highest ethical expression in the pre-exilic prophets. The extremely influential "heilsgeschichtliche Schule," represented by scholars such as Gerhard von Rad—in the U.S. by George E. Wright and John Bright—basically viewed the Old Testament as a record of the failure of a faith community to live up to the demands of its own religion. The influence of this school of thought on generations of teachers and preachers in Christian circles can hardly be underestimated. Naturally, a negative "take" on Jonah fits very well with this understanding. Jonah becomes one more example that bears out the bigotry of the period in which he lived. As a person who refuses to accept the extravagance of God's grace, Jonah stands condemned together with Jonah's people by many a Christian interpreter. The judgment rendered on Jonah, and on Judah of the fifth and fourth centuries, thus leads the Christian community all too easily to continue on a road of prejudice and anti-Jewish sentiment and practice, which paradoxically denies the very spirit of the lesson of grace understood to be the essential message of Jonah.[3]

A second line of interpretation is one that takes seriously the dangers of Christian anti-Judaism and the strictures on Christian biblical interpretation in a post-Holocaust world. The lesson of Jonah remains one of God's grace, but it is grace that is poured out on an entirely unacceptable crowd, since Nineveh represents not only evil in general, but in particular destructive activity against God's people. "Nineveh is the destroyer of Jerusalem, the concentration camp for God's people" (Lacocque and Lacocque 1990: 139). Moreover, in this understanding, the grace and goodwill of God toward Nineveh stand in stark contrast to the sufferings and deprivation of God's people. The question is one of *theodicy*. Jonah's anger is then entirely understandable, since the divine justice exhibited toward Nineveh is unacceptable for the believer, any believer.[4] The closing question of the book takes on a renewed sharpness in this reading. Should God indeed have mercy toward the Ninevehs of this world? And if God is merciful as Jonah claims, then what is an appropriate response on the part of those who are most vulnerable to Nineveh's destructive tendencies?

Yet another line of understanding is followed by those who view the book as a teaching about repentance. George Landes suggests this interpretation in several essays. Landes argues that the central message of Jonah is the provision of a model of repentance for Israel to follow. "The readers are invited to acknowledge what Jonah has refused to accept: that they cannot be continuing recipients of the divine delivering grace without manifesting the fruits of repentance" (Landes 1978: 148; cf. 1976). In reading the book in this manner Landes joins traditional Jewish understandings, which connect Jonah with Yom Kippur.

My presentation in this volume is grounded in a desire to understand Jonah and the message it contains on multiple levels. It is to my mind doubtful whether the search for a single message or The Truth of Jonah will yield a fruitful understanding of this text. At the same time, I repudiate traditional Christian interpretations that see Jonah as a bigoted member of a bigoted faith community, on the principle that any interpretation that has implications that may lead to Auschwitz, even in embryo, is to be eschewed. Such interpretations have murderous implications that "murderers will in time spell out" (Littell 1975: 110). The most productive way to read and understand Jonah, in my opinion, is to acknowledge its abiding ambiguities and to highlight sets of themes and ideas that do not exclude one another (cf. the analysis of Magonet 1983). If I focus here on the theme of repentance, it is in order to underline this theme as *one* of the central ideas that surfaces with significance in Jonah, as well as to honor George Landes and his perspective on the Book of Jonah.

> *Jonah 3:*[5]
> *(1) Then the word of Adonai happened to Jonah a second time:*
> *(2) Arise, go to Nineveh*
> *that great city,*
> *and cry to it the cry*
> *that I myself will speak to you.*
> *(3) Then Jonah arose*

and went to Nineveh
according to the word of Adonai;
and Nineveh was a godawful big city
of three days' walk across.
(4) Then Jonah began to go into the city
one day's walk
and he cried and said:
forty more days and Nineveh will be overturned!
(5) Then they believed, the men of Nineveh, in God;
they cried out a fast,
they dressed in sacks,
from great to small.
(6) And word came to the king of Nineveh,
and he arose from his throne
he took off his robe;
and he covered himself with a sack
and sat in ashes.
(7) And he had it called around in Nineveh:
By decree of the king and his nobles:
No human or beast,
cattle or flock
shall taste a bite,
graze, or drink a drop.
(8) They shall cover themselves with sacks,
human and beast,
and they shall cry mightily to God.
And they shall turn,
everyone from their evil way
and from the violence that is in their hands.
(9) Who knows,
God may turn and repent
and turn from his fierce anger
and we will not perish.
(10) When God saw their deeds
that they turned from their evil ways,
God repented of the evil
he had said to do them
and did not do it.

II. JONAH AMONG THE PROPHETS

Jonah was a prophet. The name of the prophet is that of a "real" prophet, Jonah Ben Amittai, who is mentioned in 2 Kgs 14:25. *That* Jonah Ben Amittai promised restoration, which came to pass in the Northern Kingdom in the early part of the eighth century B.C.E. The name of the city, Nineveh, is "real" also. Nineveh was the capital of Assyria for at least a century in its heyday. Moreover the Book of Jonah is placed within the prophetic section of the literature in the Hebrew Bible. This seems clear enough.

Yet, the classification of Jonah with the rest of the prophetic literature has caused commentators numerous headaches. For Jonah is not a prophet like any of the other "writing" prophets. His name is provided but not the time of his prophecy. He is the only prophet we know of who was asked to prophesy in a foreign country. He is the only prophet that we know of who fled in the opposite direction of the place in which he was to speak. The book named after him consists for the most part of a narrative and has only the merest hint of prophetic speech. The prophet, though chastened and obedient at one stage of the story, returns to his old rebellious self and opposes God once more at the end.

Moreover, the narrative is filled by unusual divine interventions: storm, fish, plant, and worm all conspire to teach Jonah the lesson that we do not know he ever learned. The miraculous aspects are more reminiscent of the Elijah/Elisha material, material with which Jonah has other elements in common. Yet, there is also much to distinguish Jonah from the legends that grew around those two northern prophets. It is hard to make Jonah, both prophet and book, fit interpreters' understandings of prophets and prophecy.

The historical context for the actual composition of the book is another cause for concern. Although scholars generally agree on a postexilic date, there is no agreement on a precise dating. Nor do different time settings guarantee deeper insight. As Jack Sasson (1990) observes ruefully, "In the case of Jonah, whether we place it in the early fifth century or in the late third century B.C.E. we gain little insight either into the text or into the selected period." As if the book has modeled itself on its main character, it turns rebellious and refuses to yield meaning regarding the question of its actual historical context. Perhaps it is time to stop asking historical questions, and to take with utter seriousness the nature of the book as a *māšāl* in a prophetic context.

The canonizers of the Hebrew Bible had apparently no difficulty with placing the book in the midst of the prophetic literature. So, we may do best to understand the teaching of Jonah in the context of prophecy in ancient Israel. This is not to say that "history" has no part to play in our understanding of the book. The "reality" of the eighth-century setting is significant insofar as it provides a background for the reality of prophecy in Israel, embodied in Jonah, as well as for the actual existence of an oppressive, violent Assyria, destructive to Israel, embodied in Nineveh. The reality of violent Nineveh also keeps us mindful of the violence that raged intermittently but regularly against the Israel of the Bible across the centuries of its existence. Moreover, violent Nineveh found its counterparts in subsequent centuries of violence against Judaism and the Jews. The teaching one derives today from Jonah must take this context into account also.

Martin Buber (1949: 104) argued many years ago that the Jonah narrative is the story that reveals the essence of the prophetic task in ancient Israel. "The true prophet," Buber states, "does not announce an immutable decree. He speaks into the power of decision lying in the moment." Thus a proclamation of disaster, such as that of Jonah, according to Buber, is designed to bring about the repentance, or "turning," that it does in Nineveh. Jonah, in Buber's view, is the paradigm of the prophetic nature and task.[6] The audience is not told exactly what Adonai tells Jonah to proclaim to Nineveh, only that he is to "cry" the "cry" that Adonai will tell him. On this command Jonah "cries" that Nineveh will be a ruin in forty days. The prophet cries his cry of disaster, the people must make their decision in the face of his cry. The theme of repentance, then, has its proper setting in the prophetic literature.[7]

Finally, in addition to the context of the Book of Jonah in prophecy, there is the reality of its present placement in the canon. Jonah is wedged between Obadiah, which is in part an announcement of the destruction of Edom, and Micah, which prophecies disaster to befall Jerusalem. Following Micah, Nahum presents a vivid picture of the violence of Nineveh and also declares its doom. These texts may at least raise the question, "But what if ...?" What if the people made a radical turn; would devastation still happen? Jonah sits in the midst of these doomsayers to underscore in its inimitable, satirical way that doom is not immutable. Doom is neither immutable for Edom, nor for Nineveh, nor for Jerusalem. If even Nineveh could turn from its evil ways, how much more so is this a possibility for the community that understands itself to be in covenant with God.

III.   JONAH'S TURN

Jonah 3 provides a drama in three stages.[8] First Adonai instructs Jonah once more to do his job and prophesy in Nineveh, and Jonah does as he is told (vv. 1–4). In the next stage, the Ninevites respond by repentance in word and deed (vv. 5–9). In the last stage, God sees what is going on in Nineveh, and repents in turn, so that nothing comes of the predicted ruin of Nineveh (v. 10). A story that can be restated in simple terms, however, is not always a story simply told, nor is it necessarily a simple story. What are some of the complexities and ambiguities in this section of Jonah?

Jonah means "dove." Jonah Ben Amittai (Jonah 1:1) means "dove son-of-faithfulness." The storyteller uses irony, of course, for here is no faithful proclaimer of God's will but rather a rebel, a run-away, who goes and cries the god-cry to Nineveh only because trying anything else proved futile. Hardly a *son of faithfulness*, this dove. Dove son-of-faithfulness in the days of Jeroboam had promised restoration and it came to pass; this Jonah promises ruin and it does not come to pass. Hardly a *dove*, this son-of-faithfulness. Ironically, as of Jonah 3 when the prophet is faithful, the text omits his "faithfulness" parentage (3:1), highlighting a continuing contrast between name and message.[9]

In the first stage, a series of verbs for speaking and crying dominate. On the word of Adonai Jonah cries out his cry. As already noted, the text provides no information about the congruence of Adonai's instruction and Jonah's words. "Cry to it the cry that I will speak to you" (v. 2) is filled in by "he cried and said: 'Forty more days and Nineveh will be overturned'" (v. 4), leaving ambiguity as to whether this announcement is in actual agreement with the word of Adonai. This gap in information is made more acute because the prophet omits any typical prophetic introduction to his words, such as "Thus says Adonai ...."

Verbs for movement are also central to the passage: combinations of the verbs "arise" (*qûm*), "go/walk" (*hālak*), and "go into" (*bô'*) keep occurring in the first four verses. The final verb of this stage, "overturned" (v. 4), provides a violent climax to the commotion that runs through this episode. The speech/cry coupled with the intensity of movement lends a note of urgency. This urgency is underlined, moreover, by words related to time. "The second time" in verse 1 introduces the time element. The measure of Nineveh is taken in terms of the "days" it takes to "walk" across it, joining time and movement. Jonah "walks" only "one day" and announces the overturn of the city in "forty days." The time spans are clearly symbolic, three days and forty days indicating numbers of special significance. In addition, the word "day" is employed in a mode that moves it from a greater to a smaller number and once again to a greater, this time exceeding the first, thereby creating a sense of interrupted expansion: three days become one day and finally forty days. Three days' walking turns into a one-day's walk, which ends in forty days of total upheaval, or forty days of anticipation before the final upheaval. The text is not clear on the latter and leaves the matter to the imagination.

Finally, "city" and "Nineveh" are central to this section. Together they are mentioned a total of seven times. In addition, the size of the city is underlined the first three times it occurs. First, Nineveh is called "the great city" (cf. 1:2). At the second mention of the city, it may be its monstrous nature that is emphasized together with its dimensions. It is difficult to render *ʿîr gĕdôlâ lēʾlōhîm* of verse 3 in English. Nineveh is not only large, it is godawful big.[10] Nineveh, after all, is a symbol of all the crushing, godawful, monstrous violence that ever beset Israel. Size resurfaces with the more specific mention of the length of time it took to traverse this city: three-days' walking. Monstrous, incredibly awful, incredibly big. Into the midst of this horror goes "dove," striding one day's journey, crying his cry of unmitigated disaster. God has spoken, Jonah has cried, Nineveh will fall.

As virtually every commentator notes, the word that the prophet uses for Nineveh's impending destruction (v. 4) is the same verb employed in the biblical text in a number of places for the annihilation of Sodom and Gomorrah (cf. Gen 19:21, 25, 29; Deut 29:22; Jer 20:16; Lam 4:6). But the root *hpk* can also be used in a positive sense (cf. Exod 14:5, where it is used of a change of heart in human beings).[11] Trible (1994: 180) observes that Jonah's utterance "abounds in unstable properties" and "invites characters and readers to exploit meanings." There will indeed be an "overturning" of Nineveh albeit not in a way that the obvious meaning of the text indicates. As noted, the announcement leaves open when the fall of Nineveh will take place: is it going to be after forty days? Or is it going to be a gradual decline over the next forty days?

IV. NINEVEH'S TURN

The Ninevites, in any case, are not going to wait and see. The first word of verse 5 abruptly cuts into the cry of the prophet, who is not even halfway into his task: *wayya ʾămînû* ("And they believed ..."). To make sure that the listener is aware of just who it is that "believed," the words "the men of Nineveh" are added before the text moves to say "in God." Jonah's cry had not included a call to belief, but the men of Nineveh believe nevertheless. They believe in the one indicated in verse 5 by the general word for deity, *ʾĕlōhîm*, rather than by the sacred Name known to Israel. The important point to make is not that the Ninevites' belief is grounded in a special relationship with Israel's God, but rather that they trust the word of Jonah to be God's word. The Ninevites understand Jonah as prophet to be speaking for God, on God's behalf, and they therefore do not believe in Jonah but in God. Their conviction finds expression in activity: "they cried out a fast." The verb "cry" formally links this stage with the previous one where the same root dominated. This time the object of the cry is a fast, accompanied by appropriate behavior in dress and demeanor. The inhabitants of Nineveh leave nothing to chance and engage to the last person ("from great to small") in this rite.

The opening word of the episode, *wayya ʾămînû* relieves some of the intensity built up in the previous lines, and creates at the same time ambiguity and expectations of its own. By providing no motivation for the instant conversion, in contrast to the instance of the sailors in chapter one (1:16), the text leaves the audience with a permanent gap in its knowledge and draws it directly into the drama that is unfolding.[12] As huge and monstrous as Nineveh's barbaric cruelty had been, so outsized and total is this reversal. If repentance is one of the major themes of the book of Jonah, then nothing but the turning around of one of the most wicked places ever known illustrates the point.

The fact that the initiative for the fast is taken by the people of the city is significant in more ways than one. Of course, the terminology of "great and small" is inclusive in terms of embracing old and young, rich and poor, the mighty and the weak. But also and more importantly, the conversion begins with the populace, rather than with their leaders. The words "from great to small" create an expectant pause. Is the palace included in the "great?" Or, does it remain to be seen whether the palace will join the proceedings? Palaces and administrations are not generally known for heeding the common folk on such a road. It would be all too easy to write off the movement as some kind of mass hysteria. Yet, without the participation of the leadership, chances are that it may all come to nothing.

Only from verse six does it become apparent that the king has yet to become engaged, and as earlier "word" came to Jonah, "word" now reaches the king. Word came from Adonai to Jonah, it went from Jonah to the people, and it goes from the people to the king. (Or, is it from Jonah himself that word finally reaches the king?) The effect on the king is certainly powerful. As the word from Adonai caused Jonah to go into motion ("he arose, he went, he began to go into" [vv. 3–4]), so the word that came to the king sets the king in motion. Similarity does not prevent contrast: unlike Jonah, the king arises in order to sit down. In between these two actions he divests himself of the accouterments of royalty in order to join in the posture of penitence. The first nouns in verse 6 connote royal status: *throne* and *robe*; the second set of nouns conveys acts of penitence that put the king on a level with his people: *sack* and *ashes*. As with Jonah, the king's activities end in speech: Jonah got up to walk and speak, the king gets up to sit down and speak. Thus the word does not stop at the king but comes back to the people, in a proclamation containing further instructions (vv. 7–8). Two negative commands, not eating or drinking, are followed by two positive actions, covering and crying. The fast is made more specific and the inclusivity applies not only to people but also extends to beasts. The stain of Nineveh's violence has spread to the entire community and affects also the ones not responsible, the children and the animals. The children were already included in the popular fast, but the royal leader wisely adds the beasts.[13]

Prayer was a traditional accompaniment of fasting, so perhaps we may assume it was included in the fast called by the Ninevites. Nevertheless, just to make sure, the royal decree spells out that there must be a crying out to God. Here the verb "cry" occurs for the last time, not only in this chapter but in the entire book. The word that has come to

Jonah and has been cried in Nineveh, which had a radical effect on the people and reached the king, which in its turn caused a word to come from king to people, now goes back to God in the form of a cry. In the process, terms for speech, "word" and "cry," have taken on a number of different shades of meaning. With its final use, the verb "cry" is brought home and can be put to rest. All the crying done so far, by the sailors to their God, and to Adonai (1:5, 14), by Jonah to Adonai (2:3), and by Jonah to Nineveh (3:4), has led up to this moment of the "mighty cry" for mercy, on the part of the Ninevites and their animals. The inclusion of the animals even at this point conjures up an image of howling for pardon.

One more instruction follows. Fasting is appropriate, humbling one-self and crying mightily to God is necessary, but all of it would mean little if there were no true turning away from what is going on in this city of violence.

Nineveh had disappeared from the map by the time the Book of Jonah was composed. It offers no "real" threat to the community that had suffered in previous centuries from its "evil ways" and the "violence of their hands." Yet its violence and monstrous cruelty had become proverbial, and by using such a place as a paradigm the storyteller can make the point about repentance strongly.

Two turns actually are required in verse 8. The first is an implied turning to God. Covered in sacks, human and animals together cry with all their might to God, that is to say they pray. If this is a turning *toward*, the next turn is a turn *away from*. Specifically, the decree is for all to *turn from* their evil way and the violence in their hands.

Evil, *rāʿâ*, is a word that has occurred already in Jonah in connection with Nineveh (1:2). "His/their evil way" in verse 8 in a general man-ner indicates the destructiveness that reigns there. The next phrase, "and from the violence (*ḥāmās*) that is in their hands," basically re-peats the first phrase but with a more specific content as to what consti-tutes these evil ways. The word *ḥāmās* is a concrete and specific term in Hebrew indicating violence that is done by the powerful to those without power, by the strong to the weak; the victims of *ḥāmās* are the poor, the needy, the weak, those without a helper, the widow, orphan, and stranger. When violence is "in the hands," it is physical violence that is intended. *Ḥāmās* is used a number of times in connection with the shedding of blood, particularly of the innocent, and can be used in the context of hostility among nations. Joel 4:19, for example, announces the destruction of Egypt and Edom because of the *ḥāmās* done to Judah, where they shed the blood of the innocent (cf. Obad 10). In terms of Nineveh we may assume that the violence of the city is both an internal and an external matter; it concerns violence within its communal life and also violence as it is turned outward to its neighbors. The victims of the latter type of *ḥāmās* certainly included Israel. In turning away from *ḥāmās* it is also this particular violence that is renounced and for which Nineveh repents.

The destructive habits of the city, and by extension of the entire Assyrian empire, are elaborately and evocatively described by the prophet Nahum who spoke of Nineveh as a "city of bloodshed" with "piles of dead, heaps of corpses, dead bodies without end." (Nah 3:1–3 NRSV). Nahum ends his indictment with a question: "Against whom has not come / your evil continuously?" (Nah 3:19). From inscriptions we learn of the custom of leading conquered leaders by a leash attached to a ring through their lips. Esarhaddon describes proudly a procession of vanquished nobles with the decapitated heads of their princes around their necks, while musicians play a merry tune (see Parrot 1955). Nineveh in the biblical world was a name that had become synonymous with barbaric and gross violence, a place that is truly in need of turning in another direction, both for its own sake and for the sake of others. In Jonah 3:2–7, "Nineveh" occurs seven times, with at least one mention in each verse and two occurrences in verse 3. The city's name sounds like the ominous clanging of a bell that rings impending disaster: Nineveh, Nineveh, Nineveh!

The name of the city disappears from the chapter when the royal decree is issued that the people "shall turn." From this point on the root *šûb* comes to the fore and it stays in the center through the last stage of the drama in this chapter. The people are compelled by their royal master to "turn away from" (v. 8) so that an opening can be created for God also to "turn away from" (v. 9). If the people turn from their *rā ʿâ* ("evil") perhaps God too will turn from the *rā ʿâ* God is planning to do to them. *Mî yôdēaʿ* ("who knows?"). The Ninevites "believed" (v. 5), a construction that implicitly compares them to Israel and Israel's ancestor Abram (Gen 15:6 and Exod 14:31), and they have engaged in appropriate acts of repentance. "Instead of feeling helpless and ultimately unconcerned about an event over which they have no control, they reflect upon their past; they review their foul deeds; they unravel the image of their wicked soul, and they mourn" (Lacocque and Lacocque 1990: 124). And, in addition, they are willing to bank on the possibility of grace. It is as if they had heard Amos admonish them:

> *Hate evil and love good,*
> *and establish justice in the gate;*
> *it may be that the Lord, the God of hosts,*
> *will be gracious to the remnant of Jacob.*
> (Amos 5:15 NRSV)

Or, as if the words of Joel had reached them:

> *Yet even now, says the Lord,*
> *return to me with all your heart,*
> *with fasting, weeping, and with mourning;*
> *rend your hearts and not your clothing.*
> *Return to the Lord, your God,*
> *for he is gracious and merciful,*
> *slow to anger, and abounding in steadfast love,*
> *and relents from punishing.*
> *Who knows whether he will not turn and relent ...?*
> (Joel 2:12–14 NRSV)

Or, as if they were well aware of the words of Jeremiah:

> *At one moment I may declare concerning a nation or a king-*
> *dom, that I will pluck up and break down and destroy it, but*
> *if that nation, concerning which I have spoken, turns from*
> *its evil, I will change my mind about the disaster that I in-*
> *tended to bring on it. (Jer 18:7–8 NRSV)*[14]

The king of Nineveh is echoing such biblical texts. Of course, it is not Nineveh that is familiar with these words and their theme; it is the people of God's covenant who have heard, repeated over and over, if not by one prophet then by another, God's unremitting plea for the community to return to the ways of justice and righteousness, a plea that constitutes a call to return to God. And God's promise to be gracious and to turn from anger even as the people have turned from their evil, that too has been heard by the community that is expected to reflect both God's grace and God's justice. So then, if the Ninevites, notorious violators of all laws of justice and mercy, could respond like this, if the king, a chief of perpetrator of evil, could issue such a call for repentance, and throw himself and his people on the mercy of God, then what is to be expected of the community that is "in the know" about the need for a turning and the certainty of grace? When Jonah utters his *yāda 'tî* ("I know"; 4:2), it is also offered as a conviction in the face of the uncertainty of Nineveh's *mî yôdēa'* ("who knows?"). Jonah *knows* what God is like, whereas the Ninevites could only engage in a wager. That Jonah is not pleased about this confirmation of his conviction is another story.

Nineveh, in any case, goes with its wager. If they turn, then God may turn, so the reasoning goes. "Who knows, God may turn and repent and turn ... and we will not perish." A bold statement, intensifying and enriching an earlier saying in the book (cf. 1:6). But whether God turns or not, Nineveh is already en route toward goodness, in a radical reversal from its wickedness and violence. So Nineveh is "overturned" after all. And not only Nineveh is turned upside down by its repentance, but so are the ideas of those who thought they knew what prophecy was all about. Where others might have heard only the certainty of disaster, Nineveh heard the possibility of liberation.

V. GOD'S TURN

The last stage of the drama unfolds in terse repetitive language. "God saw their deeds, that they turned from their evil way ..." (v. 10). The text omits to note that God *heard* the cry of Nineveh and proceeds directly to God's observing of the actions: "God *saw* their *deeds*." God's observing is not in the first place of a mood, or a sentiment, or an appropriate religious rite; as often in the Bible, God seems to have little interest in religion. The entire idea behind a fast is that God will pay attention, will *see*. But the community of God's heart had to be reminded many times that religious rites alone, even when appropriate, even when purely and devotedly practiced, do not suffice to make the life of the community acceptable to God. Isaiah 58, for example, offers an extended diatribe on the necessity of a change in oppressive practices. Self-affliction, according to the words of that text, is offensive if one is at the same time afflicting others. It is the "turning" of Nineveh that God observes and to which God responds.

There is a kind of chain-reaction here as the Lacocques call it. On seeing the turning of Nineveh, God is said to "repent" (*n-ḥ-m*; "relent," "repent"), a verb that in Hebrew also means "to comfort." In the end, God is comforted because there was also a *mî yôdēaʿ* on God's side. God was the one leaving the possibility open for new things to happen in Nineveh by sending a prophet there. And it worked, for once it worked! And if it could work in Nineveh, perhaps it can work for the community of God's choosing.

The last verse of the chapter is full of the root *ʿ-ś-h*. The deeds of the Ninevites, heretofore a cause of loathing on the part of any who love justice, are now the cause for a new deed of God. This new deed, and it constitutes God's change of mind, is to go back on God's word and to refrain from action: "God repented of the evil he said to do them, and did not do it" (3:10). This text is not the only place in the Bible where God is said to repent. But this is the only place where God is said to repent of divine punishment planned for a group outside of the covenant community (see Willis 1994; Dozeman 1989). With this last verse the twists and turns of the chapter are complete, and the tale of Nineveh's repentance has unwound itself in full. At its opening a disobedient prophet turned into an obedient spokesperson for God. His announcement of doom created a reaction of belief, an unexpected turn of events. Next, words of doom were turned into words of hope and the possibility of liberation by the pagan, barbaric, Ninevites. Finally, God's repentance overturns God's own word. God has spoken, the prophet has cried, and Nineveh does not fall.

Who are the intended listeners to this story? Not the Ninevites, not Assyria, not non-Israelites. Surely the story is told in the first instance to the community by whom and for whom the texts of the Hebrew Bible were composed. Is not this teaching intended to provide comfort to a community that was no stranger to the practice of violence and oppression in its own midst? (Witness the fervor with which Isaiah 58 denounces such practices.) If wicked, despicable, Nineveh could turn away from its evil, and God in response refrained from doing it harm, how much more so could these things happen in the beloved community. If Nineveh could repent, surely the covenant people can do the same? If Nineveh could turn from the injustice in its midst, surely the covenant people are capable of the same turn? And, even more significant, if God is pleased with the actions of such as the Ninevites, how much more so will God be pleased with those whom God has called into close relationship with God's very self.

As Christian listeners, we are latecomers to the story. We too understand ourselves to be called into close relationship with the God of Israel. Only recently, partly under the influence of sustained efforts to take seriously Christian participation in the Shoah and events that led up to it, are discernible changes taking place in Christian approaches to the Hebrew Bible. Changed perspectives include an understanding of the possibilities for violence that lie embedded in a negative appreciation of the religion of the postexilic community in Judah, and by implication of Judaism. As Christian readers today, we take our place in the story of Jonah most appropriately as Ninevites. As Nineveh was, we are marked by our history of violence. The prophetic warning of destruction may perhaps by us too be understood as a chance to repent and turn from the violence in our hands. And for us, as for the Ninevites, the *"mî yôdēaʿ"* may leave open the miraculous possibility of grace, even now.

It is no small thing when people who were bent on the destruction both of their neighbor and of the fabric of their communal life turn around and move in a new direction. No small thing indeed, the conversion of Nineveh. Not a new teaching in Israel is conversion, but an old teaching taught in a new form; like a beast dressed in a sack, it provides an unexpected sight, an outrageous picture, but certainly one to pause for and pay it attention.

NOTES

1. I take the title for this essay from a remark by André and Pierre-Emmanuel Lacocque (1990: 123) when they observe that while the conversion of Nineveh is not the goal of the book of Jonah, it is by the same token "no small thing."
2. For a clear illustration of such an analysis, one example may suffice. After discussing the glorious vision of universalism present in certain biblical texts from the postexilic period, William M. Pickard (1974) remarks: "Unfortunately, however, the exile had exactly the opposite effect on many Hebrews. Whereas for some the vision of God was enlarged, for others it was narrowed. For the first group the exile pointed in the direction of universalism. For the second group it pointed in the direction of exclusivism." And further: "One can readily see how this approach

to the reestablishment of the covenant, however sincere it might have been, quickly developed into smugness and bigotry."

3. See, for example, Martin Luther's discussion in his commentary on Jonah (Luther: 1974). It is not surprising that, according to a recent survey of literature on Jonah, Jewish interpretation is generally more sympathetic to the prophet while Christian interpretation is inclined to render him a negative judgment (Hoffer and Wright 1994: 144–50).

4. As stated by the Lacocques (1990: 164–65): "God is right and Jonah is right. But their respective stances are mutually exclusive. Who will tip the balance one way or the other? Voicing doubt as to God's justice and equanimity may appear more 'Jewish,' and pleading for it more 'Christian.' Perhaps the book of Jonah takes us to the very heart of the Jewish-Christian problem. If so, we must, like the author of the biblical book, leave the narrative without conclusion. Jonah-Israel does not surrender to the theological rationality of an argument that will satisfy the mind in general while it is nothing other than a slap in the face of the victim in particular."

5. My translation of Jonah 3 in short phrases follows the Hebrew accent marks and is, in general, based on the Buber/Rosenzweig principles of translating the Bible. These principles have recently been advocated by Everett Fox in the USA.

6. Buber discusses Jonah in the context of interpreting Amos and his judgment speeches. To Buber, "Human and divine turning correspond one to the other; not as if it were in the power of the first to bring about the second, such ethical magic being far removed from Biblical thought, but 'Who knows'" (Buber 1949: 104). Adele Berlin (1976) also understands Jonah to be a prophetic book, albeit for a different reason. She views Jonah as a prophet who suffers from "la condition prophetique," as one whose credibility is damaged.

7. For a contemporary analysis of Jonah in light of the repentance theme, see Godhart (1985).

8. There are at least two possibilities for the extent of the unit. One may end it at the last verse of chapter three, leaving God and divine repentance in the limelight. The unit is then also framed by divine initiative. Or one can draw in Jonah's reaction (4:1–2), which is tempting because of the twist on the word *rā'â* ("evil"). Nineveh's "evil" weighs on Jonah and his people; the stay of execution and pardon of Nineveh's evil is thus "evil" to Jonah:

> *4 (1) But it was evil to Jonah,*
> *a great evil,*
> *and it burned him up.*
> *(2) So he prayed to Adonai and said:*

Sure, Adonai, did I not say this
when still in my own country?
That is why I fled earlier to Tarshish.
For I know that you are a God
compassionate and gracious,
slow to anger,
full of devotion and repenting of evil.

On this view there are three perspectives on evil in this unit: the evil perpetrated by Nineveh; the evil God plans to do them; and the evil felt by Jonah in response to God's repeal of the evil God had planned. For a discussion on *rā'â* and the variations of its usage, see Magonet (1983: 22–25). As Magonet (1983: 25) observes, the author uses "what is overtly a very precise and economical technique of word usage, but at the same time succeeds in conveying reverberations and ambiguities that dissolve any oversimplified reading of the story."

9. See also Paul Kahn who suggests a tension between *Yonah* and *Amittai*, the first providing a soft, the other a stark image. This tension "articulates a basic conflict in the book, the conflict between love and justice" (Kahn 1994: 89).

10. If I were writing in Dutch there might be opportunity to render the phrase in a more neutral fashion: "godsallemachtig groot" is what I have in mind. In English the word "godawful" is negative, which provides a chance to give the size of Nineveh another slant. Yet the expression may well be ambiguous in Hebrew. It is used in a positive sense in Gen 23:6 and Ps 80:11, for example. The expression in Gen 30:8; Exod 9:28 and 1 Sam 14:15 lends itself more easily to the notion of "terrifying." For other possibilities, see Trible (1994: 178) and also Day (1990: 34) who suggests: a "godalmighty big city."

11. For the same change on God's part, see Hos 11:8.

12. For such gaps and their significance, see Trible (1994: 182).

13. Sackcloth or hair shirts were garments worn during times of mourning or penitence in the nations surrounding Israel as well as in ancient Israel itself. It is not exactly clear what sort of covering "sackcloth" indicates, partial or total, nor what made up the material, although goat-hair seems to be one possibility. It would appear that certain groups of folk might have such a garment available for special times of mourning and penitence and that for others the impromptu nature of the occasion would demand a more makeshift outfit. Since the word *śaq* is also used for grain-bags (Gen 42:25), it would be entirely possible that for large scale engagement in mourning and/or fasts these bags would used for the practice with an opening cut or torn at the closed end. I prefer to render the word with "sack" in English to indicate the linguistic connection between

the word in the original and the translation. The Akkadian word *šaqqu* reads as *šaq* in Hebrew, and came into the modern European languages via the Greek *saccos*, and the Latin *saccus*.

The practice of involving beasts in human rituals of mourning is also known among the Greeks and the Persians (Herodotus 9:24).

14. See also Jer 25:5; 26:3 and 36:3, 7. As the Lacocques (1990: 131) point out, these texts are conditioned by the covenantal relationship that is in place between God and community: "There is nothing in Jeremiah or Ezekiel to make us extend that which is valid for God's people to God's foes."

REFERENCES

Berlin, A.
1976   Rejoinder to John A. Miles Jr., With Some Observations on the
            Nature of the Book of Jonah. *Jewish Quarterly Review* 66:
            227–35.
Buber, M.
1949   *The Prophetic Faith*. New York: Harper and Row.
Day, J.
1990   Problems in the Interpretation of the Book of Jonah. Pp. 32–47
            in *In Quest of the Past: Studies on Israelite Religion, Literature
            and Prophetism*, ed. A. S. Van Der Woude. Leiden: Brill.
Dozeman, T. B.
1989   Inner-Biblical Interpretation of Yahweh's Gracious and Com-
            passionate Character. *Journal of Biblical Literature* 108: 208–19.
Godhart, S.
1985   Sacrifice and Repentance in the Story of Jonah. *Semeia* 33:
            43–63.
Hoffer, V., and Wright, R. A.
1994   A Jewish and Christian Reading of Jonah: How (Dis-)Similar.
            Sewanee Theological Review 37: 144–50.
Kahn, P.
1994   An Analysis of the Book of Jonah. *Judaism* 43: 87–100.
Lacocque, A., and Lacocque, P.-E.
1990   *Jonah: A Psycho-Religious Approach to the Prophet*. Colum-
            bia, SC: University of South Carolina.
Landes, G. M.
1976   The Book of Jonah. Pp. 448–90 in *The Interpreter's Dictionary
            of the Bible—Supplementary Volume*, ed. K. Crim. Nashville:
            Abingdon.
1978   Jonah: A *Māšāl*? Pp. 137–58 in *Israelite Wisdom: Theological
            and Literary Essays in Honor of Samuel Terrien*, eds. J. G.

Gammie, W. A. Brueggemann, W. L. Humphreys, and J. M. Ward. Missoula, MT: Scholars.

Littell, F.
1975   *The Crucifixion of the Jews*. Macon, GA: Mercer University.

Luther, M.
1974   *Lectures on the Minor Prophets II: Jonah, Habakkuk*. Luther's Works 19. Ed. H. C. Oswald. St. Louis: Concordia.

Magonet, J.
1983   *Form and Meaning: Studies in Literary Techniques in the Book of Jonah*. Sheffield: Almond.

Parrot, A.
1955   *Nineveh and the Old Testament*. London: SCM.

Pickard, W. M.
1975   *Rather Die Than Live—Jonah*. New York: Board of Global Ministries, The United Methodist Church.

Sasson, J. M.
1990   *Jonah: A New Translation with Introduction, Commentary and Interpretation*. Anchor Bible 24B. New York: Doubleday.

Trible, P.
1994   *Rhetorical Criticism: Context, Method, and the Book of Jonah*. Minneapolis: Fortress.

Willis, J. T.
1994   The "Repentance" of God in the Books of Samuel, Jeremiah and Jonah. *Horizons in Biblical Theology* 16: 156–75.

15 A Fifth Century Christian Commentary on Jonah

S. C. WINTER

For the past two decades we biblical scholars have availed our selves of a smorgasbord of methods of biblical interpretation. With this has come increasing awareness of how method affects (effects!) interpretation. This awareness has brought with it renewed interest in the methods of biblical interpretation from antiquity. Indeed allegorical interpretation, associated with Alexandria and very familiar to modern scholars from the works of Philo and Origen, has attracted considerable attention from literary critics as well as biblical scholars.

Also familiar, but less studied, are the works of exegetes who were sharply opposed to allegorical interpretation, seeing it as a fanciful distortion of the text. This method of interpretation, utilized by allegory's most adamant opponents, is known to us only from works of Christians primarily associated with Antioch-on-Orontes. A thorough and systematic grasp of their method and how it shaped the theology of the school, comparable to our understanding of allegory as a method, has eluded the modern scholar. The Christian theologians and exegetes who wrote against allegory did hold doctrinal tenets in common and their historical conception of the Bible placed great value on ancient Israel and on Judaism. Scarcity of extant texts, however, has made it difficult to reconstruct the link between their doctrinal positions and their exegetical method. The school, therefore, has remained geographically-not methodologically-defined as "the Antiochene School."

We possess few Antiochene Christian texts because Christian theologians at Antioch of the fourth and fifth centuries wrote for the losing side in the Christological controversies, the debates in which theologians attempted to define in philosophical categories how divinity and humanity combined in Jesus Christ. The Christological controversies culminated in decisions by a series of councils of bishops on the "correct" formulations, and these were subsequently adopted as creeds and tests of orthodoxy. At key junctures Antiochene positions were rejected as heretical and Antiochene theologians declared heresiarchs, originators of and teachers of heresy, with the result that few Antiochene Christian writings survive to the twentieth century.

Among the leading biblical interpreters of the Antiochene school were Paul of Samosata (*fl.* 260), Lucian of Antioch (of the Lucianic recension of the LXX, d. 312), Diodore of Tarsus (*fl.* 378–394), Theodore of Mopsuestia (350–428), John Chrysostom (d. 407), and Theodoret of Cyrrhus (ca. 393– ca. 466). Recently, discovery and reattribution of some Antiochene commentaries, especially the commentaries on the Psalms by Theodore of Mopsuestia (Devreesse 1939) and Diodore of Tarsus (Olivier 1980), have made it possible to take a new look at the exegetical principles of Christian theologians at Antioch. Alongside the commentaries, opinions attributed to Theodore of Mopsuestia, preserved in the writings of Nestorian Syrian theologians for whom Theodore's interpretations became normative, have acquired renewed importance.[1] Examination of Antiochene Christian commentaries on Psalms shows that the commentators worked with well-defined exegetical principles and within common traditions of interpretation, and so may properly be called a "school." The evidence also suggests strongly that Christian exegetes learned their method and appropriated traditions from a Jewish school of exegesis, with which, as late as the fourth or fifth century, they remained in conversation.

This paper will discuss the Antiochene Christian commentary on Jonah contained in a commentary on the Twelve Prophets attributed to Theodore of Mopsuestia. This commentary on Jonah offers a perspective on the Antiochene school that extends the perspective gained from study of the commentaries on Psalms because in it two features of Antiochene Christian exegesis, peripheral in the commentaries on Psalms, emerge centrally. These features are Antiochene typology and a connection between Antiochene Christian exegetical method and Hellenistic moral philosophy. I examine both features for the light they can shed on the origins of the school and the generation of the method.

The *Commentary on the Twelve Prophets* is presently extant in five known manuscripts (Sprenger 1977: 5–11). In addition a fragment (containing commentary on Hos 2:16) in the Greek catena to the Twelve

Prophets belongs to the work (Sprenger 1977: 9), as do some Syriac fragments that Eduard Sachau dated to the sixth century (Sprenger 1977: 36). Attribution of the commentary to Theodore of Mopsuestia was questioned in the nineteenth century, but is presently accepted, erroneously in my opinion.[2] Hence I shall refer to the author of the commentary as "the author" or "the commentator." The interpretation presented in the commentary, however, is completely consonant with Antiochene method known to us from commentaries on psalms, and its attribution to Theodore assures us that it is Antiochene. The *Commentary on the Twelve Prophets* may date from the late fourth to mid fifth century (the time of Theodore) or perhaps earlier. I am very pleased to contribute this paper to the volume in honor of my teacher and colleague George Landes in appreciation for his deep commitment to scholarship, to the field of biblical studies, and to his students.

I. SOME PRINCIPLES

Antiochene Christian commentators approached the Bible as Hellenistic historians would, viewing the text as a history comprising narrative (*historia*) interspersed with speeches (prophecies). At that time the study and writing of history was considered a branch of rhetoric (Fornara 1983: 2 n. 6), and hence the framework of analysis in the commentary is that of rhetoric. The prophets themselves were viewed as orators whose gift of prophecy permitted them to deliver prophecies appropriate to the future as well as the past. And the prophet addressed each prophecy, like a speech, to hearers in a single precise setting.

The rhetoric that exerted influence on exegesis was in the form of school exercises. In the third century B.C.E., with the decline of the Greek *polis*, Greek oratory, previously central to democratic assembly, began to lose its political function and to assume a function primarily in the schools. By the first century B.C.E. teachers of rhetoric developed programs of preliminary rhetorical exercises (*progymnasmata*), which included such forms as "narrative," "abstract question," "description," "character sketch," "comparison," "refutation and confirmation."[3] Some scholars refer to this development in rhetoric as literary rhetoric (Kennedy 1980: 108–19). These formal exercises had lasting impact in literature; the rhetorical "narrative" influenced Greek romances and "description" eventually influenced medieval poetics.

Literary analysis of prophecy as rhetoric permeates Antiochene Christian commentaries. Perhaps this is to be expected, first because rhetorical schools were the locus of literary criticism, and second because Antioch was home to a tradition of rhetoric. The most prominent Antiochene orator and teacher of rhetoric, Libanius (314–93), numbered both Christian commentators and the son of the *nasi* ʾ in Tiberias among his students.[4]

One of the rhetorical exercises was the "character sketch" (*ēethopoiia*). In the exercise of *ēethopoiia* the student of rhetoric declaimed from a precise situation, often taking on the persona of a well-known figure.[5] The student endeavored to convey the assigned figure as convincingly as possible in the appropriate predetermined setting. This technique of *ēethopoiia* apparently shaped the Antiochene concept of prophecy (Ramsay 1911: 433). The Antiochenes understood the act of prophesying to be in many instances a "taking on of the persona" of some individual from another time and place, and speaking prophetic words as that person. All of the psalms were considered prophecies of David, but in many instances David "took on the persona" of an individual from another time to give the prophecy. Thus one commentary on the Psalms calls Psalm 67 a "character sketch" (*ēethopoiia*). The commentator explains that David composed Psalm 67 when he was moving the ark, but took on the character of Moses, putting himself in the situation of Moses and the people of Israel in the desert (Devreesse 1939: 429).[6]

Consistent with their concept of the Bible as *historia*, that is, as narrative and speeches, Antiochene Christian commentators assumed that the Bible had only one meaning; this was what they called "the sense" or "gist" of the text (*dianoia, ennoia*).[7] This single sense of the text, however, was not the same as its literal meaning, that is, its meaning on the lexical level. A prophet, like any good orator, embellished his presentation with flowery metaphorical language, and thus on the lexical level the language of the text may be figurative. It was the *sense* of the text that was inspired and sacrosanct, but this depended neither on the precise wording of the text nor even on the language in which it was read. The sense of the text carried over in translation, and a paraphrase might convey the sense to the contemporary reader more clearly than the original. Indeed Antiochene commentaries customarily included a paraphrase in verse-by-verse commentary.

This Antiochene concept of the text differs sharply from that of the exegetes who employed allegory, an approach that presupposed that several levels of meaning inhere in the text. For exegetes of the allegorical school the lexical level of the text was inspired and sacrosanct. How unimportant the lexical level of the text could be to the Antiochenes is evident in our commentator's discussion of the destination of Jonah's ship. The commentator explains, "[b]ut *Tharseis* [for *Tharsis* in LXX (Rahlf's 1935)] some said means Tarsus, erring, it seems, on account of the closeness in pronunciation. For Tarsus is not a maritime city, but divine scripture is accustomed to give this appellation to indicate maritime cities, as in this by the blessed David, 'as when with a violent wind[8] you shatter ships of Tarshish' [Ps 48:8; LXX 47:8], which therefore is able to express the maritime city that has ships moored beside it. Since Tarsus is situated so far from the sea it appears in no way to fit. On the other hand, some others said it was Rhodes. But I consider all of this precision of language to be superfluous to the matter at hand, inasmuch as the tale of the prophet is surely equally valid whichever anyone considers the city to be"(Sprenger 1977: 177–78).[9]

II. INTERPRETIVE FIGURES

Unlike most of their Christian contemporaries, who took most prophecy to pertain directly to Christ, Antiochene Christian commentators understood almost all biblical prophecy (of which the Psalms were among the most important) to pertain to ancient Israel. The Antiochenes took only four to eight psalms to prophesy Christ. They are Psalms 2, 8, 45 and 110, to which some added Psalms 5 (Olivier 1980: 27–28), LXX Psalm 9 (= MT 9 and 10; Olivier 1980: 50–51), Psalm 72 (=LXX 71; Devreesse 1939: 469–70), and Psalm 117 (=LXX 116; *PG* 55.327.1).[10] Antiochene Christian commentators also understood a handful of other passages, mostly from the Twelve Prophets, in some way to prophesy Christ. These include Gen 49:11 (Devreesse 1948:5–25), Isa 7:14 (Chrysostom *PG* 55.355.5), Joel 2:28–32, Amos 9:11–12, Mic 5:2, Zech 9:9, Mal 3:1 (considered a prophecy of John the Baptist), Mal 4:5–6, and the book of Jonah. They assigned to the psalms *hypotheses* or "topics," brief summaries of the historical setting and purpose of the psalm prophecy, mostly pertaining to the Maccabees, Hezekiah, the Jewish people (especially leaving for exile, in Babylon, or upon return), and David—individuals and events who, except for David, have little direct significance for Christianity.[11] Antiochene Christian traditions of interpretation were so strongly held that the "topic" assigned to a psalm could override the interpretation of that psalm in the New Testament. Interpretation of Psalm 22 illustrates this. The New Testament Gospels depict Jesus reciting Ps 22:2 just before he dies, and they weave references to Ps 22:7–9, 19 into the passion narrative. Most other Christians of the fourth and fifth centuries interpreted Psalm 22 to be a prophecy about the crucifixion of Jesus. Antiochene Christian commentators, however, state that Psalm 22 clearly pertains to David, and that all that the New Testament is doing is depicting Jesus reciting Ps 22:2 just as any pious person who was suffering might recite it (Olivier 1980: 126–37; Devreesse 1939: 120–22).

The exegetical approach most commonly associated in people's minds with Antiochene interpretation is typology. Yet typology, far from being the hallmark of Antiochene exegesis, is in fact mentioned extremely rarely in the extant commentary literature. It is only one in a class of literary devices occasionally employed—which I shall call interpretive figures—that permitted the Antiochene "sense" of scripture to refer to two distinct times or situations, and thus enabled the Antiochene Christian exegetes to stretch the single sense they assigned to prophecies to include references to Christ and Christianity. Scripture still had only one sense, but the use of these interpretive figures gives the sense a certain duality, allowing the single sense to refer simultaneously to two distinct historical moments, rather as a metaphor compresses in tension two referents. It must be emphasized that the use of any of the figures like typology is fairly rare in the extant commentary literature.

One of these figures permitted the commentators to interpret some prophecies as being fulfilled twice, once in ancient Israel and a second time in connection with Christ. Diodore of Tarsus, for example, states that certain phrases in Psalm 22 (verse 9 and verse 19) fit Christ (Olivier 1980: 126–27). And according to the *Commentary on the Twelve Prophets*, Amos 9:11 prophesies the time of Zerubbabel and the time of Christ, Joel 2:28–29 is to comfort to people in exile and prophesies the giving of the spirit to early Christians, Zech 9:9 prophesies Zerubbabel and Christ, and Mic 5:1–2 prophesies Zerubbabel and Christ.

The commentators refer to this figure in two ways. Some commentators say that the second event, the one pertaining to Christ, "more authoritatively fulfills" the prophecy (*kyriōteron ekbainein*) (Olivier 1980: 126–27). Others say that the prophecy is overstated or excessive (*hyperbolikōs*) in connection with the first event; that is, it contains a surplus of meaning that is appropriately fulfilled in the second. The commentator states, for example, that it is clear that in the first instance Zech 9:9 is about Zerubbabel and that it is astounding that some twist the sense (*dianoia*) of the prophecy by breaking it up into fragments, some of which concern Zerubbabel, other of which concern Christ. In such a rendering the prophecy speaks first of Zerubbabel, then of Christ, then of Zerubbabel again and then again of Christ. That is, these interpretations divide the prophecy among several "topics" so it is no longer a single prophecy (Sprenger 1977: 367). The commentator goes on to explain that the prophecy, rather than being fragmented, is "more overstated" (*hyperbolikōteron*) with reference to its immediate setting (Zerubbabel). In discussing how the prophecy applies also to Christ, the commentator paraphrases the phrase from the NT Letter to the Hebrews "for the law having the shadow of all good things to come" (Heb 10:1) as "the law had a shadow of everything pertaining to Christ" (Sprenger 1977: 367).[12]

A second figure, called "riddle" (Greek: *ainygma*) makes a correspondence between the historical referent and a moral reality. With this figure the text is almost viewed as having two levels. The serpent in Genesis 3 is an example of *ainygma*: the exegete explains that there was actually a serpent, this is the sense of the text, but that the devil acted through it, in a figural interpretation.[13] The term is used differently by John Chrysostom, who designates as *ainygma* a verse or verses of prophecy fulfilled at a time different from the rest of the prophecy. For example, according to Chrysostom, Psalm 118 (LXX 117) was fulfilled upon the people's return from exile, except for verse 22 which was fulfilled later, in the life of Christ. Hence Chrysostom called v. 22 an *ainygma* that was incomprehensible to those to whom Psalm 118 was directed.[14] Similarly Chrysostom notes that Isa 7:14, which he takes as a prophecy of the birth of Jesus inserted into a prophecy directed to the time of Isaiah, was clearly an *ainygma* and incomprehensible to Isaiah's hearers (*PG* 55.335.5).

Typology is yet another figure. One of the rare instances in extant commentary literature where typology is discussed is in fact the relatively long introduction that precedes the verse-by-verse commentary on Jonah. Typology, the commentary explains, is "a certain imitation of events" (*tis mimesis tōn pragmatōn*) (Sprenger 1977: 172). It has been proposed that typological correspondences, "imitations of events," originated with concepts of restoration expressed in Jewish literature of the Second Temple Period (Goppelt 1982: 32–41), and that early Christians built upon this. Indeed writing about the events concerning Christ of which events in Jonah are the type, the commentator speaks of them as "the restoration that is to come" (Sprenger 1977: 169). In this "imitation of events" Antiochene Christians saw a direct connection between the events of ancient Israel and Christianity. Just as Moses led the people out of slavery in Egypt, the commentator continues, so Christ released us from sin and death. And as Moses lifted up the bronze serpent,[15] so Christ was lifted up. Just as Jonah preached to the Gentiles, so the church eventually turned to the Gentiles and they receive salvation (Sprenger 1977: 172).

After the introduction, however, Christ and Christianity are not mentioned. The focus of the verse-by-verse commentary is Jonah and the Ninevites, not the connection with Christianity. In the verse-by-verse commentary the author discusses only Jonah in his historical setting. Indeed at points the commentary corresponds to statements in rabbinic midrash.[16] According to the commentary Jonah hesitates to go to Nineveh because he knows that since he is unknown to the Ninevites, his reputation among them will rest on this prophecy; when the Ninevites repent and the overthrow of the city is averted, they will consider him a liar and a cheat (Sprenger 1977: 179, 187). The tradition that the Israelites considered Jonah to be a false prophet is found in rabbinic midrash.[17] A second explanation given by the commentary for Jonah's hesitation corresponds to an explanation given in the Mekhilta. According to the commentary, Jonah was disheartened at the command to go to Nineveh and lamented because comparison with the Ninevites might make his people seem worthy of divine retribution (Sprenger 1977: 175). The substance of this explanation is found concisely stated in the Mekhilta (Pisḥa I, 80–82): "But Jonah thought: I will go outside of the land, where the Shekinah does not reveal itself. For since the Gentiles are more inclined to repent, I might be causing Israel to be condemned" (Lauterbach 1933: 7). Lauterbach (1933: 7 n. 7) explains, "By contrast with the Ninevites who would readily listen to the prophet and repent, Israel would stand condemned for not so readily listening to the prophets." The commentary on Jonah attributes to Jonah additional distress, stating that Jonah knows that the promise of God will be extended to the Gentiles (in the time of Christ) and his people will be dispossessed as heirs to the kingdom of God (Sprenger 1977: 175).

The commentary on Jonah has a remarkable instance where the Antiochene Christian traditions override an interpretation in the New Testament. Matt 12:40 attributes to Jesus, "just as Jonah was three days in the belly of the whale, the Son of Man will be three days and nights in the heart of the earth" (discussed in Landes 1983). But the author of the commentary on Jonah states that Jonah's three days in the belly of the whale and the New Testament's three days between the crucifixion and resurrection of Jesus is not where the correspondence between Jonah and Christianity is to be found. It is to be found in the extension of God's mercy to the Gentiles in both instances (Sprenger 1977: 172). Thus the author privileges the tradition closer to that found in the Mekhilta over that explicitly stated in the New Testament. That there are no specifically Christian traditions in the verse-by-verse commentary strongly suggests that much of the commentary may have been taken directly, unchanged from Jewish tradition.

The commentary on Jonah adds to our information about interpretations that Christians at Antioch held in common with Jewish traditions, and it contributes evidence to the thesis that Antiochene Christians learned their exegetical method from a Jewish school. The commentary on Jonah, however, also provides evidence of theological principles that would have separated such a school from Rabbinic Judaism and most forms of Christianity. These principles derived from Hellenistic moral philosophy.

III. THE DIVINE PHILOSOPHER

It was observed above that Antiochene commentators viewed the Bible as history and rhetoric, and made use of rhetorical categories in exegesis. But the commentary on Jonah makes clear that the context of Antiochene use of rhetoric was not primarily school rhetoric, but rhetoric as employed in the service of Hellenistic moral philosophy. Speechmaking was important to the Hellenistic philosophers because they considered hearing to be the best means for moral instruction. Hence rhetoric was cultivated in schools of moral philosophy. That Antiochene Christian exegetes emphasized moral instruction in connection with biblical prophecy is evident from the topics they assigned to the Psalms. In the introduction to one commentary on Psalms the commentator writes, "the subject matter of the psalms as a whole is divided into two categories: ethical and doctrinal. The ethical category has the following subdivisions: Some of the psalms correct the moral disposition of the individual, others of the Jewish people only, still others of all human beings in general" (Olivier 1980: 4).[18] The commentary on Jonah, however, illuminates another dimension of the Antiochene Christian school's debt to Hellenistic moral philosophy.

During the Hellenistic period moral philosophy, the pursuit of ethics, was detached from the philosophical endeavor as a whole. Despite their differences in other areas of philosophy, there was a fair amount of agreement among the various schools, principally Epicurean, Stoic, Cynic, and Platonist, concerning moral instruction (Malherbe 1986: 12). The moral philosophers exerted themselves to disseminate their teachings, presenting them in various settings; hence their teachings were widely accessible. Malherbe writes:

> [t]he settings in which philosophy was taught contributed to this popularization of philosophical ethics. Philosophers were invited to deliver discourses on moral topics in the salons of the wealthy; some of them spoke, when invited, to gatherings in the forum or such places as the public baths; and others were attached to the homes of persons of means or joined the retinues of governmental officials. Other philosophers taught in their own homes or in rented quarters, while still others, like the Epicureans, withdrew from society to form philosophic communities. Some Stoics, but especially Cynics, preached in the marketplaces and on street corners, where they urged all who passed by to listen to them as they spoke of virtue .... Philosophers such as Musonius Rufus and Epictetus also conducted schools ... (Malherbe 1986: 13).

Their emphasis on the importance of prophecy for teaching and moral instruction shows the degree to which the Antiochene Christian exegetes treated the prophets as moral philosophers. Indeed the author of the commentary on Jonah writes of Jonah's situation as one God intended for the "teaching and psychagogy of all the prophets" (Sprenger 1977: 173).

The moral philosophers viewed the individual as a rational subject, capable of choosing good and rejecting evil, though not without struggle and assistance. A common theme of the Hellenistic moral philosophers is that of the crisis of an individual at a moral crossroads. The commentary on Jonah depicts just such a crossroads in its discussion of the response of the Ninevites to Jonah's proclamation; the language of moral choice permeates that discussion. Jonah foresees the Ninevites "assenting to a turn for the better" (Sprenger 1977: 173); they "incline to that which is right" (Sprenger 1977: 174). The Ninevites may "incline for the better ..., incline for the worse" (Sprenger 1977: 174).[19] When they repent, they are described as "renouncing the worse and inclining toward the better" (Sprenger 1977: 187).

The concern for the self-improvement of their followers on the part of the moral philosophers led them to develop a system of care called psychagogy, which "included what today is meant by spiritual exercises, psychotherapy, and psychological and pastoral counseling" (Malherbe 1992: 301). Psychagogy, Malherbe explains, had been developed because "[c]onversion to philosophy required a radical reorientation entailing social, intellectual, and moral transformation or readjustment which often resulted in confusion, bewilderment, and sometimes depression. Philosophic teachers therefore took great pains to analyze the conditions of their followers in order to treat them appropriately and effectively" (Malherbe 1992: 302).

There are two mentions of psychagogy in the introduction to the commentary on Jonah. The commentator writes of God wishing to give psychagogy (an aorist infinitive *psychagōgēsai*) to those who were disposed to it (Sprenger 1977: 173) and refers to what happened to Jonah as "for teaching and psychagogy of all the prophets through which he persuaded them by deeds that the events of the time of Christ will truly come to pass" (Sprenger 1977: 174). In both instances God is the direct agent of the psychagogy. God wills or intends the psychagogy.

The commentator makes use of the term again in the verse-by-verse commentary on Jonah 4. The commentary states that Jonah mourned deeply because he had now been shown to be a liar and a cheat, since his prophecy of doom had not come to pass (Sprenger 1977: 187). Evidently Jonah is in just that confused, bewildered and depressed state that would require psychagogy, for, the commentator continues, Jonah tells God that he foresaw that the Ninevites would repent and he would be shown to be a liar and a cheat (Sprenger 1977: 187). God's response, appointing a plant that grows up and delights Jonah, the commentator describes as psychagogy: "this delighted the prophet, [who] apparently [was] unexpectedly enjoying both the sight and the use of the plant that grew up. And as he was having much enjoyment in the matter [and] thence it seemed somehow to bring psychagogy" (Sprenger 1977: 188). The plant, according to the commentary, was a device to move Jonah out of his despair. And it continues, describing Jonah telling God after the plant dies, "I thought that I had the plant as a psychagogy because I experienced such oppression" (Sprenger 1977: 189).

By this use of the term psychagogy, the philosopher's art of training and healing the follower, with God as the agent of the psychagogy, the commentary casts God as a moral philosopher. The relationships of human beings to God, especially the prophets to God, are those of the followers to the moral philosopher. It may be that the commentary envisions the prophet's relationship with God as that of philosopher with follower because the prophets are understood to be so close to God.

The pairing of moral philosopher with follower evokes another concept—already encountered in connection with typology—the concept of *mimēsis*, which played a central role in the moral philosopher's training of followers. Both the philosophers themselves and significant individuals from the past were to be imitated as part of the process of moral instruction. Seneca (ca. 4 B.C.E.–65 C.E.), for example, recommended that one call upon for assistance in learning moral conduct "men who teach us by their lives, men who tell us what we ought to do and then prove it by practice, who show us what we should avoid, and then are never caught doing that which they have ordered us to avoid" (Malherbe 1989: 64). Plutarch's (ca. 50–ca. 120) *Parallel Lives*, biographies of significant figures from Greece and Rome, illustrated virtuous conduct and explored the factors that brought it out in these individuals. The rhetorical concept of taking on the person is based on the value of imitating, of putting oneself into the situation of the one whose persona one takes on.

The relationship between God and prophet was conceptualized as that of philosopher and student, a relationship of *mimēsis*. The command to be holy (Lev 19:2) commands emulation; "The way to holiness ... was for Israelites, individually and collectively, to emulate God's attributes" (Levine 1989: 256). The Hellenistic philosophers, however, taught their students to imitate them as a means to become identical to them in virtue. Applying this model of imitation to God implies that God may be, not just emulated but, imitated. This conceptualization minimizes the distinction between divine and human to a degree unacceptable to Rabbinic Judaism. This very optimistic view of human perfectibility is evident in the emphasis on the humanity of Jesus expressed in the Antiochene Christian Christologies, for which they were condemned in the councils of the fourth and fifth centuries. The theme of God as teacher is strongly evident in the heirs to the Antiochene Christian School, the Nestorian School (Macina 1983).

IV. CONCLUSION

The commentary on Jonah illustrates concretely both the close connection of Antiochene Christian exegesis with Jewish traditions of interpretation and its debt to Hellenistic moral philosophy. Antiochene Christian commentaries on the Psalms suggest strongly that Christian exegetes learned both their method and many of their traditions of interpretation from a Jewish school of exegesis. The persistence of uniquely Antiochene Christian traditions of interpretation, together with the fact that most of the traditions ignore Jesus, shows them unlikely to have originated with Christians in Antioch. The Christian commentaries on the Psalms contain occasional but heated refutations of Jewish "topics" for some psalms, yet ignore divergent interpretations propounded by Christian writers outside Antioch. This selectivity suggests that the topics with which the Christian commentators were in debate were propounded by Jews in Antioch and, because these debates appear in the commentaries only occasionally, that Christians and Jews in Antioch were in agreement on most topics. Because the topics and the method based on rhetoric are inseparable (the topics rely on the concept of the prophet taking on the person of another figure), we may speculate that they originated with a Jewish school that stood in the same relation to Antiochene Christians as the school of Philo did to Origen in Alexandria, except that Antiochene Christians evidently remained closely associated with the Jewish school as late as the early fifth century.[20]

Like the Antiochene Christian commentaries on the Psalms, the commentary on Jonah suggests that Antiochene Christian commentaries took their interpretations directly from a Hellenistic Jewish school of interpretation. The commentary on Jonah raises new questions in this regard. In the discussion of Zech 9:9 the author writes about the views of other interpreters in the present tense (present participles), "those who twist the meaning ..." (Sprenger 1977: 367). In the discussion of Jonah's destination, however, the commentator employs past tense (aorist), "some said [*ephasan*] ... others said [*ephasan*]" (Sprenger 1977: 177–78). The commentator's use of the past tense suggests the debate is no longer current, raising the possibility that the commentator was consulting written sources. This raises the intriguing question for further study of what kind of written sources Antiochene Christian commentators had available to them and incorporated into their commentaries.

The commentary on Jonah fills out the picture of the Antiochene Christian School as one holding strongly to Jewish traditions of exegesis in its adaptation of Hellenistic philosophy. Yet the concept of God as moral philosopher puts the school at variance with rabbinic perspectives, for the goal of the moral philosopher was to teach followers through imitation of him (or her) to become his or her equal in the art of the moral life. The commentary on Jonah suggests that the Antiochene School saw the human imitating God in the same way that the follower should imitate the teacher. It is worth exploring further whether this concept of God as divine philosopher derived from a form of Hellenistic Judaism. This would tell us a great deal about why this branch of Hellenistic Judaism was not incorporated into Jewish tradition. The tenet that human beings can imitate God the way the follower imitates a teacher erodes the boundary between human and divine in a manner rejected by Judaism and eventually by most forms of Christianity.

NOTES

1. Most important are the commentaries of Isho'dadh of Merv, *fl.* 850, and Bar Hebraeus, 1226–1286.
2. A full analysis of the matter of authorship requires a discussion of Greek syntax with which I shall not burden this paper. Briefly stated, comparison of the commentary on the Twelve Prophets with Theodore's *Commentary on Psalms* shows enormous differences in style and word usage,

especially with religious terms. For example, Theodore, and Diodore, refer to God simply as *ho theos* and to Christ simply as *ho Christos* (commentary on Pss 2, 8, 45 [LXX 44] for each). The commentator on the Twelve Prophets refers to God as *despotēs kyrios* (*despotēs* the translation of *ʾādôn*) and Christ as *despotēs Christos* (*ʾādôn*). Theodore analyzes each psalm in detail, discussing each verse and sometimes partial verses, separately, and concludes each section of verse-by-verse commentary on the Psalms with a paraphrase. The commentary on the Twelve Prophets often treats several verses at a time and gives a paraphrase at the beginning of the verse-by-verse commentary. Also, the wholesale invocation of the figure of authoritative fulfillment in the comment on Zech 9:9 (see Part II below) contrasts sharply with Theodore's meticulous treatment of "topics" in the *Commentary on Psalms*.

3.   Greek terms for the forms of the preliminary rhetorical exercises are *diēgēma* (narrative), *thesis* (abstract question), *ekphrasis* (description), *ēethopoiia* (character sketch), *sygkrisis* (comparison), *anaskeuē* and *kataskeuē* (refutation and confirmation).

4.   The eight letters from Libanius to the *nasi ʾ* are translated in Meeks and Wilken (1978: 60–63).

5.   "Topics" (*hypotheses*), brief summaries describing the historical setting and issues that each prophecy of David (i.e., psalm) addressed, were assigned to all of the psalms, and there was fair agreement among Antiochene commentators as to correct topics. In the schools students learned designated "topics" for Greek tragedies. Comedy and poetry likewise were assigned topics. A close parallel to the topics that Antiochene commentators assigned to the Psalms can be found in the topics assigned to the speeches of Demosthenes by the Antiochene rhetor Libanius. These topics described the historical setting and content of a speech and explained points of scholarly interest (e.g., whether the speech was ever given). Christoph Schäublin (1974: 92–94) summarizes the precedents in Hellenistic literature and rhetoric thoroughly, and points out the parallel involving Libanius' topics for Demosthenes' speeches.

6.   Ramsay (1911: 433) writes, "The view thus set forth of David's method of psalm composition strongly resembles and was not improbably suggested to Theodore by the rhetorical exercises familiar in the schools of his pagan contemporaries. The student of oratory in them was often bidden to compose a speech befitting some character of history or romance at some specified juncture of his fortunes."

7.   The *dianoia* is the "thought expressed," the "meaning of a word or passage" (L & S *dianoia* IV). The Antiochene commentators employ also *ennoia* for the "thought" (expressed in a passage) in contrast to the diction (*lexis*) of a passage (L & S *ennoia* III). The *Letter to Aristeas* men-

tions the "physical sense of the law" (*"hē physikē dianoia tou nomou"*; Aristeas 171).

8. Text of the LXX: *en pneumati biaiō̦ syntripseis ploia Tharsis* (LXX 47:8).

9. Translations from the commentary on Jonah are mine.

10. *Contra* Pirot (1913: 249) who, writing before Devreeesse's critical edition of Theodore's *Commentary on the Psalms*, has Theodore taking Psalm 55 (LXX 54) as a prophecy of Christ. In Devreesse's edition, however, Theodore writes that David takes on the *persona* of Onias in Psalm 55.

11. Topics cover various situations from David's life. The other topics are Jeremiah, moral and didactic themes, ancient deeds, Moses, singers in the temple, songs of praise and victory, Christ and the church, the virtuous in Babylon, creation, and reunification of the twelve tribes after exile in Babylon. Psalm 45, interpreted as the marriage of Christ and the church, is of course an extended metaphor or allegory; but that allegory is the "sense" of the text, the only level of meaning the text has (Devreesse 1939: 277–78).

12. The commentator paraphrases Heb 10:1 also in connection with Joel 2:28–29 (Sprenger 1977: 96).

13. M.-J Rondeau (1969: 5–33; 153–88; 1970: 5–33). The entire introduction is translated by Froehlich (1984: 88–94). The translation of the prologue contains some errors ("Hezekiah" is rendered by "Ezekiel").
    The commentator's explanation of Joel 2:28–32 combines Diodore's concept of *ekbainein kyriōteron* with Chrysostom's concept of *ainygma*. He explains that Joel's prophecy is *hyperbolikōs* as well as an *ainygma* in the initial setting (*procheiros*) (Sprenger 1977: 96).

14. New Testament writers cite two passages from Psalm 118: verse 22 ("The stone which the builders rejected has become the head of the corner"; Ps 118:22–23 cited in Mark 12:10–11) and verse 25 ("Blessed is the one who enters in the name of the Lord"; Ps 118:25–26 cited in Matt 21:9; Luke 19:38; John 12:13). For Theodore and Diodore, Psalm 118 concerns the people after the return from exile (Olivier 1980: lxxxiii). Unfortunately Diodore's comments on Psalm 118 are not (yet) available, and Theodore's are not extant. In the Latin *Epitome* of Theodore's commentary, Psalm 118 is treated as Theodore treats Psalm 22; Jesus may recite it as any just person suffering might. The *Epitome* states that the Lord applies the verse to himself "most suitably" (*Quod Dominus noster in euangelio suae personae accomodavit aptissime*).

15. Num 21:4–9 and Wis Sol 16:5–6. The reference occurs in the NT (the commentary cites John 3:13–15).

16. The tradition found in *Midrash Tehellim* 26.7 that "Jonah, while still alive, entered into his glory, into the Garden of Eden" (Braude 1959: 363) may have influenced Christian conceptions of Jonah. But as Ginzberg (1928:

351) observes, "[i]t is, however, possible that the Messianic part attributed to Jonah (= the son of the widow of Zarephath) is a Jewish adaptation of the Christian view which considers him a prototype of Jesus." The Christian introduction, like *Midrash Rabbah* on Exod 4:3, groups Jonah with reluctant prophets Moses and Jeremiah but does not mention Balaam (Sprenger 1977: 173).

17. *Pirqei de Rabbi Eliezar.*
18. My translation. The two categories are not intended to be exhaustive. The introduction goes on, "There is also another topic for the psalms, the Babylonian captivity" (Olivier 1980: 5).
19. A rationalism permeates the commentary suggesting that the intended readers would have been at least amateurs in philosophy. The commentator presents the sense of each verse in terms of what is reasonable, rational, and logical, accepting interpretations deemed "reasonable," "fitting," and "appropriate," and rejecting those deemed "ridiculous." The commentator analyzes biblical figures as individuals motivated by reason and assumes that the reader approaches the text through reason. Noting that scripture is sometimes abbreviated, the commentator leaves the reader to deduce consequences. For example, the reader must deduce what it was that God commanded Jonah to preach in Nineveh in Jonah 1:2 (Sprenger 1977: 177).
20. Robert Wilken argues that Antiochene Christians as late as the early fifth century attended synagogue and observed the holidays (Wilken 1983: 75–79).

REFERENCES

Braude, W. G.
    1959   *The Midrash on Psalms.* 2 vols. New Haven: Yale University.
Devreesse, R.
    1939   *Le Commentaire de Théodore de Mopsueste sur les Psaumes.* Studi e Testi 93. Vatican City: Biblioteca Apostolica Vaticana.
    1948   *Essai sur Théodore de Mopsueste.* Studi e Testi 141. Vatican City: Biblioteca Apostolica Vaticana.
Fornara, C. W.
    1983   *The Nature of History in Ancient Greece and Rome.* Berkeley, CA: University of California.
Froehlich, K. ed. and transl.
    1984   *Biblical Interpretation in the Early Church.* Philadelphia: Fortress.
Ginzberg, L.
    1928   *The Legends of the Jews.* Vol. VI. Philadelphia: Jewish Publication Society.

Goppelt, L.
1982   *Typos: The Typological Interpretation of the Old Testament in the New.* Trans. D. H. Madvig, from German. Grand Rapids, MI: Eerdmans.

Kennedy, G. A.
1980   *Classical Rhetoric and its Christian and Secular Tradition from Ancient to Modern Times.* Chapel Hill, North Carolina: University of North Carolina.

Landes, G. M.
1983   Matthew 12:40 as an Interpretation of "The Sign of Jonah" Against its Biblical Background. Pp. 665–84 in *The Word of the Lord Shall Go Forth: Essays in Honor of David Noel Freedman in Celebration of his Sixtieth Birthday*, eds. C. L. Meyers and M. O'Connor. Winona Lake, IN: Eisenbrauns.

Lauterbach, J. Z.
1933–35   *The Mekilta de-Rabbi Ishmael.* Trans. J. Z. Lauterbach, from Hebrew. Philadelphia: Jewish Publication Society.

Levine, B. A.,
1989   *Leviticus: The Traditional Hebrew Text with the New JPS Translation.* Philadelphia: The Jewish Publication Society.

Macina, R.
1983   L'homme à l'école de Dieu. D'Antioche à Nisibis. Profil hermeneutique, théologique et kerygmatique du movement scholiaste nestorien. *Proche Orient Chrétien* 33: 39–103.

Malherbe, A. J.
1992   Hellenistic Moralists and the New Testament. Pp. 267–333 in *Aufsteig und Niedergang der Römischen Welt,* II.26.1. Ed. W. Haase. Berlin: De Gruyter.

1986   *Moral Exhortation: A Greco-Roman Sourcebook.* Philadelphia: Westminster.

Meeks, W. A. and Wilken, R. L.
1978   *Jews and Christians in Antioch.* Society of Biblical Literature Sources for Biblical Study 13. Missoula, MT: Scholars.

Olivier, J.-M.
1980   *Diodoris Tarsensis Commentarii in Psalmos I; Commentarii in Psalmos I–L.* Corpus Christianorum Series Graeca 6. Turnhout: Brepols.

PG
1859   *Theodorus Mopsuestenus. Patrologia Graeca* 66, ed. J. P. Migne. Paris.

1862   *S. Joannes Chrysostomus. Patrologia Graeca* 55, ed. J. P. Migne. Paris.

Pirot, L.
1913   *L'oeuvre exégétique de Théodore de Mopsueste.* Rome: Pontifical Biblical Institute.

Ramsay, R. L.
1911   Theodore of Mopsuestia and Saint Columban on the Psalms. *Zeitschrift für Celtische Philologie* 8: 421–51.

Rondeau, M.-J.
1969   Le Commentaire des Psaumes de Diodore de Tarse et l'exégèse antique du psaume 109/110. *Revue de l'histoire des religions* 176: 153–88.

1970   Le Commentaire des Psaumes de Diodore de Tarse et l'exégèse antique du psaume 109/110. *Revue de l'histoire des religions* 177: 5–33.

Schäublin, C.
1974   *Untersuchungen zur Methode und Herkunft der Antiochenischen Exegese.* Theoph. 23. Köln-Bonn: Peter Hanstein.

Sprenger, H. N.
1977   *Theodori Mopsuesteni Commentarius in XII Prophetas.* Göttingen Orientforschung V Reihe, vol 1. Wiesbaden: Harrassowitz.

Vaccari, A. S. I.
1920   La ΘΕΩΡΙΑ nella scuola esegetica d'Antiochia. *Biblica* 1: 3–36.

Wiles, M.
1970   Theodore of Mopsuestia as Representative of the Antiochene School. Pp. 489–510 in *The Cambridge History of the Bible,* vol 1. Cambridge: Cambridge University.

Wilken, R. L.
1983   *John Chrysostom and the Jews.* Berkeley: University of California.

<u>16</u> Issues in Contemporary Translation: Late Modern Vantages and Lessons from Past Epochs

GERALD T. SHEPPARD

F or nine years at the beginning of my teaching career, I had the privilege of teaching Old Testament alongside George Landes at Union Theological Seminary. Later, I was elected to the Biblical Colloquium, where George has been a longstanding member. He, in many ways, represented the best of the tradition associated with that group, originally created by students and colleagues of William Foxwell Albright. In addition to publishing in a variety of areas, George also showed great interest in biblical translation. He contributed, with obvious gifts and precision, to the translation of the New Revised Standard Version (hereafter NRSV) of the Bible, now a standard in many if not most Protestant churches. Occasionally we discussed issues of translation and interpretation, especially when it concerned translating a biblical text that was itself an anachronistic blend of traditions from disparate times and places. George understood more clearly than do many other scholars today an important question faced by translators. How do we as translators take into account the fact that the meaning and translation of a *biblical* text might differ substantially from the meaning and translation of *prebiblical* texts? (By "prebiblical texts" I mean texts that we today can reconstruct from the Bible, and that we can assess as original, though disassembled, parts of it). To that question we might add a second—how might a translation of a biblical text help its modern readers interpret critically a prior history of Jewish and Christian interpretation of that same biblical text in centuries past? This latter problem becomes particularly acute when we consider how differently from those of earlier epochs modern readers of Scripture may see the implicit historical references that belong to the words of a biblical text. In sum, I want to raise some issues for translation that take into account the questions we must answer prior to deciding criteria for a translation. These issues include matters as seemingly innocent and neutral as a philological appeal to the meaning of words in a biblical text or in a prebiblical text belonging to the tradition history of that biblical text.

This essay will be concerned to deepen these questions and allow for a variety of plausible practical answers, depending on the goals of translators. On the first question, I will focus on only one issue, a distinction I want to draw between vagueness and functional ambiguity of words in a text and potentially a translation. Second, I will move in an entirely different direction and raise the problem of historical reference by considering a case of premodern translation, namely, *The Book of Psalmes: Englished both in Prose and Metre. With annotations, opening the words and sentences, by conference with other scriptures* (Amsterdam: Giles Thorp, 1612), by a brilliant Protestant, Hebraic scholar, Henry Ainsworth (1570–1622). I will try to show that premodern translation need not be "precritical" even in how it answers our questions. I would like to imagine that if George Landes, himself an ordained Presbyterian minister, were only a few centuries older and if he lived in Amsterdam, despite the British separatist Henry Ainsworth's heated conflict with the Scottish Presbyterian appointee to the English Reformed Church in the same city, George and Ainsworth would have been friends. By describing aspects of a highly sophisticated premodern translation, I want to examine the question of implied historical references in biblical texts and translations as well as some implications worth consideration by late modern or postmodern translators of the Bible today.

I

The distinction between the simple vagueness and the functional ambiguity of words partly grows out of discussions I have had with George Landes (but the weaknesses of my formulation are all my own). Whether the meaning of a word is simply *vague* or *functionally ambiguous* depends entirely on the word's literary-historical context and the text's social employment. Since the form of a text can be variously envisioned by readers and used in various ways, translators must choose a particular form and function even when they try to allow for a plurality of possibilities. In this essay, I am particularly interested in the choice that seeks to view a text as part of Jewish and/or Christian Scriptures. Texts as Scripture are employed by communities of faith as a normative "witness/testimony" to the secret things that God has revealed to them and to their children afar off (cf. Deut 29:29; 31:24–27). That option need not be a matter of piety, since its literary consequences may have nothing to do with one's own religious faith.

1. Simple Vagueness

Simple vagueness is present when a word that we must translate in a particular text is not clearly defined, grasped, or understood. In any text, it may be argued, vagueness of words occurs when words or morphological parts of them are *in context* unreadable, irrelevant, or only known by highly speculative hypotheses. The clarity of a word in an earlier context may in a later context become itself otiose, unexploited, utterly foreign, controverted, or undigested. The use of a plural form of the Hebrew word *ʾĕlōhîm*, literally, "gods," for "God" in most of Jewish Scripture may well illustrate this situation. Conversely, words once clear to any ordinary reader may now be vague, due to the loss of historical information, even to the most extraordinary modern scholar. In that case, we could simply offer only one precise possibility; we could harmonize the vagueness in terms of clearer words nearby and according to the context as a whole; we could transliterate it from Hebrew into English letters; or we could choose some equally vague English word to mark the problem in the text. In the case of a vague phrase in Ps 2:12a, the NRSV chooses one of several plausible and clear translations—"kiss his feet"—then adds a footnote, "Meaning of Heb in verses 11b and 12a is uncertain." The New Jewish Publication Society translation (hereafter, NJPS) suggests, "pay homage in good faith," with a footnote, "Meaning of Heb. uncertain." Likewise, the frequent word *selâ* is simply transliterated from Hebrew as "Selah" (cf. the last word in Ps 3:3, 5, 7) both in the NRSV and in the NJPS. The latter adds a note, "A liturgical direction of uncertain meaning."

A more complex example of what would have originally been clear but became vague can be seen by setting alongside each other two proposals: (1) the philological appeals made by Frank Cross and David Noel Freedman, both founding members of the Biblical Colloquium, in their reconstruction of the original "Song of the Sea," and (2) the proposal of Brevard Childs, also a member of the Biblical Colloquium, on the same song partially preserved in Exodus 15. Cross and Freedman propose that the verb *qāpĕ ʾû* in the original song probably signified that "the deeps *churned*" (Exod 15:8) in a storm, so that the Egyptian pursuers of the Hebrew slaves fell off their barges into turbulent and deep waters (Cross and Freedman 1955; Cross 1968). This reading finds support both in the antiquity and independence of the original song, attested partly by lexical parallels with northern Canaanite, Ugaritic mythological texts, and in its complementarity with other motifs of the song itself (e.g., v. 5, the Egyptian pursuers "went down into the depths like a stone").

Features that were once clear in the original prebiblical song have become increasingly vague centuries later, however, when this same text became part of a longer biblical narrative. In its biblical context, a prose notation (v. 19) follows the song, repeating claims in the prose that now precedes the song. There we hear that God "brought back the waters" on the Egyptians after Israel had "walked through the sea on dry ground." In light of this context, which now gives us a song explicitly sung by Moses and Miriam, we should not be surprised when translators render our verb in 15:8 in exactly the opposite meaning from that argued for by Cross and Freedman. Modern translations may read "the deeps *congealed*" (NRSV) or "the deeps *froze*" (NJPS), understanding the verb analogously to how it is used in Job 10:10. Childs (1974: 243 n. 8, 244–48) has established the cogency of this move. It is important to note that the biblical editors did not harmonize the ancient Hebrew words of the older song in its later biblical context—the song still exists in most of its original, unaltered language. The semantic potential of its words, however, has been reassessed, even rehistoricized, as is evident *by the context* that these editors gave to it. Childs ought not to debate philologically on the same level with Cross and Freedman. The two philological arguments pursue two subtly different texts that are closely related diachronically, but not identical in time, space, context, and social function. While these scholars need each other philologically, they are not translating precisely the same text.

2. Functional Ambiguity

A word that is *functionally ambiguous* in its context presents a very different problem. In contrast to vagueness, functional ambiguity occurs when the word itself is familar but the context employs it in a way that sets into motion a delimited oscillation of the referent. The context: (1) delimits somewhat the word's possible referents, and (2) elicits and requires a search for the referent. In Psalm 2, we find a recapitulation of the promise to David in 2 Samuel 7 regarding a future son in his dynasty against whom the nations will conspire. This person is called "his (God's) anointed" (NRSV, 2:2). This same word could be translated "messiah" or "Messiah" or in Greek, "Christ." The word could be taken as merely a metaphor for any king who receives God's blessing. The Good News Bible eliminates all of this ambiguity by translating the word with the phrase, "the king he chose." If the word in context is *supposed* to be ambiguous, these translators have radically changed the potential significance of the psalm.

The term "his anointed" (Ps 2:2) appears in a context in the Book of Psalms that is highly suggestive, in my view. The word belongs to a psalm that, together with Psalm 1, forms a postexilic introduction to the book of Psalms. Psalm 2 within the book resonates explicitly with Psalm 89, which also cites 2 Samuel 7, just before an intercessory prayer assigned to Moses, Psalm 90, with an extraordinarily positive response from God in Psalm 91. Whatever its origin and original meaning, Psalm 2 in the book of Psalms appears as a messianic promise of a future son of David, despite the destruction of "the throne" and "crown" of the Davidic monarchy, as Psalm 89 so vividly attests (vv. 39, 44). In other words, rather than being vague, the Hebrew word for "his anointed" stimulates the need for interpretation. One option is to preserve the ambiguity by a literalistic translation of the word, as do both the NRSV and NJPS ("His anointed," with "His" capitalized to link it explicitly to "the Lord" earlier in the same verse). This "anointed one" could, in theory, be David's immediate son, Solomon (cf. Psalm 72), or some other Davidic or messianic king. The psalm's later Jewish readers could and did understand it as "the Messiah," though the word "anointed one" is never explicitly used with the definite article within Jewish Scripture in reference to a prophetically promised future person. But only readers who know that "anointed one" and "messiah" translate the same word can entertain such possibilities.

Another more subtle example of functional ambiguity concerns the identity of the suffering "servant" in Isaiah 53. If we take the servant song out of its context in the book of Isaiah and try to reconstruct it as a prebiblical tradition in the postexilic period, we may seek to rediscover the identify of the servant, which was perhaps originally clear. We might speculate that the servant was really Deutero-Isaiah, as is common in many modern commentaries. In the scroll of Isaiah, however, the context of this song has at least secondarily made the referent functionally ambiguous, within the limits of a particular pattern of descriptive characterizations. Moreover, the context has also deepened the demand for interpretation by implying that this "servant" has significance for the sake of the redemption of Israel. So, later Jewish interpreters heard the resultant biblical text well when they sought reasonably and endlessly to identify that person in time and space: Moses? Joshua? Elijah? Zerubbabel?

While this biblical text remains understandably non-Messianic for most Jews, it became Messianic for Christians only because their Messiah was, in fact, crucified. The crucified Messiah fit the pattern of resemblances in Isaiah 53 far more than did *their own* earlier messianic expectations from Scripture. By holding the ambiguity of the Isaiah text together with the senseless death of their Messiah, text and event illuminated each other—an ancient text became an unambiguous prophecy of a meaningful death of the Messiah. The biblical text came to be heard in an entirely new way, as messianic promise fulfilled in history by the atoning death of Jesus Christ. The truth of this interpretation requires a spiritual acquiescence for its justification and could never be proved by history or grammar alone. Irenaeus admits the same in the second century C.E. when he states, "Every prophecy is enigmatic and ambiguous for human minds before it is fulfilled. But when the time has arrived and the prediction has come true, then prophecies find their clear and unambiguous interpretation" (*Against Heresies* IV.26.1; Froehlich 1984: 44). Only if a translator distinguishes to some degree differences between simple vagueness and functional ambiguity of words in Scripture can contemporary readers comprehend and critically consider centuries of Christian "literal sense" interpretation or Jewish "midrashic" modes of making sense of the same text.

II

Translation obviously belongs to the art of interpretation and interpretation presupposes a mode of perception on the part of readers. Edward Greenstein (1989: 57) cogently reminds us as readers, "Perception is itself an interpretive faculty, an active, though largely automatic, implementation of our prior models, presuppositions, and analytic strategies." For this reason, readers in earlier epochs may use the same English words as we use, while knowing these words in radically different ways from our perception of them. Admittedly my response to this problem will seek a text-oriented description instead of a solution primarily from a reader-response perspective.

I want to consider specifically the pressure a text ought to exert on any competent reader, or how a particular text and its social function can engender proper expectations, with its own commensurate rewards and disappointments. We can explore some contours to this problem by comparing our familiar English translations of the Psalms with Ainsworth's English translation of the Psalms, made at the beginning of the seventeenth century, before any conspicuous emergence of the Modern Age. We will begin this comparison with a confession of the sins of modernity: we now have inherited a legacy of misunderstanding the past, aided and abetted by a false confidence about the meaning of words. A primary example is the impressive, nineteenth century *History of Interpretation* by Oxford historian, Frederic W. Farrar. He evaluates premodern interpretation positively only when it anticipates modern historical-critical insights or seems to focus on "the author's intent" (Farrar 1979, orig. 1886: 27, 33). Contemporary counterparts to Farrar's *History* are as common as the *Cambridge History of the Bible* (Wiles 1970: 488–89). The logical fallacy that supports Farrar is subtle and easily underestimated.

1. The Fallacy of a False Intimacy with Words

We can clarify the difficulty of comparing the modern and the premodern by considering Michel Foucault's attempt to describe the transition from premodern to modern perceptions. Foucault observes "two great discontinuities in the *episteme* of Western culture," by which he seeks to describe a dramatic alteration in the cultural understanding of what is elemental and in what spatial organization or configuration our knowledge of the world belongs. Foucault recognises various "discontinuities" between the Classical Age, which emerges full-blown after the Reformation in the middle of the seventeenth century, and the Modern Age, which takes hold after the beginning of the nineteenth century (Foucault 1991: 34–75). (He senses another epistemological shift starting with the 1960s, the characteristics of which he believes have not yet become fully apparent [1991: 386–87].) Concerning Ainsworth's day, Foucault observes, "At the beginning of the seventeenth century, during the period that has been termed, rightly or wrongly, the Baroque, thought ceases to move in the element of resemblance." In brief, "The age of resemblance is drawing to a close" (1991: 51). Foucault (1991: 55) describes this modification of the entire *episteme* in Western Europe in more practical terms as follows:

> The activity of the mind ... will therefore no longer consist in *drawing things together*, in setting out a quest for everything that might reveal some sort of kinship, attraction, or secretly shared nature within them, but, on the contrary, in *discriminating*, that is, in establishing their identities, then the inevitability of the connections with all the successive degrees of a series.

In other words, Foucault sees in the Classical Age a systemic change in the dominant *episteme* in Western Europe. The new *episteme* involved a radically different understanding of historical references within a text, and therefore of what historical criticism might be. In his view, "the seventeenth century marks the disappearance of the old superstitious or magical beliefs and the entry of nature, at long last, into the scientific order" (Foucault 1991: 54). There arose a preoccupation with "tables," for example, by which things can be assigned their place within an "order" of related elements. Some signs of this same disposition can be seen in Ainsworth's various "tables" at the end of his book and in other concordances of "commonplaces" familiar in the seventeenth century (Kolb 1987: 151–53; Sheppard 1989: xlii–lxxl). "Commonplaces" were key words or phrases integral to one's proper ability to grasp the literal sense of Scripture by hearing together the words or grammar of a biblical text and its subject matter of revelation. In contrast to the "complete" concordances of the modern period, they were predecessors, to a degree, of what became in the modern period "Biblical Theology," as distinguished from Dogmatic or Church Theology. They were usually listed at the beginnings of each sub-section of biblical passages in a commentary, or highlighted by cross-references, or they formed the basis of a concordance. Ainsworth takes the latter two options in his book, within his annotations, and in a short, selective concordance of words, which he appends to his book.

Foucault describes the subsequent loss of confidence with this established mode of description and its alleged coherence during the nineteenth century, when perspectives emerged that culminated in "the Modern Age." For Foucault (1991: xxiii) the epitome of this transition was when,

> the theory of representation [dominant in the Classical Age] disappears as the universal foundation of all possible orders; language as the spontaneous *tabula*, the primary grip of things, as an indispensable link between representation and things, is eclipsed in its turn; a profound historicity penetrates into the heart of things, isolates and defines them in their own coherence, imposes upon them the forms of order implied by the continuity of time.

This modern historicism, replete with its own new insights and new limitations, has itself recently come under siege. Today the awkward and popular term "postmodern" betrays at least a confidence that we participate in a transition from modern sensibilities toward some other possible configurations of reality across a broad cultural horizon.

2. Ainsworth and His The Psalms (1612)

Ainsworth stands among the most learned non-Jewish Hebraists of his period (Katchen 1984: 35; Moody 1982: 203, 208). He offers both prose and metrical translations, and he appends very detailed annotations to each psalm. These annotations shed light on the underlying hermeneutical aims of Ainsworth's translation, which would be hard to discern by examining the translations alone. The vastness of Ainsworth's book, as well as of this subject generally, requires that I make some rather drastic decisions at the outset of this discussion. I will not attempt here to survey many of the relevant areas. Fortunately, others have already made impressive strides in that regard (Holladay 1993; Lewalski 1979; Steinmetz 1990). Instead, I will consider in detail a few issues related to historical references and how they have been understood differently in the Modern Period.

Ainsworth's work on Psalms deserves far more attention than it has received. He pursued academic work at the "Puritan" Emmanuel College at Cambridge, but fled under pressures from the Church of England, without graduating from Cambridge, to reside in Amsterdam in 1593 as a Protestant "separatist." Among his Christian friends in exile were John Robinson and William Brewster, whose congregation was in Leiden. In July, 1620, members of the Leiden congregation set sail on the Speedwell for England, and, then, on the Mayflower went on to found Plymouth Colony. They took with them Ainsworth's *Psalms,* which gains attention in the following account of their departure,

> They that stayed at Leyden feasted us that were to go at our pastor's house, [it] being large, where we refreshed ourselves, with singing Psalms, making joyful melody in our hearts as well as with the voice, there being many of our congregation very expert in music; and indeed it was the sweetest melody that ever mine ears heard (Pratt 1941: 6; Winslow 1968: 90).

The widespread use of Ainsworth's *Psalms* both in England and in the New England Colonies gained it contemporary literary attention. In "The Courtship of Miles Standish," Henry Wadsworth Longfellow describes John Alden's chance encounter with Priscilla, who is sitting alone and singing the 100th Psalm,

> Open wide on her lap the well-worn psalm-book of Ainsworth,
> Printed in Amsterdam, the words and the music together,
> Rough-hewn, angular notes, like stones in the wall of a churchyard,
> Darkened and overhung by the running vine of the verses.

On the title page of Ainsworth's *Psalms* we immediately find a hint about his typically Protestant perspective. There he describes his annotations as "opening the words and sentences, by conference with other Scriptures." This subtitle reflects the practical consequences of the Protestant principle that Scripture interprets Scripture, presented as an alternative to reliance upon the Church's teaching *magisterium* as the decisive norm of interpretation. By the sixteenth century the Latin based word "conference" began to replace the word "collation" as a technical term for explaining texts by the comparison and addition of information from other related texts. In his 1647 *Body of Doctrine*, Bishop Ussher explains, "By ... conference of other places, the true reading may be discerned." Therefore, one goal of this essay is to consider how such conferencing of Scripture with Scripture indicates something essential to the nature of what Ainsworth thinks he is translating. Implicit in my way of asking that question is the suggestion that there is no single objective method of translating but only strategies of translation dependent on the answer to a prior question about how a text makes "sense" for those who want to read it in their own tongue.

3. Understanding Ainsworth's Translation by Way of a Modern Misunderstanding

In order to illustrate some of these problems as concretely as possible for the subject of psalm translation, let me cite two negative examples from an otherwise outstanding scholarly assessment of *The Bay Psalm Book* of 1640, the first book and Psalter published in the American Colonies. In his *The Enigma of the Bay Psalm Book* (1956), Zoltán Haraszti highlights several positive features of the metrical psalm translations of *The Bay Psalm Book*, despite much earlier criticism by other scholars, who find them both uneven in quality and derivative. Haraszti makes several sweeping judgments about the recognition of historical criticism and historical references in the Psalms among seventeenth century Protestant interpreters, including Ainsworth specifically.

Haraszti (1956: 38–39) begins his description of both Ainsworth's *Psalms* and *The Bay Psalm Book* with the glittering generality, "It is doubtful that the problems of 'higher criticism' worried them much." He contrasts this situation with that of the Reformers who were open to the new ideas of humanism and detected some historical features indicative of a more complex tradition history. Haraszti cites Calvin's observation, "He who collected the Psalms into one volume, whether Ezra or someone else ...." Regretting the subsequent loss of this earlier openness to historical complexity, Haraszti concludes that "by the seventeenth century a dogmatic revival set in, which insisted on David's authorship of all the psalms." After a detailed treatment of several psalms in the *Bay Psalm Book*, including comparisons with Ainsworth's *Psalms*, he opines,

> One may justly ask how they could explain Psalms 126 and 137 without recognizing their post-Exilic origin or account for the repetitions of certain psalms and for the use of "Jehovah" in some of the books and "Elohim" in others, without realizing that the Psalter was a composite of earlier collections (Haraszti 1956: 39).

To these disappointments, he adds,

> Only Ainsworth's translation marked the fivefold division, but the prose versions too added the "finis" clause after Psalm 72. At that point Ainsworth noted that "Davids prayers are not set last in order." However, it was only in the next generation that scholars, led by Grotius, began to discuss in earnest *these contradictions and confusions* (Haraszti 1956: 39–40, my emphasis).

Before taking up some of Haraszti's specific observations, we might first consider his overarching comment about the apparent lack of anxiety about "higher criticism" among the seventeenth-century Protestant interpreters. *The Oxford English Dictionary* (Vol 2, 1971: 1181) indicates that what had previously been called "Grammar" began to be called "Criticism" only during the last half of the seventeenth century. Further, English usage of the term "higher criticism" begins only in the nineteenth century, in R. Keith's English translation and publication in 1836 of Hengstenberg's *Christology of the Old Testament*. In W. Robertson Smith's famous lectures in defence of historical criticism, delivered to an assembly of Scottish Presbyterians in 1881, the term "higher criticism" was still new enough to require definition. He explained that a "series of questions affecting the composition, the editing, and the collecting of the sacred books" is "usually distinguished from the verbal criticism of the text by the name of Higher or Historical Criticism" (Smith 1881: 104–5). Neither Baruch Spinoza nor John Locke, both born in 1632, had yet presented even an embryonic approach to Scripture that might later be identified with the label of "modern" or "higher criticism" (Drury 1989: 1–20; Reventlow 1984; Shaffer 1975). Clearly, the term "higher criticism" would have been unfamiliar to Ainsworth and his contemporaries. That fact in itself, however, might not necessarily warrant our calling them, according to our own conventions, "uncritical" or even "precritical" in their use of texts or in their practice of translation.

4. Ainsworth as a Seventeenth Century Translator and Commentator

In order to understand Ainsworth's translation and commentary on the Psalms, we need to see him at the end of the Classical Age in the Netherlands. This was a time when many intellectuals and artists became aware that they were participating in a transitional period as momentous as the one many of us feel we are experiencing today. One impressive sign of this consciousness of a change in perspective can be seen in the artistic development of the famous Dutch "still life," a term not used for such art until the mid-seventeenth century. In this period, items portrayed as on tables—in the paintings of Pieter and Willem Claesz, Antonio de Pereda, Pieter Boel, Georg Flegel, Nicolas Gillis, Foris van Dijck, for example—included such things as half-eaten food, insects or cats leaping onto the remains, plates precariously ready to fall off, unattended remains of peels, shells, or dead plants alongside the living, and even skulls, dishevelled books, and citations from Ecclesiastes about the vapour and vanity of life. Art historian Norbert Schneider describes in detail how these efforts "teach us ... inconspicuously and implicitly, about historical changes in attitudes towards the capabilities of human perception" (Schneider 1990: 18).

Ainsworth, as one of the most gifted of biblical scholars in the first half of the seventeenth century, deserves our full appreciation precisely because he exhibits, against this increasing tide, the full maturity and fruition of a perspective not yet put in serious jeopardy by the later triumphant "modern" alternatives. He affords us an exciting opportunity to examine what a genius in the late premodern period is capable of perceiving in the words of a biblical text and what he is not. We can compare and contrast with modern perceptions how Ainsworth responds to the evidence of resemblance and difference in a text, including, of course, overt as well as subtle historical references in the Bible. We must ask carefully *how* and perhaps *if* Ainsworth shares the same biblical text with us, when we presume to see how differently he interprets it. We need to be alert to how each of us might envision differently the elements of a shared text, so that we become aware of what we will most easily "see" and "know" in uniquely different ways. Hearing a psalm form-critically in the modern period may properly envision only an originally oral text of a prebiblical prayer in ancient Israel. This is not identical with a written textual "psalm" within a "prophetic" biblical book of Psalms within the intertext of Jewish or Christian Scriptures. In our efforts to interpret the history of interpretation, what could be more elementary than the question of whether what is being interpreted is actually the same text?

Furthermore, we must recognize that a shift in our form of knowing the same things affects how we use and what we signify by ordinary labels, such as, "author," "history," "text," "intent," and "translation." As scholars who stand today once again in a period of disequilibrium between epochs of confidence, we may be in an advantageous position, and more able than some who preceded us, to understand a fresh textual interpretation in the distant and recent past for the sake of a new future.

5. "Authorship," "History," and the "Meaning" of Biblical Psalms

My strategy here will be, first, to respond to Haraszti's specific assessments of the seventeenth-century translations by considering the evidence of Ainsworth's effort. Afterwards, I will suggest a more general, alternative strategy for judging premodern "exposition" and its implications for a later, modern "exegesis" (Sheppard 1989: llxvii; Terry 1890: 19). At the outset, Haraszti asserts flatly that "a dogmatic revival" in this period "insisted on David's authorship of all the psalms." Contradicting this assertion is Ainsworth's statement that when Psalm titles "signifie the writers" or "inditers," they indicate not only David but also Asaph, Heman, Aethan, and Moses (Ainsworth 1612: 346–47). Ainsworth's list is further significant because he omits from it Solomon (Pss 72:1: 127:1) and Korah (Pss 42:1; 44:1; 45:1; 46:1; 47:1; 48:1;

49:1; 84:1; 85:1; 87:1; 88:1). His translation deals with these figures in a different way. As did ancient interpreters of the Bible, Ainsworth has made a historical and critical decision based on a grammatical ambiguity: All these superscriptions link familiar names by the same prepositional morpheme (*lamed*), which could be translated either "by" (signifying a designated writer or speaker), or "to"/"for" (signifying either some indirect association or the person concerning whom a prayer is prayed). While most psalms are "of David," these others are "to the sons of Korah" or "for Solomon." The Authorized Version of 1611, *The Bay Psalm Book*, and many other English translations maintained similar distinctions. In this matter, Ainsworth's translation is dynamic rather than concerned with retaining the text's ambiguity in a formal-equivalence translation, to use a modern distinction.

If we ask what criteria led Ainsworth and most of his predecessors to these historical conclusions, we find in his annotations evidence that he looks to the books of Chronicles for this information. There he learns David appointed the Asaphites to be authors of psalms, according to 1 Chr 25:1, but the Korahites were assigned only the role of "doorkeepers," without an explicit vocation for composing psalms (1 Chr 26:1). For that reason, several psalms have been written by an unnamed person for some use by the Korahites: "to these sonns of Korah this and sundry other Psalms are commended" (annotation on Ps 42:1). Similarly, in his table "Of the Titles of the Psalms," he states (1612: 348) the sons of Korah "have eleven psalmes directed unto them."

For some psalms without superscriptions, Ainsworth notes the New Testament citation of them as words by David. Ainsworth (1612: 347) speculates on unnamed psalms, "some of these the holy Ghost witnesseth that David wrote them, Act.4.25. Heb.4.7. and so we may judge of the rest." This comment harmonizes away any possible conflict in historical assumptions between New Testament usage and the book of Psalms itself. The effect is to put the New Testament on a par with the Old Testament and to reinforce the place of Psalms as a part of Christian Scripture. It does not argue "historically" in a strict modern sense, nor does the attribution to David anchor the meaning of these psalms to a distinct psychology and overarching "intent" of David. The speculative nature of his conclusion, "so we may judge the rest," shows that these untitled psalms belong fully to the Psalms of David, but authorship itself is not necessarily the key to meaning.

Ainsworth's conception of authorship and its import for interpreting the text differs in other ways from similar concerns that would arise in the modern period. The annotations themselves show that the relationship of Psalms to David is for Ainsworth far more significant as a clue regarding how each psalm relates to rest of Scripture, or how other Scriptures can be cited to "open" its words, than as a strictly historical reference to events occurring in the pre-history of the text itself. Another sign of this difference is Ainsworth's frequent use of the term "inditer" for our modern term "author." Here Ainsworth implies he perceives a biblical "author" in terms of someone who "dictates" or composes orally. In Ainsworth's own day, lectures were customarily recorded and edited by others, though published under the name of the lecturer. The preface to William Perkins' commentary on Galatians well illustrates this practice. This preface attests to a self-conscious awareness of a complex process of recording addresses, their transmission, the editing of them by others, and the "author's" examination of the results. Books were often developed from speeches or sermons that "were taken by some diligent auditors, and perused by himself" (Cudsworth 1617: preface; see Sheppard 1989).

The term "inditer" itself suggests a primary emphasis on the voice of a person as the vehicle for his or her published words. While there was substantial fidelity to the words actually spoken, books were edited by auditors, who would not record or retain every single word precisely as it had been originally spoken. Ainsworth applies this model to the psalms' ascriptions. In my view, Ainsworth has put emphasis on the human "authority" of these biblical traditions primarily in so far as they identify whole books or blocks of tradition with a known biblical figure. Authorship in this sense serves as a demarcation of the prevailing and authoritative human voice in a book, indicative of that particular textual territory specifically pertaining to individual books or collections of books.

For Ainsworth, Perkins, and others in the sixteenth and seventeenth century, the process was less important than the result; the opposite became true for modern historicists. Ainsworth and his colleagues, instead of focusing on the historical "origins" of a "unit" of "biblical tradition," preferred to talk about "the circumstances of the place [or 'text']." By the term "place" they spoke commonly of words located within a larger territory of literature, unlike our modern disposition to speak more abstractly and non-contextually of "texts." "The circumstances" of a place concerned any specific historical information that might illuminate the grammatical and semantic use of words. A good example can be found in Ainsworth's annotations on Psalm 74. This is one of the rare instances I could find where he shows some fleeting interest in a complex prehistory to the book of Psalms. On the superscription to Psalm 71 Ainsworth proposes:

> Of Asaph ... **If Asaph (who lived in Davids dayes) made this psalm, it was a prophesie of troubles to come. If some other prophet made it, when calamities were on Israel; then was it committed to** Asaphs posteritie **the singers, caled by their fathers name; as** Aaron's posteritie, **are caled** Aaron. 1.Chron. 12.27. [The use of boldface type here, and in the quotations below, is Ainsworth's own.]

The reason for Ainsworth's judgment that the words of this psalm pertain to circumstances centuries after David and the "trouble to come ... when calamities were on Israel," can be found in his annotations. Ainsworth sees that the psalmist pleads with God about the Temple in flames (v. 7), an event that belongs to the historical aftermath of the Babylonian conquest, destruction of the temple, and exile of Judah. These events constitute the "circumstances of the place" regardless of authorship. Since the superscription appears to identify an incongruent author or inditer, however, Ainsworth allows for two possibilities. The psalm could have been prophetically written for later circumstances, and 1 Chr 25:1 confirms the prophetic nature of the Davidic psalms. Or, "some other [much later] prophet made it," and simply "committed it to Asaph's posteritie." To speak of having "committed it to Asaph" implies assigning it to the inditer, Asaph! This is quite a different matter than the case of psalms "directed unto ..." as in Ainsworth's assignment of the Korahite psalms, as already discussed. At least in theory, nothing would prevent him from saying the same of a Davidic psalm. This latter type of move utilizes the very same logic that underlies modern historical criticism's designation of Isa 40–66 as written by "Deutero-Isaiah" and "Trito-Isaiah." What is for Haraszti the most obvious about a biblical text is the least obvious to Ainsworth. Yet, both Haraszti and Ainsworth actually translate with the same historical features in mind. As Foucault has demonstrated, however, they "know" and perceive the implications of this same data in very different ways.

Recall that Haraszti further criticizes Ainsworth and other seventeenth century commentators on psalms by the derisive comment, "One may justly ask how they could explain Psalms 126 and 137 without recognizing their post-Exilic origin." Historical references to the exile or postexilic period seem so obvious to Haraszti that he can only imagine that a "dogmatic" assumption of Davidic authorship could have prevented Ainsworth and others from seeing these features. Haraszti presupposes that historical references necessitate a postexilic date for these psalms and, therefore, provide the semantic key to their true meaning. Perhaps even if Haraszti looked carefully at Ainsworth's annotations of these two psalms, he might have still overlooked how Ainsworth fully confirms the postexilic "circumstances" of both Psalms 126 and 137. On the word, "the captivitie," in the untitled Ps 126:1, Ainsworth clarifies the sense as follows: **"that is,** the multitude of captives **returning from bondage"** and, further, **"The return from Babels bondage, figured their redemption by Christ. Isa. 10,21,22, Rom. 9.27."** The biblical text itself does not name Babylon explicitly at all, but Ainsworth freely does, and he knows the nation of Babylon only plays this role centuries later than the time of David. On the later reference to "our captivitie" in v. 4, Ainsworth further collates this verse with Ezek 11:24–25, recalling the words of a prophet overtly identified with the postexilic period long after David, and one who makes a direct appeal to captivity in Babylon.

In Ainsworth's annotations to Psalm 137, which mentions people in despair "by the river of Babylon," he does not hesitate to "conference" this text with Jer 25:11–12 and confirms it as the place where "were the Jewes captives." He states for verse 1, **"In that captivity, they lamented as in this psalm is shewed."** But these observations offer no historical help in determining who wrote this untitled psalm. As indicated in the annotation to Ps 74:1, because the psalmist is a prophet he may speak in terms of circumstances far into the future. The question of the historical "origins" of these psalms remains of much less importance than the historical "circumstances," since these "circumstances" that are referenced by the psalm govern critically the provenance of language within the psalm. For neither Psalm 126 nor Psalm 137 does Ainsworth feel the need to address the problem of the "origins" of these psalms. Nonetheless, "the circumstances of the place" clarifies the historical reference of the words in the Psalm, and the words ought to be grammatically and semantically illuminated by words and circumstances pertaining to postexilic events as found elsewhere in Scripture. Never is "the author's intent" used as an historicist norm in the way that has become commonplace in the modern period; a verse of Scripture might just as likely be introduced with the words, "the Holy Spirit says." The most consistent goal is not, however, a spiritual or pneumatic rendering but an effort to retain the "plain sense" of a text in its translation. How this text makes sense differently to Jews and Christians becomes yet another major issue. At least, we are reminded, once more, that Ainsworth and his peers knew the import of "historical" traces in these psalms in a way differing from how the modern period came to know them. Perhaps the conviction regarding the prophetic nature of the book of Psalms provides the next logical step in our effort to understand why Ainsworth and other Christian scholars made the choices they did in early English Psalm translations.

6. Conferencing: "History," Grammar, and Key Word Resonances in the Translation of a Prophetic Text

Ainsworth's use of "conferencing" in his annotations to "open" words for the sake of his translation presupposes a uniquely prophetic character to the nature of the biblical text itself. If, to the contrary, the meaning of the Bible is, to use a modern example, essentially a "message" being sent from a sender (author) to a receiver (reader), then dynamic-equivalence translation ought to win the day. Even here one liability is that such a translation of the Bible might become a bland resource of "information." For this reason, translators employing dynamic equivalence in United Bible Society work are advised to include imperative and emotive expressions in their renderings of "kernel meanings" of biblical verses in "the target language" (Nida and Tabor 1974: 24). If, however, the language of the Bible is less telegraphic, and can be identified as prophetic speech, then the language's actual form may play a more significant role in biblical texts than is allowed by even the best dynamic-equivalence translation. The text's actual form may establish a pattern of resemblances between one biblical text and another, or between the biblical text and the subject matter of the text: the Torah for Jews, or the Torah and Gospel for Christians. Edward Greenstein persuasively describes some limitations to modern dynamic equivalence for the retention of resonance, on a strictly literary level, in the translation of an extended textual unit. Greenstein (1989: 85–118) also points out the additional role of resonance, or interplay of formal elements, that the translation of Buber and Rosenzweig sought to retain in order to make midrashic interpretation comprehensible to a German reader of the Bible. As a rough analogy, we might say that Ainsworth sought to make Christian "literal sense" interpretation comprehensible, much as did Buber and Rosenzweig for midrash. "Literal sense" interpretation, as we shall see, often traded upon a different set of resonances than midrash. However, Ainsworth's aim is complicated by his desire, also, to acknowledge in varying degrees the possession of this book by Jewish interpreters, who still have a claim upon it, in a manner both similar to and distinct from his own.

Evidence of Ainsworth's allowance for Jewish interpretation can be found in his reliance on Jewish grammatical helps, his use of the Targums throughout his Psalms, and, later, his extensive use of citations from the Mishnah and Talmud in his annotations to the Pentateuch. Ainsworth's reliance on rabbinic tradition evoked outrage from his antagonist John Paget of the English Reformed Church in Amsterdam. Paget and Ainsworth became embroiled in a dispute over ecclesiology, elaboration of which lies beyond the scope of this essay. In the middle of that heated debate, Paget wrote an extensive pamphlet entitled, "An Admonition Touching Talmudique & Rabinical Allegations." In it, Paget complains, "Mr. A, it was much beyond my expectations, when as I met with your allegations of Rabbines against me in this controversy." Paget (1618: 339–59) chides Ainsworth, "The Rabbines may say they have made you rich: that your Annotations are enriched with their traditions ..." but, "It is too much that you approve of them in so great a measure." Though we have almost no historical information about Ainsworth's life in Amsterdam, we do know his house and church lay outside the old city in what became the Jewish neighborhood. Jews who fled persecution in other parts of Europe populated this area, just as Ainsworth himself had sought refuge from England when the independent churches were under siege. A subtle hint of Ainsworth's positive relationship to Jewish rabbis can perhaps be seen in his careful insistence that in Ps 2:1, David prophetically "marvel(s) at the rage and folly of Jewes and Gentiles, in persecuting Christ and his Church." The citation from Acts 4:35 [actually 4:25], repeats this phrase, "Jews and Gentiles." This phrase at least broadens the blame for Jesus' death by including Gentiles, unlike an earlier tendency by some Reformers to assign the guilt simply to "Jews." By contrast, Isaac Watts begins his hymnic version of Psalm 2, "Why did the Jews proclaim their Rage" (Bishop 1962: lxiv).

A significant point is that Ainsworth saw in Jewish interpretation a concern, similar to his own, with the prophetic nature of the Psalms. In his occasional dependence on Jewish tradition and especially his use of the "Chaldee," or Aramaic Targums, he finds help in determining which psalms he should take to be messianic in a Christian sense, although other evaluative factors also enter in and prove more decisive. He does not cite the Targums for Psalm 2, although he clearly interprets it in his translation as a prophecy of Christ. Ainsworth even volunteers "his Christ" for "his anointed" in v. 2. In contrast to his ample citations of Mishnah and Talmud in his work on the Pentateuch, Ainsworth's annotations to the psalms make only rare reference to Jewish tradition outside of the Targums.

Ainsworth's treatment of Psalm 22 provides an example of his approach. He annotates the superscription of Psalm 22 mentioning the word "Aejaleth," and comments, "**Some Jewes have interpreted it**, morning starr; **which (although the word be no where ells found in scripture, for a starr;) agreeth also to our Lord Christ who is intituled**, the bright morning starr, Rev.22.16." Elsewhere he notes Targumic messianic references, as with the annotation to the first verse of Psalm 21, "**This Psalm, as the former, gratulateth the victory and salvation of Christ; and is by the Chaldee paraphrast applied to the reign of** King Messias."

The mere fact that the Targum makes reference to "Messias" does not always determine what Ainsworth will do with a psalm as a whole. For example, on Ps 80:16, "and the son," he remarks, "**By** the son, **may be meant** Christ, **as the Chaldee paraphrast plainly sayth**, the King Messias." Yet, with the exception of the phrase, "man of thy right hand," in v. 18, Ainsworth finds no christological overtones throughout this psalm. Also, use of the Targums will not tell us whether a messianic psalm will be understood by Ainsworth expressly as verbal prophecy or, as in the case of Psalm 45 and 72, only as typologically open to messianic interpretation. In sum, we find in Ainsworth some signs of an engagement with Jewish interpretation regarding the prophetic import of the Psalms from a congenial but distinctly Christian perspective.

Ainsworth's emphasis on the prophetic dimension of Scripture and on the effective hearing of God's voice accords well with a position found in the lengthy response to the Council of Trent by William Whitaker, one of Ainsworth's teachers at Cambridge. Whitaker (1968: 296) cites a Roman Catholic view of Scripture that justifies reliance on the teaching traditions of the Church alongside Scripture, "The scripture is not the voice of God; that is, it does not proceed immediately from God, but is delivered mediately to us through others." His answer is, "The prophets and apostles were only the organs of God [citing Heb 1:1 and 2 Pet 1:21] ... Therefore scripture is the voice of the Spirit, and consequently the voice of God." This understanding of the ultimate voice of Scripture as God's voice, regardless of its overstated simplicity, resists any reduction of the Bible to either an isolated "message" from a human author or an aesthetic system of signs. Wilfred Cantwell Smith (1992: 21–44) has recently raised this same issue for Scriptures in most religions in his *What is Scripture? A Comparative Approach*. Similarly, George Steiner (1988: 94–98) criticizes *The Literary Guide to the Bible* for reducing the Bible to merely aesthetic or symbolic literature.

We have already seen with Ainsworth's interpretation of Psalm 137 that a psalm's prophetic character shifts the weight of interpretation away from a focus on the social location of the writer to the historical "circumstances" attendant to the words themselves. The concern is less with the biography of the original speaker and the identity of the target audience than with the clarity of a particular voice that has become particularly articulate in language enlivened by implicit and explicit references to the ephemeral circumstances of a specific historical event. For Ainsworth the point of Psalm 137 is not that a prophet can predict future events, but that a prophet here bears witness to the import of the Torah upon the effective circumstances of the psalm's events. So, Ainsworth does not annotate Psalm 137 in the future tense, any more than he translates verbs in the psalm as prophetic perfects. At this level of translation, other verses of Scripture "conference" with this psalm in order to illuminate its words grammatically and historically. Later, we will consider other dimensions of conferencing related to how "Scripture interprets Scripture." For the moment, it is enough to see that Ainsworth clearly understands this psalm to reveal through prophecy the reality of the historical events themselves: "In this captivity, they lamented as in this psalm is shewed."

On the basis of the prophetic character of Scripture in general, Ainsworth also allows for radically different "circumstances of the place" even within the same psalm. For example, the superscription of Psalm 51 identifies the following prayer of penitence as David's words after Nathan the prophet confronted him regarding his taking Bathsheba. Premodern interpreters generally recognized that the last two verses suddenly refer to circumstances in the period of the exile, after the destruction of Jerusalem. Modern critics usually conclude that they are a postexilic addition to an earlier psalm. They contain a request of God, "build-thou, the walls of Jerusalem" (Ainsworth, v. 20) and look for a time when sacrifices can be offered once more in the temple. In his annotations, Ainsworth clarifies, **"for the building up of these [walls], dooth David here pray."** On the next verse, he relates the circumstances **"when the walls of Jerusalem were unbuilded"** to the postexilic period. He cites Neh 1:3 and recounts how God "sharply blamed" the people, who lived in the postexilic period, for not rebuilding these walls, recalling also Hag 1:2, 4, 8, 9, and 2:1. Again the circumstances of the place inform the translator's lexical understanding of the grammar and semantic force of the words.

Ainsworth routinely tries to make sense of difficult terms both by appeal to their occurrence elsewhere in Scripture and by making use of conferencing to "open" the meaning of words in a psalm according to the circumstance of a place. So, for "their bands" in Ps 2:3 he observes, **"These were signs of subjection/ Jer.27.2.3.6.7."** Likewise, he states that historical "circumstances of the text" help him choose "anger" in 2:5 from among the options for the same Hebrew word: "ire, outward in the face, grame [an antiquated Anglo-Saxon English word, meaning "anger" or "wrath"], grimnes [grimness] **or** feircenes **of** countenance." At his best, Ainsworth relies on the "circumstances of the text" as a clue to how he "conferences" words and expressions with language from passages sharing in the same circumstances of the place elsewhere in Scripture. At his worst, Ainsworth will uncritically let New Testament citations of the Old Testament determine issues of Hebrew grammatical usage, crediting the Holy Spirit for such insight (rather than viewing it as simply noteworthy evidence of how ancient Jewish-Christian translators read Hebrew). Still, I think Ainsworth's prophetic understanding of the psalms better recognizes the nature of Jewish and Christian Scriptures than does any modern tendency to find in the Psalms only a badly edited collection of ancient prayers.

Finally, another understandable role for an inner-biblical "conferencing" of texts is to show the cumulative effect of certain key words throughout the entire Christian Bible. These words served to establish continuity in the understanding of biblical revelation. They might belong to practical matters of faith or point to the essential content of more complex doctrines. Sometimes these terms simply indicated ideas that have persisted from Jewish Scripture into the Greek of the New Testament. They could also indicate topics where a Christian understanding from the New Testament deviated from what remains unchanged in the Old Testament alone. In the last instance, the translation retains a claim that Ainsworth sees modified by the New Testament. Ainsworth's annotation on Ps 2:7, "I wil tel, the decree [*'el ḥōq*]," illustrates both his conferencing for the sake of grammar and his effort to pursue a Hebrew word in a doctrinal direction well beyond its immediate contextual usage in Psalm 2. He comments:

> The decree] **Here the Hebrue** el [*'el*], **seemeth to be used for** eth [*'et*]: **as** el haderech, 2 Chon.6.27, **is the same that** eth haderech, 1 King.8.36. **We may also read it thus,** I wil tel of the decree; el **being many times used for** of; **as** Gen.20,2, Job.42,7, 2 King.19,32, Ier.51.60, **So the Greek pro (answering the Hebrue** el,) **is used for** of, **or** concerning, Heb.1,7,&4,13. decree] prescript law or statute. **The Hebrue** Chok, **actually denoteth the** rules decrees **and** ordinances **about Gods worship; as the** decree of the Passover, Exo.12,24,43; **the** decree **of dressing the lamps** Exod.27,21, **of Priests office and garments**, Exo.29,9,**of their washing**, Exod.30,21, **of the sacrifices**, Lev.3,17, & 6,18,22, **and many other things about gods service. So may here be taken, that Christ** preacheth the decree **or** rule **of serving God, fulfilled of us by fayth and obedience to his gospel, when these legal ordinance had an end.** Iohn.4,21 &c.

Obviously he offers in this final comment an assurance to Christians that they are to fulfill the demands of the ritual law by a spiritual obedience to the Gospel rather than through legal observance.

In a related manner, Ainsworth frequently provides word studies pertinent to a particular verse based on occurrences throughout the Old Testament, often including Greek counterparts in the New Testament. At the end of his Psalter he provides: "A Table, directing to some principal things, observed in the Annotations of the Psalms." Among the words he lists that recall his annotations on Psalms 1–2 are the following: for "blessed," for "wicked," for "synners," and for "scornful" in 1:1; for "walking" as "conversation" in 1:1 and 56:14; for "way" as "course of life or religion" in 1:1 and 25:4; for "sitting" in 1:1 and 102:13; for "seat" or "chaire" in 1:1 and in 107:4; for "meditate" in 1:2 and 55:3; for "brooks" and for "Dooing, **for** yeelding fruit"; for "knowing" in 1:6; for "Christ" or "anointed" in 2:2; for "Lord, Adonai" in 2:4; for "Sion, **the mount**" in 2:6; for "decree" or "statute," as noted above, and for "tel" with the sense of "preach" in 2:7; for "heritage" in 2:8; for "gladnes" in 2:11; and for "kyssing" in 2:12.

In the annotations themselves, Ainsworth tries to cross-reference a word or phrase to the place elsewhere in his annotations where he has provided the fullest study of it. Usually, he "collates" words from the Old Testament first. Then follows attention to occurrences of the same or similar words translated into the Greek of the New Testament. By this means, he shows how the same theological language of Christian Scripture can be found in both Testaments, despite the differences between Hebrew and Greek. From a modern perspective, we know of both the dangers and the serious significance to such word studies. We are aware of a Christian tendency to read into Old Testament words and phrase ideas developed only in the New. Still, Ainsworth reminds us that the larger canonical context of Scripture provides a primary arena in which theological language finds its definition, necessity, and sense of direction.

The evidence from Ainsworth's translation and annotations shows that his translation is attentive to a Christian, literal-sense mode of using Scripture to interpret Scripture. For that reason he seeks to translate some Hebrew words concordantly, but not others, by rendering the Hebrew consistently with the same English word. For purpose of illustration, I will consider a few examples in comparison with Buber's translation of the Psalms. Ainsworth translates the Hebrew root *h-g-h,* which occurs in Ps 1:2 and in Ps 2:1, as "meditate" in both places, thus emphasizing that we, the readers, are commanded to meditate daily on the Torah in contrast to the nations who "meditate vanity." In the annotation to Ps 2:1 Ainsworth notes the difference in "the time" (imperfect) of the verb *h-g-h* from that of its predecessor "rage" (*r-g-š*) (in the perfect). He observes that in the New Testament usage of this verse, "the holy Ghost in Act.4:25 keepeth like time here" (as in the preceding verb, "rage"), but then justifies his own usage simply by stating, "I follow/ according to the propriety of our tongue." Buber's translation is more sophisticated in that he allows for the contextual change in the semantic import of the root verb in these two places, but still retains resonance through alliteration, so in Ps 1:2 he uses, "murmelt," while in 2:1, "murren Nationen." On psalm superscriptions, however, Buber retains strictly the syntactical ambiguity in the titles referring to Solomon and the sons of Korah ("von Schlomo" and "von den Korachsohnen"). Ainsworth, we saw earlier, resolves the ambiguity in these cases in favour of viewing them as Davidic psalms "for Solomon" and "for the sons of Korah." Buber, also, retains a literal resonance seen between Ps 2:2 and Ps 89:51. The resonance occurs between the promise to "his anointed" (*seinen Gesalbten*) in Ps 2:2 on the one hand, and the complaint to God regarding "your anointed" (*deines Gesalbten*), based on the same promises to David, in Ps 89:51 on the other hand. Ainsworth's approach to this case differs. Ainsworth translates the former instance as "his Christ," since Psalm 2 is among the few verbally overt messianic psalms for him. He retains "thine anointed" in Psalm 89, however, where the prayer most clearly states that God has "profaned his [the earthly king's] crown to the earth" (v. 39; Ainsworth, v. 40). At a minimum, the reasons and means of retaining resonance vary with assumptions regarding how Jews and Christians, respectively, can best hear the text as Scripture.

In sum, no theory of translation can do justice to Jewish or Christian Scripture if it ignores or gives only a naively modern response to these issues. At the end of the Modern Age, these issues confront us with a freshness as never before. We need to think carefully about the difference between the vagueness and the ambiguity of words in a specific context, the role of resonance within the intertext of Scripture, and the persistence of "the circumstances of the place" as distinct from merely the modern concern with historical origins. Otherwise, we will reinvent the Bible under a simplistically pious notion of secular objectivity. Under those terms, we could probably never understand why so many centuries of interpreters, including my esteemed colleague, George Landes, poured so much of themselves into the effort to understand a text, but claim to have gotten even more out of it.

REFERENCES

Ainsworth, H.
1612   *The Psalmes: Englished both in Prose and Metre. With Annotations, opening the words and sentences by conference with other scriptures.* Amsterdam: Giles Thorp.
n.d.   Of Davids Life and Acts. In some later editions of his *Psalms,* but not in the original edition of 1612.

Bishop, S. L.
1962   *Isaac Watts: Hymns and Spiritual Songs, 1707–1748.* London: The Faith Press.

Buber, M.
1975   *Das Buch der Preisungen.* Heidelberg: Lambert Schneider.

Childs, B. S.
1979   *The Book of Exodus: A Critical Theological Commentary.* Old Testament Library. Philadelphia: Westminster.

Cross, F., Jr.
1968   The Song of the Sea and Canaanite Myth. *Journal for Theology and the Church* 5: 1–25.

Cross, F., Jr., and Freedman, D. N.
1955   The Song of Miriam. *Journal of Near Eastern Studies* 14: 237–50.

Cudsworth, C.
1617   To the Courteous Reader. In *A Commentarie or Exposition Upon the five first Chapters of the Epistle to the Galatians*, by W. Perkins. London: John Legatt.

Drury, J.
1989   *Critics of the Bible, 1724–1873.* Cambridge: Cambridge University.

Farrar, F. W.
1979   *History of Interpretation.* Grand Rapids: Baker. London original, 1886.

Foucault, M.
1973   *The Order of Things: An Archaeology of the Human Sciences.* Trans. from French. New York City: Vintage Books.

Froehlich, K.
1984	*Biblical Interpretation in the Early Church.* Philadelphia: Fortress.

Greenstein, E. L.
1989	*Essays on Biblical Translation.* Brown Judaic Studies 92. Atlanta: Scholars.

Haraszti, Z.
1956	*The Enigma of the Bay Psalm Book.* Chicago: University of Chicago.

Holladay, W.
1993	*The Psalms Through Three Thousand Years: Prayerbook of a Cloud of Witnesses.* Minneapolis: Fortress.

Katchen, A. L.
1984	*Christian Hebraists and Dutch Rabbis.* Cambridge: Harvard University.

Kolb, R.
1987	Teaching the Text: The Commonplace Method in Sixteenth Century Lutheran Biblical Commentary. *Bibliothèque d' Humanism et Renaissance* 49/3: 571–85.

Lewalski, B. L. K.
1979	*Protestant Poetics and the Seventeenth-Century Religious Lyric.* Princeton: Princeton University.

Moody, M. E.
1982	"A Man of a Thousand": The Reputation and Character of Henry Ainsworth 1569/70–1622. *Huntington Library Quarterly* 45/3: 200–14.

Nida, E., and Tabor, C. R.
1974	*The Theory and Practice of Translation.* Leiden: Brill.

Paget, J.
1618	*An Arrow Against the Separation of the Brownists. Also an Admonition Touching Talmudique & Rabbinic allegations.* Amsterdam: Veseler.

Pratt, W. S.
1941	*The Music of the Pilgrims: A Description of the Psalm-book brought to Plymouth in 1620.* Boston: Oliver Ditson.

Reventlow, H. G.
1984	*The Authority of the Bible and the Rise of the Modern World.* Philadelphia: Fortress.

Schneider, N.
1990	*The Art of the Still Life: Still Life Painting in the Early Modern Period.* Trans. H. Beyer, from German. Köln: Taschen.

Shaffer, E. S.
  1975   *Kubla Khan and the Fall of Jerusalem: the Mythological School in Biblical Criticism and Secular Literature, 1770–1880.* New York City: Cambridge University.

Sheppard, G. T.
  1989   Between Reformation and Modern Commentary: The Perception of the Scope of Biblical Books. Pp. xlii–lxxl in *William Perkins' A Commentary on Galatians (1617), with Introductory Essays*, ed. G. T. Sheppard. New York City: Pilgrim.

Smith, W. C.
  1993   *What is Scripture? A Comparative Approach.* Minneapolis, MN: Fortress.

Smith, W. R.
  1881   *The Old Testament in the Jewish Church.* Edinburgh: Adam and Charles Black.

Steiner, G.
  1988   Review of *The Literary Guide to the Bible*, eds. R. Alter and F. Kermode. *The New Yorker* January 11: 94–98.

Steinmetz, D. C.
  1990   *The Bible in the Sixteenth Century.* Durham: Duke University.

Terry, M. S.
  1890   *Biblical Hermeneutics: A Treatise on the Interpretation of the Old and New Testaments.* New York City: Eaton & Mains.

Whitaker, W.
  1968   *A Disputation on Holy Scripture.* New York City: Johnson Reprint Corporation. Latin original, 1588.

Wiles, M. F.
  1970   Origin as Biblical Scholar. Pp. 454–89 in *The Cambridge History of the Bible: Vol.1, From the Beginnings to Jerome*, eds. P. R. Ackroyd and C. F. Evans.Cambridge: Cambridge University.

Winslow, E.
  1968   *Hypocrisie Unmasked: A True Relation of the Proceedings of the Governor and Company of Massachusetts Against Samuel Gorton of Rhode Island.* New York: B. Franklin. Original edition, London 1646.

N.a.
  1956b   *The Bay Psalm Book: A Facsimile Reprint of the First Edition of 1640.* Chicago: University of Chicago.

17 The Tradition of Mosaic Judges: Past Approaches and New Directions

STEPHEN L. COOK

In keeping with the theme of this volume, I propose to inquire into the place of philological and archaeological methods in contemporary biblical scholarship through a specific textual study. An examination of the tradition about Mosaic judges in Exodus 18 may serve to illustrate the history and current significance of philological and related critical methods. Past criticism of Exodus 18 has included both the philological and archaeological approach championed by W. F. Albright, the teacher of our honoree, George Landes, and the challenge to this approach by the German, form-critical school, an approach applied to this text in a well-known study by Rolf Knierim. At the same time, Exodus 18 and related texts turn out to be readily susceptible to newer tradition-historical and sociological approaches, approaches that must continue to rely on philological knowledge and analysis. Applying these newer methods to Exodus 18 breaks new ground in understanding the judicial traditions standing behind Deuteronomism and the preexilic judiciary system that these traditions advocated.

Both of the approaches to Exodus 18 associated with Albright and Knierim have increased our understanding, yet neither does full justice to the text and its tradition of Mosaic judges. I want to argue that Exodus 18 is best approached, rather, in terms of a new stance that recognizes that it exhibits at least the following three features. First, in Exodus 18 we are dealing with an ongoing tradition, rich with potential meaning, that was found relevant not merely in one historical setting but that crystallized several times in the Hebrew Bible under various historical circumstances. Second, Exodus 18 coheres with groups of related traditions as part of a continuum or "stream" with a fixed diction and a definite theological orientation. And third, the tradition stream with which Exodus 18 is linked was borne by specific groups of tradents with a social and religious provenance that must be distinguished within that of Israel's larger society. Recognition of the place of Exodus 18 in a larger stream of tradition and of its social provenance reveals its actual intentionality and its significance in the development of biblical Yahwism.

George Landes has impressed on us all the significance of close philological work on the Hebrew Bible. His love and mastery of Hebrew philology was certainly unmistakably clear to me while serving as his junior colleague during the last several years before his retirement from Union Seminary. Historical criticism achieved many of its gains through such philological study. And I am convinced that future avenues of investigation will continue to rely heavily on this tool; the approaches that I apply to the problem of the Mosaic judges below draw both on philological analysis and on archaeology's umbrella rubric, sociology. At the same time as they draw on time tested tools, these new avenues of research may avoid some of the pitfalls of the past. Specifically, it is hoped that these newer directions are leading away from older historical-critical tendencies either to make the problem of the authenticity of a text's surface presentation the paramount concern (Albright) or to stress the ensnarement of texts' authors in given historical contingencies (Knierim).

I. PAST GAINS IN THE STUDY OF EXODUS 18

Since the contemporary place of the methods advocated by W. F. Albright is the general theme of this volume, it is appropriate to begin with two of his articles that have been most influential on the scholarly study of Exodus 18: "Jethro, Hobab and Reuel in Early Hebrew Tradition" (1963) and "The Judicial Reform of Jehoshaphat" (1950). These articles do not constitute detailed exegetical treatments. They do suit the purpose, nevertheless, of illustrating an Albrightian approach to Exodus 18 and to the preexilic judicial system.

In his 1963 article, which treats Exodus 18 and related texts, Albright's main concern is to determine the identities and relationships of the presettlement, Kenite figures Reuel, Jethro, and Hobab. He argues that by analyzing the texts and names at issue, reasonable sense can be made of the biblical presentation as we now have it, without either harmonizing or fragmenting the texts (Albright 1963: 4–5). From his subsequent argument, it is clear that by the phrase "analyze the texts" Albright means combining philological, text-critical, and archaeological methods to clarify and appreciate the texts' surface presentation. Applying these methods, he concludes that Reuel is a clan name, and that Jethro and Hobab are separate persons, Moses's father-in-law and son-in-law respectively. "Both Hobab and Jethro belonged to the clan of Reuel," he writes; "the West-Semitic nomads were as a rule endogamous, so one would expect Moses' son-in-law and father-in-law both to come from the same clan" (Albright 1963: 7). Simply put, then, Albright's approach can be summarized as oriented toward explicating Israelite history as it is straightforwardly referenced by the biblical text. To say that Albright is oriented toward such a surface reading does not at all mean he accepts the biblical text's presentation uncritically. It does mean, however, that he tends, at least in this article, to relate the events narrated by the text, its literal sense, closely to the text's historical sense. The narrative and its historical background are held in close proximity.

In his second article under consideration, "The Judicial Reform of Jehoshaphat," Albright uncovers several facets of Israel's sociology that remain valuable for tracing the history of the tradition of Mosaic judges. The article undertakes an historical appraisal of the Chronicler's account of Jehoshaphat's reform. Correctly rehabilitating Chronicles' historical value, Albright recognizes that 2 Chr 19:4–11 authentically depicts an historical change in Israel's judicial system, a change that came with Israel's development as a monarchic state.[1] Of course, Albright does not make the connection that this judicial change forms the setting of Exodus 18, with its tradition of Mosaic judges. That discovery represents a main contribution of Knierim's study ten years later. Albright does correctly note, however, how Jehoshaphat grappled with "Mosaic" institutions and traditions in launching his reform. His new system began to move away from Israel's prestate judicial system, which was in the hands of the lineage heads of village Israel:

> The civil code preserved in fragmentary form by
> Deuteronomy antedates the institution of royal judges by
> Jehoshaphat. In this old civil code there are many refer-

ences (e.g., 19:12; 21:2–3, 4, 6, 19–20; 22:15–16, 18; 25:7–9) to the judicial function of the elders (Albright 1950: 77; cf. Wilson 1983b: 237, 246).

I argue below that Exodus 18 grapples with the same judicial change seen in 2 Chronicles 19. It does so from a different angle, however, that of the village elders' conservative reaction to the monarchy's progressivism.

Despite some of Albright's keen historical and sociological insights in his articles under consideration, the depth of his penetration was hindered by his disinterest in tradition-history. An initial problem associated with this disinterest is his tendency to identify biblical Israel and biblical faith with historical Israelite history and religion (see Albright 1963: 10–11). Because he assumes this identification, he misses the distinctiveness within Israel of the minority traditions behind biblical religion, which religion only flowered in the wake of the reforms of Hezekiah and Josiah.

A correlative problem is Albright's treatment of J and E. He identifies these sources as merely two alternate representatives of a base narrative that was central to Israel's religion. J and E are two "closely related ... bodies of material," "normal alternatives" of Israel's official, ancient traditions (Albright 1963: 2, 10). More specifically, Albright singles out Exod 2:11–25; 18; and Num 10:29–32 in his "Jethro, Hobab and Reuel" article as examples of biblical narratives often considered to be in tension that should instead be viewed as stemming from Israel's common tradition-store. For Albright, these Kenite traditions are thus one of "several bodies of material in the Pentateuch which appear homogeneous to me but which are usually considered to be highly composite" (Albright 1963: 3).

Regardless of the reasonableness of his specific arguments about the compatibility of the Kenite narratives, the general position that Albright defends on J and E is problematic. Specifically, his view that J and E are basically twin versions of Israel's general tradition compounds his anachronism of picturing biblical Yahwism as normative in Israel as early as the tenth century (Albright 1963: 9–11). Further, and along the same lines, his position misses the value of the E source as a distinctive exemplar of the tradition stream behind biblical Yahwism, a minority *traditio* within preexilic Israelite society.

Rolf Knierim (1961) presents a very different approach than that of Albright in his seminal study of Exodus 18 as reflecting a reorganization of Israel's judicial system. Whereas Albright (1963: 10–11) values the Kenite narratives as ancient traditions preserved early on and "unaffected appreciably by later transmission," Knierim's focus is the opposite. He finds the key to Exodus 18's meaning precisely in later, monarchic-period transmission and reuse of the earlier Kenite traditions. Several clues within Exodus 18 initially betray the narrative's mooring in later times. Verse 23b's reference to satisfied litigants returning to "their place in peace" signals a setting in the postsettlement period for the new judicial institution of the chapter. Also, later hearers would have imagined their own circumstances when v. 22a states that Israel's new Mosaic judges will judge the people בכל־עת ("at all times"; cf. v. 26a). (See Knierim 1961: 156.) Most telling, however, is the military idiom of vv. 21b and 25b, which does not fit with old Israel's legal system and thus betrays that Exodus 18 played a role in explaining how monarchic-period military officers had begun to exercise judicial authority (Knierim 1961: 150–51, 155, 167–71).

When Knierim moves to pin down the postsettlement historical setting in which Exodus 18 had its relevance, he lands on the monarchic period and on the creation of a state judicial system, a societal reorganization that eventually led to the repression of premonarchic judicial institutions. Knierim (1961: 161–62) maintains that Exodus 18's pressing concern is with "the basic sanctioning and legitimation of this royal, statist judicial institution ... and this perhaps with a definite accent over against the older, legal forms of Israelite justice." Knierim finds the report of Jehoshaphat's reform in 2 Chr 19:4–11 to be one of our earliest attestations of this monarchic reorganization of the judiciary. He argues that Jehoshaphat's judicial reorganization corresponds structurally to the system outlined in Exodus 18, and he thus concludes that Exodus 18 justifies the reorganization by grounding it in an action of Moses soon after the exodus. "The etiology was most needed where, in view of public life's incorporation into a state, it was an issue of the sacral legitimation of a 'reorganization of the justice system' that suspended the traditional, patriarchal jurisdiction or at least repressed or modified it" (Knierim 1961: 166).

Knierim's detailed form-critical recovery of the depth dimension of Exodus 18 represents a classic scholarly breakthrough and greatly illu-

mines the nature of the text. At the same time, nevertheless, his treatment fails fully to elucidate Exodus 18 largely because he downplays
the significance both of the history of the scriptural tradition of Mosaic
judges that lies behind this passage and this tradition's impact in the
passage's composition. This neglect of the inner-scriptural development of the tradition of Exodus 18 is first visible in Knierim's lack of
treatment of Numbers 11 in his article. Where he does mention Numbers 11, it is to say that it is largely unconnected to our text (Knierim
1961: 157 n. 24). This conclusion seems unlikely, due to the strong
links between these passages. They share the motif of the burden of
the people on Moses, which he cannot bear "alone" (Num 11:14, 17;
Exod 18:18), the idea of a selection of leaders from among the people
for the relief of Moses (Num 11:16; Exod 18:21, 25), the identical
clause וְנָשְׂאוּ אִתְּךָ ("they will share your load"; Num 11:17; Exod 18:22),
and a report that Moses carried out the recommended decentralization
of his office (Num 11:24–25; Exod 18:24–27).[2]

Exod 18:13–27 and Num 11:14–30 must be connected. They either
share the same independent tradition in common, or they are dependent in some way on each other. Knierim's objection that Numbers 11
deals with prophetic, not judicial, issues does not carry much weight
(Knierim 1961: 157 n. 24). As elaborated below, Numbers 11 involves the reinforcement of the leadership role of lineage heads in Israel. It is specifically the people's "elders and officers" that are singled
out to be Mosaic leaders (Num 11:16). And the leadership role of
Israel's elders had a significant judicial component, which would be
presupposed by the ancient hearers of Numbers 11.[3] Thus, the tradition of Moses's relief through the appointment of Mosaic elders/judges
should be accepted as a common thread linking Numbers 11 and Exodus 18, although the judicial aspect of the tradition was only stressed
explicitly in the latter text.

Since Exod 18:13–27 and Num 11:14–30 both reflect the same tradition of Mosaic judges, and since both passages are attributable to E, I
suggest that the later passage in Exodus 18 knows of and reuses the
earlier passage in Numbers.[4] This hypothesis, to be developed below,
represents a challenge to Knierim's etiological interpretation of the
function of Exodus 18. It would be understandable how an old,
prescriptural Moses tradition could be manipulated in service of the
acute etiological concern that Knierim reconstructs. But if the E writ-

ers of Exodus 18 are drawing on their own *scriptural* tradition that occurs in an earlier face of E in Numbers 11, they would not have treated the tradition in such a way, merely as an object of manipulation or a means for expressing a pressing concern. Rather, a scriptural tradition would have brought its own meaning and intentionality to bear on the contemporary scene in which it was recalled. In other words, such a tradition would have had a crucial "kerygmatic" impact in E's composition of the narrative of Exodus 18 that should not be underestimated. B. S. Childs' comment is an understatement, "I doubt that the etiological factor was the decisive factor in the formulation of the tradition" (Childs 1974: 324).[5]

A final problem with Knierim's etiological thesis should be observed. Although he recognizes that Exodus 18 belongs to E, Knierim does not treat the problem of the relation of Exodus 18's intended function to the general orientation and specific viewpoints of the E strand.[6] Against Knierim, it seems highly unlikely that an E-strand pericope such as Exodus 18 functioned to justify the emerging, centralized judicial system of Israel as a state. The E-strand and related sources aimed to temper and decentralize human rule over Israel not to account for and justify it. The E stance is precisely not that of advocate of Israel's monarchy. Thus, Terence Fretheim (1962: 260) sees in the E source a "strong affirmation of charismatic and democratic leadership." By the same token, Alan Jenks (1992: 480) states that the E source views monarchy as a "potentially dangerous institution" that prophetic leaders should hold in check.[7] Texts related to E such as Hos 8:4, 10; 13:10–11; Mic 4:9; and Deut 17:16 epitomize this characteristic view.[8] For these texts, God only allowed Israel to adopt a monarchical, state administrative system as a concession, and provided strong caveats and strictures in order to temper it. Not only the idea of a monarch, but the whole idea of a state system was suspect for these sources. Thus, the Hosean texts cited express dissatisfaction with Israel's שׂרים ("officers") along with the מלך ("king") (also see Hos 3:4; 5:10).

II. MOSES'S RELIEF AS AN E-STREAM TRADITION

The problems in Albright's and Knierim's analyses of Exodus 18 can be addressed by a new tradition-historical approach to the text. This new direction in scholarship recognizes that the traditions of the

Pentateuchal E-strand in general, and Exodus 18 in particular, are part of a larger continuum or "stream" of related traditions borne by specific groups of tradents. In technical terms, the E source and Exodus 18 belong to a *traditio*, specifically the *traditio* that lies behind Deuteronomism and the book of Deuteronomy. Fortunately, enough scholarly work has been done on the case for including E among proto-Deuteronomic traditions as to make detailed arguments for applying this model here unnecessary. As Fretheim (1962: 261) writes, "While much work remains to be done on the antecedents of the Deuteronomic tradition, numerous ties with E suggest a common ... provenance: the Sinaitic covenant; the Mosaic office; key theological emphases; the antimonarchic perspective; and a religious interpretation of history that merges narrative and parenesis."[9]

Scholars have long grouped other specific biblical writings with E as additional traditions related to Deuteronomism. The especially strong consensus about the affinity of both Hosea and Jeremiah with E and Deuteronomy seems established. In addition, H. Nasuti (1988) has argued persuasively that this same stream also encompasses the Psalms of Asaph (Pss 50, 73–83). In research in progress, I am currently working to detail arguments for including much of the Book of Micah in this stream as well. J. Levenson's work has already indicated the need for such a specific investigation of Micah's links to "Sinai" theology. Aided by W. Beyerlin's 1959 study of the Mican traditions, Levenson (1987: 195–200) finds specifically in Micah a definite example of the existence of a Mosaic/Sinaitic orientation in a southern prophet. Other scholars have focused on particular parts of Micah, and have concluded that they strongly betray E-related traditions (Burkitt 1926: 159–61; Eissfeldt 1962: 259–68; van der Woude 1971: 365–78).[10]

Lacking a better term, I shall call the tradition complex at issue the "E-stream." This designation appreciates the Elohist-strand's place toward the early end of the continuum and the "Ephraimite" provenance of several of the complex's literary deposits. Unlike the term "Ephraimite," however, this designation should not be construed as suggesting a geographical categorization of the stream.[11]

This essay is not the place for any further general argumentation about the existence and nature of the E-stream. What is appropriate here, rather, is to take the E-stream's existence as a hypothesis and to test it as a model for elucidating the particular tradition of Mosaic judges.

In this section, I thus want to sketch the outlines and progression of this tradition's history. As suggested in the introduction, presenting this history allows for more critical understandings of how the tradition functioned at various stages of its life and of the identity of its tradents and their role as bearers of biblical Yahwism.

The E narrative of Num 11:16–30 stands near the beginning of the history of the E-stream tradition of Mosaic judges, and it is an appropriate starting point for tracing the tradition. This is the text that first distinguishes Mosaic judges from judges in general within Israelite society. It is important to observe carefully what it depicts. A new social role is not created here; rather, a group of individuals is singled out who already possess the known social role of lineage head (vv. 16, 24). Neither is their selection part of any change in social systems—indeed, the judicial system is not even mentioned in Numbers 11. The appointee group will remain kin-group elders and continue to perform the leadership tasks, including that of judge, associated with that social role. What will distinguish the selected appointees is a new, sacral recognition of their role.

Verse 24 says the seventy, selected elders are "stationed" at the covenant tent; and the verb עמד ("station") here connotes being installed within the covenant. (Compare the use of the verb for Joash's and Josiah's taking their stand within the covenant in 2 Kgs 11:14; 23:3.)[12] Further, Yahweh gives the new group a special imputation of the spirit that is upon Moses (vv. 17, 25). Thus, they receive the sanction and regularization of having their role in the culture as elders incorporated within the structures of the Mosaic/E-stream covenant. At the same time, they receive the authority and power to carry out the role by becoming Mosaic figures, being given the spirit associated with Moses.[13]

Exod 18:13–27 at first appears to be a mere variation of this story in Numbers 11, but examination soon reveals that something rather different is going on in the Exodus text than in its parallel in Numbers. Although Knierim's thesis of Exodus 18's etiological function is problematic, several clues within the Exodus pericope do show the correctness of his correlation of the passage with the circumstances of the development of a centralized, state administrative and judicial system in Judah. The E narrative of Exodus 18 presents a stage beyond Numbers 11, which is still associated with prestate, lineage-based Israelite society and must represent an earlier face of E.[14]

Unlike Numbers 11, Exodus 18 deals with a reorganization of Israel's judiciary, not just its sacralization: new lower judges are to be appointed who will attend to minor disputes (vv. 21–22, 25–26). The appointment of such full-time, vocational judges (vv. 22a, 26a) breaks with the older, local practice of judging as a part-time role of elders.[15] Further, the hierarchical, tiered system of Exodus 18 (vv. 22b, 26b) looks like a state-period innovation different from village Israel's free exercise of legal authority within gatherings open to all owners of inherited land.[16] Finally, although vv. 21b and 25b seem to be additions to Exodus 18, they nonetheless show that the judicial appointees of the pericope were at least secondarily identified with שׂרים ("officers"), monarchic officials unknown to village Israel.[17]

Why then did the E-stream tradition of Moses's relief (Numbers 11) resurface in Exod 18:13–27, within its circumstances of the monarchic development of Israel into a state? An initial clue is given by the syntax of v. 23, which sets up a condition. The prosperity of Judah's monarchs, Judah's chief justices who lead the people in Moses's stead,[18] is not guaranteed but conditional. They will endure only if they adhere to the instructions presented in vv. 19–22. Although these instructions are a concession to Israel's new reality as a state and permit the creation of a centralized judicial system, this concession also applies strong caveats and tempering. Exodus 18 aims far more to contain the new monarchic judiciary than etiologically to legitimize it.

Exodus 18 first modulates royal judicial-prerogative by its general orientation and by the motivation it depicts as appropriate for Judah's monarchs in affecting judicial reform. The occasion of systemic reorganization in Exodus 18 is that Moses is overburdened (v. 18). The solution of reorganization is thus oriented towards a *decentralization* of centrally held judicial power (v. 23).[19] Contrast the thrust of Jehoshaphat's reform depicted in 2 Chr 19:4–11, against which Exodus 18 may well be reacting. Jehoshaphat is not overburdened, but establishes a new judicial system that *extends* central judicial authority over the land, starting with the fortified cities where the state already had footholds of control (v. 5). By the same token, Exodus 18 says that Moses's motivation in implementing the new system should be a desire for time to fulfill his covenant duties (vv. 19–20). Jehoshaphat's drive in 2 Chr 19:4–11, by contrast, could be mistaken for a desire for monarchic achievement and renown.[20]

The idiom of vv. 21, 25 again tempers the emerging, new judicial institution by specifying that its representatives should be chosen from among those already pretested in the covenant role of local judge. Earlier, Numbers 11 had already applied covenantal reinforcement and regularization to Israelite culture's practice of having lineage heads fill judicial roles. Circles of village elders were to bear E-stream judicial tradition in their local administration of justice. Exod 18:21 now specifies that the new, professional judges are to be chosen out of candidates from this particular pool. The specification that the new judges are to be שׂנאי בצע ("those who hate dishonest gain") signals this stricture. This diction is typically used in the Hebrew Bible in reference to those already in a position to wield judgment.[21] Thus, the new judicial appointees are to be chosen from among those who have already shown themselves to be faithful in the local judicial roles they have played as village elders.

Exod 18:22 further clarifies how the new judiciary must retain a sacral character. It is Moses who appoints the judges, and it is the Mosaic office itself that is apportioned to them. Thus, the appointees remain obligated to conform to the covenantal criteria associated with their office by Numbers 11. As Childs (1974: 325) observes, "The tradition [of Exodus 18] connects this [monarchic-judicial] office with the original Mosaic one and finds therein a warrant for demanding covenant responsibility in the administration of justice."

Unfortunately, in the view of later E-stream proponents, the attempt in Exodus 18 to temper and apply caveats to the state judicial system was unsuccessful. The newer system's excesses are castigated in particular by Micah and his circle. Micah's eighth-century reaction to the failure of the ideal of the Mosaic judge in monarchic Judah is recorded in several texts.

Mic 3:1–4, for example, levels a reproach and a threat against Jerusalem's establishment. This reproach zeros in on the establishment's responsibility for legal justice, and thus it raises the E-stream concern for judicial ethics that we have in Exodus 18. Although this concern will be spelled out more concretely in Mic 3:9–12, its centrality and mooring in the E-stream in Micah are already suggested here. Specifically, note Micah's use of the term המשפט ("the justice," Mic 3:1). This is most probably a reference to the specific legal customs of the Mosaic covenant tradition, on which Exod 18:15–16, 20;

21:1 (E) focus.[22] Further, Mic 3:1 assigns responsibility for justice to Israel's ראשׁים ("heads"). This is the same tenet of the E-stream that we see in Numbers 11 and Exodus 18. Numbers 11 makes clear that it is to lineage heads that the Mosaic office is distributed. Exodus 18 later insisted that this covenant role of Mosaic judge must be maintained even if Israel wants to adopt a new state administrative and judicial system. Exod 18:25 thus applies the term ראשׁים ("heads") to its judicial appointees, expressing an admonition that they carry on the tradition of the faithful Mosaic judge.[23]

A second Mican text, Mic 3:9–12, even better exemplifies the reaction within the E-stream to the Judean state's breach of the strictures of Exodus 18. The two-part judgment oracle of Mic 3:9–12 was probably delivered a decade or two before the Assyrian crisis of 701 B.C.E. Like Micah's prophecy against the mercenary prophets, which it directly follows, the oracle concentrates on problems internal to Israel. The oracle's threat of complete destruction in v. 12 immediately links the passage to the E-stream's theology of a conditional covenant. The idiom of the verse confirms this link.

The E-stream Book of Jeremiah takes Mic 3:12 as a precedent for Jeremiah's anti-Zion stance (Jer 26:18). Outside of Jeremiah, the verse's distinctive term עי ("ruin," also see Mic 1:6) occurs only in a wisdom text, Job 30:24, and in Ps 79:1, at the beginning of an Asaphite psalm. Nasuti's analysis of Psalm 79 suggests that its provenance was within the E-stream and that its tradents were the same pro-Deuteronomic supporters of Jeremiah that valued Mic 3:12. Indeed, Psalm 79, which probably postdates Jeremiah's time, seems to lament the fulfillment of Micah's and Jeremiah's prediction of Jerusalem's destruction.[24] The dependence of Jeremiah 26 and Psalm 79 on Mic 3:9–12 helps situate Micah firmly within the E-stream. That Ps 79:1 describes God's land, now ruined by the nations' invasion, using the same נחלה ("inheritance") terminology found in Micah (e.g., Mic 2:2) further supports this tradition-historical placement.

Turning back now to the oracle's invective in vv. 9–11, it is immediately clear that its diction strongly reintroduces the E-stream tradition of Mosaic judges. The focus of the pericope is wide enough to include the abuse of office in general, and v. 9 repeats the E-stream terminology for Israel's overall leadership found in Mic 3:1. More explicitly than Mic 3:1–4, however, this pericope centers on those abusing judicial responsibilities. The first bicolon of Mic 3:11 names the immediate and specific officials involved in miscarrying justice: the "priests" and "heads." These are the same officials that Deuteronomy identifies as the ultimate arbiters of Yahweh's judicial will (e.g., Deut 17:9). Of particular interest here, of course, is Micah's renewed address of the monarchic judges as ראשׁים ("heads"), his way of pinning them with responsibility for their Mosaic, sacral role.

The charges that Mic 3:11a levels against Jerusalem's judges are also from the E-stream. In the first colon, Micah charges Jacob's "heads" with giving "judgment for a bribe," a direct betrayal of the office of Mosaic judge (Exod 18:21). Although Micah's diction is not identical to that of Exod 18:21 here, he is clearly using an alternative E-stream expression. A concern about judges taking a שׁחד ("bribe") characterizes such texts as Exod 23:8 (E) and Deut 16:18–19 (cf. Levenson 1987: 197).[25]

In sum, Micah does not evaluate his addressees using objective, performance criteria, such as poor administrative functioning, nor is he introducing into Israel an innovative concern for social ethics. He indicts Jerusalem's judges, rather, on the basis of an ancient sacral role, which they have accepted and then betrayed. Knierim (1961: 158–59) is correct here: "We have in Micah 3 ... the actual existence of an institution of judges, who are associated with sacral occupations, whose praxis is clearly subject to sacral criteria, who thus also possess sacral legitimation, and whose representatives are made up of the leaders of tribes and clans. We surmise with good grounds that the institution of representatives of the Mosaic judicial office designated in Exodus 18 is visible here."

Long after Micah's time, near the endpoint of the E-stream, the tradition of Mosaic judges crystallizes once again in Deut 1:9–18. The appearance of the Mosaic-judges tradition here is assured; Deuteronomy 1 draws directly on the language of both Numbers 11 and Exodus 18 (see Knierim 1961: 167; Mayes 1979: 118; Weinfeld 1991: 139). Deut 1:9 is practically a quotation of Num 11:14, לא־אוכל (אנכי) לבדי (לשׂאת) ("I am not able to bear [the burden] alone"; cf. Deut 1:12; Exod 18:18). Again, the hyperbolic language of Deut 1:10 recalls that of Num 11:22. Further, Deut 1:15 and Exod 18:25 use almost exactly the same language to describe Moses's selection of appointees as "heads" of the people: ואתן (ויתן) אתם ראשׁים עליכם (על־העם) ("and I [/he] appointed them heads over you [/over the people]"). The same verse, Deut 1:15, also duplicates the military diction of Exod 18:21b, 25b, "leaders of thousands, and of hundreds, of fifties, and of tens." Fascinatingly, Deuteronomy combines this levy terminology from Exodus with an additional designation of the appointees as שׁטרים ("officers"), a term taken from Num 11:16. Finally, Deut 1:17 depicts the same judicial "referral" process that was set forth in Exod 18:22, 26.

Just as Micah's use of the Mosaic-judges tradition came at a stage removed from that in Exodus 18, so the tradition's appearance in Deuteronomy 1 goes beyond Micah's stage. Chapter 1 of Deuteronomy is part of a late preface to the book that recapitulates the beginning of Israel's story in order to come to terms with Israel's history as a whole given the crisis of the exile (cf. Deut 4:27). One way in which the preface accounts for this crisis of existence is by fixing responsibility for the exile.[26]

Confirming the validity of Micah's warnings, Deut 1:9–18 links Israel's ultimate failure to the abandonment of the ideal of Mosaic judges within the state judiciary. Deut 1:13 and 15 thus restate the requirement that Israel's monarchic leaders were supposed to continue as lineage ראשׁים ("heads"), despite Israel's adoption of a new state judicial system. Just as Exod 18:25 specified, they were not supposed to abandon the covenantal regularization that Numbers 11 had applied to this role. Deut 1:16–17 even goes beyond Exodus 18 in having Moses explicitly charge the new state judges to continue the ethical conduct required of a Mosaic judge, for which character they were selected in the first place (Deut 1:13, 15; Exod 18:21, 25). "You shall not show partiality in judgment; you shall hear the small and the great alike. You shall not fear human beings, for [covenant] justice belongs to God."

The implication of Deut 1:9–18, of course, is that the Mosaic role was not respected by Judah's state judiciary, and this was one reason for the exile. Thus the Deuteronomic preface places responsibility for the exile not only with Judah's and Israel's kings, as the Deuteronomistic History does, but also with the larger monarchic administrative system. Indeed, the Israelites as a whole must share in the culpability, since they colluded in the implementation of Judah's new judicial administration. In Deut 1:13, Moses has the people themselves nominate the state judges that are to be appointed. This is in contrast to Num 11:16, 24; Exod 18:21, 25; and 2 Chr 19:5, 8 where the judges are selected by Moses/the king (Mayes 1979: 119; Weinfeld 1991: 139; Knoppers 1994: 73). Deut 1:14 then states that when "Moses" finished proposing the new state system, "You answered me and said, 'The thing which you have said to do is good.'" Such criticism of the people for allowing, elsewhere even demanding, a monarchic, state government is very much in keeping with the general stance of the E-stream. Thus, before the destruction of the northern kingdom, Hos 13:10 sarcastically asks, "Where now is your king, that he may save you / And all your officers, that they may judge you / Of whom you requested, 'Give me a king and officers'? //" (cf. 1 Sam 8:7; 10:19; Mic 4:9).[27]

III. THE SOCIAL PROVENANCE OF THE MOSAIC-JUDGES TRADITION

I noted in this essay's initial section that Albright's article about Jehoshaphat's reform helpfully sketched some key aspects of Israelite judicial history. In particular, the article mentions the historical shift that took place in Israel and Judah away from a village-based judicial system, whose representatives were lineage heads, to a state-based system administered by royal appointees. Albright (1950: 75) was correct: "That the administration of civil justice was transferred long before the Exile from the 'elders' to royally appointed judges may be taken as certain, since there are innumerable historical parallels." Further, Albright even correctly suggested how Israel's shift in judicial systems at first drew on the resources of the older system but eventually came into conflict with it.

> At first, we may suppose, the crown intervened in local affairs to the extent of selecting magistrates from among the "elders"; when this system failed to work satisfactorily, royal judges were sent in. There is nothing in our narrative [2 Chr 19:4–11] to indicate that Jehoshaphat went farther in this direction than to designate local dignitaries as royally appointed judges (Albright 1950: 76).

I want to return to this reconstruction now and show how it can be elaborated and illuminatingly applied with reference to Exodus 18 and the tradition of Mosaic judges. This is a move that Albright's article, written before Knierim's study, could not yet make.

The exhortations of Exodus 18 correlate with the initial phase of judicial change in Israel, where the state attempted to co-opt the resources of the older legal system. The admonitions of the passage were issued at a time when it was still hoped that social progress might be modulated by E-stream values. As the previous section has made clear, however, by the time of Micah such hopes had proved misplaced. Social change had progressed farther, to the point where some E-stream injunctions looked obsolete to state officials and where some local clan heads felt betrayed. Those magistrates selected from among the village elders of Judah did not act in accordance with the mandates of the E-stream, at least not in the view of groups such as the Mican circle. The failure of these state magistrates, exacerbated by the fact of royal appointments of judges from outside the old, village system, was creating a judiciary that looked less and less "Mosaic" in character.

The tradition-historical links between Exodus 18 and Micah that philological analysis identified in the previous section pave the way for further clarification of the sociology of the Mosaic-judges tradition, and thus for deeper probings into the social roots of the E-stream. Form- and tradition-critical methods are intended to unearth the *Sitze im Leben* of biblical traditions, and they deliver on this promise when applied to Micah's prophecies about Judah's judiciary.

Observe first the language that Micah uses in indicting the judiciary of his time. The felt burden for his country folk expressed by his passionate words, including his term עמי ("my people"; Mic 3:3; cf. 1:9; 2:8–9), strongly suggests that beyond his role as a prophet, Micah had an additional role in Israel that is directly relevant to the discussion at hand.[28] Micah's repeated reference to "my people" together with other evidence, such as his clan-based language (e.g., his funerary language), have suggested to scholars that he was himself one of old Israel's lineage elders, a judge in village Israel's administrative system.[29] H. W. Wolff has argued this case in an especially convincing manner. As Wolff (1990: 7) states, "Micah's active defense of those whom he calls 'my people' is not the concern of a solitary, small landowner or even that of an (exceptionally) righteous estate owner who has regard for the distress of the little people; rather, it is best understood as that of an elder."[30] If this suggestion is accurate, it is remarkable. It would mean that Micah did not merely trade in the E-stream and its ideal of the Mosaic judge, as the last section demonstrated; Micah was actually a genuine, old-style Mosaic judge himself.

The development of Judah as a state by Micah's time challenged his traditional, village judicial role. In his conflicts in Jerusalem, Micah in fact was forced to compete with contemporaries who held overlapping administrative and legal roles (Knierim 1961: 164; Wolff 1978: 79; 1990: 7, 105).[31] The situation was further complicated in that the Jerusalem officials and landgrabbers of Micah's time were largely the descendants of clan elders similar to the prophet himself. As Albright mentions, part of the process of overlaying one judicial system with another in Judah involved some of the clan elders of Israel's older system being allowed to retain power and being placed in positions of authority in the newer state system. This is stated explicitly in 2 Chr 19:8, where Jehoshaphat incorporates some of Israel's lineage "heads" (ראשי האבות) into the new, state judicial system, even into its highest courts. Thus, in attacking many of the nobles of Jerusalem, Micah consciously confronts figures who in an earlier historical period would have been his colleagues and counterparts (Hillers 1984: 33).[32]

The language of Micah's oracles clearly reflects his consciousness that the state system of Judah had co-opted groups of elders from within Israel's village networks. As discussed, Mic 3:1 and 3:9 apply prestate leadership terms such as קצין ("field commander") and ראש ("tribal chief") to eighth century Jerusalem's leadership. The terms מלך ("king") and שרים ("officers," cf. Isa 1:23), the nomenclature of state-based leadership, are lacking here (Mays 1976: 78; Wolff 1990: 98).[33] Micah's choice of terms for Judah's contemporary state establishment means more than simply that he operated with and advocated premonarchic leadership depictions. Aware that some of Jerusalem's establishment actually derived from authentic leading lineages within Judah, he tries to hold members of the establishment responsible for the legal customs of the Mosaic covenant based on this their ancestry. To his way of thinking, their social roots should have linked them with responsibility for the E-stream (Mic 3:1).

Micah's argument here is a clear clue to the sociological roots of the E-stream in the prestate period, before Micah's time. When, in Mic 3:1, the prophet's indignant question assumes a link between lineage "heads" and "the justice" (of the E-stream), he *repristinates* a prestate sociology in which such heads were responsible for sacral administration of the Mosaic covenant in the clan and village (cf. Knierim 1961: 158–59; Hillers 1984: 42). This repristination means that the role of

Micah-like figures—that is, of some of the elders/judges of the land—
as E-stream tradents must go back in time to Israel's existence as villages.

The two-part judgment oracle in Mic 3:5–8 helps to corroborate the
above reconstructed social background of the Mosaic-judges tradition
and the E-stream. The oracle's special rhetorical conclusion in v. 8 in
particular relates Mic 3:5–8 to the tradition of Mosaic judges. Micah
claims in v. 8 that, in contrast to Jerusalem's mercenary prophets, he is
filled with "justice" and "might." In using these two terms, Micah
describes himself as an authentic Mosaic judge. Clan elders were considered the custodians of מִשְׁפָּט ("justice"). They were the ones who
pronounced verdicts in the village gate. Again, in taking up his legal
role, Micah is aided by גְבוּרָה ("might"). Micah uses this term in its
meaning of "clan influence." Note how Ruth 2:1 similarly uses the
term to describe Boaz's high social standing among the Ephrathites.
(Judg 6:5 also uses the same vocabulary to describe the judge Gideon
as a member of the rural aristocracy.) Just as Boaz was aided by his
clan standing in the legal process of Ruth 4:1–12, Micah must have
been empowered by his village-system position in pursuing justice
(Kosmala 1975: 374; Hubbard 1988: 133). Micah's claim of this clan-
based judicial role is central to the conflicts behind Micah 3. Micah
challenges Jerusalem's ruling stratum not from within their state system, but based on the prerogatives of his role in a differing, overlapping social system—namely, a system rooted in the clan structures of
village Israel.

Within Mic 3:8, the words אֶת־רוּחַ יהוה ("with the spirit of Yahweh")
are particularly informative of the sociology of Micah. This phrase
forms part of Micah's personal claim of authority in the verse. The
phrase may be an addition to the earliest poetry of the oracle—its syntax is admittedly prosaic and its presence weighs down the meter of its
colon a bit. Upon examination, however, it becomes apparent that the
phrase is completely in line with E-stream perspectives. Thus if it was
not part of the passage's original poetry, its addition, which may well
have been early, authentically elaborates the Mican school's understanding of the term כֹּחַ ("power"). When Micah links himself with
Yahweh's spirit in this way, he identifies himself with the particular
tradition and social status of the Mosaic judge. This self-identification
is clear from Num 11:16–30, discussed in the previous section. In

conformity with Num 11:17, 25, the Mican brand of elder was specially empowered by Yahweh's spirit sacrally to perform their administrative and judicial roles within old Israel. This stress on the significance of being linked with Yahweh's spirit characterized the E-stream throughout its history. Thus, after Micah's time, the Deuteronomistic history still stresses the "spirit" language of Numbers 11.[34]

The link of Mic 3:8 to Num 11:16–30 suggests the fruitfulness of turning again to the latter text with an eye to any specifically sociological clues that it may contain. In fact, Numbers 11 provides a fascinating piece of evidence as to the actual institutional setting within old, village Israel of the tradition of Mosaic judges and of the E-stream. The clarification of Micah's dual role as both prophet and elder that has been developed above helps to resolve much previous scholarly confusion about this evidence.

In picturing village Israel's elders being stationed around the "tent of assembly" and prophesying, Numbers 11 highlights the significance of this locale in their sacral empowerment. The tent of assembly, then, may possibly be a symbol of the actual prestate institution of the Mosaic judges, the forebears of the prophet Micah. It is true that vv. 26–29 of Numbers 11 provide a caveat against reducing divine inspiration to a mere institutional function. Nevertheless, Num 11:16–17, 24–25 clearly and positively derive the inspired leadership of Israel's Mosaic elders from a traditional post at the assembly tent.

The nature of the tent of assembly in Numbers 11 can be clarified by examining its overall character within the E-stream. Examination reveals that the stream knows of two different wilderness tents. One of these tents was associated with Micah-like elders, and it was quite distinct from the cultic tent (P's "tabernacle") associated with the sacrificing priests.[35] The non-P-source Pentateuchal texts that mention a "tent of assembly" are: Exod 33:7; Num 11:16; 12:4; and Deut 31:14. All of these texts are often assigned to either the E source or a Deuteronomic source.[36] In contrast to P's tabernacle, these E and D texts describe a tent that is outside Israel's encampment, not at its center, that is associated with oracles and tribal decision making, not priests and sacrifices, and that has nothing to do with housing the ark. Haran's thesis is correct: "This tent has nothing in common with any temple ... it is nowhere associated with priests (or Levites), still less with sacrifices or permanent rituals, or indeed with any cult in the priestly sense of the word" (Haran 1985: 267). Rather, the E-strand references of the Pentateuch link the tent of assembly with the transmission and application of the norms and penalties of the covenant.

Haran (1985: 271) has successfully established the thesis that "the tent of מועד ['assembly'] and the ark are two institutions derived from different social and spiritual spheres of ancient Israelite life ... each of which evolved its own particular symbols and rites." Haran and other scholars do not go far enough, however, when they assign the tent of assembly simply to the sphere of prophecy as opposed to that of priesthood. The sphere of prophecy encompassed many social groups in Israel. Based on the above examination of the tradition of Mosaic judges, the assembly tent is more critically assigned as the bailiwick of the Mican brand of prophet. The E-stream traditions, such as that of the Mosaic judges, were borne, in part at least, by groups of "elders of the land" (cf. Jer 26:17–18), Micah's forebears, who represented this institution of the covenant. A fruitful avenue for future research will be to clarify further, perhaps based on cross-cultural parallels, the actual social form that the covenant assembly (or assemblies), symbolized by the wilderness tent, took in the villages of prestate Israel.

IV. METHODOLOGICAL CONCLUSIONS

Having elucidated the tradition of Mosaic judges as a component of the E-stream with its social roots in old Israel's covenant assembly, some final observations are in order about methodology in light of this volume's general theme. Although the contemporary, scholarly methods employed here in examining Exodus 18 have moved in new directions from the practice of the American school of biblical scholarship of the 1950s and 1960s, central tools used by this school remain basic resources. Tradition-history criticism continues to rely particularly on philological methods in its task of placing a biblical pericope or pericopes in the context of a definite tradition stream. Thus, the analysis here depended on isolating details of linguistic expression and idiomatic usage in linking texts in Numbers, Exodus, Micah, and Deuteronomy to the fixed diction of their common *traditio*.

The above analysis has accepted the full depth-dimension of Exodus 18. It has also correlated its historical questions with the pericope's social background of monarchic judicial reform, rather than with its narrative references. In these ways, its methodology has moved in a form-critical direction, away from an Albrightian one. At the same time, some definite, late-modern vantages have been taken that also distinguish the analysis from the form-critical school of the 1950s and 1960s. Understanding Exodus 18 was found to depend heavily on appreciating the canonical context of the tradition of the pericope. That the Mosaic-judges complex behind Exodus 18 is a scriptural tradition means a mere etiological concern cannot explain its meaning. Rather, Exodus 18 represents one point along a trajectory in which its tradition continually challenged its bearers and their audience to be true to the Mosaic ideal of justice.

NOTES

1.   The historical sketch of the Mosaic-judges tradition drawn below requires that the type of systemic social change depicted in 2 Chr 19:4–11 was a historical reality in Judah. Although this sketch does not also require the historical accuracy of the details of the Chronicler's account, or even that Judah's change of judicial systems be linked specifically to Jehoshaphat, both of these possibilities are credible. Indeed, a broad scholarly consensus has developed that accepts Albright's defense of the historical veracity of 2 Chr 19:4–11. For examples, see Mayes (1979: 261–69), Myers (1965: 99–117), Williamson (1982: 277–91), Wilson (1983a: 39–69; 1983b: 229–48, esp. pp. 244–45). It should be noted, however, that over against this consensus, Gary N. Knoppers in a 1994 article argues that the issue of the historical reliability of 2 Chr 19:4–11 is complicated by two significant factors. The account is more fully characterized by the Chronicler's own language and compositional shaping than hitherto recognized. And the account is literarily indebted to Exod 18:13–27 and Deut 1:9–18, compromising the value of these texts for corroborating its historical presentation. See Knoppers (1994: 59–80). Knoppers' work encourages a healthy skepticism about the details of Chronicles, but it in no way calls into question the reality of ninth century judicial reorganization in Judah. Several arguments made below help establish this dating of the implementation of the new state judicial system at issue. This judicial reorganization must have been initiated before the time of Micah, whose eighth century oracles presuppose the system and pronounce its failure. The discovery that reflections of the new judiciary are manifest in Exodus 18 (E) pushes the system's time of initiation back even farther to a period no later than the E source. Given these parameters, the Chronicler's assignment of the reorganization to the time of Jehoshaphat

appears rather trustworthy. Even Knoppers, who stresses the Chronicler's creative, programmatic mode in the composition of 2 Chr 19:4–11, has to note that he may have had good reasons for using Jehoshaphat's reign as the place for depicting his juridical ideal (Knoppers 1994: 68).

2. As Childs (1974: 324–25) writes, "The connection of Num. 11 with Ex. 18 is assured by the common theme of Moses' inability to carry the load of the entire people and a means being provided for sharing the responsibility." Further attesting to the connection of Numbers 11 with Exodus 18, Deut 1:9–18 conflates both passages in its recapitulation of the tradition of Mosaic judges. As in Numbers 11, but unlike Exodus 18, Deuteronomy 1 places the tradition's origin after the events at Horeb, and connects it with the people's rebelliousness and their myriad number. As in Exodus 18, but unlike Numbers 11, Deuteronomy 1 is specifically concerned with Israel's judiciary, and it uses the language of the levy system in describing the hierarchical ordering of the new Mosaic appointees. Further evidence for this conflation in Deuteronomy 1 appears below.

3. On Numbers 11 as oriented towards the judicial sphere, see Reviv (1982: 572). On the kin-group elders as old Israel's judges, see Köhler (1956: 127–50), McKenzie (1964: 100–104), Mendenhall (1976: 143–44), Wilson (1983b: 234–40). On the association of ecstatic prophecy with the elders in Numbers 11, see n. 13 below. Elsewhere in his article, Knierim recognizes that tribal and clan heads were specifically assigned the function of administration of justice in village Israel's public life (Knierim 1961: 158).

4. Arguments for ascribing Exodus 18 to E are given in n. 6 below. On the attribution to E of at least Num 11:16–17, 24b–30, the narrative of Moses's appointment of the seventy elders, see Gray (1903: 98–99, 113, 115), Driver (1910: 62), and Jenks (1992: 480). The narrative, Num 11:16–17, 24b–30, contains E's concept of a sacred tent outside the camp (vv. 26, 30; cf. Num 12:4 [E]; Exod 33:7 [E]). It also exhibits E's distinctive association of the theophanic cloud with that tent (v. 25; cf. Num 12:5 [E]; Exod 33:9–10 [E]). Again, the narrative includes E's diction about Joshua as Moses's מְשָׁרֵת ("attendant"; v. 28; cf. Exod 24:13 [E]; 33:11 [E]). And further, it stresses prophecy in a manner characteristic of E (vv. 25–29; cf., e.g., Gen 20:7, 17). Finally, there is an idealization of Moses and the Mosaic office in the narrative that is also indicative of E (vv. 17, 25, 28; cf. Num 12:7–8 [E]).

5. On the need to distinguish and appreciate specifically canonical traditions and their historical growth and development within the broader tradition-historical enterprise, see Childs (1992: 97–106).

6. Knierim assumes that Exodus 18 was shaped primarily by the E source

(see especially Knierim 1961: 154). Although he does not focus on arguing this assumption, it does tally well with several characteristics of the passage. The narrative uses the name אלהים ("God") at key points, and exclusively in vv. 13–27 (see Driver 1910: 31; Noth 1962: 146; Campbell and O'Brien 1993: 187 n. 57). It deals with the Kenite "Jethro" (cf. Exod 3:1 [E]; 4:18 [E]) as opposed to J's figure(s), "Hobab son of Reuel" and "Reuel" (Exod 2:18 [J]; Num 10:29 [J]; see Bentzen 1952: 25, 47). And it presents Moses not only as a judge but also as a prophet (vv. 16b, 20), in keeping with E's stress on the Mosaic foundation of legitimate prophecy (e.g., Num 12:6–8; cf. Deut 18:15–19; see Knierim 1961: 155, 156).

7. Jenks cites as evidence E's presentation of Balaam as a model of how an inspired prophet must resist a king's command if it challenges divine authority (Num 22:38 [E]).

8. The ties of texts such as Hosea and Micah to the E-strand are treated in the next section in connection with the proposed idea of an "E-stream."

9. On E's scholarly status, see further Jenks' recent summary: "It is difficult ... to separate E from 'proto-Deuteronomic' materials because of the similarity in outlook" (Jenks 1992: 480).

10. Also see Eissfeldt (1953: 7–8) and Willis (1974: 64–76). In my view, these scholars are mistaken in assigning a northern provenance to these texts near the end of Micah. They have rightly discerned the presence of the E-stream in this part of the book, but, based on presuppositions about the stream's geography, have been too quick to trace these sections to north Israel.

11. I am very much indebted to my former teacher, Robert R. Wilson, for the theoretical apparatus that I am applying here. Confining the E-stream to the northern kingdom, Wilson (1980: 17–18, 135–252) designates it as "Ephraimite." In my view, however, this geographical restriction of the E-stream is too narrow. Knierim's breakthrough tying Exodus 18 to societal developments in Judah helps to show that the E-stream is not of a purely northern origin. See Knierim's comments on this (Knierim 1961: 159 n. 31); and cf. Noth (1972: 230).

12. See "עמד," BDB: 764 Qal 7. b. Further support for a covenantal interpretation of the installation in Num 11:16–30 is provided by Exod 24:1–2, 9–11. In this E text, the seventy elders are specifically portrayed as participating with Moses in a covenant meal on the sacred mountain.

13. Note that the story of the installation of the seventy elders here does not form any sort of etiology aimed at legitimizing ecstatic prophets, as Noth and von Rad argued. The sign of the spirit merely attests to the divine sanctioning of the seventy's new covenantal office, and it empowers them for their covenantal duties as Mosaic figures. Thus, the sign is given only

once, and v. 25 states that the elders did not prophesy again. See Wilson (1980: 153–54), Van Seters (1985: 359).

14. Note that the clear change in social backgrounds between Num 11:16–30 on the one hand and Exod 18:13–27 and Deut 1:9–18 on the other belies Van Seters' unique argument that the Numbers and Exodus texts are a late set of related episodes derived from the Deuteronomic text (Van Seters 1985: 358–60). As argued below, the Exodus and Deuteronomic texts both have backgrounds in Judah's state-based judicial system, a later development beyond the lineage-system background of Num 11:16–30. A similar objection would apply to Reviv's argument for the priority of Exod 18:13–27 over Num 11:16–30 (Reviv 1982: 566–75).

15. Knierim (1961: 151); see n. 4 above.

16. Knierim (1961: 161) writes, "That the institution of Exodus 18 in fact fits better in the royal than in the amphictyonic period follows from the fact that the structure of profane administration of justice in the gate on the one hand and of sacral administration of justice at the shrines on the other hand is downright distinct from the structure of the institution for large and small cases .... Exodus 18 ... indicates a unified judicial institution organized from the top down, which is known from the royal period and presupposes the nationalization of the justice system." Also see Wilson (1983b: 234–35, 238, 239).

17. As Knierim (1961: 170, cf. p. 168) concludes, "The שׂרים are always royal high-officials. They have in part military, in part judicial competence, often both together." For convincing arguments that vv. 21b and 25b are additions to Exodus 18, see Knierim (1961: 155, 167–68).

18. That the Judean kings were supposed to act as supreme representatives of the Mosaic office of judge is clear from texts such as Mic 4:14 (Eng.: 5:1). Cf. Knierim (1961: 156–57, 160–61).

19. Compare Wilson's interpretation of Deut 16:18–20 and 17:2–7 as "attempts to reform the sort of hierarchical legal system attributed to Jehoshaphat" (Wilson 1983b: 246). In the ideal Deuteronomic state, most judicial matters are to be handled locally.

20. See Knoppers' observation: "The renovation of the judiciary in Chronicles evinces Jehoshaphat's return to bold leadership and piety following a period of regression (2 Chr 18:1–19:4a). It marks a greater royal say in the organization of justice within Judah and Jerusalem" (Knoppers 1994: 72). Thus Knoppers (1994: 73) is correct to conclude that "Moses decentralizes his power, while Jehoshaphat extends his power in Jerusalem and the fortified cities of Judah. Given these fundamental differences, I fail to see why Exod 18:13–27 would be written as an etiology for Jehoshaphat's judicial reform." As argued above, Knierim's etiological thesis is an inadequate interpretation of Exodus 18. I disagree with

Knoppers, however, that the differences between the Exodus and Chronicles accounts are linked to their relative historical chronology. These differences are better dealt with in terms of the differing intentionalities at stake. Exodus 18's tradition of Mosaic judges aims to temper the excesses possible in pro-monarchic stances, such as that of the Chronicler.

21. As Knierim states, the שׂנְאֵי בֶצַע ("those who hate dishonest gain") are associated chiefly with the sphere of administration of justice (cf. 1 Sam 8:3; Isa 33:15; Jer 6:13; 8:10; 22:17; Ezek 22:12–13, 27; 33:31; Hab 2:9). Knierim further notes that the phrase אַנְשֵׁי אֱמֶת ("men of truth") is also mostly used of those known as honest witnesses and judges in the practice of justice at the gates. (Cf. Prov 14:25; 29:14; Ezek 18:8–9; Zech 7:9; 8:16, 19.) See Knierim (1961: 149–50).

22. Thus Leslie Allen (1976: 306) writes, "It was the terms of [Yahweh's] covenant that the custodians of law and order were meant to enforce."

23. See Beyerlin (1959: 52–54). The terminology linked to state officials, שָׂרִים ("officers"), in v. 25b (also v. 21b) does not contradict this thesis. As mentioned in n. 17, these clauses appear to be post-E glosses. The language of vv. 2–4a of Micah 3 is mostly too general to be of help in confirming the oracle's E-stream *traditio*. The usage מַעֲלָל ("deed") in v. 4b, however, is more evidential. In its meaning of "evil practice" this term is especially frequent in the E-stream prophet Jeremiah.

24. See Nasuti (1988: 94), and cf. Allen (1976: 321), Mays (1976: 92), Wolff (1990: 109).

25. For more examples, compare the language of 1 Sam 8:3 and Deut 10:17; 27:25. The E-stream language continues in the invective against the priests in the second colon of Mic 3:11a. The verb ירה ("teach") has a distinct sense here that is characteristic of the *traditio*. It is in E-stream texts that this verb is used in its finite form specifically of teaching authoritative torah (see Exod 24:12 [E]). Even more telling is Deuteronomy's linking of this instruction idiom to the teaching role of the levitical priests (Deut 17:10, 11; 24:8; 33:10; cf. Hos 4:6). Micah's language reflects this linkage. He thus charges the Levites of his time with failure to comply with a Deuteronomic directive, a directive later crystallized in writing in Deut 17:10, 11. See BDB: 435 section C. 5. b; Wagner (1990: 343–44).

26. On the exilic dating of this part of Deuteronomy, see Noth (1981: 12–13, 79), von Rad (1966: 12), Weinfeld (1991: 14).

27. My reading here follows *BHS* n. b-b to Hos 13:10; cf. Knierim (1961: 170 n. 64). Verse 11 continues, "I gave you a king in my anger, / and took him away in my wrath.//"

28. On the possibility of one person taking on multiple roles in a society, see D. L. Petersen's discussion of role enactment (Petersen 1981).

29. On this suggestion, see J. Levenson's brief references to Micah's conservative theology having its social roots in the rural provinces and among Judah's old clans (Levenson 1987: 198, 200, 203).

30. Cf. Wolff (1990: 59, 75). (I plan to lay out the arguments for Micah as a kin-group head more fully in a future study.) The book of Micah thus attests to how the elders of the land perdured as a social group during the monarchic period. They not only retained some of their localized functions in the countryside, such as their judicial function in the city gate, but also retained a concern to exert a direct influence in the affairs of Judah as whole.

31. Compare Wilson (1983b: 240–41), and Itumeleng J. Mosala's discussion, drawing on South African evidence, of the tension between the ruling class and the class of elders in a tributary system (Mosala 1989: 81).

32. Compare John Andrew Dearman's statement that in the newer, monarchic system, "the traditional authority of the local assembly would now be overlaid and circumscribed by the authority of the appointed officials. In many cases the appointees would have been drawn from the local assembly, thus elevating a community leader above his peers. A local citizen taking a case to the gate could find his/her case adjudicated by people whose interests ran against his" (Dearman 1988: 144). Albrecht Alt (1959: 374 n. 2), in his well-known analysis of Micah's sociology, allows that members of well-to-do families in the land of Judah participated in the exploitations of the new, state administrative system, and the resultant destruction of the old Israelite order. He underestimates the significance of this, however, in arguing that they thus became colluders in "the society of the Jerusalem nobles" and could scarcely be viewed any longer as "authentic Judeans."

33. A similar phenomenon occurs in Mic 4:14–5:1 (Eng.: 5:1–2). That the Mican group could have used monarchic terms here, but avoided them, is shown by the occurrence of the term מֶלֶךְ ("king") in Mic 1:1, 14; 2:13; 4:9; 6:5 and by the occurrence of the term שַׂר ("officer") in Mic 7:3.

34. On the basis of this, Wolff (1990: 91–92, 96) attributes the occurrence of this language in Mic 3:8 to Deuteronomistic circles of the early sixth century.

35. Menahem Haran (1985: 263 n. 5) gives a long list of scholars, including Wellhausen, Holzinger, Driver, Eissfeldt, and Pedersen, who have mistakenly viewed E's tent as cultic in essence and as housing the ark. Haran does believe that E and D assume the existence of a cultic tent, housing the ark, within the camp. He argues, however, that such a cultic tent must be distinguished from the tent outside the camp on which E and D focus their attention (Haran 1985: 263–69).

36. See Koch (1974: 123–25), Friedman (1992: 299–300), Haran (1985: 262), Childs (1974: 590), Levine (1993: 130).

REFERENCES

Albright, W. F.
1950   The Judicial Reform of Jehoshaphat. Pp. 61–82 in *Alexander Marx Jubilee Volume*. New York: The Jewish Theological Seminary of America.
1963   Jethro, Hobab and Reuel in Early Hebrew Tradition. *Catholic Biblical Quarterly* 25: 1–11.

Allen, L. C.
1976   *The Books of Joel, Obadiah, Jonah, and Micah*. New International Commentary on the Old Testament. Grand Rapids, MI: Eerdmans.

Alt, A.
1959   Micha 2,1–5: ΓΗΣ ΑΝΑΔΑΣΜΟΣ in Juda. Pp. 373–81 in *Kleine Schriften zur Geschichte des Volkes Israel*. Vol. 3, ed. M. Noth. München: Beck.

BDB
1907   Brown, F.; Driver, S. R.; and Briggs, C. A., *Hebrew and English Lexicon of the Old Testament*. Oxford: Clarendon.

Bentzen, A.
1952   *Introduction to the Old Testament*. Vol. 2. 2nd ed. Copenhagen: G. E. C. Gad.

Beyerlin, W.
1959   *Die Kulttraditionen Israels in der Verkündigung des Propheten Micah*. Forschungen zur Religion und Literatur des Alten und Neuen Testaments 62. Göttingen: Vandenhoeck und Ruprecht.

BHS
1977   *Biblia Hebraica Stuttgartensia*, ed. K. Elliger and W. Rudolph. Stuttgart: Deutsche Bibelstiftung.

Burkitt, F. C.
1926   Micah 6 and 7 a Northern Prophecy. *Journal of Biblical Literature* 45: 159–61.

Campbell, A. F., and O'Brien, M. A.
1993   *Sources of the Pentateuch: Texts, Introductions, Annotations*. Minneapolis: Fortress.

Childs, B. S.
1974   *The Book of Exodus*. Old Testament Library. Philadelphia: Westminster.
1992   *Biblical Theology of the Old and New Testaments: Theological Reflection on the Christian Bible*. Minneapolis: Fortress.

Dearman, J. A.
1988   *Property Rights in the Eighth-Century Prophets: The Conflict*

and Its Background. Society of Biblical Literature Dissertation
Series 106. Atlanta: Scholars.

Driver, S. R.
1910   An Introduction to the Literature of the Old Testament. New
            York: Scribner's.

Eissfeldt, O.
1953   Der Gott Karmel. Sitzungsberichte der preussischen Akademie
            der Wissenschaften. Berlin: Akademie.
1962   Ein Psalm aus Nord-Israel. Micha 7, 7–20. Zeitschrift der
            deutschen morgenländischen Gesellschaft 112: 259–68.

Fretheim, T.
1962   Elohist. Pp. 259–63 in Interpreter's Dictionary of the Bible,
            Supplementary Volume, ed. K. Crim. Nashville: Abingdon.

Friedman, R. E.
1992   Tabernacle. Pp. 292–300 in Anchor Bible Dictionary. Vol. 6,
            ed. D. N. Freedman. New York, NY: Doubleday.

Gray, G. B.
1903   Numbers. International Critical Commentary. New York:
            Scribner's.

Haran, M.
1985   Temples and Temple Service in Ancient Israel: An Inquiry into
            Biblical Cult Phenomena and the Historical Setting of the Priestly
            School. Winona Lake, IN: Eisenbrauns.

Hillers, D. R.
1984   Micah. Hermeneia. Philadelphia: Fortress.

Hubbard, R. L., Jr.
1988   The Book of Ruth. New International Commentary on the Old
            Testament. Grand Rapids, MI: Eerdmans.

Jenks, A. W.
1992   Elohist. Pp. 478–82 in Anchor Bible Dictionary. Vol. 2, ed. D.
            N. Freedman. New York, NY: Doubleday.

Knierim, R.
1961   Exodus 18 und die Neuordnung der mosäischen Gerichtsbarkeit.
            Zeitschrift für die alttestamentliche Wissenschaft 73: 146–71.

Knoppers, G. N.
1994   Jehoshaphat's Judiciary and "the Scroll of YHWH's Torah."
            Journal of Biblical Literature 113: 59–80.

Koch, K.
1974   אהל. Pp. 118–30 in Theological Dictionary of the Old Testa-
            ment. Vol. 1, eds. G. J. Botterweck and H. Ringgren. Grand
            Rapids, MI: Eerdmans.

Köhler, L.
1956   *Hebrew Man*. Trans. P. Ackroyd, from German. New York:
          Abingdon.
Kosmala, H.
1975   גבר. Pp. 367–82 in *Theological Dictionary of the Old Testa-
          ment*. Vol. 2, eds. G. J. Botterweck and H. Ringgren. Grand
          Rapids, MI: Eerdmans.
Levenson, J.
1987   *Sinai and Zion*. San Francisco: Harper & Row.
Levine, B. A.
1993   *Numbers 1–20: A New Translation with Introduction and Com-
          mentary*. Anchor Bible 4. New York: Doubleday.
Mayes, A. D. H.
1979   *Deuteronomy*. New Century Bible. Grand Rapids, MI:
          Eerdmans.
Mays, J. L.
1976   *Micah: A Commentary*. Old Testament Library. Philadelphia:
          Westminster.
McKenzie, D. A.
1964   Judicial Procedure at the Town Gate. *Vetus Testamentum* 14:
          100–4.
Mendenhall, G. E.
1976   Social Organization in Early Israel. Pp. 132–51 in *Magnalia
          Dei: The Mighty Acts of God*, ed. F. M. Cross, et al. Garden
          City, NY: Doubleday.
Mosala, I. J.
1989   *Biblical Hermeneutics and Black Theology in South Africa*.
          Grand Rapids, MI: Eerdmans.
Myers, J.
1965   *II Chronicles*. Anchor Bible 12. Garden City, NY: Doubleday.
Nasuti, H.
1988   *Tradition History and the Psalms of Asaph*. Society of Biblical
          Literature Dissertation Series 88. Atlanta: Scholars.
Noth, M.
1962   *Exodus*. Old Testament Library. Philadelphia: Westminster.
1972   *A History of Pentateuchal Traditions*. Trans. B. W. Anderson,
          from German. Englewood Cliffs, NJ: Prentice-Hall.
1981   *The Deuteronomistic History*. JSOT Supplement Series 15.
          Trans. E. W. Nicholson, from German. Sheffield: JSOT.
Petersen, D. L.
1981   *The Roles of Israel's Prophets*. JSOT Supplement Series 17.
          Sheffield: JSOT.

von Rad, G.
1966   *Deuteronomy.* Old Testament Library. Philadelphia: Westminster.

Reviv, H.
1982   The Traditions Concerning the Inception of the Legal System in Israel: Significance and Dating. *Zeitschrift für die alttestamentliche Wissenschaft* 94: 566–75.

van der Woude, A. S.
1971   Deutero-Micha: Ein Prophet aus Nord-Israel? *Nederlands theologisch tijdschrift* 25: 365–78.

Van Seters, J.
1985   Etiology in the Moses Tradition: The Case of Exodus 18. *Hebrew Annual Review* 9: 355–61.

Wagner, S.
1990   ירה III. Pp. 339–47 in *Theological Dictionary of the Old Testament.* Vol. 6, eds. G. J. Botterweck and H. Ringgren. Grand Rapids, MI: Eerdmans.

Weinfeld, M.
1991   *Deuteronomy 1–11.* Anchor Bible 5. New York: Doubleday.

Williamson, H. G. M.
1982   *1 and 2 Chronicles.* New Century Bible. Grand Rapids, MI: Eerdmans.

Willis, J. T.
1974   A Reapplied Prophetic Hope Oracle. Pp. 64–76 in *Studies on Prophecy*, ed. G. W. Anderson, *et al.* Supplements to Vetus Testamentum 26. Leiden: Brill.

Wilson, R. R.
1980   *Prophecy and Society in Ancient Israel.* Philadelphia: Fortress.
1983a   Enforcing the Covenant: The Mechanisms of Judicial Authority in Early Israel. Pp. 39–69 in *The Quest for the Kingdom of God: Studies in Honor of George E. Mendenhall*, ed. H. B. Huffmon *et al.* Winona Lake, IN: Eisenbrauns.
1983b   Israel's Judicial System in the Preexilic Period. *Jewish Quarterly Review* 74: 229–48.

Wolff, H. W.
1978   Micah the Moreshite—The Prophet and His Background. Pp. 77–84 in *Israelite Wisdom: Theological and Literary Essays in Honor of Samuel Terrien*, ed. J. Gammie, et al. Missoula, MT: Scholars Press for Union Theological Seminary, New York.
1990   *Micah: A Commentary.* Continental Commentaries. Trans. G. Stansell, from German. Minneapolis, MN: Augsburg.

18 Intertextuality and Canon

JAMES A. SANDERS

It is a distinct pleasure to dedicate the following *étude* to my colleague of twelve years, George M. Landes. I often think it was those twelve years with George on the Union Seminary faculty that taught me what real collegiality is about. Thank you, George, and may you and Carol Marie enjoy long life with the health to continue to be productive.

The term "intertextuality" is currently used in three basic but distinct senses: the interrelation of blocks of text (large or small) in close proximity; the function of older literature cited or in some way alluded to in later literature; and the interrelation of text and reader. The reader is in essence a human text with his/her own hermeneutics and psychological texture, engaging a literary text. There are other ways in which the term is used, but these seem to be the most common uses (see Boyarin 1990: 12, 135 n. 2).

My own interest in intertextuality, which dates from well before the term came into common usage, has been largely in its second sense, the function of older literature in a newer writing where the older is called upon, usually, to authenticate or illumine a point the writer or speaker wants to make. The modes whereby this happens in Early Jewish and Christian literature are basically seven in number: 1) quotation with formula; 2) quotation without formula; 3) weaving of familiar phrases into a new composition; 4) paraphrasing or facilitating the meaning of the older in the new, usually for clarification in the terms of the later language; 5) allusion, usually to authoritative events and persons of the community's past; 6) echoes of key terms and ideas of an older writing in the new; and 7) reflection of the literary structure of the older in the structure of the new (see Sanders 1992a: 323–36). These modes illustrate the adaptability of literature that got onto a tenure track toward canon by repetition/recitation in ever changing situations and conditions in the community's on-going life.[1]

316

The third way in which the term is used is a part of the human experience, which in post-modern terms is a conscious admission of human limitations, subjectivity, and indeterminacy (see Sanders 1995a).

It is the first sense noted above that is usually at play when the focus is on the so-called final forms of canons.[2] The word "canon" itself connotes two quite different senses of the term: *norma normans*, where focus is on the function of a community's authoritative or canonical literature (in the seven modes listed above), the sense operative in most of the writer's work to date;[3] and *norma normata*, where focus is on the structure of canons effected by the phenomenon of canonical "closure."

Comparison of canons of Jewish Scripture can be very informative. When the early churches had the temerity to add to Jewish Scripture their own growing corpus of sectarian writings, they appended them to a Jewish corpus called Torah, Prophets (Luke 24:27), "and other writings" (prologue to Sirach), and they did so before the phenomenon of closure came about. For decades it was thought that closure occurred at a "council" of rabbis that met at the Palestinian coastal town of Yavneh or Jamnia after the fall of the Second Jewish Commonwealth and the expulsion of Jews from the largely destroyed city of Jerusalem. Jack P. Lewis' study of the references in rabbinic literature to Jamnia proved clearly, however, that while there was indeed a gathering of surviving Pharisees at Yavneh after 70 of the common era, it was not a canonizing council in any sense that Christians should or Jews would attribute to it. Many things about Judaism, including Torah and Scripture, were discussed at Yavneh, but few decisions were made of an authoritative nature, and none that could be called comparable to such ecclesial decisions familiar in later Church councils. Judaism was not and is not structured in such a hierarchical way (Lewis 1964).

Such councils would only have been able to ratify what was happening in the communities among the people. It is now commonplace to suggest that the Jewish canon was not "closed" until the middle of the second century after the Bar Kochba revolt, with firm evidence coming even later.[4] And it is not certain at what date the Jewish canon was generally viewed as tripartite, perhaps not until the talmudic period (Pettit 1993). The quadripartite Christian canons, seen already in some so-called LXX codices, clearly contradict the Jewish tripartite sequence; whether the Christian sequence of First Testament books in the LXX was done in blatant contradiction of the emerging Jewish sequence, or vice versa, has not been proved. The likelihood is that by the time codices came into common use, displacing scrolls, thereby highlighting the issue of the order of books, the two forms of Judaism, Rabbinic and Christian, had gone their separate ways and arranged their Bibles to suit their quite distinct needs and views of the Abraham/Sarah religion.

THE DEAD SEA SCROLLS

The Dead Sea Scrolls have impacted biblical studies in a number of ways, and one of those has been a dramatic revision in understanding the history of Early Judaism (from the fall of the first temple to the Babylonians to the fall of the second to Rome). The consensus before the impact of the Scrolls was that formulated by George Foot Moore of Harvard, namely, that Judaism in that period was made up of two major types: normative Judaism, expressed in the Pharisaic/rabbinic form of Judaism, on the one hand, and heterodox Judaism expressed in the apocrypha and pseudepigrapha, Philo, etc., on the other. In 1973, Prof. Michael Stone of Hebrew University published an article in *The Scientific American* that was almost immediately accepted in the field as "right"; he then followed the article with a book (Stone 1973; 1980). It has now become commonplace to speak of Judaisms in the Early Jewish period. Early Judaism was pluralistic with the strength and influence of the Pharisees in the pre-destruction period debated still (see Schwartz 1994). The Torah and Prophets were set and stabilized probably by the time of Ezra and Nehemiah in the middle of the fifth century B.C.E., at which time it was believed by some Jews (by no means all), particularly those who became known as Pharisees, that prophecy or revelation had ceased.

Jewish literature that was later added to the Torah and Prophets varied considerably in the Early Jewish period as may be seen from the various codices of the LXX and in the Qumran literature. The Jewish canon as it is known from the Talmud and from medieval codices is only a fraction of the Jewish religious literature that was available and used in authoritative ways by different communities in the Early Jewish period, when Judaism was highly pluralistic. This has always been known from various LXX codices, but now, in light of the Dead Sea Scrolls and their trove of heretofore unknown Jewish religious literature, the sheer amount of it appears little short of massive (see Charlesworth 1983; 1985; Martinez 1994; Wise, Abegg and Cook 1996). How many of these writings functioned canonically for this or that Jewish community before the fall of Jerusalem in 70 C.E. has yet to be determined.

THE STRUCTURE OF A CANON (*NORMA NORMATA*)

The accompanying chart (Lundberg and Reed 1991: 3) offers a simple comparison of four lists of current canons of the First Christian Testament with the Tanak or Jewish canon (as found in the first four editions of *Biblia Hebraica*). The difference in the messages conveyed by the variant orders of biblical books between the Tanak and the Christian canons is radical. Exploring those differences is the main purpose of the present study, which is, in effect, an exercise in the study of the phenomenon of canon as *norma normata*, as well as an exercise in intertextuality, in the first sense noted above.[5]

The Jewish canon is tripartite in structure; the Christian "Old Testament" is quadripartite in structure. The contents of the Protestant First Testament are precisely the same as those of the Tanak. This was due to the Hebraica Veritas principle set forth by Jerome (and to a large degree followed by him in the Latin text of the Vulgate), and then followed by Luther (see Sanders 1995b). What issued was a Christian First Testament that violated the structures of both the Tanak and the Septuagint (insofar as the structure of the pre-Christian "Old Testament" in Greek can be known, since Septuagint manuscripts were preserved only by the churches).

The Pentateuch is stable in all canons of the First Testament. In the Jewish tripartite canon the Pentateuch or Torah is followed by the Prophets, then the Writings. In the Christian canons the Pentateuch is followed by books suggesting the history of ancient Israel and Judah, and the beginnings of Judaism in the postexilic period, with the "historical novels," Ruth and Esther, inserted at appropriate chronological points to flesh out the history; the historical books are then followed by the poetic/wisdom books; then finally the prophetic corpus comes last in Christian canons. Each arrangement or structure makes its own theological statement, even though the actual texts are basically the same.[6]

Within each section of Jewish and Christian canons, after the Torah or Pentateuch, there are variations in order, both according to available

TABLE 1. Comparison Between the Jewish Canon and
Four Canons of the Old Testament.

Jewish	Protestant	Roman Catholic	Greek Orthodox	Russian Orthodox
TANAK	OLD TESTAMENT	OLD TESTAMENT	OLD TESTAMENT	OLD TESTAMENT
Torah	Pentateuch	Pentateuch	Pentateuch	Pentateuch
Genesis	Genesis	Genesis	Genesis	Genesis
Exodus	Exodus	Exodus	Exodus	Exodus
Leviticus	Leviticus	Leviticus	Leviticus	Leviticus
Numbers	Numbers	Numbers	Numbers	Numbers
Deuteronomy	Deuteronomy	Deuteronomy	Deuteronomy	Deuteronomy
Prophets	Historical Books	Historical Books	Historical Books	Historical Books
Joshua	Joshua	Joshua	Joshua	Joshua
Judges	Judges	Judges	Judges	Judges
Samuel	Ruth	Ruth	Ruth	Ruth
Kings	1&2 Samuel	1&2 Samuel	1–4 Kingdoms	1&2 Samuel
Isaiah	1&2 Kings	1&2 Kings	1&2 Paralipomenon	1&2 Kings
Jeremiah	1&2 Chronicles	1&2 Chronicles	1 Esdras	1&2 Chronicles
Ezekiel	Ezra	Ezra	2 Esdras (Ezra-	1 Esdras (Ezra-
Twelve Prophets	Nehemiah	Nehemiah	Nehemiah)	Nehemiah)
Hosea	Esther	Tobit	Tobit	2–3 Esdras
Joel		Judith	Esther + Additions	(Apocryphal)
Amos		Esther + Additions	1–3 Maccabees	Tobit
Obadiah		1&2 Maccabees		Judith
Jonah				Esther + Additions
Micah				1–3 Maccabees
Nahum				
Habakkuk				
Zephaniah				
Haggai				
Zechariah				
Malachi				
	Poetry/Wisdom	Poetry/Wisdom	Poetry/Wisdom	Poetry/Wisdom
	Job	Job	Job	Job
	Psalms	Psalms	Psalms + Psalm 151	Psalms + Psalm 151
	Proverbs	Proverbs	Proverbs	Prayer of Manasseh
	Ecclesiastes	Ecclesiastes	Ecclesiastes	Ecclesiastes
	Song of Songs	Song of Songs	Song of Songs	Song of Songs
		Wisdom of Solomon	Wisdom of Solomon	Wisdom of Solomon
		Ecclesiasticus	Ecclesiasticus	Ecclesiasticus
Writings	Prophets	Prophets	Prophets	Prophets
Psalms	Isaiah	Isaiah	Isaiah	Isaiah
Job	Jeremiah	Jeremiah	Jeremiah	Jeremiah
Proverbs	Lamentations	Lamentations	Lamentations	Lamentations
Ruth	Ezekiel	Baruch and Letter	Baruch and Letter	Baruch and Letter
Song of Songs	Daniel	of Jeremiah	of Jeremiah	of Jeremiah
Ecclesiastes	Hosea	Ezekiel	Ezekiel	Ezekiel
Lamentations	Joel	Daniel with the	Daniel with the	Daniel + Additions
Esther	Amos	Prayer of Azariah,	Prayer of Azariah,	(as in Greek
Daniel	Obadiah	Song of the Three	Song of the Three	Bible)
Ezra—Nehemiah	Jonah	Young Men,	Young Men,	Hosea
Chronicles	Micah	Susanna, Bel and	Susanna, Bel and	Joel
	Nahum	the Dragon	the Dragon	Amos
	Habakkuk	Hosea	Hosea	Obadiah
	Zephaniah	Joel	Joel	Jonah
	Haggai	Amos	Amos	Micah
	Zechariah	Obadiah	Obadiah	Nahum
	Malachi	Jonah	Jonah	Habakkuk
		Micah	Micah	Zephaniah
		Nahum	Nahum	Haggai
		Habakkuk	Habakkuk	Zechariah
		Zephaniah	Zephaniah	Malachi
		Haggai	Haggai	
		Zechariah	Zechariah	
		Malachi	Malachi	

ancient canonical lists and the available manuscripts. As Israel Yeivin (1980) has indicated, there is no stability in the order of books after Genesis to Kings, that is, in the Torah and Early Prophets, in Hebrew Bible lists and manuscripts. What is clear is that prior to the technological advance from the use of scrolls to the use of the codex, the only clear sequence of books would have been the story line from Genesis to Kings. If a member of the Qumran community, for instance, goofed because it was late perhaps, and had grown dark, and replaced a scroll of Judges in the cubbyhole before Joshua, there was no problem. He would simply put it back in its right place the next morning when there was sufficient light to see where it should go; or he wouldn't bother because it made no difference since the story line was so clear. But after Kings, beginning with the major prophets, the sequence of books varied, with the tripartite order in the Jewish canon, and the quadripartite order in the Christian, remaining constant (see Swete 1968; Leiman 1976; Beckwith 1985; McDonald 1995).

THE JEWISH CANON

The structure of the Jewish canon makes a statement about history that is quite clear even if one has only a basic knowledge of the textual content of the Tanak. The story line that runs from Genesis through Kings is rather remarkable in itself, and needs to be noted in any discussion of nationalism, universalism, or monotheism in the Bible. In the ancient Near East, as well as in the Greek classical world, the human story was always told in terms of the relations of deities and humans. In the Bible the most important actor in "history" was God: "In the beginning God created ...." Gen 1–11 sets the universal stage for God's work in the world, and through Israel. Most creation accounts in the ancient Near East show clearly a) the need of humans to understand that God or the gods created a secure place against the threats of chaos for humans to dwell, and b) that humanity was created in large part to be servants to the gods (see Clifford 1994). The "rage for order," which seems to be an integral part of the human psyche, can be seen in the need of humans to engage in annual or regular myth-and-ritual exercises designed to reassure the faithful of these two points, a) cosmic order and b) the place of humans in that order. In the Bible creation means bringing order out of chaos, and only God could do that. Asserting that humans are made in the image of God assures humanity of a rightful and responsible place in that order.

The biblical gospel story of salvation or redemption begins in Genesis 12, with a pastoral call by God on Abraham and Sarah, in which God invited them to sacrifice their birth-given identity and take on a new one. Along with the invitation went two promises: land and progeny. Those promises are fulfilled in a dramatically climactic way in 1 Kings 10 when the Queen of Sheba paid a call on Solomon. She came calling ostensibly to witness for herself Solomon's famed wisdom, but the reader does well to remember that Solomon's wisdom was a gift of God (1 Kgs 3:12–13). What the good queen did, for the implied reader, was to provide an international witness to God's having fulfilled the two promises, made to the patriarchs, of land and progeny. If one looks for tangible, observable fulfillment in the Bible, there is no portion of it that provides a story of fulfillment quite like 1 Kings 10. Everything in Jerusalem was of gold; silver was as common as stones (1 Kgs 10:27). But God appointed satans, or testers, for Solomon, and he failed them all. Beginning in 1 Kings 11 everything went downhill. The United Kingdom of David and Solomon split asunder. The Northern Kingdom fell to the Assyrians in 722 B.C.E., and the Southern Kingdom to Babylonia in 587 B.C.E. And that is where the story line of Genesis to Kings leads, defeat. 2 Kings 25 ends in ignominy and shame: the only status the exiled King Jehoichin had was what the Babylonian monarch, Evil Merodach, deigned to give him; he had naught but God's promises, and they had apparently failed.

The story that began with the universal God's promises to Abraham and Sarah reaches marvelous, stunning fulfillment, only to be lost entirely by the end of the story. And that is all by way of a running history that the Bible offers, until one reaches the end of the Tanak (in most lists and some manuscripts) when "history" is resumed and revised in the books of Ezra/Nehemiah and Chronicles. And even there (2 Chr 36), Israel's continued existence is shown to be dependent on the good graces and policies of Cyrus, king of Persia. In fact it may be said that much of the Bible, of whatever canon, is an effort to explain defeats: the defeats of the united, northern and southern kingdoms, the defeat of the Second Jewish Commonwealth, and the crucifixion of the master/teacher from the Galilee.

In the light of that observation, the fact that the prophetic corpus follows immediately after the Book of Kings makes its own statement.

Following Kings in the Jewish canon are the Books of the Three (major prophets) and the Book of the Twelve (minor prophets), fifteen case histories, as it were, to validate the lesson the Deuteronomist makes about the message of Torah: a) it is not God who let us down in these defeats; b) it is we who had let God down by polytheism and idolatry; c) but if in destitution we take what the prophets said to heart, God will restore us and every gift God has given us, bigger and better than before; and d) remember that God had sent prophets, early and often, to tell us how it really is in the divine economy. Those four points are clearly made in Deut 29–31, but they ring true to the general message of the Torah and the Early Prophets (see Sanders 1989). In fact, the Torah makes it abundantly clear that God is the God of risings and fallings, victories and defeats, what we humans might call good and what we might call evil (e.g., Deut 32:39). And it makes it clear also that God can convert the evil we do and turn it into good (e.g., Gen 50:20), just as the good we think we do, at one point in time, may turn out later to be what we would call evil (Eccl 9:11). There is but One God; there is no other. These are the tenets of monotheism hardest to grasp, but the Torah and the Prophets make these points time and again with utter clarity.

Then if one scrutinizes the Writings of the Jewish canon (the Ketuvim) one sees many musings and meditations on those and other points found in the Torah and the Prophets—indeed, how to live out life and understand it in the belief in One God of All—but no further speculation, as in the prophets, about what God will do next. The one possible exception is the Book of Daniel, which Christian canons include in the Prophets. But that depends on the hermeneutic one brings to Daniel. For the Jew it is a wonderfully inspiring wisdom story on how brave, young Jews can practice monotheism in the court of a foreign king, who himself will experience his fallings, just as he has experienced his risings and momentary dominance over Jews. For the Jew it fits well in the Ketuvim following Esther, which tells of how a brave, young Jewess practiced monotheism (without mentioning God's name) in the court of a foreign king. Christians bring a different hermeneutic to Daniel, see in it a foretelling of the Son of Man (7:13), and place it in the prophetic corpus. The speculative element is definitely there, as well as the inspiring stories about brave young believers, but each group brings with it the hermeneutic that highlights the one or the other.

THE COMMUNITY AND THE INDIVIDUAL

A major strain that runs through the Bible is that of the tension between corporate worth and responsibility, and individual worth and responsibility. Semitic culture generally stresses the corporate, and Greek or European culture the individual—neither to the exclusion of the other, of course. The concept of covenant is a corporate concept. The covenants God made with Noah, Abraham, and Moses were corporate in concept; those individual figures in fact represent the corporate relation God had with humanity, and with Israel. The pre-exilic prophets declaimed judgment on the two kingdoms corporately; it was a one-hundred percent judgment God was leveling against his own people.

It is understandable why these prophetic writings would be included in the canon, because they explained, in advance, the reasons for the defeats. But they also explained how God can work through fallings to bring about risings, or indeed death to bring about life. These would have been picked up and read, again and again, in the surviving Jewish communities in exile because they made sense of the evil that had befallen them, but also gave them hope for new life as Jews. Such literature thus got on a sort of tenure track toward canon. The folk in pre-exilic times, the so-called false prophets, who claimed that God, or Egypt, would save the old institutions and send the Babylonians away, would simply have been set aside as so much dust in the mouth if reread in a prisoner-of-war camp in Babylonia. A later theologian from Tarsus will say, "None was righteous, no not one" (Rom 3:10, echoing Eccl 7:20), which reflects the indictments of the pre-exilic prophets generally, as well as Deuteronomic theology.

INDIVIDUAL RESPONSIBILITY

Beginning apparently in the late pre-exilic period debates arose about individual responsibility within the corporate, and how to understand that. The disintegration of the experience called Israel meant that those who retained their Yahwistic identity in destitution needed assurances that they would not have to continue to pay for the sins of their ancestors, as Torah clearly states they might (Exod 34:7). First Jeremiah, then Ezekiel insisted that the people stop citing the old proverb about how, though the ancestors ate sour grapes, it was the children that paid for it (Jer 31:29; Ezekiel 18). Later the rabbis would discuss the contradiction and debate whether Ezekiel "soiled the hands," that is, was inspired or authoritative.

The Book of Job stands as a major exilic statement refuting the efforts of Job's friends to apply pre-exilic, prophetic, corporate views of sin to Job as an individual; their efforts to say that Job's suffering proved he had earlier been sinful were duplicated and matched many times in Early Judaism in the doctrine of *pur'anut*, a form of meritocracy that argues that comfort indicates God's favor and deprivation indicates God's disfavor (see Sanders 1955). Most of the Bible, from the Pentateuch to whatever canonical end, is fundamentally about the grace of God and refutes meritocracy, but it has reasserted itself in both Judaism and Christianity as a companion (Yang-Yin?) to the ideas of individual worth and responsibility which arose in the early exilic period.

A major feature of biblical literature is its dialogical nature. When it came time to assert the worth and responsibility of individuals in historical perspective, the Chronicler revised the Genesis-Kings story and upgraded the records of those who, in the earlier Kings version, were described as blatantly sinful. For instance, Chronicles does not even mention David's affair with Bathsheba. And where Second Kings makes Manasseh the scapegoat for all that went wrong in pre-exilic times, indeed the principal reason God sent Nebuchadnezzar and the Babylonians to punish the nation as a whole for the sins of their kings (2 Kgs 21:1–18), Chronicles reports that King Manasseh repented. His repentance was accepted by God, and he was restored (2 Chr 33:13).

Chronicles in its turn failed to record Manasseh's prayer of repentance, but that was supplied in later Early Judaism in the "apocryphal" Prayer of Manasseh. The prayer is found in Greek and Russian Orthodox Bibles as canonical, testifying to a major tenet of Judaism, God's great mercy in accepting the repentance of even the worst of sinners (Sanders 1991). It is understandable that this became a major Jewish doctrine, since Jews have been scattered in dispersion in all kinds of conditions ever since the Exile, and have needed to know that they do not have to continue to pay for the sins of ancestors (Ezek 18:21–23). Nay, even the worst sinner's repentance is accepted by God.

As one leafs through the Ketuvim, the third section of the Jewish canon, one is struck by how much focus there is on individual worth and responsibility. While the Talmud (Baba Bathra 14b) lists Chronicles as last in the Ketuvim, all the classical Tiberian Masoretic manuscripts, as well as Spanish manuscripts of the Hebrew Bible, put Chronicles first. In fact, the oldest complete Hebrew Bible in the world, a manuscript dating from 1005 C.E. called Leningradensis, which has formed the text base of the last two editions of Biblia Hebraica, and will be the text base of the fifth (Biblia Hebraica Quinta), has Chronicles first in the Ketuvim despite the fact that the third and fourth editions of Biblia Hebraica printed editions continue to print it last (as in the Talmud list and in German and French mss) (see Beck, Freedman, and Sanders 1998).

The placement of Chronicles makes a statement in itself. After the message of the Torah and the Prophets has been conveyed (the four points above), the Writings shift gears entirely and focus on the fact that it is possible for individuals to obey and please God. A major tenet of Judaism is that it is possible to obey and please God.[7] To begin the Ketuvim with the Chronicler's reconsidered view of history, wherein individual worth and responsibility is stressed, prepares one to hear clearly the theme of the first psalm in the Psalter, which immediately follows Chronicles: "Blessed is the person who walks not in the counsel of the wicked … but whose desire is in the Torah of Yahweh" (Ps 1:1).[8] Views of individual worth and responsibility were always seen as operating within the corporate, and some Jews were more Hellenized than others. Therefore, many who fully celebrated the idea of God's presence being with Israel as a people (Emanuel) could not accept the idea of God's being incarnate in one Jew; that was going too far toward Hellenism, and was the basic, fundamental reason for Pharisaic/rabbinic Jewish rejection of eventual Christian claims about Christ.

ANONYMITY AND PSEUDEPIGRAPHY

Another aspect of the strain between the corporate and the individual is in the fact that most of the Bible is anonymous. This is true of both testaments. We actually have no idea who wrote most of the Bible. Because modern, critical study of the Bible is a result of the Renaissance of Greek culture in Europe, biblical criticism attempts to wrest from the biblical text, studied in its ancient historical contexts, authorial intentionality. This was undoubtedly in response to the call Baruch Spinoza issued in 1670 to write the history of the formation of the biblical text (see Sanders 1995a; Sanders 1995b). Spinoza had claimed that the truth of the Bible would be found in a history of its literary formation. His call spoke directly to the Renaissance mind, with its emphasis on the worth and responsibility of the individual, because it meant historically reconstructing the origins of the Bible through its individual authors. And a great deal about the formation of the Bible has been learned, despite the shifts in perspective that take place every decade or so and the differences in concept and method according to the school of thought the scholar adheres to.

But the fact remains that most of the Bible is anonymous literature despite the efforts of the past three hundred years of critical study of its formation. It was under pre-Christian Greek influence and pressure that Jews felt the need to attach well-known names from its past to whole books. The whole Psalter began to be attributed to David despite the numerous superscriptions to individual psalms attributing them to others (even Solomon, Psalm 72), all of Proverbs and all the sayings in Ecclesiastes to Solomon, all the Torah to Moses, etc. In other words, the Semitic emphasis on shared literature belonging to the community meant that the Bible's anonymous literature became, in Greek-European terms, pseudepigraphic literature.

While Paul wrote some of the letters attributed (even by critical scholarship) to him, we actually have no idea who wrote the Gospels. The Gospels, like the entire Bible, are basically Semitic in origin, but under Greek influence it was felt necessary to attribute discrete literary units to individual names. One often hears comments from layfolk to the effect that we would know much more about the Third Gospel if we only knew who Luke was. In the popular mind, he was the companion of Paul mentioned in Colossians (4:14), "Luke, the beloved physician." I sometimes refrain from disabusing layfolk of their understanding that the Third Gospel was written by a physician, and a beloved one at that. At other times, I mention the fact that Henry Cadbury, one of the truly great NT scholars of the early part of the century, wrote his dissertation at Harvard showing that neither Luke nor Acts contains vocabulary from the medical world of ancient Greece or the Hellenistic world. Cadbury had done a thorough search of all relevant Greek literature of the era before he wrote the study. My teacher, Samuel

Sandmel, once remarked that Henry Cadbury got his doctorate by depriving Luke of his. The story simply underscores how much the "modern" mind is influenced by the Greek emphasis on individual worth and responsibility, and the conviction that truth lies there, because of the Renaissance (see Sanders 1992c).

CHRISTIAN CANONS

Christian canons differ markedly from the Jewish. Despite the fact that Jerome, followed by Luther, made translations of the First Testament (more or less) directly from the Hebrew, Christian canons kept what they had inherited from the Septuagint of the order and arrangements of the books. Jerome placed the larger "pluses" of the Greek forms of Esther and Daniel, as well as the books in the Septuagint that did not survive in the Jewish canon, into a section he called "Apocrypha." In the cases of Esther and Daniel, he named the long "pluses" of the Greek "Addenda ad Esther (or) ad Daniel." It in effect violated the integrity of the Greek forms of those books. Recent translations have restored the Greek Esther to its full integrity by placing the shorter Hebrew Esther in the canonical part of the translation, and the full Greek Esther in the apocryphal section (e.g., Traduction Oecuménique de la Bible [1976]; Revised English Bible [1992]).

The structure of Christian Bibles conveys its message also. The same basic theology obtains in both Jewish and Christian canons: God is One, indeed the God of risings and fallings, life and death; and the Pentateuch and Historical Books, the first two sections of Christian canons, are designed in large measure to explain the defeats suffered by ancient Israel. But the history of each has quite a different thrust. Whereas the Jewish canon eliminates speculation beginning after the Exile about what God would do next, or even in the distant future, the Christian view of Israel's history is that God continued to be active in human affairs well after Ezra and Nehemiah. Whereas the Pharisees and later rabbis believed that prophecy or revelation had ceased at the time of Ezra, other Jewish communities, those that produced most of the Apocrypha and Pseudepigrapha, the Qumran literature, and the Christian, firmly did not believe that prophecy or revelation had ceased. On the contrary, those Jewish groups produced literature of comfort for Jews under many eras of persecution, particularly the Seleucid and the Roman; and that comfort was expressed precisely in speculation about how God and the heavenly hosts were going to bring justice and salvation to surviving Jews (see Sanders 1975; Talmon 1991).

That view of "history" prevails in Christian canons. Ruth and Esther were placed in the "Historical Books," as were the "apocryphal" books that could be thought of as "historical"—1–3 Esdras, Tobit, Judith, and the Books of the Maccabees. This had the effect of lengthening the history of God's work with ancient Israel and Early Judaism down almost to the point where hanging the Gospels and Acts (Christian sacred history) onto that earlier sacred history would seem appropriate and believable. God's work was continuing. This is a major theme in Luke/Acts, which is clearly theocentric in hermeneutic, where the Gospel may be understood as God's Work in Christ, and the Book of Acts as God's Continuing Work in the Early Churches (see Evans and Sanders 1993:4–14). As with the community at Qumran, prophecy or revelation had definitely not ceased in the time of Ezra and Nehemiah.

Finally, Christian canons place the Prophets last, just before the Gospels. Whereas the prophetic corpus in the Jewish canon functions to explain monotheism in the risings and fallings, and risings again, of ancient Israel and Early Judaism, in the Christian canon it serves to foretell Christ and the Church, also in fallings and risings (crucifixion, resurrection, birth of the church). The different locations in the two structures suggest the hermeneutics by which the books of the Prophets were to be read in the two communities. In the Jewish canon the prophets explain how it is in the divine economy, with hope for the fulfillment of God's promises, especially the return to the Land. In the Christian, they are poised to point to the Gospel of Jesus Christ. If one goes through the prophetic or Haftarah passages that are read in synagogue liturgy in conjunction with the annual lectionary for reading the Torah through each year, one sees that the message of hope is considerably more prominent than that of indictment and judgment, just as Christian lectionaries tend to select portions from the Prophets that support the Gospel lesson each week.[9]

The structure of a canon conveys a message of its own and suggests the hermeneutic by which the community reads or hears the actual texts themselves. Jewish and Christian canons may have largely the same basic text of the First Testament, even the exact same books as in the Protestant canon, but they present two different Bibles through their respective structures. The first meaning of intertextuality, noted above, is as important in studying Scripture as canon as the other two.

NOTES

1. See the writer's "Adaptable for Life: The Nature and Function of Canon" in Sanders (1987a: 9–39), and the seven characteristics of canon noted in Sanders (1984).

2. Most of Brevard Childs' work is focussed on the final form of the Canon of the Reformation (see Childs 1985).

3. Since Sanders 1959. See Sanders 1992b and 1995a. Gerald Sheppard calls canon as *norma normans* "canon 1" and *norma normata* "canon 2" (Sheppard 1987).

4. See McDonald (1996: 92–94), Beckwith (1985: 274–337); and the writer's review of Beckwith (Sanders 1987b). And see now David Carr's in-depth study of "the diversity of Scriptural structures in Second Temple Judaism" (Carr 1996).

5. Most of the present writer's work in the concept of canon has been in canon as function, that is, as *norma normans*. The discussion in Sanders (1972) touched on the issue of *norma normata* to the extent that it probed the question why Joshua (the story of fulfillment of the promise of the Land) begins the prophetic corpus and did not conclude the Pentateuch, or Torah *in sensu stricto*, Judaism's very charter. See Sanders (1995a).

6. Some LXX translations indicate different *Vorlagen*, or concepts if not *Vorlagen*, of the text at hand—notably, Jeremiah and Proverbs, but also Samuel, Exod 35–40, and Isaiah.

7. Pre-exilic royal psalms after the fall of Jerusalem were read by and for individual Jews, as speaking directly for the lay person and having nothing to do with royal entries, and the like; see Evans and Sanders (1993: 140–53).

8. Unfortunately the NRSV, following its mandate to use inclusive language, pluralized the word ʾîš (usually translated "man," really "person") and translates, "Happy are those who do not ...." This compromises the focus of the psalm, and of much of the Psalter as read in Early Judaism in totally different *Sitze im Leben*, which is largely on individual worth and responsibility, understood within the corporate covenant of Israel as God's people.

9. Christian abuse of the prophetic indictments against ancient Israel and Judah, as indictments against all Jews, is a travesty that requires full exposure and discussion. See the writer's "Hermeneutics of Translation" (Sanders 1998).

REFERENCES

Beck, A.; Freedman, D.N.; and Sanders, J., eds.
1998   *The Leningrad Codex: A Facsimile Edition*. Grand Rapids, MI:
        Eerdmans.
Beckwith, R.
1985   *The Old Testament Canon of the New Testament Church*. Grand
        Rapids, MI: Eerdmans.
Boyarin, D.
1990   *Intertextuality and the Reading of Midrash*. Bloomington: Indi-
        ana University.
Carr, D.
1996   Canonization in the Context of Community: An Outline of the
        Formation of the Tanakh and the Christian Bible. Pp. 22–64 in
        *A Gift of God in Due Season: Essays on Scripture and Commu-
        nity in Honor of James A. Sanders*, ed. R. D. Weis and D. M.
        Carr. Sheffield: Sheffield Academic.
Charlesworth, J. H., ed.
1983   *The Old Testament Pseudepigrapha*. Vol. 1. Garden City:
        Doubleday.
1985   *The Old Testament Pseudepigrapha*. Vol. 2. Garden City:
        Doubleday.
Childs, B. S.
1985   *Old Testament Theology in a Canonical Context*. Minneapolis:
        Fortress.
Clifford, R. J.
1994   *Creation Accounts in the Ancient Near East and in the Bible*.
        Catholic Biblical Quarterly Monograph Series 26. Washington,
        DC: Catholic Biblical Association.
Evans, C., and Sanders, J. A.
1993   *Luke and Scripture*. Minneapolis: Fortress.
Leiman, S.
1976   *The Canonization of Hebrew Scripture: The Talmudic and
        Midrashic Evidence*. Hamden: Archon Books.
Lewis, J.P.
1964   What Do We Mean by Jabneh? *Journal of Bible and Religion*
        32: 125–32.
Lundberg, M., and Reed, S.
1991   What Do We Mean by the Bible? *The Folio: The Newsletter of
        the Ancient Biblical Manuscript Center for Preservation and
        Research* 11/1: 3.

McDonald, L. M.
    1996   *The Formation of the Christian Biblical Canon.* 2nd ed. Peabody:
             Hendrickson.
Martinez, F. G.
    1994   *The Dead Sea Scrolls Translated.* Leiden: Brill.
Pettit, P.
    1993   The Place of Scripture Citation in the Mishnah. Unpublished
             Ph.D. Dissertation, Claremont Graduate School.
Sanders, J. A.
    1955   *Suffering as Divine Discipline in the Old Testament and Post-
             Biblical Judaism. Colgate Rochester Divinity School Bulletin*
             xxviii (Special Issue): 105–16.
    1959   Habakkuk in Qumran, Paul and the OT. *Journal of Religion* 39:
             232–44.
    1972   *Torah and Canon.* Philadelphia: Fortress.
    1975   Torah and Christ. *Interpretation* 29: 372–90.
    1984   Canonical Criticism: An Introduction. Pp. 341–62 in *Le Canon
             de l'Ancien Testament,* eds. J.-D. Kaestli and O. Wermelinger.
             Genève: Labor et Fides.
    1987a   Adaptable for Life: The Nature and Function of Canon. Pp. 9–39
             in *From Sacred Story to Sacred Text.* Minneapolis: Fortress.
    1987b   Review of *The Old Testament Canon of the New Testament
             Church,* by R. Beckwith. *Theology Today* 44: 131–34.
    1989   Deuteronomy. Pp. 89–102 in *The Books of the Bible.* Vol. 1, ed.
             B. W. Anderson. New York: Scribner's.
    1991   Introduction and Annotations to The Prayer of Manasseh. Pp.
             AP 281–82 in *The New Oxford Annotated Bible: New Revised
             Standard Version,* eds. B. Metzger and R. Murphy. New York:
             Oxford.
    1992a   The Dead Sea Scrolls and Biblical Studies. Pp 323–36 in *Sha ʾarei
             Talmon,* eds. M. Fishbane and E. Tov. Winona Lake, IN: Eisen-
             brauns.
    1992b   Canon. Pp. 837–52 in *The Anchor Bible Dictionary.* Vol. 1, ed.
             D. N. Freedman, et al. New York: Doubleday.
    1992c   Communities and Canon. Pp. 91–100 in *The Oxford Study Bible:
             Revised English Bible with the Apocrypha,* eds. M. J. Suggs,
             K. D. Sakenfeld, and J. R. Mueller. New York: Oxford.
    1993   A Hermeneutic Fabric: Psalm 118 in Luke's Entrance Narra-
             tive. Pp. 140–53 in *Luke and Scripture,* by C. Evans and J. Sand-
             ers. Minneapolis: Fortress.
    1995a   Scripture as Canon for Post-Modern Times. *Biblical Theology
             Bulletin* 25/2: 56–63.

1995b   Hermeneutics of Text Criticism. *Textus* 18: 1–26.

1998   Hermeneutics of Translation. *Explorations* 12/2: 1.

Schwartz, D.

1994   MMT, Josephus and the Pharisees (S205). P. 401 in *1994 SBL Abstracts*. Chico, CA: Scholars.

Sheppard, G.

1986   Canon. Pp. 62–69 in *The Encylopedia of Religion*. Vol. 3, ed. Mircea Eliade. New York: Macmillan.

Stone, M.

1973   Judaism at the Time of Christ. *Scientific American* 288: 80–87.

1980   *Scriptures, Sects and Visions*. Minneapolis: Fortress.

Swete, H.B.

1968   *An Introduction to the Old Testament in Greek*. New York: KTAV.

Talmon, S.

1991   Oral Tradition and Written Transmission, or the Heard and the Seen Word in Judaism of the Second Temple Period. Pp. 121–58 in *Jesus and the Oral Gospel Tradition. Journal for the Study of the New Testament*–Supplement Series 64. Ed. H. Wansbrough. Sheffield: JSOT.

Wise, M., Abegg, M., and Cook, E.

1995   *The Dead Sea Scrolls: A Comprehensive New Translation. San Francisco*: Harper.

Yeivin, I.

1980   *Introduction to the Tiberian Masorah*. Masoretic Studies 5. Atlanta: Scholars.

INDEX